Maths for the future

Maths for the future

JIM MILLER

*Deputy Headteacher, Redewood School, Newcastle upon Tyne
and Principal Examiner in GCSE Mathematics*

GRAHAM NEWMAN

*Deputy Headteacher, Prestwich Community High School, Bury,
Moderator and Chief Examiner in GCSE Mathematics*

Nelson

Nelson
Nelson House
Mayfield Road
Walton-on-Thames
Surrey
KT12 5PL
United Kingdom

First published by Nelson 2000

ISBN 0-17-431530-9
04 03 02 01 00/9 8 7 6 5 4 3 2 1

Typeset by Mathematical Composition Setters Ltd, Salisbury, United Kingdom
Printed and bound in China by L. Rex Printing Co., Ltd.

Acknowledgements

The authors and publishers would like to acknowledge with thanks:
   The Guinness Book of Records (Guinness Publishing Ltd) and
   The Kingfisher Science Encyclopedia (Kingfisher Books) as sources
   for the interesting facts throughout this book;
   *Isle of Man map extract reproduced with kind permission of Michelin from
   their Road Atlas of Great Britain, 1993 edition. Authorisation no 93–887.*

The authors and publishers would like to thank the following Examination Groups and
Boards for permission to reproduce the questions included in this book:
   Welsh Joint Education Committee [WJEC]
   Foundation and London Examinations [EDEXCEL]
   Assessment and Qualifications Alliance [AQA]
   Oxford Cambridge and RSA Examinations [OCR]
   Midlands Examining Group [MEG]
   Northern Examinations and Assessment Board [NEAB, formerly NEA and
   NREB]
   Southern Examining Group [SEG]

Every effort has been made to trace all the copyright holders, but where this has not been
possible the publisher will be pleased to make any necessary arrangements at the first opportunity.

CONTENTS

Preface

Number

1 Using numbers

Mental mathematics; Pen and paper methods; Calculator methods; Number size; Indices; Equivalent fractions; Mixed and improper fractions; Cancelling fractions; Simple addition and subtraction of fractions; Simple multiplication and division of fractions; Using fractions; Using decimals; Using a calculator; Rounding; Decimal places; Significant figures; Estimation; Standard form; Appropriate accuracy; Review; Ideas for investigations

2 Percentages

Percentages; Finding percentages; Increase and decrease by a percentage; VAT; Credit agreements; Simple interest; Compound interest; Wages and salaries; Expressing in percentages; Inverse percentages; Review; Ideas for investigations

3 Number relations

Ratio; Proportional parts; Direct proportion; Inverse proportion; House insurance; Speed; Average speed; Foreign currencies; Directed numbers; Number types; Squares and cubes; Products of primes; Review; Ideas for investigations

Algebra

4 Patterns and relationships

Use of simple formulas; Substituting into a formula; Relationships: number patterns; Writing formulas for relationships; Use of calculators; Use of memory; Rules of indices; Simplifying algebraic expressions; Brackets; Multiplying brackets; Factorising algebraic expressions; Sequences; Methods of generating sequences; Further sequences; Review; Ideas for investigations

Handling Data

PREFACE

Mathematics is an essential part of our lives. You may need mathematics for your employment or as part of a search for better qualifications, or perhaps you are interested in exploring the applications and uses of mathematics. This book is designed to guide you and give you a better appreciation of what mathematics can do for you.

This book is written specifically to correspond to the Mathematics GCSE criteria. In particular, it is aimed at those students who wish to continue to study mathematics up to GCSE grade C, perhaps in search of a better GCSE grade. However, it also offers ample opportunity for practice in mathematics which is used in a range of applications, and is therefore suited to other vocational numeracy and mathematics courses.

To make it easy to use, the book is divided into four sections, each of three chapters, which broadly cover Number; Algebra; Shape, Space and Measure; and Handling Data. These are the four sections of the GCSE criteria that are covered by the GCSE syllabuses. To enable you to use the book for reference there is both a contents list and an index.

Each chapter is divided into clear sections, providing you with ample worked examples and graded exercises, some of which include questions from GCSE examination papers. Each chapter closes with a few ideas for investigations, which could assist you to meet the coursework requirements of GCSE. Answers to all questions are included at the end of the book.

USING NUMBERS

Numbers have been used to pass on information for many thousands of years. Prehistoric man has left some records which show they counted using, primarily, the fingers on one hand: that is, in fives. Throughout history numbers have been used in calculations to combine information. Numbers also summarise information. There are many different ways of doing calculations, but they are usually grouped into three methods:

1 Mental mathematics. All the calculations are done in your head; only the answer is written down. Mental mathematics is also used in estimating the accuracy of answers calculated by other means.

2 Pen and paper methods. Calculations are done without the aid of a calculator. Calculations are broken down into easier steps, and written out on paper. This makes it easier to do the problems.

3 Calculator methods. Using the power of today's modern calculators.

1.1 Mental mathematics

In doing calculations mentally it sometimes helps to see the problem 'in your head'. You would then do it in the same way as you would do it on paper. You can also use the value of the numbers, and number patterns, to help you work out the problems more easily.

Example   345 + 173
Add the units first: $5 + 3 = 8$ *That is*
Add the tens next: $4 + 7 = 11$ *1 ten and*
                                               1 hundred.

Add the hundreds: $3 + 1 + 1 = 5$
Answer: 518

Example   5 + 17 + 36 + 3 + 15
Units: $(7 + 3) + (5 + 5) + 6 = 10 + 10 + 6 = 26$
Tens: $1 + 3 + 1 + 2 = 7$
Answer: 76   *Use the patterns*
                                 in the numbers.

Example $7000 \div 20$
             $700\cancel{0} \div 2\cancel{0}$
             $= 700 \div 2$ *Divide each*
             $= 350$ *number by 10.*

Example 30×0.04

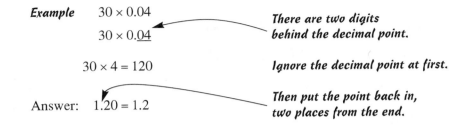

$30 \times 0.\underline{04}$ *There are two digits behind the decimal point.*

$30 \times 4 = 120$ *Ignore the decimal point at first.*

Answer: $1.20 = 1.2$ *Then put the point back in, two places from the end.*

Exercise 1

You must only write down the answers. All working out needs to be done in your head.

1 What do the even numbers less than 10 add up to?

2 A 90-minute video tape is used for a programme of 55 minutes' duration.
   How much time is left on the tape?

3 There are 41 houses on one side of the street, and 28 houses on the other side. How many houses are there altogether?

4 The hours Jenny worked each day in one week are: 8, 5, 7, 6, 5, 3. How many hours did she work altogether?

5 How much longer is 723 mm than 589 mm?

6 Find the total of £435, £274, and £309.

7 There are 86 eggs that are to be packed into boxes of six. How many eggs will be left over?

8 How many minutes are there in seven hours?

Exercise 2

1 There are 6000 people who have each paid £20 to attend a concert. How much money is this altogether?

2 A radio charity show asks 4000 people to donate 50p each. How much will this amount to?

3 An outing for 200 students will cost £4000. What is the cost for each student?

4 There are 9000 company shares that are to be divided among 30 people. How many shares will each person receive?

5 A box contains 8000 microchips. Each microchip weighs 0.2 g. What is the total weight of the microchips?

6 A 200 kg bag of powder is to be divided into sachets containing 0.05 g. How many sachets will there be?

7 A bottle of oil contains 0.8 litres. How many litres will there be in 50 bottles?

8 How many 20p coins can you get in exchange for £70?

1.2 Pen and paper methods

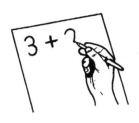

There are many times in real life when we need to do a calculation without a calculator. It is useful, then, to write the problem out. You will have to do problems like this in your non-calculator paper.

Example $600 - 45$

First borrow using the six:	Then using the ten:	Then subtract:
$^5\cancel{6}{}^1 0\ 0$	$^5\cancel{6}{}^{1}\cancel{9}{}\cancel{0}{}^1 0$	$^5\cancel{6}{}^{1}\cancel{9}{}\cancel{0}{}^1 0$
$-\quad 4\ 5$	$-\quad 4\ 5$	$-\quad 4\ 5$
		$5\ 5\ 5$

Example 438×27
This is $(438 \times 7) + (438 \times 20)$
or $(438 \times 7) + (438 \times 2 \times 10)$

Which can be done in one sum:

$$
\begin{array}{r}
4\ 3\ 8 \\
\times\ \ 7 \\
\hline
3\ 0\ 6\ 6
\end{array}
\qquad
\begin{array}{r}
4\ 3\ 8 \\
\times\ \ 2 \\
\hline
8\ 7\ 6 \times 10 = 8760
\end{array}
\qquad
\begin{array}{r}
438 \\
\times\ 27 \\
\hline
3066 \\
8760 \\
\hline
11826
\end{array}
$$

So $438 \times 27 = 3066 + 8760 = 11826$.

When doing division with large numbers it is sometimes useful to write out a times table.

1 × 42 = 42
2 × 42 = 84
3 × 42 = 126
4 × 42 = 168
5 × 42 = 210
6 × 42 = 252
7 × 42 = 294
8 × 42 = 336
9 × 42 = 378
10 × 42 = 420

Example $672 \div 8$

$$
8\ \overline{)\ 6\ 7{}^3 2}\ \ \overset{8\ \ 4}{}
$$

The remainder (67 − 64 = 3) is carried on to the next digit.

Example $1056 \div 42$

$$42\ \overline{)\ 1\ 0\ 5\ 6}$$

$$42\ \overline{)\ 1\ 0\ 5{}^{21}6}\ \ \overset{2}{}$$ *105 ÷ 42 = 2 r21*

$$42\ \overline{)\ 1\ 0\ 5\ 6}\ \ \overset{2\ \ 5\ \ r6}{}$$ *216 ÷ 42 = 5 r6*

So $1056 \div 42 = 25$ with remainder 6.

Exercise 3

Do not use a calculator with these questions. You may use pen and paper to work them out. Set out your calculations clearly.

1   A piece of wood of length 700 mm has 135 mm cut off. What length remains?

2   In a college there are 1435 male students and 1473 female students. How many students attend the college?

3 A workshop takes delivery of 196 tyres. How many cars can have their four tyres changed?

4 There are 12 items in one dozen. How many make 25 dozen?

5 A football pool's win of £1312 is to be divided amongst 16 workers. How much will each receive?

6 A coach has 42 seats; 165 students are expected on a field trip. How many coaches are needed?

7 A lorry is delivering 318 boxes of crisps. There are 48 packets of crisps in each box. How many packets are there altogether?

8 How many felt-tip pens are needed to fill 244 boxes?

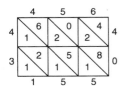

This method of calculation was used in India during the twelfth century. To do 456 × 34 set the digits around the outside of the grid. Multiplying each pair of digits together, placing the answers inside the grid. Then add along the diagonals, starting from the right; this gives the answer around the outside: 15 504!

1.3 Calculator methods

Many people believe that using a calculator has made mathematics easier. Calculators may have made calculations easier to do, but we still have to understand which buttons to press to get the correct answer, and in which order.

The first telephone was invented by Alexander Graham Bell in 1876.

Example A telephone bill is made up of:
(a) a call charge of 110 units at 5.5p per unit
(b) a rental line charge of £25.80.

What is the total bill?

(a) $110 \times 5.5 = 605$ ← *This answer is in pence. We need to write this as £6.05 before adding the rental charge.*

(b) £6.05 + £25.80 = £31.85

Example Jenny has a basic pay rate of £3.10 per hour. She gets 'time and a half' for overtime. In one week Jenny works 36 hours, plus five hours overtime. What is her total wage for the week?

Normal rate:	$36 \times £3.10 =$	£111.60
Overtime rate:	$5 \times 1.5 \times £3.10 =$	£ 23.25
		£134.85

Time-and-a-half rate is 1.5 × normal rate.

Exercise 4

The first gas light was put into a house in Cornwall, in 1872. London received its first gas street-lighting 15 years later.

1 What is the total cost of four rulers at 65p each, and three pens at £1.20 each?

2 An adult ticket for an amusement park is £15.60. Children pay half the adult price. What is the total entry fee for five adults and three children?

3 A video club will give one video free for every six bought. How many videos will be *bought* out of a stock of 105?

4 A car uses one litre of petrol every six miles. Petrol costs 44p per litre. How much will it cost, in petrol, to make a journey of 300 miles?

5 Remi buys a video recorder. The deposit is £45. The 24 monthly payments are £5.25 each. What is the total cost of Remi's video recorder?

6 The maximum mortgage a couple can obtain is (larger salary $\times 2\frac{1}{2}$) + (smaller salary $\times 1$). A couple earn £25 600 and £12 000. What is the maximum mortgage they can obtain?

7 Building insurance is £2.50 per £1000 value; house contents insurance is £6.50 per £1000 value. What is the total cost of insuring a house valued at £80 000, with contents estimated at a value of £60 000?

8 Stanley's gas bill is made up of a quarterly charge of £8.83 plus 1.32 pence per kwh. He uses 8500 kwh in the quarter. What is Stanley's total bill?

Exercise 5

Each of these questions is slightly longer. Remember to write down all your working out, even the calculations you do on the calculator.

1 An assistant earns £3.60 per hour for a basic week of 35 hours, overtime is paid at 'time and a half'. Calculate his total weekly wage if he works the following hours:

Mon. 7 h	Tue. 6 h	Wed. $7\frac{1}{2}$ h	Thu. 8 h	Fri. $6\frac{1}{2}$ h	Sat. (overtime) 5 h

2 What will be the date in exactly 40 weeks from March 3rd?

3 An electronics supplier has the following delivery charges: an initial charge of £5.30 plus 15p for each of the first 50 items, 10p for each of the next 50 items, and 5p for each item thereafter. What would be the delivery charge on (a) 30 items (b) 75 items (c) 118 items?

4 These are the readings from an electricity meter over a quarterly period. The cost of each unit used is 6.6 pence. To this should be added a quarterly charge of £8.83.

Present	Previous
72248E	71118

   (a) What is the total bill?

   (b) The present reading is an estimate. It should have been 72008. What should the total bill have been?

5 Martin is booking an adventure holiday for a group of families. There are seven adults and nine children: two under 5, one aged 6, one aged 8, two aged 9, two aged 12, and one aged 13.

The cost of the holiday is advertised as follows:

Adult rates	Week 1	Week2	Children
2 nights	£56	£52	Under 5: free
Each additional night	£25	£23	5–9 years: $\frac{1}{2}$ price
7 nights	£180	£165	10–13 years: $\frac{2}{3}$ price

Martin needs to book seven nights the first week, and five nights the second week. Calculate the total bill for the group.

1.4 Number size

The Egyptians were excellent mathematicians for their time; they used a system not unlike our own:

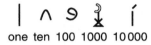

one ten 100 1000 10 000

So 12 343 should be written:

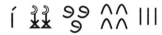

When dealing with whole numbers we need to have an understanding of the size of numbers. The number 342604523857 has 12 digits, which can be grouped in threes:

342	602	523	857
billions	millions	thousands	hundreds/tens/units

Example   Write in figures the number 'forty-two million, four thousand and fourteen'.

Forty-two million =	42 000 000
Four thousand =	4 000
Fourteen =	14
	42 004 014

The usual convention nowadays is that one billion is a thousand million. However, the old UK meaning used to be that one billion was a million million.

Example   Add a quarter of a million to three-quarters of a thousand.

One million is 1 000 000. One quarter is	$1\,000\,000 \div 4 =$	250 000
One thousand is 1000. Three-quarters is	$1000 \div 4 \times 3 =$	750
		250 750

Exercise 6

Write the following numbers in figures:

1 One hundred thousand and ten.

2 Three million, one hundred and five thousand, four hundred.

3 One million, thirty thousand, two hundred and fifty.

4 Four hundred and ten thousand, and six.

5 Five million, two thousand, five hundred and nine.

6 Four million, eight hundred and five thousand, and seventy-eight.

Write the following numbers in words, as in questions 1–6:

7 205 103	**8** 4 030 120	**9** 990 009
10 8 750 003	**11** 7 006 207	**12** 5 100 550

13 Rearrange these cheque numbers into numerical order, smallest first:

605431 650547 649531 631427 650001 609495

14 Rearrange these file reference numbers into order of size, largest first:

2435721 2404321 3571453 3600005
2314373 2450401 2837431

15 Add a quarter of a thousand and half a million.

16 What is twice half a million?

17 Write in figures the number which is three-quarters of a million.

18 Five people share £$\frac{1}{4}$ million equally. How much will each receive?

19 A salary is described as '22$\frac{3}{4}$K', where K is 1000. Write the salary as a 5-digit number.

20 A company is bought out for £35$\frac{3}{4}$ million. Write this amount in figures.

The highest bid in a corporation take-over was $21 billion for RJR Nabisco Inc. In 1988. The largest company in 1997 was the Ford Motor Company, with assets of $222 billion

---

1.5 Indices

Repeated multiplication is something that occurs in mathematics:

$$2 \times 2 \times 2 \times 2 \times 2 = 32$$

Rather than write out these long problems there is a shorthand way of writing them:

$2 \times 2 \times 2 \times 2 \times 2$ is written as $2^5 = 32$

index number

The **index** tells us how many of these numbers we need to multiply together:

$$2^3 = 8, \qquad 2^2 = 4, \qquad 2^1 = 2$$

We also have **negative** indices:

$$2^{-1} = \tfrac{1}{2}, \qquad 2^{-2} = \tfrac{1}{4}, \text{ etc.}$$

A negative index is another shorthand code to tell us to put 'one over' the answer, that is to write down the inverse. For 2^{-5}:

First work out $2^5 = 2 \times 2 \times 2 \times 2 \times 2 = 32$.

Then write it as $\tfrac{1}{32}$. So $2^{-5} = \tfrac{1}{32}$.

A **zero** index always gives an answer of 1: $2^0 = 1$, $3^0 = 1$, $100^0 = 1$.

Example Work out (a) 4^3 (b) 2^6 (c) 3^{-2}

(a) $4^3 = 4 \times 4 \times 4 = 64$

(b) $2^6 = 2 \times 2 \times 2 \times 2 \times 2 \times 2 = 64$

(c) $3^{-2} = \tfrac{1}{3^2} = \tfrac{1}{9}$ *The negative index tells us to put 'one over' the answer.*

The largest named number is the centillion, which is a hundredth power of a million, or 1 followed by 600 noughts. A googol is 10^{100}.

To save us some time there is a button on some scientific calculators to help us work out indices: $\boxed{y^x}$

To work out 2^5 press: $\boxed{2}$ $\boxed{y^x}$ $\boxed{5}$ $\boxed{=}$

To work out 2^{-5} press: $\boxed{2}$ $\boxed{y^x}$ $\boxed{5}$ $\boxed{\pm}$ $\boxed{=}$

Note: A scientific calculator will give a negative index calculation as a decimal, not a fraction.

Exercise 7   Work out each of the following:

1 3^4	**2** 2^4	**3** 2^3	**4** 0^2	**5** 5^3
6 1^4	**7** 3^6	**8** 5^5	**9** 8^2	**10** 15^3
11 13^2	**12** 7^0	**13** 2^1	**14** 3^2	**15** 6^4
16 2^4	**17** 9^4	**18** 5^6	**19** 7^4	**20** 3^0
21 2^{-3}	**22** 6^{-1}	**23** 3^{-4}	**24** 10^{-3}	**25** 1^{-1}
26 7^{-2}	**27** 3^{-5}	**28** 8^{-2}	**29** 3^{-3}	**30** 4^0

Find the missing index:

31 $3^? = 27$ **32** $10^? = 1000$ **33** $4^? = 4096$ **34** $11^? = 1331$

35 $2^? = 32$ **36** $9^? = 729$ **37** $6^? = 216$ **38** $5^? = 125$

39 $2^? = 1024$ **40** $12^? = 1728$

Example   Work out (a) 2×3^2 (b) $5^2 \times 4^3$ (c) $4^4 \div 2^3$

     (a) $2 \times 3^2 = 2 \times 3 \times 3 = 2 \times 9 = 18$

     (b) $5^2 \times 4^3 = 5 \times 5 \times 4 \times 4 \times 4 = 25 \times 64 = 1600$

     (c) $4^4 \div 23 = 256 \div 8 = 32$

Exercise 8   Work out each of the following:

1 $2^4 \times 2^2$ **2** $4^3 \div 2^2$ **3** $4^2 \times 2^4$ **4** $3^2 \times 2^3$ **5** $8^4 \div 4^4$

6 5×6^2 **7** 3×5^3 **8** $4^5 \times 3^4$ **9** $6^3 \times 8^2$ **10** $5^4 \div 5^2$

1.6   Equivalent fractions

Fractions are parts of a whole.

This fraction is represented by 4 out of the 12 rectangles, that is $\frac{4}{12}$. It is also $\frac{2}{6}$, and $\frac{1}{3}$ of the whole shape.

The Egyptians also used fractions in hieroglyphics: they represented a number as a fraction by giving it a 'halo'.

$\frac{1}{4}$ $\frac{1}{24}$

$$\frac{1}{3} = \frac{2}{6} = \frac{4}{12}$$

These fractions are **equivalent** fractions, they have the same value. There are many other fractions which are equivalent to these, for example: $\frac{10}{30} = \frac{200}{600} = \frac{16}{48}$

Example   Find three fractions equivalent to $\frac{3}{7}$.

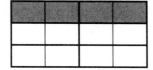

(a) $\dfrac{3}{7} \overset{\times 2}{\underset{\times 2}{=}} \dfrac{6}{14}$ (b) $\dfrac{3}{7} \overset{\times 3}{\underset{\times 3}{=}} \dfrac{9}{21}$ (c) $\dfrac{3}{7} \overset{\times 4}{\underset{\times 4}{=}} \dfrac{12}{28}$

Example   Complete these equivalent fractions:

(a) $\dfrac{2}{5} = \dfrac{?}{10}$ (b) $\dfrac{7}{10} = \dfrac{84}{?}$ (c) $\dfrac{12}{15} = \dfrac{?}{5}$

We do this by first finding the link between the equivalent fractions.

(a) $\dfrac{2}{5} = \dfrac{?}{10}$ **The link is: ×2 (since 10 ÷ 5 = 2).**

$$\dfrac{2}{5} \overset{\times 2}{\underset{\times 2}{=}} \dfrac{4}{10}$$

(b) $\dfrac{2}{5} = \dfrac{84}{?}$ **The link is: ×12 (since 84 ÷ 7 = 12).**

$$\dfrac{7}{10} \overset{\times 12}{\underset{\times 12}{=}} \dfrac{84}{120}$$

(c) $\dfrac{12}{15} = \dfrac{?}{5}$ **The link is: ÷3 (since 15 ÷ 5 = 3).**

$$\dfrac{12}{15} \overset{\div 3}{\underset{\div 3}{=}} \dfrac{4}{5}$$

Exercise 9   Write down a fraction representing the shaded part of each diagram:

1

2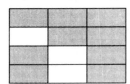

3

4

Complete the equivalent fractions:

5 $\dfrac{2}{3} = \dfrac{6}{?}$ **6** $\dfrac{2}{5} = \dfrac{?}{20}$ **7** $\dfrac{1}{2} = \dfrac{?}{4}$ **8** $\dfrac{7}{10} = \dfrac{70}{?}$

9 $\dfrac{90}{100} = \dfrac{?}{10}$ **10** $\dfrac{15}{9} = \dfrac{?}{81}$ **11** $\dfrac{18}{21} = \dfrac{6}{?}$ **12** $\dfrac{4}{3} = \dfrac{?}{12}$

13 $\dfrac{24}{36} = \dfrac{6}{?}$ **14** $\dfrac{3}{8} = \dfrac{?}{240}$ **15** $\dfrac{7}{12} = \dfrac{84}{?}$ **16** $\dfrac{2}{3} = \dfrac{?}{24}$

1.7 Mixed and improper fractions

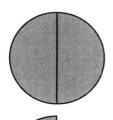

This is the fraction $\frac{3}{2}$ or three halves. This is called an **improper** fraction. It is also one whole circle and one half, i.e. $1\frac{1}{2}$. This is called a **mixed** fraction. When doing fraction calculations we sometimes need to change between mixed and improper fractions.

Example   Change $2\frac{3}{4}$ to to an improper fraction.

$$2\frac{3}{4} = (2 \times \tfrac{4}{4}) + \tfrac{3}{4} = \tfrac{8}{4} + \tfrac{3}{4} = \tfrac{11}{4}$$ $\frac{4}{4}$ *is the same as one whole.*

Example   Change into mixed fractions: (a) $\dfrac{20}{3}$ (b) $\dfrac{52}{7}$

(a) $\begin{array}{r} 6 \ \ r2 \\ 3 \overline{)2\ 0} \end{array}$ Answer: $6\frac{2}{3}$ (b) $\begin{array}{r} 7 \ \ r3 \\ 7 \overline{)5\ 2} \end{array}$ Answer: $7\frac{3}{7}$

Exercise 10   Change into improper fractions:

1 $1\frac{5}{6}$ **2** $6\frac{2}{3}$ **3** $7\frac{5}{6}$ **4** $2\frac{1}{6}$ **5** $8\frac{1}{5}$

6 $7\frac{2}{3}$ **7** $8\frac{3}{5}$ **8** $5\frac{7}{10}$ **9** $5\frac{5}{9}$ **10** $3\frac{7}{8}$

Exercise 11   Change into mixed numbers:

1 $\dfrac{49}{8}$ **2** $\dfrac{53}{6}$ **3** $\dfrac{33}{10}$ **4** $\dfrac{77}{9}$ **5** $\dfrac{23}{4}$

6 $\dfrac{84}{11}$ **7** $\dfrac{29}{5}$ **8** $\dfrac{60}{11}$ **9** $\dfrac{59}{12}$ **10** $\dfrac{40}{7}$

1.8 Cancelling fractions

When doing fraction calculations it is usually helpful to write the answer 'in its simplest form'. This means we need to reduce the numbers in the fraction, wherever possible.

Example   Write these fractions in their simplest form:

(a) $\dfrac{5}{20}$ (b) $\dfrac{84}{10}$

(a) $\dfrac{5}{20} \overset{\div 5}{\underset{\div 5}{=}} \dfrac{1}{4}$ *Divide by the largest number which is a factor of both numbers: 5.*

(b) $\frac{84}{10} = 8\frac{4}{10}$ *Write this as a mixed fraction.*

$= 8\frac{2}{5}$ *Simplify the fraction part.*

Exercise 12

Write each fraction in its simplest form:

1 $\frac{6}{16}$ **2** $\frac{21}{28}$ **3** $\frac{16}{24}$ **4** $\frac{3}{18}$ **5** $\frac{22}{55}$

6 $\frac{36}{84}$ **7** $\frac{30}{45}$ **8** $\frac{18}{24}$ **9** $\frac{20}{32}$ **10** $\frac{24}{60}$

1.9 Simple addition and subtraction of fractions

The most common fractions are those with multiples of 2 in the denominators; $\frac{1}{2}$, $\frac{1}{4}$, $\frac{1}{8}$, $\frac{1}{16}$. An imperial ruler divides inches into these fractions: they are easy to change between when measuring inches.

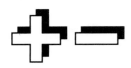

When adding or subtracting fractions with the same denominators (lower numbers) we do not need to change the fractions.

Example   Work out (a) $\dfrac{5}{6} - \dfrac{1}{6}$ (b) $\dfrac{7}{10} + \dfrac{9}{10}$

(a) $\dfrac{5}{6} - \dfrac{1}{6} = \dfrac{4}{6}$ *Simply subtract one-sixth from five-sixths.*

         $= \dfrac{2}{3}$ *Simplify your answer if possible.*

(b) $\dfrac{5}{10} + \dfrac{9}{10} = \dfrac{14}{10}$ *As we have the same denominator we can add.*

         $= 1\frac{4}{10}$ *Write as a mixed fraction where possible.*

         $= 1\frac{2}{5}$ *Simplify.*

When using fractions with *different* denominators we need to change the fractions, so that they will each have the same denominator, before we can add or subtract.

Example $\dfrac{1}{4} + \dfrac{3}{16}$

$\dfrac{1}{4} \overset{\times 4}{\underset{\times 4}{=}} \dfrac{4}{16}$ *Change $\frac{1}{4}$ into $\frac{?}{16}$: the link is $\times 4$.*

So $\dfrac{1}{4} + \dfrac{3}{16} = \dfrac{4}{16} + \dfrac{3}{16} = \dfrac{7}{16}$

Example $\dfrac{2}{3} - \dfrac{1}{4}$

We cannot change thirds into quarters, or quarters into thirds.
We can change them *both* into twelfths, since 3 and 4 both divide into 12.

$\dfrac{2}{3} = \dfrac{?}{12}, \dfrac{2}{3} \overset{\times 4}{\underset{\times 4}{=}} \dfrac{8}{12}$

$\dfrac{1}{4} = \dfrac{?}{12}, \dfrac{1}{4} \overset{\times 3}{\underset{\times 3}{=}} \dfrac{3}{12}$ So $\dfrac{8}{12} - \dfrac{3}{12} = \dfrac{5}{12}$.

Example $1\frac{1}{2} + 5\frac{1}{4}$

When we are adding or subtracting mixed numbers, we deal with the whole numbers first, and then the fractions:

$1 + 5 = 6$ and $\frac{1}{2} + \frac{1}{4} = \frac{3}{4}$

So $1\frac{1}{2} + 5\frac{1}{4} = 6\frac{3}{4}$.

Exercise 13

It is only since the mid 1980s that calculators have been able to do fraction calculations. For many years they were only able to calculate using decimals.

1 $\frac{1}{3} + \frac{1}{3}$ **2** $\frac{5}{10} - \frac{3}{10}$ **3** $\frac{1}{5} + \frac{3}{5}$ **4** $\frac{3}{8} - \frac{1}{8}$

5 $\frac{9}{10} + \frac{7}{10}$ **6** $\frac{5}{7} + \frac{5}{7}$ **7** $\frac{1}{8} + \frac{1}{16}$ **8** $1\frac{1}{2} - 1\frac{1}{4}$

9 $\frac{3}{4} + \frac{3}{16}$ **10** $\frac{1}{6} + \frac{11}{12}$ **11** $\frac{1}{4} + \frac{7}{8}$ **12** $1\frac{3}{8} - \frac{11}{16}$

13 $9\frac{3}{4} - 1\frac{2}{3}$ **14** $6\frac{5}{8} - 3\frac{1}{2}$ **15** $5\frac{3}{16} + 2\frac{1}{4}$ **16** $5\frac{5}{16} + 2\frac{1}{4}$

1.10   Simple multiplication and division of fractions

Example   (a) $\dfrac{1}{3} \times \dfrac{6}{7}$ (b) $3\frac{1}{3} \times 4\frac{2}{5}$

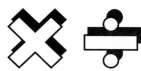

(a) $\dfrac{1}{3} \times \dfrac{6}{7} = \dfrac{1 \times 6}{3 \times 7} = \dfrac{6}{21} = \dfrac{2}{7}$ *Multiply the numerators, and then the denominators.*

(b) $3\frac{1}{3} \times 4\frac{2}{5}$

    $= \frac{10}{3} \times \frac{22}{5}$ *When multiplying mixed fractions first change them into improper fractions.*

    $= \frac{220}{15}$ *Then multiply,*

    $= 14\frac{10}{15}$ *re-write as a mixed number,*

    $= 14\frac{2}{3}$ *and finally simplify.*

Exercise 14

1 $\frac{1}{7} \times \frac{7}{10}$ **2** $\frac{7}{8} \times \frac{5}{7}$ **3** $\frac{2}{15} \times \frac{1}{2}$

4 $\frac{14}{15} \times \frac{2}{7}$ **5** $\frac{4}{5} \times \frac{1}{16}$ **6** $\frac{3}{4} \times \frac{1}{12}$

7 $\frac{6}{7} \times \frac{2}{3}$ **8** $\frac{5}{11} \times \frac{22}{35}$ **9** $\frac{7}{12} \times 4\frac{4}{5}$

10 $2\frac{2}{5} \times \frac{1}{2}$ **11** $\frac{1}{11} \times 8\frac{1}{4}$ **12** $4\frac{4}{5} \times 6\frac{1}{4}$

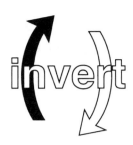

Example   (a) $\dfrac{5}{9} \div \dfrac{2}{3}$ (b) $3\tfrac{1}{2} \div 1\tfrac{3}{4}$

We change division problems into multiplication problems by writing down the inverse of the divisor. We then work them out in the same way as the problems in the previous exercise.

(a) $\dfrac{5}{9} \div \dfrac{2}{3} = \dfrac{5}{9} \times \dfrac{3}{2}$ **Invert the second fraction.**
Leave the first fraction as written.

$= \dfrac{15}{18} = \dfrac{5}{6}$

(b) $3\tfrac{1}{2} \div 1\tfrac{3}{4} = \tfrac{7}{2} \div \tfrac{7}{4}$ **Change to improper fractions before inverting the second fraction.**

$= \tfrac{7}{2} \times \tfrac{4}{7} = \tfrac{28}{14} = 2$

Exercise 15

1 $\tfrac{9}{16} \div \tfrac{3}{4}$ **2** $\tfrac{2}{3} \div \tfrac{4}{9}$ **3** $\tfrac{3}{4} \div \tfrac{5}{8}$ **4** $\tfrac{5}{9} \div \tfrac{2}{3}$

5 $\tfrac{5}{6} \div \tfrac{1}{8}$ **6** $3\tfrac{1}{2} \div \tfrac{3}{4}$ **7** $4\tfrac{1}{3} \div \tfrac{1}{4}$ **8** $4\tfrac{1}{8} \div 2\tfrac{1}{4}$

9 $4\tfrac{1}{5} \div 1\tfrac{1}{3}$ **10** $4\tfrac{7}{8} \div 2\tfrac{3}{5}$ **11** $3\tfrac{1}{7} \div 2\tfrac{4}{9}$ **12** $10\tfrac{2}{3} \div 3\tfrac{1}{3}$

1.11 Using fractions

Now we have the skills to use fractions in problems. To find a fraction *of* a quantity we *multiply* by that fraction.

Example   How many minutes are there in $\tfrac{2}{3}$ of 2 hours?

2 hours = 120 minutes

$\tfrac{2}{3}$ of 2 hours $= \tfrac{2}{3} \times 120 = \tfrac{2 \times 120}{3} = \tfrac{240}{3} = 80$ minutes

Example   A train carried 273 passengers; of these $\tfrac{2}{7}$ travelled first class. How many passengers travelled first class?

$\tfrac{2}{7}$ of 273 $= \tfrac{2}{7} \times 273 = \tfrac{546}{7} = 78$ passengers

Example   A student has £86. He spends £24 on an evening meal. What fraction of the original amount has he left?

Amount left = £86 − £24 = £62.

Fraction is $\tfrac{62}{86} = \tfrac{31}{43}$.

Some calculators can do fraction calculations. If you have such a calculator do each question by pen and paper method first, then use your calculator to check your answer.

Exercise 16

Write out each question as a fraction problem. Find the answer, giving any fractions in their simplest form.

1. What is the value of $\frac{1}{12}$ of 180?
2. There are 48 chocolates in a box. Of these $\frac{5}{12}$ have hard centres. How many chocolates have hard centres?
3. A student spends, on average, £48 per week. Of this $\frac{3}{16}$ is spent on bus fares, and $\frac{1}{8}$ on lunches. What is the actual amount spent on (a) bus fares (b) lunches?
4. Which is the larger weight: $\frac{3}{5}$ of 18 kg or $\frac{2}{3}$ of 15 kg?
5. Of 144 rail passengers who were surveyed, 16 claimed their train was regularly late. What is this, as a fraction of the total number of passengers in the survey?
6. During a 30-week holiday season, $\frac{3}{7}$ of the days were wet. How many dry days were there?
7. A salesman had 144 brushes. He sold $\frac{5}{12}$ at 90p each, and $\frac{4}{7}$ of the remainder at 60p each. How much money did he take?
8. Of 204 imported cars, $\frac{7}{12}$ were Japanese. How many imported cars were *not* Japanese?

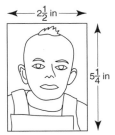

Example How many bricks will be needed to build a wall that is eight bricks high?

$$8 \times 3\frac{3}{4} = \frac{8}{1} \times \frac{15}{4} = \frac{120}{4} = 30 \text{ bricks}$$

In the past, the sign " was used to mean inches, but this is no longer very common, e.g. $3\frac{1}{8}$".

Example The cylinder has a diameter of $3\frac{1}{8}$ in. The hole has a diameter of $5\frac{3}{4}$ in. What is the maximum width of the gap between the two?

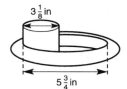

$$5\frac{3}{4} - 3\frac{1}{8} = 2\frac{6}{8} - \frac{1}{8} = 2\frac{5}{8} \text{ in} \quad \text{— } \textit{Change the denominator.}$$

Exercise 17

1. Two pipes, of lengths $3\frac{1}{4}$ ft and $4\frac{3}{8}$ ft, are put end to end. What is their total length?
2. If $2\frac{1}{4}$ bags of compost are needed for each hanging basket, how many bags are needed for 12 hanging baskets?
3. What is the length of the perimeter of this portrait sketch?

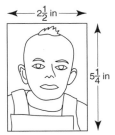

4. A path is to be laid which is $9\frac{2}{3}$ slabs long, and $2\frac{1}{2}$ slabs wide. How many paving slabs will need to be bought, assuming there is no waste? (Paving slabs can be cut to size.)

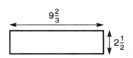

5 A glass rod, $5\frac{7}{8}$ in long, has a length of $1\frac{3}{16}$ in cut off. What length is left?

6 Maclad, a stallion, is $14\frac{3}{4}$ hands high. Millady, a filly, is $10\frac{3}{8}$ hands high. What is the difference in their heights?

7 A recipe requires $1\frac{1}{4}$ cucumbers. How many cucumbers are needed to make six times the quantity stated?

8 A mechanic can fit a car tow-bar in $1\frac{1}{3}$ hours. He has 14 tow-bars to fit. How long will it take him?

1.12 Using decimals

Decimals similar to those we use today originated 2000 years ago in China. In using the abacus, it was easy to add extra wires for the decimal parts.

We have already used some decimals in the earlier part of this chapter. Decimals are like fractions; they show parts of a whole.

$$\begin{array}{cccc} & \frac{1}{10} & \frac{1}{100} & \frac{1}{1000} \\ 0. & 4 & 6 & 5 \end{array} = \frac{4}{10} + \frac{6}{100} + \frac{5}{1000}$$

$$12.7 = 12\frac{7}{10}$$

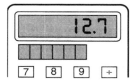

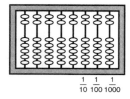

$$\frac{1}{10}\ \frac{1}{100}\ \frac{1}{1000}$$

They are easier to use than fractions, because all decimal numbers are a fraction or multiple of some power of **ten**.

Most decimal calculations are done on a calculator. In this section you will be reminded of the pen and paper methods for doing decimal calculations. You could be asked to do decimal calculations on your non-calculator paper.

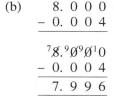

Get the point?

Example   (a) $3.1 + 45 + 0.001$ (b) $8 - 0.004$

(a)
$$\begin{array}{r} 3.1 \\ 45.0 \\ +\ \ 0.001 \\ \hline 48.101 \end{array}$$

Write out the addition problem vertically. Make sure you keep the decimal points in a line underneath each other (45 can be written as 45.0).

(b)
$$\begin{array}{r} 8.\ 0\ 0\ 0 \\ -\ 0.\ 0\ 0\ 4 \end{array}$$

Write 8 as 8.0 to begin with. Then add as many 0s as you need to make the two decimals the same length.

$$\begin{array}{r} {}^{7}8.{}^{9}\cancel{0}{}^{9}\cancel{0}{}^{1}0 \\ -\ 0.\ 0\ 0\ 4 \\ \hline 7.\ 9\ 9\ 6 \end{array}$$

Exercise 18

1 $0.9 + 4.7$ **2** $4.2 + 0.8 + 3.5$

3 $4.1 - 2.7$ **4** $20.01 - 3.6$

5 $12.03 + 96.6 + 9.1$ **6** $9.9 - 1.07$

7 $36 - 0.36$ **8** $7.57 + 29.05 + 103.6$

9 $15 + 1.34 + 0.21$ **10** $0.9 + 672.3 + 83.21$

Example   (a) 3×0.03 (b) 0.651×2.4

First count how many digits there are after the decimal point.

(a) $3 \times 0.\underline{03}$ (b) $0.\underline{651} \times 2.\underline{4}$

Number of digits: 2   Number of digits: $3 + 1 = 4$

$3 \times 3 = 9$

$$\begin{array}{r} 651 \\ \times\ 24 \\ \hline 2604 \\ 13020 \\ \hline 15624 \end{array}$$

Ignore the decimal point, and do the multiplication.

Make sure there are the same number of digits after the decimal point as there were at the start,

On the Continent the decimal point is represented by a comma, and not a dot, as it is in this country

Answer: 0.09   Answer: 1.5624

Example   (a) $120 \div 0.004$ (b) $1.25 \div 5$

(a) $120 \div 0.004$

The first person to use a decimal point was Francesco Pellos, in the year that Columbus discovered America, 1492.

$$= \frac{120}{0.004} \begin{array}{c} \times 1000 \\ \times 1000 \end{array} = \frac{120\,000}{4}$$

First multiply by 1000, to change 0.004 into a whole number; multiply both numerator and denominator.

$$\begin{array}{r} 30\,000 \\ 4\,\overline{)\,120\,000} \end{array}$$

Then divide as normal.

Answer: 30 000

(b) $$\begin{array}{r} 0.2\ 5 \\ 5\,\overline{)\,1.2^25} \end{array}$$

If you are dividing by a whole number there is no need to multiply.

Answer: 0.25

Exercise 19

1 1.2×0.4	**2** 6×1.23	**3** $14 \div 0.8$	**4** $238 \div 0.7$
5 $16.94 \div 1.4$	**6** $42 \div 0.03$	**7** 6.03×11	**8** $6.82 \div 1.1$
9 311×0.12	**10** $0.252 \div 2.1$	**11** 0.81×16	**12** 0.72×48.7

Are you as quick as a calculator?

In 1980 Mrs Shakuntala Devi of India took 28 seconds to work out mentally:

$$7686369774870 \times 2465099945779$$

Her correct answer was: 18947668177995426773730!!!

1.13 Using a calculator

Throughout this book you will be shown sensible ways of using calculators. Calculators and indices were discussed earlier in this chapter. The use of brackets and memory will be looked at in detail in chapter 4.

In using calculators we have to make sure we enter the numbers in the correct order.

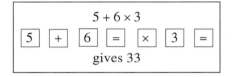

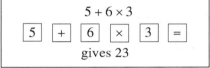

Which answer is correct?

Mathematicians have agreed a correct order for doing calculations. All $\times$ or $\div$ calculations are done first, from left to right. Then $+$ or $-$ calculations are done, from left to right.

Be careful! Some calculators do this automatically for you, others do not.

Check: $2 + 3 \times 5 - 4 \times 2$

Enter:
$\boxed{2}$ $\boxed{+}$ $\boxed{3}$ $\boxed{\times}$ $\boxed{5}$ $\boxed{-}$ $\boxed{4}$ $\boxed{\times}$ $\boxed{2}$ $\boxed{=}$

If your calculator follows the correct order you should get the correct answer of 9. If not, you will need to help it: $2 + 3 \times 5 - 4 \times 2$

$= \boxed{2}$ $\boxed{+}$ $\boxed{15}$ $\boxed{-}$ $\boxed{8}$ $\boxed{=}$ $\boxed{9}$

Exercise 20 Work out these calculations:

1 $8 - 6 \div 2$	**2** $12 + 9 \div 3$	**3** $18 \div 9 + 9$
4 $36 \div 9 \times 3$	**5** $6 \div 3 \times 8$	**6** $33 - 27 \div 3$
7 $35 - 6 \times 4$	**8** $3 + 4 \times 5$	**9** $18 \div 9 + 6$
10 $27 - 9 \div 3$	**11** $7 \times 2 - 2 \times 6$	**12** $10 + 3 \times 4 - 17$

1.14 Rounding

Numbers are rounded off to make them easier to handle and compare.

ATHLETICS
ATTENDENCE

132, 863

This headline is rarely seen in newspapers. The figures are normally rounded off.

This attendance figure has been rounded off to the nearest thousand.

ATHLETICS
ATTENDENCE

133,000

We round *up* if the number is halfway or more to the next rounding number. We round *down* if the number is less than halfway to the next rounding number.

Example   Round these three numbers, 2345, 2660, 2750: (a) to the nearest 1000 (b) to the nearest 100.

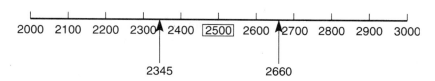

(a) If we need to round these numbers to the nearest thousand:
2345 is *less* than halfway (2500), so 2345 is rounded *down* to 2000.
2660 is *more* than halfway (2500), so 2660 is rounded *up* to 3000.
2750 is also rounded to 3000.

(b) Rounding to the nearest hundred is done in the same way:
2345 → 2300; 2660 → 2700
But 2750 is halfway between 2600 and 2700, so we round up to 2700.

Rounded to the nearest hundred million light-years, the most distant heavenly body is a quasar, at 13 200 million light-years

---

Exercise 21

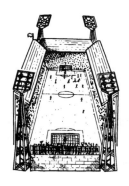

Round off each of the numbers (a) to the nearest 1000 (b) to the nearest 100.

1 41 341	**2** 5750	**3** 84 210
4 66 666	**5** 7586	**6** 3050
7 43 216	**8** 5131.5	**9** 47 198
10 1005.9	**11** 1175.6	**12** 1088.8

13 One summer the number of visitors to a museum was 23 893. Write this figure to the nearest thousand.

14 The attendance at a football match was 12 846. Write this figure to the nearest 100.

15 A house extension is estimated to cost £18 986. Write this quotation to the nearest 100.

Example   Jenny needs 16 litres of paint, which is sold in 5-litre tins. How many tins will she buy?

To the nearest 5, 16 rounds off to 15 (three tins), but this will not leave her with enough paint. We need to round up in this type of situation. She will need four tins (20 litres).

Example   Derek has £85 in 1 coins. He wants to change the coins for £10 notes. For how many notes will he exchange the coins?

£85 rounds up to £90, but Derek hasn't got £90! He will round down to £80, i.e. eight £10 notes.

Exercise 22

1 Tom has £2.59. He needs 20p coins. How many 20p coins will he get for £2.59?

2 Barbara needs 61 tiles for a bathroom wall. The tiles come in boxes of five. How many boxes will she need?

3 A taxi will carry a maximum of five persons. How many similar taxis are needed to take 71 disabled youngsters on a day's outing?

4 An empty tank has a capacity of 85 litres. How many 8-litre containers can you empty into the tank before it overflows?

5 A college orders pens in boxes of ten. It needs three pens for each of its 144 members of staff. How many boxes will need to be ordered?

6 Potting compost is sold in 4-kg bags. If 22 kg are needed for new plants, how many bags will need to be bought?

7 Eggs are sold in boxes of six. If 89 eggs have been laid, how many full boxes will be sold?

8 The number of people allowed in a lift is ten. How many trips will the lift need to make to transport (a) 48 people (b) 62 people?

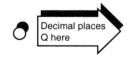

85 Litres

1.15 Decimal places

One way of rounding numbers is by using decimal places (d.p.).

```
32.0    3     2
  ↑     ↑     ↑
 1st   2nd   3rd decimal place
```

Decimal places
Q here

Example   23.147 Round this number off to (a) 2 d.p. (b) 1 d.p.

(a)   23.15   *The 5 is in the 2nd decimal place. As 7 is more than halfway to the next digit we have rounded up.*

(b)   23.1   *Since in the original number the 4 is less than halfway to the next digit we round down.*

Exercise 23   Round these numbers off to (a) 2 d.p. (b) 3 d.p.

1 3.8597   **2** 9.4185   **3** 29.8314   **4** 0.013 79   **5** 0.9753
6 6.4074   **7** 50.9137   **8** 4.8864   **9** 36.057 57   **10** 9.094

Round off to the number of decimal places given in brackets:

11 7.215 (2)   **12** 95.786 (1)   **13** 68.89 (1)   **14** 29.971 (2)   **15** 0.78567 (4)

1.16 Significant figures

Another way of rounding numbers is by using significant figures (s.f.). We can round off either whole numbers or decimals.

Order of significance

```
3   5 . 0   2   7
↑   ↑   ↑   ↑   ↑
1st 2nd 3rd 4th 5th
```

To round off decimals to significant figures we do almost the same as when rounding to decimal places.

Example   Round off 35.027 to (a) 3 s.f. (b) 4 s.f.

```
3   5 . 0   2   7        (a) 35.0        (b) 35.03
↑   ↑   ↑   ↑   ↑                ↑                ↑
1st 2nd 3rd 4th 5th          3rd s.f.        4th s.f.
```

In rounding off significant figures with whole numbers we need to know the value of the significant figures:

```
1   4   5   7 . 3   2
↑   ↑   ↑   ↑   ↑   ↑
1st 2nd 3rd 4th 5th 6th
```
The 1st significant figure is the thousands figure.
The 2nd significant figure is the hundreds.
The 3rd significant figure is the tens, etc.

To round off to 1 significant figure, we would round off to the nearest thousand: 1000
To round off to 2 significant figures, we would round off to the nearest hundred: 1500
To round off to 3 significant figures, we would round off to the nearest ten: 1460

Example   Round off 339.45 (a) to 1 s.f. (b) to 3 s.f. (c) to 4 s.f.

(a) The 1st significant figure is to the nearest hundred: 300
(b) The 3rd significant figure is to the nearest unit: 339
(c) The 4th significant figure is to the first decimal place: 339.5

Example   Round off 0.00718 to (a) 1 s.f. (b) 2 s.f.

(a) 0.007   (b) 0.0072

Exercise 24   Round off these numbers to (a) 1 s.f. (b) 3 s.f.

1 29.05   **2** 5653   **3** 73 423   **4** 0.037 51   **5** 23.51

6 15.435   **7** 62.84   **8** 0.080 99   **9** 467.5   **10** 4090.09

Round off to the number of significant figures given in the brackets:

11 0.1255 (3)   **12** 14.7 (1)   **13** 0.6593 (2)

14 289.5 (2)   **15** 4227 (1)

1.17 Estimation

Estimates of the circumference of the earth (in miles) are: Aristotle (fourth century BC) 40,000; Archimedes (third century BC) 30,000; Eratosthenes (second century BC) 25,000. True distance: 24850-24900.

There are many times when we may want to estimate the answer to a calculation. We can make such estimates easier to do without a calculator by rounding all the numbers to one significant figure before carrying out the calculation.

Example   Estimate the answer to (a) 218.5×4.9 (b) $\dfrac{44 \times 2.32}{21.7 \times 7.5}$

Start by rounding all the numbers to 1 significant figure.

(a) 218.5×4.9 becomes $200 \times 5 = 1000$

(b) $\dfrac{44 \times 2.32}{21.7 \times 7.5}$ becomes $\dfrac{40 \times 2}{20 \times 8} = \dfrac{80}{160} = \dfrac{1}{2}$

Exercise 25   Find an estimated answer to each of the following:

1 34.89×2.97 **2** 4.2×53.8 **3** $\dfrac{51 \times 33.2}{2.6}$

4 $\dfrac{22 \times 43}{14 \times 18}$ **5** $\dfrac{38 \times 17}{4.5}$ **6** $\dfrac{3870}{1.78 \times 2.34}$

7 $\dfrac{28.4 \times 38.5}{5.5 \times 2.1}$ **8** $\dfrac{30.2 \times 714.3}{4.98 \times 19.4}$ **9** $\dfrac{74.3 \times 58.2}{5.1 \times 6.6}$

10 $\dfrac{33 \times 1.45}{12.6 \times 8.5}$ **11** $\dfrac{318.2 \times 898.3}{6.24 \times 3.19}$ **12** $\dfrac{38.5 \times 82.7}{2.02 \times 1.95}$

1.18 Standard form

The first person to use standard form to advance mathematics was John Napier, who published the first set of logarithm tables in 1614. These have now been replaced with the modern calculator.

Standard form is a way of representing large numbers on a calculator.

If you see $\boxed{3.8737 \ \ 07}$ on a calculator this means:

3.8737×10^7 or $3.8737 \times 10 \times 10 \times 10 \times 10 \times 10 \times 10 \times 10$

In standard form there are two parts to each number:

(i)   the decimal part, with the decimal point after the first digit,
(ii) the power of ten by which we should multiply the decimal to change it back to an ordinary number.

Example   Write as ordinary numbers:
(a) 5.231×10^6 (b) $1.09\ 05$ (c) 1.423×10^{-4}

(a) $5.231 \times 10^6 = 5.231 \times 1\ 000\ 000 = 5\ 231\ 000$

(b) $1.09\ 05 = 1.09 \times 100\ 000 = 109\ 000$

(c) $1.423 \times 10^{-4} = 1.423 \times 0.0001 = 0.000\ 142\ 3$

Exercise 26

Write each of the following numbers as ordinary numbers.

1 7.5×10^{-4} 2 9.8×10^{-3} 3 3.75×10^{-5}

4 1.6×10^6 5 1.01×10^{-3} 6 7.63×10^5

7 6.2×10^3 8 7.0×10^4 9 9.21×10^{-3}

10 9.83×10^6

Example   Write these numbers in standard form:
(a) 31420   (b) 0.0432   (c) 0.0052

(a) $31420 = 3.142 \times 10\ 000 = 3.142 \times 10^4$

(b) $0.0432 = 4.32 \div 100 = 4.32 \times 10^{-2}$

(c) $0.0052 = 5.2 \div 1000 = 5.2 \times 10^{-3}$

Exercise 27

Write each of the following numbers in standard form:

1 0.07	2 4500	3 0.35
4 800 000	5 0.008	6 0.027
7 24 000	8 0.0069	9 4000
10 14 000	11 0.000 008 5	12 0.0009

The mass of the sun is 1.9889×10^{27} tonnes, compared with the mass of the earth at 5.974×10^{18} tonnes.

You can also put standard form numbers into your calculator to answer problems.

Use the $\boxed{EE}$ or $\boxed{EXP}$ button on your calculator.

For example, you would put in 2.1×10^{-2} as $\boxed{2}\ \boxed{\cdot}\ \boxed{1}\ \boxed{EXP}\ \boxed{2}\ \boxed{+/-}$.

Exercise 28

Use your calculator to work out these problems. The answer to each question should be written (a) in standard form (b) as an ordinary number.

The weight of a graviton is 7.6×10^{-67} g, which is considerably lighter than the neutrino, which weighs 1.8×10^{-32} g.

1 $(1.3 \times 10^3) \times (6 \times 10^{-7})$ 2 $(6 \times 10^6) \times (2 \times 10^2)$

3 $(4 \times 10^8) \times (6 \times 10^{-3})$ 4 $(8 \times 10^{-3}) \times (4 \times 10^{-4})$

5 $(4.8 \times 10^3) \times (8 \times 10^{-4})$ 6 $(6 \times 10^5) \times (2 \times 10^2)$

7 $(6 \times 10^5) \times (2 \times 10^{-3})$ 8 $(7.2 \times 10^{-7}) \times (9 \times 10^3)$

1.19 Appropriate accuracy

There is sometimes a limit on the accuracy of an answer. This happens when the numbers we use in a calculation have already been rounded.

Example   4.32 and 5.47 have both been rounded to 2 decimal places. Write down a reliable answer to 4.32 × 5.47.

4.32 × 5.47 = 23.6304   *But this is inaccurate to two or more decimal places.*

Answer: 23.6   *Round off to one decimal place.*

Example   5420 and 5.47 have both been rounded to 3 significant figures. Write down an accurate answer to 5420 ÷ 5.47.

5420 ÷ 5.47 = 973.07   *An accurate answer needs to be written to 2 significant figures.*

Answer: 970

A reasonable answer should have no more significant figures than that of any of the numbers in the calculation.

Exercise 29   Write down an answer, expressed to an appropriate accuracy. Each of the numbers below has been rounded.

1 12.97 × 0.35   **2** 0.612 × 20.471
3 136.74 ÷ 8.60   **4** 3.142 × 5.217
5 2130 ÷ 3.57 (3 s.f.)   **6** 6.213 × 15.24 (4 s.f.)
7 54 200 ÷ 43.2 (3 s.f.) **8** 142.2 ÷ 7.2
9 10.23 × 5.10   **10** 12 ÷ 0.020 (2 s.f.)

11 Write down a reliable figure for the perimeter of the bedroom.

12 A field has dimensions of 48 m by 36 m, to the nearest metre. Write down a reliable figure for the area of the field.

13 The circumference of a lamp shade is 38 cm, to the nearest centimetre. What length of material would you buy to add a frill round 20 similar lampshades?

14 The diameter of a circular pond is 2.37 m. To find the circumference use $C = \pi D$, where π is 3.14, to 2 decimal places. Write a reliable answer for the circumference.

15 The classroom of a college measures 8.4 m by 5.3 m. What is the total floor area of 12 similar classrooms? Write your answer to an appropriate accuracy.

Note: Normally we write down the full and complete answer to a mathematical problem. We only write down an answer appropriately

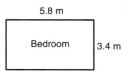
5.8 m

Bedroom   3.4 m

38 cm

rounded when we have a practical situation where the figures have previously been rounded. In your working out always show your complete answer, followed by your appropriately rounded answer.

Review

Exercise 30

Do not use a calculator in this exercise.

Work out mentally:

1 How much longer is 627 mm than 439 mm?

2 Find the total of £327, £503, £239.

3 If 78 pens are to be placed into boxes of eight pens each, how many pens are left over?

4 A thimble weighs 8.5 g. What is the total weight of six of these thimbles?

5 A 200 ml bag of blood is emptied in drips of 0.2 ml. How many drips will a full bag hold?

You may use pen and paper methods to work out the answers to these remaining questions.

6 A graphical calculator costs £35. How much will 238 graphical calculators cost?

7 A local politician shares out 2103 local addresses equally amongst her 48 party volunteers. Any remaining she will visit herself. How many will the politician visit?

8 A sunflower is 933 mm tall. In a week it grows another 487 mm. How tall is it now?

9 A piece of wood, 600 mm in length, has 188 mm cut off. What length remains?

10 How many seconds are there in a day?

Without using a calculator, *estimate* the answers to these problems:

11 3.81×847

12 $689.6 \div 23.98$

13 $\dfrac{41.87 \times 56.56}{3.04 \times 19.8}$

14 $\dfrac{38}{1.95 \times 2.1}$

15 $\dfrac{81 \times 152}{41.3 \times 2.2}$

Exercise 31

1 Add £$\frac{1}{2}$M to £35$\frac{1}{2}$K, where K = £1000, and M is a million.

2 Write in figures the number three million, four hundred and eight thousand, and five.

3 £5 407 890. (a) Write this number in words. (b) Round off this number (i) to the nearest £1000 (ii) to the nearest £100 (iii) to 4 significant figures.

4 Work out (a) 6^5 (b) 4^{-3} (c) 3^4 (d) 5^0 (e) $5^2 \times 4^3$ (f) $9^4 \div 3^3$.

5 Work out the following. Write your answers in their simplest form.

    (a) $\frac{7}{12} = \frac{?}{36}$ (b) $\frac{1}{2} + \frac{1}{5}$ (c) $2\frac{3}{4} + 4\frac{2}{3}$ (d) $\frac{6}{7} - \frac{2}{3}$

    (e) $2\frac{1}{2} - 1\frac{1}{3}$ (f) $\frac{3}{8} \times \frac{5}{6}$ (g) $3\frac{1}{2} \times 3\frac{1}{2}$ (h) $\frac{1}{3} \div \frac{3}{4}$

6 Six nails are each of length $1\frac{2}{5}$ inch. What is the total length when the nails are placed end to end?

7 How many pieces, each $\frac{3}{5}$ yd long, can be cut from a rope $2\frac{2}{5}$ yd long?

8 Five students out of a class of 30 were not wearing trainers. What fraction were wearing trainers?

9 Which is the heavier weight: $\frac{4}{5}$ of 35 kg, or $\frac{3}{4}$ of 36 kg?

10 Round off your answers to the following to 2 decimal places:

    (a) $43.12 \div 1.4$ (b) 1.42×3.9 (c) 7.401×0.8 (d) $43.21 \div 9$

11 Round off your answers to the following to 3 significant figures:

    (a) 210×34.7 (b) $434 \div 0.7$ (c) 10.42×6.1 (d) 50.05×0.07

12 Write your answers to the following problems (i) in standard form (ii) an ordinary number:

    (a) 3.2×0.008 (b) 3200×6700 (c) $3 \times 10^{-3} \times 5 \times 10^6$

Exercise 32

The following questions are all taken from GCSE papers.

1 Do not use a calculator when answering this question. Show all your working.
Show clearly how you would obtain an *estimate* for the following calculation.

$$\frac{597 \times \sqrt{35.7}}{9.2}$$

(3 marks)
[WJEC]

2 In this question you must *not* use a calculator. You must show *all* your working.
Tom buys 67 cameras at £312 each.

    (a) Work out the total cost.   *(3 marks)*

    (b) Write down two numbers you could use to get an approximate answer to your calculation.   *(2 marks)*
[EDEXCEL]

3 (a) Calculate

$$\frac{89.6 \times 10.3}{19.7 + 9.8}$$

(*2 marks*)

(b) *Do not use your calculator in this part of the question.*
By using approximations show that your answer to (a) is about right.
You *must* show all your working. (*2 marks*)

[AQA/SEG]

4 Mark has a market stall. Mark bought 25 melons for his stall. He paid £16 for 25 melons.

(a) Work out the price Mark paid for each melon. Do *not* use a calculator and show *all* your working. (*3 marks*)

Two of the melons were bad. Mark sold the other 23 melons for 149p each.

(b) Work out the total amount for which Mark sold the melons. Do *not* use a calculator and show *all* your working. (*3 marks*)

Mark usually sells oranges for 40p each. He reduces the price to $\frac{7}{8}$ of this.

(c) Work out the new price of an orange. (*2 marks*)

Mark bought his potatoes for 30p for each kilogram. He sold the potatoes and made a profit of 40%.

(d) At what price did Mark sell the potatoes? (*3 marks*)

[EDEXCEL]

5 The table below shows the cost of hiring a ladder.

Cost for the first day	Extra cost per day for each additional day
£13.75	£2.25

A family hires the ladder. The total cost of hiring the ladder was £25. How many days did the family hire it for? (*3 marks*)

[AQA/NEAB]

6 (a) Korky cat food costs 44p a tin. Alec buys 18 tins of Korky cat food. He pays with a £10 note.
How much change should he receive? (*3 marks*)

(b) Alec's cat eats $\frac{2}{3}$ of a tin of Korky each day.
What is the least number of tins Alec needs to buy to feed his cat for 7 days? (*3 marks*)

[AQA/NEAB]

27

7 Work out

    (a) 7 squared   *(1 mark)*

    (b) 3 cubed   *(1 mark)*

    (c) 2^4 *(1 mark)*

    (d) 5×10^3 *(1 mark)*

    (e) 3.2×10^2 *(1 mark)*

                          [OCR/MEG]

8 (a) Which of the fractions $\frac{2}{3}$ and $\frac{3}{4}$ is the larger? Show your working. *(1 mark)*

    (b) Sam gives his dog $\frac{3}{4}$ of a tin of dog food each day. What is the least number of tins Sam needs to buy to feed his dog for 7 days? *(3 marks)*

                          [WJEC]

9 (a) Write down a decimal that lies between $\frac{1}{3}$ and $\frac{1}{2}$ *(1 mark)*

    (b) Which of these two fractions is the bigger? $\frac{3}{4}$ or $\frac{2}{3}$ *(2 marks)*

                          [AQA/NEAB]

10 (a) Express the number $\frac{3}{5}$ as a percentage.   *(1 mark)*

    (b) List the following in order of size, starting with the smallest.

        $\frac{2}{3}$,   0.7,   0.67,   66%   *(2 marks)*

    (c) Calculate the exact value of

        (i) $\frac{1}{2} + \frac{2}{3}$ *(1 mark)*

        (ii) $\frac{4}{5}$ of $2\frac{1}{2}$ *(1 mark)*

        (iii) $5 \div \frac{2}{3}$ *(1 mark)*

                          [OCR]

11
$$F = \frac{ab}{a - b}$$

Imran uses this formula to calculate the value of F. Imran estimates the value of F without using a calculator. $a = 49.8$ and $b = 30.6$.

    (a) (i)   Write down approximate values for a and b that Imran could use to estimate the value of F.   *(1 mark)*

        (ii) Work out the estimate for the value of F that these approximations give.   *(1 mark)*

        (iii) Use your calculator to work out the accurate value for F. Use $a = 49.8$ and $b = 30.6$. Write down all the figures on your calculator display.   *(2 marks)*

Imran works out the value of F with two new values for a and b.

    (b) Calculate the value of F when $a = 9.6 \times 10^{12}$ and $b = 4.7 \times 10^{11}$. Give your answer in standard form, correct to two significant figures.   *(3 marks)*

                          [EDEXCEL]

12 Jameed is going to use his calculator to work out the value of

$$\frac{1.9 \times 10^6}{502 \times \sqrt{0.95}}.$$

He says that the answer will be approximately 4×10^4.

(a) Write 4×10^4 as an ordinary number. *(1 mark)*

(b) *Without using your calculator*, check Jameed's approximation. Show your working. *(3 marks)*

(c) Use your calculator to find the value of $\dfrac{1.9 \times 10^6}{502 \times \sqrt{0.95}}$. Write down all the figures on the calculator display. *(2 marks)*

[OCR/MEG]

13 Last year the population of the United Kingdom was approximately 5.3×10^7.

(a) An average of £680 per person was spent on food last year in the United Kingdom.

What was the total amount spent on food last year in the United Kingdom?

Give your answer in standard form. *(3 marks)*

(b) Last year there were 1.4×10^7 car drivers in the United Kingdom. They spent a total of £1.5×10^{10} on their cars.
What was the average amount spent by each car driver? Give your answer to a suitable degree of accuracy. *(3 marks)*

[AQA/NEAB]

14 The mass of one electron is
0.000 000 000 000 000 000 000 000 91 grams.

(a) Write 0.000 000 000 000 000 000 000 000 91 in standard form. *(2 marks)*

(b) Calculate the mass of five million electrons. Give your answer, in grams, in standard form. *(3 marks)*

[EDEXCEL]

15 A white coffee costs 32 pence. Quicks Drinks gets $\frac{3}{8}$ of this cost.

(a) How much of the 32 pence does Quicks Drinks get? *(2 marks)*

Do not use a calculator in this part of the question.

(b) What is the greatest number of white coffees that could be bought for £7.20? *(3 marks)*

[EDEXCEL]

16 Tom uses his calculator to multiply 17.8 by 0.97. His answer is 18.236.

(a) *Without* finding the exact value of 17.8×0.97, explain why his answer must be wrong. *(1 mark)*

Sally estimates the value of $\dfrac{42.8 \times 63.7}{285}$ to be 8.

(b) Write down three numbers Sally could use to get her estimate.

(2 marks)
[EDEXCEL]

17 (a) Write each of the following numbers in standard form.

(i) 457 170 000 *(1 mark)*

(ii) 0.00000000656 *(1 mark)*

(b) Find, in standard form, the value of each of the following.

(i) $(8.17 \times 10^{-4}) \times (6.54 \times 10^{-5})$ *(1 mark)*

(ii) $\dfrac{3.32 \times 10^4}{7.11 \times 10^{-3}}$ *(2 marks)*

[WJEC]

18 On a computer keyboard there are 104 keys.

(a) 26 of the keys have letters on them.
What fraction of the keys on the keyboard have letters on them? (Give your answer in its simplest form.) *(2 marks)*

(b) 13 of the keys have arrows on them.
What percentage of the keys on the keyboard have arrows on them? *(2 marks)*

[AQA/NEAB]

19 (a) *Do not* use a calculator when answering this part of the question. Show all your working.
Show clearly how you would obtain an *estimate* for the following calculation.

$$\frac{610 \times 4.98}{0.213}$$

(3 marks)

(b) Use your calculator to find, correct to 3 significant figures, the value of

$$\sqrt{54.6^2 - 9.37^3}.$$

(2 marks)
[WJEC]

20 The star Sirius is 81 900 000 000 000 km from the Earth.

(a) Write 81 900 000 000 000 in standard form. *(2 marks)*

Light travels 3×10^5 km in 1 second.

(b) Calculate the number of seconds that light takes to travel from Sirius to the Earth. Give your answer in standard form correct to 2 significant figures. *(3 marks)*

[EDEXCEL]

21 (a) Work out $\dfrac{4.7 \times 20.1}{5.6 - 1.8}$

        Write down your full calculator display.   *(1 mark)*

   (b) Use estimation to check your answer.   *(2 marks)*

                                                        [AQA/NEAB]

22 *Do not* use a calculator to answer this question.

Alun has a part-time job. He is paid £18 each day he works. In 1998 he worked 148 days.

Estimate Alun's total pay for 1998. Write down your calculation and answer.   *(3 marks)*

                                                          [AQA/NEAB]

Ideas for investigations

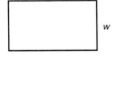

1 The area of a rectangle = length × width.
The measurements for the length and width have both been rounded to one decimal place.

Choose your own figures to work with.

   (a) What is the (i) maximum (ii) minimum length possible?

   (b) What is the (i) maximum (ii) minimum width possible?

   (c) What is the (i) maximum (ii) minimum area possible?

   (d) What is the difference between the maximum and minimum areas?

Repeat the investigation for different figures. How does your choice of figures affect your results? What happens if your figures are rounded to two decimal places? Or to one, two significant figures?

2 Multiply several powers of 2 together (e.g. $2^2 \times 2^3 \times 2^2 = 2^?$) writing your answer in index form. Repeat, with a different combination of powers of 2. Repeat with several combinations of powers of 3 (e.g. $3^3 \times 3^2 \times 3^3 \times 3^4 = 3?$). What do you find this time?

    Can you find a rule which you can easily use to find the answer in cases like this? If so, describe your rule, and show that it works for other examples/numbers.

    Can you find a rule that works when you divide two identical numbers with different powers (e.g. $3^7 \div 3^2$)?

3 Jillian collected a box of apples from her tree. She used half of them for a pudding. She then used half of the remainder for a pie. She gave three-quarters of those that were left to her children for lunch, and had two left over. How many apples did she get from the tree?

    Describe any strategies that you use (even if they don't work). Show, in detail, how you obtain the answer.

4 Susan has £200 to spend on athletics badges. She tries a number of suppliers. Susan wants to buy exactly 100 badges. For each of the following suppliers show whether it is possible to buy exactly 100 badges.

(a) Badges Incorporated: gold badges are £20 each, silver £1 each, and bronze 20p each.

(b) Signatories PLC: gold badges are £20 each, silver £1 each, and bronze are two for 50p.

(c) Make up your own companies and prices.

PERCENTAGES 2

2.1 Percentages

'One hundred' is one of the most important numbers in mathematics. In so many ways the number 100 is used in problems:

$100 \text{ cm} = 1 \text{ m}$ $100\text{p} = £1$ $3.27 = 3\frac{27}{100}$ $100\text{c} = \$1$

Percentages also use the number 100: percentages are directly linked to the number 100, since each per cent is one hundredth.

Example   Change the following percentages into (a) a decimal (b) a fraction: 17%, 20%, $12\frac{1}{2}\%$

$17\% \rightarrow \frac{17}{100} \rightarrow$ (a) 0.17 (b) $\frac{17}{100}$

$20\% \rightarrow \frac{20}{100} \rightarrow$ (a) $0.20 = 0.2$ (b) $\frac{1}{5}$

$12\frac{1}{2}\% \rightarrow \frac{12\frac{1}{2}}{100} \rightarrow$ (a) 0.125 ***On a calculator, 12.5 ÷ 100 is 0.125.***

(b) $\frac{12\frac{1}{2}}{100} \overset{\times 2}{\underset{\times 2}{=}} \frac{25}{200} = \frac{1}{8}$

Exercise 1   Write each of the percentages as (a) a decimal (b) a fraction.

1 40%	**2** 35%	**3** 15%	**4** 44%
5 27%	**6** $82\frac{1}{2}\%$	**7** $32\frac{1}{2}\%$	**8** $17\frac{1}{2}\%$
9 $4\frac{3}{4}\%$	**10** $15\frac{1}{4}\%$		

To change a decimal or a fraction into a percentage we multiply by 100.

Example   Change the following decimals into a percentage: 0.7, 0.19, 0.345

$0.7 \times 100 = 70\%$

$0.19 \times 100 = 19\%$

$0.345 \times 100 = 34.5$ or $34\frac{1}{2}\%$

Example   Change the following into a percentage: $\frac{3}{5}$, $\frac{5}{8}$, $\frac{1}{3}$

$\frac{3}{5} \times 100 = \frac{300}{5} = 60\%$

$\frac{5}{8} \times 100 = \frac{500}{8} = 62.5\%$ or $62\frac{1}{2}\%$

$\frac{1}{3} \times 100 = \frac{100}{3} = 33.33\%$ or $33\frac{1}{3}\%$

Exercise 2

Write each of the following as percentages:

1 0.3   **2** $\frac{1}{2}$ **3** 0.35   **4** $\frac{3}{8}$ **5** $\frac{4}{5}$

6 1.32   **7** 0.3125   **8** $\frac{5}{16}$ **9** $\frac{7}{12}$ **10** $\frac{15}{16}$

Example   What percentage of these diagrams are shaded?

$$\frac{1}{3} = 33\frac{1}{3}\% \qquad \frac{1}{8} = 12\frac{1}{2}\% \qquad \frac{4}{9} = 44\frac{4}{9}\%$$

Exercise 3

Write each shaded part as a percentage of the whole.

The Egyptians thought that the fraction $\frac{2}{3}$ had magical properties. Whenever they had to find $\frac{1}{3}$ of something, they always used to find $\frac{2}{3}$ and then divide by 2!

1   **2**   **3**   **4**

5   **6**   **7**   **8**

Exercise 4

Write in order of size, starting with the smallest.

1 50%, $\frac{3}{5}$, 0.4   **2** 32%, $\frac{1}{5}$, 0.35   **3** 33%, $\frac{1}{3}$, 0.3   **4** 0.80, 70%, $\frac{3}{4}$

5 28%, $\frac{7}{20}$, 0.25   **6** 63%, $\frac{3}{5}$, 0.65   **7** 59%, $\frac{9}{20}$, 0.55   **8** 75%, $\frac{5}{8}$, 0.7

2.2   Finding percentages

Percentages are always fractions of one hundred. Percentages are a convenient way of showing fractions of quantities. We frequently need to change these percentage fractions back into actual quantities.

When finding percentages of money, you may need to round off the answer to the nearest penny.

Example   Find (a) 16% of £14.00 (b) 10% of £2.25 (c) $12\frac{1}{2}$% of £59.40

(a)   16% of £14.00 = $\frac{16}{100} \times 14.00 = \frac{224}{100}$ = £2.24

(b)   10% of £2.25 = $\frac{10}{100} \times 2.25 = \frac{22.5}{100}$ = £0.225 = £0.23 to the nearest penny

(c) $12\frac{1}{2}$% of £59.40 = $\frac{12.5}{100} \times 59.40 = \frac{742.5}{100}$ = £7.425 = £7.43 to the nearest penny

We can find percentages of any quantity, including measurements.

Note: Some calculators have percentage keys. How they work depends upon the calculator. If you have a % key, find out how it works. For example to find 16% of £14.00 press the following keys:

| 1 | 4 | × | 1 | 6 | % |

Do not press | = |.

You should get the answer 2.24.

Exercise 5   Find:

1 10% of £80	**2** 15% of £7.20	**3** 20% of 80 g
4 40% of 150 mm	**5** 25% of 36 kg	**6** 10% of 30 cm
7 5% of 300 t	**8** 35% of £23	**9** 15% of £4.80
10 8% of 500 m		

2.3   Increase and decrease by a percentage

Percentages are frequently used to represent an increase or a decrease of a quantity. There are two commonly used methods for working out increase or decrease. The choice of which to use is yours!

Example   'Local Government Officers receive a $5\frac{1}{2}$% wage increase.' Shreena works for the local council. Her salary is £12 800. What will be her new salary?

Method 1:

£12 800 × $\frac{5.5}{100} = \frac{70400}{100}$ = £704 increase

New salary is £12 800 + £704 = £13 504

Or by using the calculator keys:

$$\boxed{1}\;\boxed{2}\;\boxed{8}\;\boxed{0}\;\boxed{0}\;\boxed{\times}\;\boxed{5}\;\boxed{.}\;\boxed{5}\;\boxed{\%}\;\boxed{+}$$

Note: Your calculator might work it out a different way.

Method 2:

If her present salary is represented by 100%, then an increase of $5\frac{1}{2}\%$ on this will mean a salary represented by $105\frac{1}{2}\%$. New salary is:

$$£12\,800 \times \tfrac{105.5}{100} = \tfrac{1\,350\,400}{100} = £13\,504$$

Example   SALE: 30% OFF ALL PRICES

What is the sale price of a coat normally priced at £48?

Method 1:

$$\tfrac{30}{100} \times £48 = \tfrac{£1440}{100} = £14.40 \text{ decrease}$$

Sale price is £48 − £14.40 = £33.60

Or by calculator keys: $\boxed{4}\;\boxed{8}\;\boxed{\times}\;\boxed{3}\;\boxed{0}\;\boxed{\%}\;\boxed{-}\;\boxed{=}$

But again, check whether your calculator does it this way.

Method 2:

If the normal price is represented by 100%, then a decrease of 30% leaves: 100% − 30% = 70%

Sale price: $\tfrac{70}{100} \times £48 = \tfrac{£3360}{100} = £33.60$

In 1990 the inflation rate in Nicaragua was 13 500%. The highest inflation in the UK was 26.9%, during 1974/5.

Exercise 6

In this exercise answers should be rounded to the nearest penny, if necessary.

Increase the following amounts by the percentage shown:

1 £420 by 85%   **2** 1250 g by 85%   **3** 400 g by 77%

4 £460 by 60%   **5** £250 by 30%

Decrease the following by the percentage shown:

6 240 m by 53%   **7** 3000 ml by 86%   **8** £4.50 by 35%

9 £32 by $10\frac{1}{2}\%$ **10** £9.50 by $6\frac{1}{2}\%$

Exercise 7

1 A £36 coat is reduced by $12\frac{1}{2}\%$. How much will it now cost?

2 The 50 000 population of a town has increased this year by 6%. What is the population now?

3 A dining room suite costs £625. In a sale the price is reduced by 15%. What is the sale price?

4 Mortgage payments of £230 are to be increased by $5\frac{1}{2}\%$. What will the new payments be?

5 Attendance at a play was recorded as 120 people. The following night the attendance increased by 8%. What was the attendance on the second night?

6 In one year 1500 t of potatoes were grown on a farm. The crop increased by 18% the following year by use of a fertiliser. How many tonnes were grown the following year?

7 A man pays 20% tax on earnings of £3900. How much has he left after paying tax?

8 A garage offers a 20% reduction on a £130 car service. How much will you pay?

2.4 VAT

Value Added Tax is added on to bills, prices or receipts for services. The VAT rate is set by the Chancellor of the Exchequer. $17\frac{1}{2}\%$ has been the VAT rate used recently.

Exercise 8

VAT was introduced as a result of the UK joining the EC. Before VAT the UK had Purchase Tax, which was a tax on purchases, but not services.

1 Find the $17\frac{1}{2}\%$ VAT on a £80.00 bill for a meal for four.

2 $17\frac{1}{2}\%$ VAT is added to a telephone bill for £80.60. What is the total bill?

3 A lawn mower costs £125.80 + VAT at $17\frac{1}{2}\%$. What is the total cost?

4 A table is advertised as £78 + VAT. What is the total purchase price if VAT is $17\frac{1}{2}\%$?

5 A portable TV costs £129.99 plus $17\frac{1}{2}\%$ VAT. What is the total cost of buying a portable TV?

2.5 Credit agreements

Credit agreements became popular in the 1920s, and at that time was used mainly as a way of buying cars. They used to be called Hire Purchase agreements.

A credit agreement is signed when you buy an item, but it is **rented** to you, until all payments have been made. The item is then yours to keep. Most credit agreements require you to make an initial percentage deposit, and a number of monthly payments.

£ 380

Example The credit agreement terms on the TV set are a 15% deposit, and 36 monthly payments of £12.70.

Find: (a) the total cost of the credit agreement
(b) the amount saved if the TV is bought for cash.

(a) 15% of £380   = £57.00   *Deposit*
   + 36 × £12.70 = £457.20   *Monthly payments*
   Total credit price   = £514.20

(b) Credit   = £514.20
   – Cash   = £380.00
   Amount saved   = £134.20

Exercise 9 Find: (a) the total cost of the credit agreement
(b) the difference between the cost of the credit agreement, and the cash price.

1 Photographic equipment costs £350. The credit agreement requires a 20% deposit, and 30 payments of £24.90.

2 A leather armchair normally costs £360. It can be bought on credit with 24 monthly payments of £15.50, and a deposit of 25%.

3 A kitchen table is offered with a £200 cash price, or 20% deposit with ten payments of £21 each.

4 A £225 refrigerator can also be bought with a credit agreement, requiring a deposit of 20%, and 12 monthly payments of £20.99.

Credit agreements are called Instalment Credit in other parts of the world.

5 The credit agreement for a £4950 motorbike is an initial deposit of 20%, plus 36 payments of £136.55.

6 A music centre has a price tag of £575. It can be paid for with 12 monthly payments of £45, after a deposit of 15%.

2.6   Simple interest

Simple interest calculations are used to find the *approximate* interest gained once money is invested. It is assumed in each case that the interest rate remains constant.

The world's biggest commercial bank by assets (in 1997) is the Bank of Tokyo-Mitsubishi, Japan, with assets of $692 billion.

$$I = \frac{P \times R \times T}{100} = \frac{PRT}{100}$$

where I = Interest, P = Principal (amount), R = Rate of Interest (%), T = Time (years)

Example Find the simple interest when £200 is invested for $1\frac{1}{2}$ years at an interest rate of 9.5% p.a. (p.a. means per annum, or per year).

$$I = \frac{PRT}{100} = \frac{£200 \times 9.5 \times 1.5}{100} = £28.50$$

Example   Approximately how long would it take for £300 to produce £40 simple interest at a rate of 8.25% p.a.?

In this problem we have P = £300, I = £40, R = 8.25%

$$I = \frac{PRT}{100}, \quad \text{so } £40 = \frac{£300 \times 8.25 \times T}{100}$$ *Put in the values.*

$$= 24.75 \times T$$ *As £300 × 8.25 ÷ 100 = £24.75.*

$$\text{so } T = \frac{£40}{£24.75} = 1.61 \text{ years}$$ *Divide both sides of the equation by the same amount of 24.75.*

$$= 1 \text{ year 7 months, rounded to the nearest month}$$ *0.61 years is 0.61 × 12 months*

Exercise 10

The interest in this exercise is simple interest.

1 Find the interest when £650 is invested for 6 years at 12% p.a.

2 Find the interest when £200 is invested for $3\frac{1}{2}$ years at 9% p.a.

3 Find the interest when £265 is invested for 6 months at 9% p.a.

4 Find the interest when £600 is invested for $4\frac{1}{2}$ years at $8\frac{1}{4}$% p.a.

5 Find the time it takes for an amount of £198 to produce £84 interest at $7\frac{1}{2}$% p.a.

6 Find the time it takes for an amount of £500 to produce £110 interest at 10% p.a.

7 An amount of £500 is invested for $3\frac{1}{2}$ years, and gains £123 interest. What is the rate of interest?

8 Find the interest when £150 is invested for 4 years at $12\frac{1}{2}$% p.a.

9 What amount of money has been invested when it takes $4\frac{1}{2}$ years for an amount of £105 interest to be earned, at a rate of interest of 14% p.a.?

10 Find the time it takes for an amount of £850 to produce £200 interest at 11% p.a.

2.7 Compound interest

A more accurate, and fairer way of calculating interest is by **compound** methods. Interest in many accounts is **accredited** every year, or every six months, or even every day! This means that the interest is added to the amount invested. The total will then continue to earn interest.

Example   Find the interest when £200 is invested for 3 years at an interest rate of 9.5% p.a. The interest is accredited every year.

1st year: $\dfrac{£200 \times 9.5 \times 1}{100} = £19.00$ *Total amount now £200 + £19.00 = £219.00*

2nd year: $\dfrac{£219.00 \times 9.5 \times 1}{100}$ = £20.81 **Total amount now**
£219.00 + £20.81 = £239.81.

3rd year: $\dfrac{£239.81 \times 9.5 \times 1}{100}$ = £22.78 **Total amount now**
£239.81 + £22.78 = £262.59.

Total interest earned is £262.59 − £200 = £62.59

Example Find the interest when £200 is invested for $1\frac{1}{2}$ years at an interest rate of 9.5% p.a. The interest is accredited every 6 months.

The first evidence of the use of compound interest is found in tables used by Babylonian businessmen, dated approximately 700 BC.

1st 6 months: $\dfrac{£200 \times 9.5 \times 0.5}{100}$ = £9.50 **Total amount now**
£200 + £9.50
= £209.50.

2nd 6 months: $\dfrac{£209.50 \times 9.5 \times 0.5}{100}$ = £9.95 **Total amount now**
£209.50 + £9.95
= £219.45.

3rd 6 months: $\dfrac{£219.45 \times 9.5 \times 0.5}{100}$ = £10.42 **Total amount now**
£219.45 + £10.42
= £229.87.

Total interest earned is £229.87 − £200 = £29.87

How does this compare with the example in section 2.6, where the interest was worked out by simple interest methods?
Note: In the worked example above all answers have been rounded to the nearest penny.

Exercise 11

1 £4000 is invested for $1\frac{1}{2}$ years at 10% p.a. compound interest which is accredited every 6 months. What is the total interest earned in this time?

2 £500 is invested for 3 years at 9% p.a. compound interest which is accredited annually. What is the total interest earned in this time?

3 £700 is invested for 2 years at $8\frac{1}{2}$% p.a. compound interest which is accredited every 6 months. What is the total interest earned in this time?

4 £650 is invested for 2 years at 7% p.a. compound interest which is accredited annually. What is the total interest earned in this time?

5 £180 is invested for 4 years at $10\frac{1}{2}$% p.a. compound interest which is accredited annually. What is the total interest earned in this time?

6 £80 is invested for $1\frac{1}{2}$ years at $8\frac{1}{4}$% p.a. compound interest which is accredited every 6 months. What is the total interest earned in this time?

2.8 Wages and salaries

A record salary was earned by George Soros, who was paid $1.1 billion by his company, Soros Fund Management.

If you work for someone else (rather than being self-employed) you are paid a wage, which is normally paid weekly or monthly. There are several ways in which wages are calculated:

Salary: an agreed wage for the whole year, divided equally per week or per month

Time Rate: by the number of hours worked

Piece Rate: by the number of items produced or processed, or jobs done

Commission: a percentage of the sales.

The amount paid for an hour's work during the normal working week is called the **basic rate**. Any work done outside the normal working week is **overtime**, and it's usually paid at time and a quarter, time and a half, or double time.

Example The basic rate is £5.60. Calculate the overtime rates.

Time and a quarter is £5.60 × 1.25 = £7.00   ***Time and a quarter = 1.25 × basic rate.***

Time and a half is £5.60 × 1.5 = £8.40   ***Time and a half = 1.5 × basic rate.***

Double time is £5.60 × 2 = £11.20   ***Double time = 2 × basic rate.***

TIME SHEET		
DAY	BASIC	OVERTIME
Mon.	8	
Tue.	8	
Wed.	$6\frac{1}{2}$	
Thu.	$7\frac{1}{2}$	
Fri.	7	1
Sat.		3

Example The basic rate of pay at a factory is £5.30. Overtime is paid at time and a half from Monday to Friday, and double time at the weekend. Calculate the weekly wage.

Basic rate	= 37 hours × £5.30	= £196.10
Time and a half	= 1 hour × £5.30 × 1.5	= £7.95
Double time	= 3 hours × £5.30 × 2	= £31.80

Total wage is £235.85.

Piece rate is paid by the amount of work done.

Example Martin is paid 2p for each circuit board he assembles per day, up to 500. After this he is paid 3p per board. How much does he earn if he makes 800 boards?

500 × 2p = £10.00
300 × 3p = £9.00
800 made = £19.00

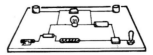

Some people are paid a commission. This is usually a percentage of the actual sales figures for a product or service. Commission is usually paid to sales people, as an incentive for them to perform better. Profits arising out of sales may be passed back to other members of the firm in the form of bonuses, which is a form of commission.

Example Selene sells perfume. She is paid a basic rate of £1.80 per hour, plus 5% commission on sales. During one week she works for 35 hours, and sells perfume to the value of £873. How much is she paid?

$35 \times £1.80 = £63$ *Basic salary*

$5\% \text{ of } £873 = \frac{5}{100} \times £873 = £43.65$ *Commision*

Total earnings = £63 + £43.65 = £106.65

Exercise 12

Calculate the weekly wage in questions 1–4.

1 A mechanic works a basic $37\frac{1}{2}$-hour week, and overtime is paid at time and a half. The basic hourly rate is £4.70 per hour. She works 5 hours overtime (a total of $42\frac{1}{2}$ hours).

2 A man on an assembly line works a basic 40-hour week. His basic rate of pay is £3.80 per hour. The 4 hours overtime worked is paid at time and a quarter.

3 Ms Fairclough is a supervisor. Her basic week is 38 hours at £4.10 per hour. She also works 5 hours overtime a week at time and a half.

4 A woman works a 38-hour basic week, at the basic rate of £4.15 per hour. Her overtime is made up of 4 hours at time and a half, and 2 hours at double time.

5 A man earns £154.44. He has worked 39 hours at the basic rate. What is his basic hourly rate?

6 Michelle earns £40.80 for 5 hours work at the weekend on double time. What basic hourly rate is she paid?

7 For each article up to a maximum of 200 a worker is paid 7p. Above this limit she is paid 8p. How much is she paid for making 360 articles?

8 Brian is paid 15p for each piece of artwork up to 100. After that he is paid a rate of 22p per piece. How much will he earn if he does 130 pieces of artwork?

9 A woman is paid 45p for each page of typing she does for a firm. What will she earn for a 250-page document?

10 A printer employs part-time staff to deliver leaflets at the rate of £4.80 for every complete 100 leaflets. How much is someone paid for delivering 1450?

11 Barry is paid £3.75 each for the express delivery of container boxes. If he delivers more than 20 in a day, he is paid an *extra* 50p per box. How much will he be paid for delivering 26 boxes?

Income Tax was first introduced in 1799 for incomes above £60 p.a.!

12 A car salesman receives 4% commission on the sale of a £8000 car. How much is this?

13 A woman is paid £80 in a week, and commission of 4% on £600. How much is she paid?

14 Bill sells cosmetics at the door. He is paid £2.05 per hour, and 15% commission on sales. How much is he paid for 5 hours work and sales of £120?

15 Val sells newspapers in the precinct. She is paid a basic rate of £2.50 per hour, and also gets $3\frac{1}{2}$% commission on sales. How much is she paid for 25 hours work, and sales of £205 during the week?

16 A man in a shoe shop earns £2.10 per hour, and commission of 8% on sales. How much is he paid for 38 hours work, and sales of £480 during the week?

2.9 **Expressing in percentages**

There will be times when you might need to express one number as a percentage of another.

Example   Colin has gained 68 marks out of 85. Write this as a percentage.

$$\tfrac{68}{85} \times 100 = 68 \div 85 \times 100 = 80\%$$ *Multiply by 100 to change a fraction to a percentage.*

Example   Sue's weekly salary has been increased from £172 to £195. Find the percentage increase, writing your answer to one decimal place.

Actual increase = £195 − £172 = £23

$$\text{Percentage increase} = \frac{\text{actual increase}}{\text{original figure}} \times 100 = \frac{£23}{£172} \times 100 = 13.4\%$$

Example   The cost of a holiday to the USA has fallen from £730 to £650. What is the percentage decrease?

Actual decrease = £730 − £650 = £80

$$\text{Percentage decrease} = \frac{\text{actual decrease}}{\text{original figure}} \times 100$$

$$= \frac{£80}{£730} \times 100$$

$$= 10.96\% \qquad \text{(to 2 d.p.)}$$

Exercise 13

1 There were 8410 people at a sports concert; 4030 were female. What percentage were male?

2 The amount of liquid in a container rises from 8 litres to 10.5 litres. What is the percentage increase?

3 It is found that 8 minutes out of every 60 minutes on television is spent on advertisements. What percentage is this?

4 Of 48 letters taken to the post, 18 are first class. What percentage are second class?

5 In a delivery of 80 apples, 12 were bad. What percentage were bad?

6 Sandra can earn £180 per week. Her net pay is £103. What percentage is this of her weekly earnings?

7 The number of students at a college rises from 1832 to 2009. What is this as a percentage increase?

8 The cost of a digital television has fallen from £180 to £108. What is the percentage decrease in price?

9 In an evening class of 30 adults, 14 are women. What percentage are (a) women (b) men?

10 A car park has 120 cars. Of these 65 are of foreign make. What percentage are (a) foreign (b) British?

Main constituents of air:

Nitrogen 78%,
Oxygen 21%,
Argon 0.9%,
Carbon Dioxide 0.01- 0.1%

2.10 Inverse percentages

Inverse percentage is used when we are given an amount *after* a percentage change, and wish to find the original amount.

Example A bathroom suit costs £305.50 after VAT at $17\frac{1}{2}\%$ has been added. Calculate the price without VAT.

The original price (without VAT) represents 100%.
The £305.50 (with VAT) represents $100\% + 17\frac{1}{2}\% = 117\frac{1}{2}\%$ of the original price.

So $117\frac{1}{2}\% \rightarrow £305.50$ *This is $117\frac{1}{2}\%$.*

$$1\% \rightarrow \frac{£305.50}{117.5}$$ *To find 1%.*

$$100\% \rightarrow \frac{£305.50}{117.5} \times 100$$ *To find 100%.*

$$= £260$$

Example After a wage increase of $6\frac{1}{2}$% a worker's salary is £8679.75. What was his salary before the increase?

$$100\% + 6\tfrac{1}{2}\% = 106\tfrac{1}{2}\%$$ ***After the increase.***

$$106.5\% \rightarrow £8679.75$$ ***This is 106.5%.***

$$1\% \rightarrow \frac{£8679.75}{106.5}$$ ***To find 1%.***

$$100\% \rightarrow \frac{£8679.75}{106.5} \times 100 = £8150$$ ***To find 100%.***

Example A car has had its price reduced by 15% to £6800. How much money has been taken off its price?

The original price is represented by 100%.

$$100\% - 15\% = 85\%$$ ***This represents a reduction of the original price.***

$$85\% \rightarrow £6800$$ ***This is 85%.***

$$1\% \rightarrow \frac{£6800}{85}$$ ***To find 1%.***

$$100\% \rightarrow \frac{£6800}{85} \times 100 = £8000$$ ***To find 100%.***

Its price has been reduced by £8000 − £6800 = £1200.

Exercise 14

1 An aeroplane ticket to Brussels has risen by 25% to £109. What was the original price of the ticket?

2 A car stereo has its price increased by $7\frac{1}{2}$% to £172. What was the original price?

3 A cooker costs £728.50 inclusive of VAT at $17\frac{1}{2}$%. What is its price without the VAT?

4 A coat has been reduced by $12\frac{1}{2}$% to £56 in a sale. What was its original price?

5 A table costs £293.75 inclusive of VAT at $17\frac{1}{2}$%. What is its price without the VAT?

6 A portfolio of shares is sold for £2112, a loss of 12%. Find the price at which they were originally bought?

7 A man weighs 220 kg, having lost 12% of his original weight. What was his original weight?

8 A building job costs £15 040 inclusive of $17\frac{1}{2}$% VAT. How much does it cost without the VAT?

9 The value of a motorbike has decreased by 32% to £2584. What was its original value?

10 The quarterly rental charge for a telephone system has been increased by 14% to £20.52 What was the charge before the increase?

Review

1 Copy and complete the table.

Decimal	Fraction	Percentage
0.9		
	$\frac{3}{8}$	
		45%
		$62\frac{1}{2}$%
	$\frac{2}{3}$	

2 Which is the greater: $\frac{2}{3}$ of £139.53, or 49% of £186?

3 Find 23% of £35.

4 Calculate $42\frac{1}{4}$% of £3500.

5 A salary of £8300 is increased by $4\frac{3}{4}$%. (a) What is the new salary? (b) By how much has it been increased?

6 If 1750 kg is decreased by 15%, what is the new weight?

7 A garage offers $12\frac{1}{2}$% off a service normally costing £160. How much will the service now cost?

8 The price of an adventure holiday is increased by $5\frac{1}{2}$% from £350. How much will it now cost?

9 Find the cost of an exhaust system priced at £56 + VAT at $17\frac{1}{2}$%.

10 A new central heating system is advertised at £946. Credit agreement terms are quoted as 17% deposit, plus monthly instalments of £39.90 over two years. How much *more* expensive is the credit price, compared with the cash price?

11 An amount of £2000 is invested for 2 years at an interest rate of 8% p.a. (a) Calculate the simple interest over 2 years. (b) Calculate the compound interest, if the interest is accredited every 6 months.

12 The cost of a gas fire is now £76.84, an increase of 13% on the original price. What was the original price of the gas fire?

13 A company makes food processors. The price of a processor is increased from £60 to £72. What is the percentage increase?

14 A train ticket was £25 a year ago, but is £29 now. What is the percentage increase?

15 A man's wages have increased by $6\frac{1}{4}$% to £127.50. What wage did he receive before the increase?

16 A woman receives a basic wage of £4.20 per hour; overtime is at time and a quarter. How much will she receive for 38 hours at basic rate and 4 hours at overtime rate?

17 A salesman receives a wage of £1.50 per hour, plus $12\frac{1}{2}$% commission on sales. What will be his wage for 35 hours work, and sales of £1850?

18 In a morning Barry is paid 50p for each machined part up to 40 parts. He is paid 70p for each part over the 40 that he machines. How much will he receive in a morning in which he makes (a) 30 parts (b) 55 parts?

Exercise 16   The following are all questions taken from GCSE papers.

1   Christopher has received his gas bill for the period June to August. The details of the bill are as follows.

        Number of units of gas used is 7939.
        The cost of one unit of gas is 1.52 pence.
        Number of days in this period is 92.
        The standing charge is 10.39 pence per day.

  (a) Find, in pounds, the total cost of the gas, including the standing charge, for the June to August period. Show your working.
(4 marks)

  (b) VAT at 5% is charged on gas bills.
      How much is Christopher's gas bill including VAT? Give your answer in pounds, correct to the nearest penny. *(2 marks)*
[WJEC]

Saxophone
£740 for cash
Credit Plan available

2   The cash price of the saxophone is £740. Tom buys the saxophone using a Credit Plan. He pays a deposit of 5% of the cash price and 12 monthly payments of £65.

Work out the difference between the cost when he used the Credit Plan and the cash price. *(3 marks)*
[EDEXCEL]

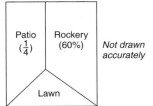

Patio ($\frac{1}{4}$) Rockery (60%) *Not drawn accurately*

Lawn

3   The diagram illustrates a garden. 60% of the garden is a rockery, $\frac{1}{4}$ of the garden is a patio.
What percentage of the garden is lawn? *(3 marks)*
[AQA/NEAB]

4   Shreena is placing an advertisement in a weekly newspaper.

> Single Column Advertisement: £3.25 for each line
> plus VAT at $17\frac{1}{2}$%.

Shreena wants to put a single column advertisement in the paper. The advertisement is 9 lines long.

  (a) Work out the total cost, including VAT, of placing a single column advertisement 9 lines long. *(4 marks)*

A 4-column advertisement is to be 8 centimetres high. The cost, in £, of this advertisement is worked out using the formula:

$$\text{Cost} = \frac{\text{Height (cm)} \times \text{Number of columns} \times 1745}{100}$$

  (b) Work out the cost, in £, of this advertisement. *(2 marks)*
[EDEXCEL]

5 Write these numbers in order of size. Start with the smallest number.

$\frac{7}{8}$ 80%   0.9 $\frac{8}{9}$ *(2 marks)*
                                                        [EDEXCEL]

6 An estate agent makes the following charge for the sale of a house.

Sale price of house	Charge by estate agent
up to £50 000	3% of the sale price
over £50 000	3% of the first £50 000 plus 2% on the remainder

Calculate the charge made by the estate agent for a house sold for
£89 000.   *(3 marks)*
                                                        [AQA/SEG]

7 Compact discs (CDs) are sold for £12 each. $\frac{2}{5}$ of the £12 goes to the
record company.

   (a)   Work out the amount of money which goes to the record
          company.   *(2 marks)*

   30% of the £12 goes to the shopkeeper.

   (b)   (i)   Write 30% as a decimal.   *(1 mark)*
          (ii)   Work out the amount of money which goes to the
                  shopkeeper.   *(2 marks)*

   For each CD sold, £0.84 goes to the singer.

   (c)   Work out the percentage of the £12 which goes to the singer.
                                                         (2 marks)

   For each CD sold, £0.24 goes to the song-writer.

   (d)   Work out the fraction of the £12 which goes to the song-writer.
          Give your fraction in its simplest form.   *(3 marks)*
                                                        [EDEXCEL]

8 (a)   A car cost £14 000 when it was new. Now it is worth £9100.
          Express its value now as a fraction of its value when it was new.
          Give your answer in its simplest form.   *(2 marks)*

   (b)   The value of another car has dropped by 20%. Its value is now
          £8200.
          What was its original value?   *(2 marks)*
                                                        [AQA/NEAB]

9 (a)   Harold invests £850 at 8% p.a. simple interest. Calculate the total
          amount of money he has at the end of three years. *(3 marks)*

   (b)   Katherine invests £600 in a simple interest account. At the end of
          two years her investment has become £684. What is the annual
          percentage rate of simple interest?   *(2 marks)*
                                                        [WJEC]

10 A 'Travel Saver Card' entitles the holder to 40% off the normal price of a journey.

(a) A particular journey normally costs £28.50.
How much would it cost with a Travel Saver Card? *(2 marks)*

(b) The Travel Saver Card price for another journey is £18.60.
What is the normal price of this journey? *(3 marks)*

[AQA/SEG]

11 (a) Alex has a part-time job. His basic rate of pay is £3.70 per hour. After he has worked 8 hours he is paid at the overtime rate. The overtime rate is one and a half times the basic rate.

(i) Calculate the amount that Alex is paid for one hour of overtime. *(1 mark)*

(ii) Calculate Alex's total pay for a day when he worked $2\frac{3}{4}$ hours overtime after completing 8 hours at the basic rate. Give your answer to a suitable degree of accuracy. *(3 marks)*

(b) In 1997 people did not pay Income Tax on the first £3800 they earned in a year. The remainder was taxed at 20%.

(i) Salma earned £5400 in 1997. Calculate the amount of tax that Salma paid. *(2 marks)*

(ii) Reshma paid £180 in tax in 1997. Calculate how much she earned. *(3 marks)*

[OCR/MEG]

12 Two shops sell the same make of calculator. At Calculators are Us, the price of a calculator is £7.50 plus VAT. At Top Calculators, the price is £8.75, this includes VAT. VAT is charged at a rate of 17.5%.
Work out the difference in cost between the two prices. *(3 marks)*

[EDEXCEL]

All Prices Down by 10%

NOW ONLY £32.40

13 In a sale a dress costs £32.40. The original price has been reduced by 10%. What was the original price? *(3 marks)*

[AQA/NEAB]

14 Class 11A has 30 pupils. 18 of these pupils are girls. What percentage of the class is girls? *(2 marks)*

[EDEXCEL]

15 £500 is invested for 2 years at 6% per annum compound interest.

(a) Work out the total interest earned over the 2 years. *(3 marks)*

£250 is invested for 3 years at 7% per annum compound interest.

(b) By what single number must £250 be multiplied to obtain the total amount at the end of the 3 years? *(1 mark)*

[EDEXCEL]

16 Sam wants to buy a Hooper washing machine. Hooper washing machines are sold in three different shops.

Washing Power	**Whytes**	**Clean Up**
$\frac{1}{4}$ OFF usual price of £330	20% OFF usual price of £320	£210 plus VAT at $17\frac{1}{2}$%

(a) Work out the cost of the washing machine in the Washing Power shop. *(2 marks)*

(b) Work out the cost of the washing machine in the Whytes shop. *(2 marks)*

(c) Work out the cost of the washing machine in the Clean Up shop. *(2 marks)*

[EDEXCEL]

Ideas for investigations

1 A couple make and sell document cases. The weekly sales figures over a period of six weeks are:

283, 297, 255, 218, 298, 323

What is the average number sold in a week?

The couple employ three workers who each expect a wage of about £120 per week for making the document cases, which are sold for £25 each. The normal working week is 36 hours, and the normal work rate is about 90 document cases per worker in a week ($2\frac{1}{2}$ per hour). To produce more will require overtime at time and a quarter, or a faster rate of working.

The manager has three options when it comes to paying the wages of the workers: (a) time-rate working (b) piece-rate working (c) a commission on the number of cases sold.

Work out the basic rate of pay under each of the three options. Use your figures to calculate the extra weekly wage bill in producing the extra document cases needed per week. Comment on the consequences of the three options: from the point of view of the workers, and the manager. Can you propose any recommendations? Can you describe any other options?

2 A man has £500, which is invested in an account. The interest rate is 10%. Calculate how long it would take to double the investment if the account is accredited at the end of (a) every year (b) every six months (c) every three months. Repeat the investigation for different interest rates (e.g. 8%, 7%, 11%, 12%).

3 Find out from your local Estate Agent or Building Society the cost of buying a house. Find the details of a house you might want to buy from the Estate Agent, along with details of other charges you may face when buying a house. (a) How much will it cost you to buy the house? (b) What will be the monthly outgoings once you have bought the house?

NUMBER R**3**ELATIONS

3.1 Ratio

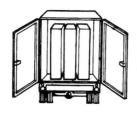

A ratio is a way of representing the relationship between two or more quantities.

Example   There are nine boxes which are divided between a van and a lorry.
The van can carry three boxes, the lorry can carry six boxes.
Represent this as a ratio in its simplest form.

The boxes are shared between the van and the lorry in the ratio 3 : 6.

3 : 6 can be simplified to become $3 : 6 = 1 : 2$
$\div 3 \quad \div 3$

This relationship tells us that the lorry is carrying twice as much as the van.

Exercise 1

Write these ratios in their simplest form:

1 2 : 8	**2** 3 : 6	**3** 18 : 12	**4** 7 : 21	**5** 5 : 20
6 4 : 6	**7** 4 : 10	**8** 42 : 49	**9** 8 : 4	**10** 15 : 30

Example   Simplify the ratios
    (a) 16 kg : 800 g   (b) £2 : 40p   (c) 10 mm : 1 m

A ratio compares two quantities which are *alike*: we first need to change the units.

(a) 16 kg : 800 g = 16000 g : 800 g = 20 : 1   ***Change all the units to grams.***

(b) £2 : 40p = 200p : 40p = 5 : 1   ***Change all the units to pence.***

(c) 10 mm : 1 m = 10 mm : 1000 mm = 1 : 100   ***Change all the units to millimetres.***

Exercise 2   Write these ratios in their simplest form.

1 £3 : 25p	**2** 55 g : 2 kg	**3** 30 cm : 1 m
4 2 km : 250 m	**5** £1.50 : 50p	**6** 10 g : 0.5 kg
7 £1.25 : 10p	**8** 4 kg : 40 g	**9** 800 cm : 4 km
10 50 g : 1 kg	**11** 10 cm : 2 mm	**12** £2.80 : £3.50

Example   Express these ratios in the form $1 : n$ (a) $2 : 3$ (b) $10 : 35$

To change a ratio into the form $1 : n$, divide both numbers by the number on the left-hand side.

(a) $2 : 3 = \dfrac{2}{2} : \dfrac{3}{2} = 1 : 1.5$ ***Divide both sides by 2.***

(b) $10 : 35 = \dfrac{10}{10} : \dfrac{35}{10} = 1 : 3.5$ ***Divide both sides by 10.***

Exercise 3   Express these ratios in the form $1 : n$

1 12 : 3	**2** 7 : 21	**3** 2 : 15	**4** 5 : 9	**5** 4 : 10
6 5 : 12	**7** 2 : 10	**8** 12 : 48	**9** 2 : 5	**10** 3 : 27

One common use of ratios in the form 1 : n is in map scales.

A ratio is a comparison between two quantities. Ratios, using fractions, can be related to decimals and percentages.

'4% of nothing is nothing. We want 12%.' Quoted during a pay dispute, The Daily Telegraph, 15th June 1982.

Example   Change the following into a decimal and a percentage:
(a) $4 : 5$ (b) $3 : 20$

Fraction	Decimal	Percentage

(a) $4 : 5 \ \rightarrow \tfrac{4}{5} \ = 4 \div 5 \ = 0.8 \ \rightarrow \times 100 = 80\%$ ***The first number is 80% of the second number.***

(b) $3 : 20 \rightarrow \tfrac{3}{20} = 3 \div 20 = 0.15 \rightarrow \times 100 = 15\%$ ***The first number is 15% of the second number.***

Exercise 4   Change the following as indicated.

ALL CHANGE

1 10 : 35 into a fraction	**2** 1 : 5 into a decimal
3 16 : 64 into a percentage	**4** 18 : 12 into a decimal
5 5 : 15 into a fraction	**6** 4 : 10 into a percentage
7 8 : 16 into a decimal	**8** 2 : 5 into a percentage
9 7 : 10 into a fraction	**10** 5 : 2 into a fraction

Example $2 : 5 = 4 : ?$ Find the missing number.

We use the relationship between the numbers to work out what the missing number is.

$2 : 5 = 4 : ?$ So we have $2 : 5 = 4 : 10$ *Both sides of the ratio are multiplied by 2.*

Example $4 : ? = 20 : 35$ Find the missing number.

We use the relationship between the numbers to work out what the missing number is.

$4 : ? = 20 : 35$ So we have $4 : 7 = 20 : 35$ *Both sides of the ratio are multiplied by 5.*

Exercise 5

'All animals are equal, but some are more equal than others.' George Orwell, Animal Farm.

Find the missing number in each question.

1 $1 : 6 = 5 : ?$ **2** $? : 20 = 3 : 4$

3 $2 : 5 = ? : 10$ **4** $1 : 9 = ? : 27$

5 $6 : 5 = ? : 10$ **6** $1 : 6 = ? : 42$

7 $? : 6 = 12 : 18$ **8** $3 : ? = 4 : 12$

9 $24 : 14 = 12 : ?$ **10** $5 : 2 = ? : 8$

Example   In a class the ratio of males : females is $1 : 2$. If there are nine males, how many females are there?

M   F   M   F
$1 : 2 = 9 : ?$

Note that the number of males has been multiplied by 9.

So $2 \times 9 = 18$ females

Exercise 6

1 Two lengths of wood are in the ratio $4 : 7$. The longer length is 35 cm. What is the shorter length?

2 Two soap packets contain powder in the ratio $3 : 10$. The smaller contains 1 kg of powder. What weight of powder does the larger packet contain?

3 An alloy contains iron and copper in the ratio $5 : 1$. A block of this alloy contains 30 kg of iron. What weight of copper does it contain?

4 In a rectangle the ratio of the width to the length is $5 : 12$. The length is 30 cm. Find the width.

5 In making concrete you need sand and cement in the ratio $4 : 1$; 30 kg of cement has been delivered. What weight of sand is needed?

6 The speed of two boats is in the ratio $9 : 4$. The speed of the second boat is 10 km/h. What is the speed of the first boat?

7 The teacher to student ratio is $1 : 18$. If a college has 180 staff, how many students are there?

8 A machine makes electrical components, of which 2 in 35 are faulty. If it has made 16 faulty components how many good ones has it made?

3.2 Proportional parts

Example Norman and his daughter have won £10 000 in a competition, which cost 80p to enter. Norman paid 50p, and his daughter paid 30p. How should they share the winnings?

$50 : 30 = 5 : 3$ *Add the parts to make 8 altogether.*

£10 000 ÷ 8 = £1250   *Divide the total by 8 to find each part.*

Norman has 5 parts, and his daughter has 3 parts:

So $5 \times £1250 : 3 \times £1250$ *Calculate their actual amounts.*

$= £6250 : £3750$

Norman's share is £6250, and his daughter's is £3750.
(Check: £6250 + £3750 = £10 000)

Exercise 7

1 Divide £35 in the ratio 4 : 3
2 Divide 600 g in the ratio 3 : 2
3 Divide £14.91 in the ratio 2 : 5
4 Divide 48.24 m in the ratio 2 : 7
5 Divide 32 cm in the ratio 3 : 5
6 Divide 48 kg in the ratio 3 : 5
7 If 75 cm is divided in the ratio 3 : 2, how long is each section?
8 The ratio of boys to girls in a youth club is 4 : 5. There are 72 members. How many boys and how many girls are there?
9 Chris needs to make 600 g of short-crust pastry. Flour and fat are needed in the ratio 2 : 1. How much flour is needed?
10 A company posts 387 letters in a week. The ratio of 1st to 2nd class letters is normally 2 : 7. How many 2nd class stamps are needed in a week?

Example Brian and Jane have divided an amount of money in the ratio 3 : 5. Brian's share is £36. How much was the original amount of money?

The ratio is 3 : 5   *Brian's share is 3 parts out of 8.*

£36 ÷ 3 = £12   *Find 1 part.*

So 8 parts (the whole) is $8 \times £12 = £96$.

Exercise 8

1 A lorry is loaded with fruit and vegetable boxes in the ratio 5 : 7. The fruit has a weight of 8.5 tonnes. What is the total weight of both fruit and vegetables?

2 A quantity of alloy is made from copper and zinc in the ratio 5 : 6. The weight of copper used is 25 kg. What will be the final weight of the alloy?

3 A rope is cut into two lengths in the ratio 3 : 4. The longer of the lengths is 113.2 metres. What was the length of the original single rope?

4 The weight of two boxes is in the ratio 4 : 5. The heavier box has a weight of 97.5 kg. What is the total weight of the two boxes?

5 A cable is cut into two sections with lengths in the ratio 3 : 5. The shorter of the two lengths is 49.5 metres. What was the length of the original cable?

6 The directors of a company share an amount of money in the ratio 1 : 2 : 3. The Managing Director, who has the greatest share, receives £4572. What is the total amount of money they have to share between them?

One and one make two,
But if one and one should marry,
Isn't it queer,
Within a year,
There's two and one to carry.

3.3 Direct proportion

Direct proportion is when two quantities are directly related; an increase in one will result in a proportionately similar increase in the other.

Example   Five similar books cost £29.95. How much will seven cost?

5 books cost £29.95.

1 book costs £29.95 ÷ 5 = £5.95. ◄——— *Always work back to one. This is called a unitary method.*

7 books cost £5.95 × 7 = £41.65.

£29.75   ?

Exercise 9

In the questions below, assume that all rates remain the same.

1 If 4 kg of sugar cost £2.12, how much will 7 kg cost?

2 Seven pencils cost 56p. How much will five pencils cost?

3 Betty takes 50 minutes to walk 4 km. How long will it take her to walk 3 km?

4 A woman is paid £18.20 for seven hours work at a Nursing Home. How much will she receive for five hours work?

5 Six razor blades cost 42p. How much will ten cost?

6 Four boxes weigh 30 kg. What weight will nine boxes be?

7 Fencing costs £10.80 for nine metres. How much will it cost for seven metres?

8 A machine makes 245 parts in 35 minutes. How many will it make in one hour?

3.4 Inverse proportion

With inverse proportion, two quantities are inversely related, and a *decrease* in one will result in a proportionately similar *increase* in the other.

The use of proportional methods for solving problems is one of the earliest techniques; both Egyptians and Greeks used it extensively.

Example   Five identical machines take 20 hours to complete production of an order for machine parts. One machine breaks down. How long will it now take to produce a similar order?

5 machines take 20 hours.

1 machine would take $20 \times 5 = 100$ hours.   ***Always work back to one.***

4 machines would take $100 \div 4 = 25$ hours.

Exercise 10

In the questions below, assume that all rates remain the same.

1   A local farmer employs 18 students in his orchard. It takes them three days to pick the apples. How long would it take 12 students?

2   Three men can paint a concert hall in 20 days. How long will it take five men?

3   Seven machines are used to complete an order in 21 hours. How long would it take three machines to complete a similar order?

4   To complete a harvest, a farmer needs two combine harvesters for six days. How long would it take if he had three combine harvesters?

5   Travelling at 30 m.p.h. it takes a car four hours for a journey. How long would the journey take at a speed of 40 m.p.h.?

6   Two secretaries can type a document between them in nine hours. How long would it take three secretaries working together?

7   Eggs are packed into boxes of six each. One hundred boxes are needed for a large order. If the eggs were to be packed into new boxes containing eight eggs each, how many of these new boxes would be needed?

8   It takes nine men 30 days to complete a contract. How long would it take 15 men?

3.5 House insurance

Once we have bought a house we need to protect it. If there is a fire, flood or storm damage an insurance policy pays for the repairs. We pay for the policy on a monthly or annual basis, whether we have damage or not. If the time comes to make a **claim** from the company for damage, they will pay the bills as long as the policy is up to date.

The cost of paying for the insurance policy is called the **premium**. House insurance can be divided into two separate policies: Buildings insurance and Contents insurance. By buildings we mean the actual structure of the house: walls, windows, roof, garage, floors and so on. The premium paid on the buildings is determined by the value of the house. The Contents insurance is for everything inside the house such as carpets and curtains, furniture, clothes, hi-fi, washing machine, and so on. This type of insurance is linked to the estimated value of the items inside the house.

House insurance normally covers a property from theft, fire, lightning, explosion, earthquake, storm and flood, riots, falling trees, subsidence, aircraft and vehicles.

Example   Richard has a house valued at £72 000, and contents estimated at a value of £75 000. His insurance company has annual charges of £1.85 per £1000 value for Buildings insurance, and £4.60 per £1000 estimated value for Contents insurance. What will be his total annual insurance bill?

Buildings: £72 000 ÷ 1000 × £1.85   = £133.20

Contents: £75 000 ÷ 1000 × £4.60   = £345.00

Total cost of insurance   = £478.20

Exercise 11

1   Marie has a house which is worth £97 500. What would the house insurance cost per year at a rate of £1.92 per £1000 value?

2   Don obtains an insurance quotation of £5.25 per £1000 for the contents of his flat. What would be the annual charge for insurance if he thinks the contents are worth about £59 600?

3   Vera has been asked to renew her Contents insurance. She estimates the value of all the contents to be £18 700, and is to be charged £0.45 per £100 insured. What will the new insurance premium be?

House insurance does not normally cover damage from coastal erosion, faulty workmanship or accidental demolition, mining, or war.

4   Martin has just bought a house for £72 900. How much will it cost him for House insurance at the rate of £1.82 per £1000?

5   Paul and Clare buy a house for £140 000. They have accumulated possessions for the house with an estimated value of £127 500. They receive quotations from an insurance company as follows: Buildings: £1.72 per £1000, Contents: £0.43 per £100. Find the total cost of insurance for the house and possessions.

3.6 Speed

This is a useful way for remembering rates in speed. From this sign you can write down these formulas:

Distance = Time × Speed

$$\text{Time} = \frac{\text{Distance}}{\text{Speed}}$$

$$\text{Speed} = \frac{\text{Distance}}{\text{Time}}$$

Example   How long will it take a greyhound to race 238 m at 17 m/s?

$$\text{Time} = \frac{\text{Distance}}{\text{Speed}} = \frac{238}{17} = 14 \text{ seconds}$$

Example   A horse takes 6 minutes to gallop 5 km.
What is the speed of the horse, in km/h?

$$\text{Speed} = \frac{\text{distance}}{\text{time}}$$

$$= \frac{5 \text{ km}}{0.1 \text{ h}}$$

remember to change units:
6 min = $\frac{6}{60}$ h = 0.1 h.

$$= 50 \text{ km/h}$$

Exercise 12

The fastest speed recorded by a jet-engined car is 1227 km/h, or 763 m.p.h.: Thrust SSC, Andy Green (GB), October 1997.

1 An aeroplane flew at 400 m.p.h. How far did it travel in (a) 2 h (b) $3\frac{1}{2}$ h?

2 A car goes at a speed of 48 m.p.h. on the motorway. How long will it take to travel (a) 60 miles (b) 72 miles?

3 A motorbike travels for four hours and goes 160 miles. What is the average speed over this distance?

4 How long does it take a go-kart to go 60 miles around a circuit at 40 m.p.h.?

5 A bird flies 259 m in seven seconds. What is its speed in metres per second?

6 Brian cycles at an average speed of 24 km/h. How far will he go in $3\frac{1}{2}$ hours?

7 A boat goes a distance of 72 nautical miles in four hours. What is its average speed, in knots (nautical miles per hour)?

8 Majid can walk at a speed of 6 km/h. How far can he walk in 30 minutes?

3.7 Average speed

When calculating **average** speed we use: Speed $= \dfrac{\text{Distance}}{\text{Time}}$, as in the previous section. When calculating average speed over *more* than one distance we need to use:

$$\text{Average speed} = \frac{\text{Total distance}}{\text{Total time}}$$

Example A car travels 2 hours at 30 m.p.h., and 100 miles at 25 m.p.h. What is the average speed for the journey?

1st part of journey: distance travelled $= 2 \times 30 = 60$ miles

2nd part of journey: time taken $= 100 \div 25 = 4$ hours

$$\text{Average speed} = \frac{\text{total distance}}{\text{total time}}$$

$$= \frac{60 + 100 \text{ miles}}{2 + 4 \text{ hours}}$$

Add the distances for the 2 parts of the journey.

Add the times for the 2 parts of the journey.

$$= \frac{160}{6} \text{ m.p.h.} = 26\tfrac{2}{3} \text{ m.p.h.}$$

Exercise 13

Find the average speed for the whole journey in the following:

1 A coach travels at 42 km/h for 4 hours, and then a distance of 105 km over 3 hours.

2 A cyclist travels at 12 km/h for 2 hours, and then at 15 km/h for 4 hours.

3 A car travels at 65 km/h for 6 hours, and then at 85 km/h for 4 hours.

4 A lorry travels at 264 km/h over 8 hours, and then at 45 km/h for 4 hours.

5 A train travels 280 km at a speed of 70 km/h, and then a distance of 480 km over 6 hours.

6 A car travels 67 km in the first hour of its journey. It then drives 392 km at an average speed of 56 km/h.

7 A cyclist travels at 12 km/h for 6 hours, and then at 9 km/h for 3 hours.

8 A coach travels at 45 km/h for 5 hours, and then 252 km at an average speed of 63 km/h.

3.8 Foreign currencies

As people travel outside the country more frequently, and as we do more trade with other countries, particularly within Europe, we need to be able to change from pounds sterling to other currencies.

The rates shown are the amounts of foreign currency you will receive for your pound on a particular day. These could change from hour to hour. The bank will also add a service charge whenever you change your money.

> To change *out* of £sterling you *multiply* by the rate.

> To change *back* to £sterling you *divide* by the rate.

TOURIST RATES

Australia 2.19 dollars
Austria 19.55 schillings
Belgium 57.26 francs
Canada 1.9945 dollars
Denmark 10.82 kroner
France 9.49 francs
Germany 2.79 marks
Greece 318 drachmae
Holland 3.14 guilders
Hong Kong 13.47 dollars
Ireland 1.04 punts
Italy 2100 lire
Malta 0.55 lire
New Zealand 3.01 dollars
Norway 10.93 kroner
Portugal 244 escudos
Spain 176 pesetas
Sweden 10.16 kronor
Switzerland 2.46 francs
Turkey 8134 lire
US 1.760 dollars

Example (a) Change £50 to dollars
  (b) Change £50IR into pounds sterling.

Paper money was an invention of the Chinese, first tried in AD 812.

(a) £50 × 1.7560 = \$87.80 **Muliply to change out of pounds.**

(b) £50IR ÷ 1.04 = £48.08 to the nearest penny. ◄ **Divide to change back into pounds.**

Exercise 14

Change the following amounts, in pounds sterling, to the currency given. Round off, if necessary, to 2 decimal places.

1 £40 to schillings **2** £65 to Italian lire **3** £480 to marks

4 £15.20 to Swedish kronor **5** £800 to French francs

6 £727 to \$US **7** £222 to pesetas **8** £135.50 to punts

Change the following into pounds sterling. Round your answers, if necessary, to the nearest penny.

9 US \$270 **10** 156 guilders **11** 522 pesetas

12 415 Swiss francs **13** 75 Belgian francs **14** 6000 drachmas

15 85 Norwegian kroner **16** 3500 escudos

Use the exchange rate given in the question:

17 A watch costs 475f in a Paris shop. If 12f = £1, what would the watch cost in pounds sterling?

18 A radio is bought in Rome for 48 000 lire. If 2000 lire is about one pound, what is the approximate cost of the radio in pounds sterling?

19 If 2.71 marks = £1, what would be the equivalent cost, in Germany, of a crate of manufactured parts, valued in this country at £9750?

20 A large cuckoo clock costs 96.25 Swiss francs. If you can get 2.75 Swiss francs for every £1, what is the cost in pounds sterling?

3.9 Directed numbers

The temperature shown is 3 °C. What temperature will be 5° below this?
The temperature will fall to −2 °C. This is a directed number.
Note: 5 is the same as + 5.

Example (a) The temperature falls by 10 °C from 6 °C. What is the temperature now?

(b) What is the difference in temperature from 3 °C to −6 °C?

(a) 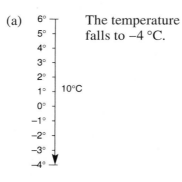 The temperature falls to −4 °C.

(b) 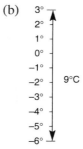 The difference in temperature is 9 °C.

The highest temperature achieved is 510 000 000 °C in the centre of a fusion test reactor in 1994. The lowest temperature is −273.15 °C, recorded in a laboratory experiment.

Exercise 15

Find the temperature when:

1 5 °C falls by 6 °C   **2** −1 °C falls by 2 °C   **3** 2 °C falls by 9 °C

4 3 °C falls by 7 °C   **5** −4 °C rises by 6 °C   **6** −2 °C rises by 7 °C

7 7 °C falls by 13 °C   **8** 5 °C falls by 8 °C   **9** −4 °C rises by 3 °C

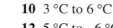

Find the difference when the temperature changes from:

10 3 °C to 6 °C   **11** 3 °C to −5 °C

12 5 °C to −6 °C   **13** −1 °C to 4 °C

14 −1° to −4 °C   **15** −2 °C to 5 °C

Example The temperature is 4 °C. It falls by 7 °C. What is the new temperature?

This problem can be shown in writing:

$$(+4 \ °C) + (−7 \ °C) = −3 \ °C \quad \text{or} \quad (+4) + (−7) = −3$$

Exercise 16

Work out the answers to these problems.

1 (−2) + (+5)   **2** (−11) + (+7)   **3** (+9) + (−17)

4 (−3) + (−1)   **5** (+4) + (−4)   **6** (−12) + (+3)

7 (−3) + (0)   **8** (−11) + (+6)   **9** (−6) + (−6)

Example   The temperature was 5 °C; it is now −2 °C.
What is the difference in temperature?

This problem can be solved by writing
(−2 °C) − (+5 °C) = −7 °C, which is a fall of 7 °C.

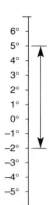

Exercise 17

Work out these differences:

1 (+3) − (+2)   **2** (+4) − (0)
3 (+5) − (−1)   **4** (−2) − (+7)
5 (−4) − (−5)   **6** (−9) − (+4)
7 (+11) − (+4)   **8** (+11) − (−4)
9 (+14) − (+21)

Example

(+4) × (−2) = −8

(+12) ÷ (+2) = +6

(−2) × (+3) = −6

(−12) ÷ (−3) = +4

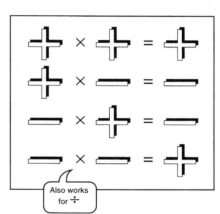

Also works for ÷

Exercise 18

Use the rules given to find the answers to:

1 +5 × +4   **2** + 8 ÷ +2   **3** −3 × +4
4 +10 ÷ −5   **5** −3 × +10   **6** −21 ÷ −3
7 +4 × −8   **8** −8 × −8   **9** −27 ÷ −3
10 −7 × −6   **11** −24 ÷ −6   **12** +6 × −9

Exercise 19

Work out:

1 (3) + (−1)   **2** (7) − (−2)   **3** (3) − (+2)
4 (−30) ÷ (+2)   **5** (−3) × (7)   **6** (−4) × (+3)
7 (−3) + (−1)   **8** (7) + (−2)   **9** (+4) + (+4)
10 (+9) × (−4)   **11** (+8) × (−5)   **12** (+18) ÷ (−3)

3.10 Number types

Factors:

A factor is a number that divides exactly into another number.
The factors of 12 are 1, 2, 3, 4, 6 and 12.

The Greeks were the first to investigate prime numbers, about the time of Pythagoras.

HCF:

The highest common factor (HCF) of the two numbers is the biggest number that will divide into both numbers exactly.
The factors of 20 are 1, 2, 4, 5, 10 and 20.
So the HCF of 12 and 20 is 4.

Multiples:

A multiple of a number is produced when that number is multiplied by another number.
Multiples of 3 are: 3, 6, 9, 12, 15, 18, ...

Prime numbers:

These are numbers which do not have any other factors other than 1 and themselves: 2, 3, 5, 7, 11, 13, ...
Note: the number 1 is *not* a prime number.

Exercise 20

1 Find all the factors of each of the following numbers:
   (a) 8   (b) 15   (c) 28   (d) 39   (e) 40   (f) 24

2 Write down three multiples of each of the following numbers:
   (a) 6   (b) 5   (c) 9   (d) 11   (e) 7

3 Find the highest common factor (HCF) of each pair of numbers:
   (a) 18, 24   (b) 9, 12   (c) 8, 16   (d) 21, 35   (e) 2, 8

4 Find three multiples of 7 that are bigger than 60.

5 Find three numbers that have a factor of 9.

6 Write out the first twenty prime numbers.

3.11 Squares and cubes

Square numbers

$1 \times 1 = \underline{1}$ $2 \times 2 = \underline{4}$ $3 \times 3 = \underline{9}$ $4 \times 4 = \underline{16}$

Cube numbers:
$$1 \times 1 \times 1 = 1$$
$$2 \times 2 \times 2 = 8$$ *These are the cube numbers.*
$$3 \times 3 \times 3 = 27$$

The square root of a number gives the number which when multiplied by itself (squared) will give the original number.

$$5 \times 5 = 25 \qquad \sqrt{25} = 5$$
5 is the square root of 25.

The cube root of a number gives the number which when cubed will give the original number.

$$4 \times 4 \times 4 = 64 \qquad \sqrt[3]{64} = 4$$

4 is the cube root of 64.

Exercise 21

1 Write out the first twenty square numbers.

2 Write out the first twenty cube numbers.

3 Find the following:
   (a) $\sqrt{49}$ (b) $\sqrt{81}$ (c) $\sqrt[3]{8}$ (d) $\sqrt[3]{125}$ (e) $\sqrt{169}$

4 The number 20 can be made from 'square sums': $20 = 16 + 4 = 4^2 + 2^2$.
   Which other numbers between 1 and 25 can be found by adding two square numbers?

5 Continue the pattern downwards:

$1^2 =$	1×1	$= ?$
$11^2 =$	11×11	$= ?$
$111^2 =$	111×111	$= ?$
$? =$	$? \times ?$	$= ?$

6 Continue the pattern downwards:

$3^2 =$	3×3	$= ?$
$33^2 =$	33×33	$= ?$
$333^2 =$	333×333	$= ?$
$? =$	$? \times ?$	$= ?$

7 Find the following, giving your answer correct to 4 decimal places.
   (a) $\sqrt{17}$ (b) $\sqrt[3]{30}$ (c) $\sqrt{8.9}$ (d) $\sqrt[3]{7.5}$ (e) $\sqrt{0.8}$

3.12   Products of primes

All numbers can be made up from products of prime numbers, that is, a number of prime numbers multiplied together.

The highest known prime number is $2^{3\,021\,377} - 1$, which is $909\,526$ digits long discovered on 27th January 1998 by Roland Clarkson (USA).

Example   Find the prime products of (a) 540   (b) 210.

Take each prime in turn, starting with the smallest (2), and divide it into the number as many times as possible. Then divide by the next prime, and the next, until the number is reduced to 1.

(a) 2) 540
    2) 270
    3) 135
    3) 45
    3) 15
    5) 5
       1

(b) 2) 210
    3) 105
    5) 35
    7) 7
) 1

Always start with 2.

Divide by prime numbers only.

So $210 = 2 \times 3 \times 5 \times 7$

So $540 = 2 \times 2 \times 3 \times 3 \times 3 \times 5 = 2^2 \times 3^3 \times 5$

Exercise 22 Express each of these numbers as a product of its prime factors:

1 36	**2** 96	**3** 1080	**4** 27	**5** 72
6 360	**7** 120	**8** 980	**9** 2940	**10** 4000
11 2600	**12** 1002	**13** 729	**14** 624	**15** 725

Review

Exercise 23 Write these ratios in their simplest form:

1 $25 : 10$	**2** $8 : 64$	**3** $18 : 63$
4 $13 : 169$	**5** $15p : £1.00$	**6** $60 \, cm : 1 \, m$
7 3 hours : 75 minutes	**8** $2 \, kg : 600 \, g$	**9** $£2.50 : 50p$

Express in the form $1 : n$

10 $12 : 3$	**11** $20 : 4$	**12** $8 : 5$	**13** $45 : 4$

14 Change $6 : 10$ into a percentage. **15** Change $3 : 10$ into a fraction.

16 Change $4 : 16$ into a fraction. **17** Change $15 : 20$ into a percentage.

18 Change $6 : 15$ into a decimal. **19** Change $70 : 150$ into a fraction.

20 Change $9 : 10$ into a decimal.

21 An alloy contains iron and copper in the ratio $5 : 2$. A quantity of alloy contains 20 kg of iron. What weight of copper does it contain?

22 In making mortar you mix sand and concrete in the ratio $6 : 1$. You need 140 kg of mortar. How much sand will you need?

23 In a rectangle the ratio of the width to the length is $5 : 7$. The length is 42 cm. Find the width.

24 Divide 48 cm in the ratio $1 : 2$

25 Divide £27 in the ratio $3 : 7$

26 Divide 61.93 kg in the ratio $2 : 9$

27 In a triangle the lengths of the sides are in the ratio 3 : 4 : 5. The perimeter is 96 cm. What is the length of each of the sides?

28 Ali, Betty and Clare share £240 in the ratio 10 : 8 : 7. How much do they each receive?

29 Seven rulers cost £1.61. How much will three rulers cost?

30 Three identical textbooks cost £17.88. How much will ten of these textbooks cost?

31 It takes seven ladies 6 hours to complete a job of work. How long would it take eight ladies?

32 Six machines will produce 840 toys in a day. How many would seven machines produce in a day?

33 Mortgage repayments are £9.10 per £1000. What are the repayments on a house costing £65 500?

34 Remi has a house valued at £38 000, and contents at an estimated value of £31 000. His insurance company has an annual charge of £1.88 per £1000 value for Buildings insurance, and £4.80 per £1000 estimated value for Contents insurance. What would be the total annual insurance bill?

35 A car travels 100 miles in 2 hours. At what average speed was the car travelling?

36 Sally can walk at a speed of 4 m.p.h. How far will she walk in $1\frac{3}{4}$ hours?

37 A car drives for 2 hours at a speed of 50 m.p.h. It then covers the remaining 95 miles of its journey in $1\frac{1}{4}$ hours. What is the average speed for the whole journey?

38 In Berlin a leather coat costs 180 marks. How much is this in pounds sterling if the exchange rate is 2.8 marks = £1?

39 A couple wish to take £350 on holiday with them to Tenerife. How many pesetas will they get if the exchange rate is £1 = 3240 pta?

40 From the numbers below list all the (a) square numbers (b) cube numbers (c) prime numbers: 2, 4, 5, 7, 8, 9, 10, 11, 13, 18, 20, 21, 25, 27, 29

Exercise 24

The following are all questions taken from GCSE papers.

1 (a) The train from London to Manchester takes 2 hours 30 minutes. This train travels at an average speed of 80 miles per hour. What is the distance from London to Manchester? (*2 marks*)

   (b) The railway company is going to buy some faster trains. These new trains will have an average speed of 100 miles per hour. How much time will be saved on the journey from London to Manchester? (*3 marks*)

[AQA/NEAB]

2 Janet and Kyra share a flat and pay all bills in the ratio 1 : 2.
    (a)   The telephone bill is £75.
        How much of this bill does Janet pay?   *(2 marks)*
    (b)   Janet's share of the electricity bill is £42.
        How much is Kyra's share of the electricity bill?   *(2 marks)*
                                         [OCR]

Medium
224 g
43p

Large
454 g
89p

3 The weights and prices of two different sizes of tomato soup are shown.
Which size of soup gives more grams per penny?   *(3 marks)*
                                         [AQA/SEG}

4 Fred has a recipe for 30 biscuits. Here is a list of ingredients for 30 biscuits.

Self-raising flour: 230 g
Butter: 150 g
Caster sugar: 100 g
Eggs: 2

Fred wants to make 45 biscuits.

    (a)   Write down his new list of ingredients for 45 biscuits.   *(3 marks)*

The recipe gives the baking temperature as 350° Fahrenheit, F. A modern oven shows baking temperature in Celsius, C.

    (b)   Use the formula $C = \dfrac{5(F - 32)}{9}$ to change 350° Fahrenheit to

        Celsius. Give your answer correct to the nearest degree.
                                            (3 marks)

Gill has only 1 kilogram of self-raising flour. She has plenty of the other ingredients.

    (c)   Work out the maximum number of biscuits that Gill could bake.
                                              (3 marks)
                                             [EDEXCEL]

5 (a)   Write down the value of 3×2^4 *(1 mark)*
    (b)   Write 36 as a product of prime factors.   *(2 marks)*
    (c) p and q are whole numbers. The lowest common multiple of p and q is 36.
        Write down the values of p and q when $p + q = 13$.   *(1 mark)*
                                             [AQA/SEG]

6 Jack shares £180 between his two children Ruth and Ben. The ratio of Ruth's share to Ben's share is 5 : 4.

    (a)   Work out how much each child is given.   *(3 marks)*

Ben then gives 10% of his share to Ruth.

    (b)   Work out the percentage of the £180 that Ruth now has.
                                               (3 marks)
                                             [EDEXCEL]

7 Kylie, Lucas and Daniel share £972 in the ratio of 11 : 9 : 7. How much does each one get? *(3 marks)*

[WJEC]

8 The following were the temperatures (in °C) in four cities at midday on 1st January.

City	London	Moscow	Oslo	Sydney
Temperature	3	−8	−12	23

(a) What was the difference in temperature between

    (i) Oslo and Sydney, *(1 mark)*

    (ii) Oslo and Moscow? *(1 mark)*

(b) By midday on the next day, the temperature in Moscow had risen by 2 °C and the temperature in London had fallen by 5 °C. What was the difference in temperature between Moscow and London at midday on 2nd January? *(2 marks)*

(c) At midday on 1st February the temperature in Moscow was −2 °C. London was 3 °C warmer than Moscow. Oslo was 8 °C colder than London. What was the temperature in Oslo at midday on 1st February? *(2 marks)*

[OCR/MEG]

LONDON
95p

ROME
2400 Lire

9 A bottle of lemonade costs 95 pence in London. In Rome, the same size bottle costs 2400 Lire. There are 3000 Lire to £1 In which city does the lemonade cost more? You should show all your working. *(3 marks)*

[AQA/NEAB]

10 (a) (i) A small bag of potatoes weighs 5 kg. A large bag of potatoes weighs 60% more than a small bag. What is the weight of a large bag of potatoes? *(2 marks)*

    (ii) The ratio of the price of a small bag of potatoes to the price of a large bag of potatoes is 3 : 4. A small bag costs 96 pence. What is the price of a large bag? *(3 marks)*

(b) Carrots are sold in bags and sacks. Bags of carrots weigh 3 kg and cost 72 pence. Sacks of carrots weigh 14 kg and cost £2.66. How much, per kilogram, is saved by buying sacks of carrots instead of buying bags of carrots? *(3 marks)*

[AQA/SEG]

11 Work out the value of (i) 5^3, (ii) $\sqrt{36}$, (iii) $2^3 \times 3^2$. *(4 marks)*

[EDEXCEL]

12 When 56 is written as the product of its prime factors in index form, we obtain $56 = 2^3 \times 7$.

(a) Write 126 as the product of its prime factors in index form.

(2 mark)

(b) Write down 126×56 as a product of prime factors in index form.

(1 mark)

(c) Write down the square root of your answer to (b) as a product of prime factors in index form

(1 mark)

[WJEC]

13 (a) Complete the boxes.

(i) $\boxed{} \times \boxed{} = \boxed{-10}$ *(1 mark)*

(ii) $\boxed{} \div \boxed{} = \boxed{-1}$ *(1 mark)*

(b) Work out $\dfrac{(-1) \times (-7) \times (+8)}{(-2)}$ *(1 mark)*

[AQA/NEAB]

14 (a) Susan changed £500 into South African Rand, when the rate of exchange was £1 = 9.90 Rand.
How many Rand did she get? *(3 marks)*

(b) During her holiday Susan spent 4005 Rand.

(i) How many Rand did she have left? *(1 mark)*

(ii) She changed her remaining Rand into pounds, when the exchange rate was £1 = 10.50 Rand.
How many pounds did she get? *(2 marks)*

[WJEC]

15 *Do not* use a calculator to answer this question.

Exchange Rate: £1 = 19.61 dollars

(a) Estimate the number of dollars you would get for £523. Write down the calculation you used to obtain your estimate.

(2 marks)

(b) Estimate the number of £s you would get for 238 dollars. Write down the calculation you used to obtain your estimate.

(3 marks)

[AQA/NEAB]

16. A shop has a sale of jackets and shirts. In the sale there are a total of 120 jackets and shirts. Shirts are to be sold at a price of £8.00 plus VAT at $17\frac{1}{2}\%$.

(a) What is the cost of buying one shirt, including the $17\frac{1}{2}\%$ VAT?

(2 marks)

The jackets and shirts are in the ratio 5 : 3.

(b) Work out the number of jackets. *(3 marks)*

(c) Calculate the percentage that are shirts. *(2 marks)*

[EDEXCEL]

17 A cake is made from fat, flour and sugar. The cake weighs 110 g. The weight of the sugar is 42 g.

(a) (i) What percentage of the cake is sugar? Give your answer correct to one decimal place. *(3 marks)*

(ii) The ratio of the weight of flour to the weight of sugar is 3 : 2. What is the weight of the flour? *(2 marks)*

(b) The weight of the cake has been given to the nearest 10 g. What is the minimum weight of the cake? *(1 mark)*

[AQA/SEG]

Ideas for investigations

1 A series of ratios are given as follows:

$$\frac{b}{a} = \frac{2}{1} = 2 \qquad\qquad \frac{c}{b} = \frac{3}{2} = 1.5 \qquad\qquad \frac{d}{c} = \frac{5}{3} = 1.6666$$

$$\frac{e}{d} = \frac{8}{5} = 1.6 \qquad\qquad \frac{f}{e} = \frac{13}{8} = 1.625$$

Continue the series of ratios until your answer remains almost unchanged (remains the same to 4 decimal places). You have then found the Golden Ratio.

Hint: The series of numbers this is based on is the Fibonacci series:

1, 1, 2, 3, 5, 8, 13, 21, 34, 55, ...

2 Investigate these two patterns of numbers, and extend the series if possible. In each case explain how the series 'works'.

$$1^3 = \ \ 1 = 1^2 - 0^2 \qquad\qquad 1^2 = 1$$
$$2^3 = \ \ 8 = 3^2 - 1^2 \qquad\qquad 2^2 = 4 = 1 + 3$$
$$3^3 = 27 = 6^2 - ?^2 \qquad\qquad 3^2 = 9 = 1 + 3 + ?$$
$$4^3 = ? \ ... \qquad\qquad\qquad 4^2 = ? \ ...$$

3 Foreign currencies: How does the pound fare?
Monitor the rise and fall of the pound against a number of other currencies, recording the data on a graph. Which currencies appear to be stable when compared to the pound? You can obtain this information from newspapers.

Also find the commission charged for (a) buying (b) selling a foreign currency at various banks. Show how much money you are left with if you were to start with £100, change it into a foreign currency, and then back to pounds again.

PATTERNS AND RELATIONSHIPS 4

4.1 Use of simple formulas

Example If one button costs 7p, then the cost of buying n of these buttons is given by the formula:

$$c = 7 \times n \qquad (\text{or } c = 7n)$$

cost → number of buttons

So the cost of six buttons is given by $c = 7 \times 6 = 42$p.
What is the cost of 20 buttons?

The formula gives $c = 7 \times 20 = 140$. We must remember that this answer is in pence. Hence the cost is 140p or £1.40.

Exercise 1

Find the cost of buying:

1 3 buttons	**2** 8 buttons	**3** 14 buttons
4 38 buttons	**5** 200 buttons	**6** 1000 buttons

Example The number of matchsticks (n) needed to make s squares is given by the formula:

$$n = 3s + 1$$

How many matchsticks are needed to make six squares?

If $s = 6$, then

$n = (3 \times 6) + 1$ ***The brackets indicate that this calculation is done first.***

$= 18 + 1$

$= 19$ matchsticks   ***Then the 1 is added.***

Exercise 2

Use the formula to find the number of matchsticks needed to make:

1 3 squares	**2** 8 squares	**3** 15 squares
4 12 squares	**5** 20 squares	**6** 52 squares

Exercise 3

1 The area of a rectangle is given by the formula $A = l \times h$, where l is the length and h is the height.
Use the formula to find the areas of these rectangles:
(a) $l = 8$ cm, $h = 5$ cm
(b) $l = 12$ m, $h = 4.5$ m
(c) $l = 2.3$ cm, $h = 3.7$ cm
(d) $l = 200$ km, $h = 150$ km

2 The perimeter of a rectangle is given by the formula $P = 2l + 2h$, where l is the length and h is the height.
Use the formula to find the perimeters of the rectangles in question 1.

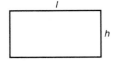

3 A ball is dropped from a window in a tall building. Its speed is given by the formula $v = 10 \times t$, where t is the time (in seconds) that it has been falling. Use the formula to find the speed of the ball after:
(a) 2 s   (b) 7 s   (c) 15 s   (d) 22 s

4 The size of the exterior angle of a regular polygon is given by the formula

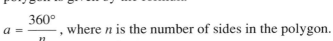

$$a = \frac{360°}{n},$$ where n is the number of sides in the polygon.

Use the formula to calculate the exterior angle of a regular polygon with:
(a) 6 sides (hexagon)
(b) 8 sides (octagon)
(c) 15 sides
(d) 4 sides (square)

5 A taxi company charges C pence for a journey of n kilometres. The formula is $C = 80 + 15n$. Find the fare for a journey of
(a) 2 km   (b) 5 km   (c) 10 km   (d) 30 km.

6 The time (t minutes) taken to travel to college depends on how far the student walks and how far the student travels on the bus. The formula for the time taken is $t = 11w + 4b$, where w is the walking distance and b is the distance travelled on the bus.

Find the time taken for these students to travel to college:
(a)   Wendy, who walks 2 km and goes 7 km on the bus.
(b)   Rashid, who walks 4 km and goes 3 km on the bus.
(c)   Annette, who walks 3 km and goes 16 km on the bus.
(d)   Michael, who walks 1 km and goes 5 km on the bus.

7 The amount of sleep (H hours approximately) that a child needs depends on its age (A years). A formula for the number of hours is given by $H = 17 - \dfrac{A}{2}$. Work out how many hours of sleep are needed by:
(a) Henrietta, aged 4
(b) Miranda, who is 6 years old
(c) Julian, who is 12
(d) Craig, a 15-year-old

4.2 Substituting into a formula

In exercise 3, you were **substituting** numbers into a formula, to work out a value of, or **evaluate**, the formula.

Example   If $v = u + 10t$, work out v when

(a) $u = 5$ and $t = 4$
(b) $u = 17.4$ and $t = 3.6$
(c) $u = 3\frac{1}{4}$ and $t = 2\frac{1}{4}$.

(a) $v = 5 + (10 \times 4)$ ← *Do the substitution first, without any working out.*
$\quad = 5 + 40$ ←
$\quad = 45$ — *Then work out the formula.*

(b) $v = 17.4 + (10 \times 3.6)$
$\quad = 17.4 + 36$
$\quad = 53.4$

(c) $v = 3\frac{1}{4} + (10 \times 2\frac{1}{4})$
$\quad = 3\frac{1}{4} + 22\frac{1}{2}$
$\quad = 25\frac{3}{4}$

The first true electronic calculator was produced in Britain by the Bell Punch Company in 1963. It had a display 20 centimetres wide, and could perform only the four basic functions of adding, subtracting, multiplying and dividing.

Note: Do not try to substitute numbers into the formula *and* do a calculation at the same time. You are likely to make errors. Invariably you will gain method marks for substituting the correct figures into the formula, so set your work out in two stages:

1   Replace letters in the formula by the correct numbers.
2   Complete the calculations.

Although it may seem unnecessary to follow these steps in the simple examples given, more complicated formulas, or numbers, can give rise to errors if such a procedure is not followed.

Exercise 4

Evaluate these formulas:

1   $P = 5 \times k$.   Find P when   (a) $k = 3$ (b) $k = 10$ (c) $k = 16$
2   $t = 30s$.   Find t when   (a) $s = 2$ (b) $s = 6$ (c) $s = 0.5$
3   $m = 2n + 10$.   Find m when   (a) $n = 4$ (b) $n = 8$ (c) $n = 1$
4   $R = \dfrac{60}{I}$.   Find R when   (a) $I = 12$ (b) $I = 30$ (c) $I = 4$
5   $v = 40 + 10t$.   Find v when   (a) $t = 5$ (b) $t = 3.5$ (c) $t = 35$
6   $q = 4r + s$.   Find q when   (a) $r = 8$ and $s = 7$ (b) $r = 20$ and $s = 20$
7   $x = 25 - \dfrac{100}{g}$.   Find x when   (a) $g = 10$ (b) $g = 50$ (c) $g = 4$
8   $A = 5j + 2k$.   Find A when $j = 4\frac{1}{3}$ and $k = \frac{5}{6}$
9   $t = (v - u)/a$.   Find t when $v = 18\frac{1}{2}$, $u = 2\frac{2}{5}$ and $a = 2$
10   $s = (a + b)/(a - b)$.   Find s when $a = 2$ and $b = 1\frac{1}{2}$

Example   Find the area of this rectangle, using the formula $A = l \times h$

Without noticing, you may write $A = 2 \times 50 = 100$

This is wrong, because the formula requires both measurements to be in the *same* units.

2 m

50 cm

In using formulas, you will need to take care to:

(i) *use the correct units in the formula,*

(ii) *adjust your answer, if necessary, to a more sensible unit.*

You can say either: or:

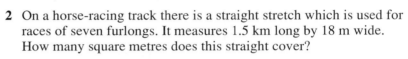

200 cm

50 cm

2 m

0.5 m

$A = 200\ \text{cm} \times 50\ \text{cm}$
  $= 10\ 000$ square centimetres
  $(10\ 000\ \text{cm}^2)$

$A = 2\ \text{m} \times 0.5\ \text{m}$
  $= 1$ square metre
  $(1\ \text{m}^2)$

Both answers are correct: $1\ \text{m}^2 = 10\ 000\ \text{cm}^2$

Exercise 5

1 Find the area of a skirting board 2.6 m long and 15 cm wide. Give your answer in (a) m^2 (b) cm^2.

2 On a horse-racing track there is a straight stretch which is used for races of seven furlongs. It measures 1.5 km long by 18 m wide. How many square metres does this straight cover?

3 A roll of wallpaper is 51 cm wide and 10.05 m long.

  (a) What is its area, in square metres, to one decimal place?

  (b) A wall is 3.8 m long and 2.5 m high. Will two rolls of wallpaper be enough to cover the wall?

4 Each quarter, Mrs Graham's gas bill is worked out from the formula $C = S + (n \times 1.6)$p, where S is the standing charge in £, and n is the number of kilowatt-hours of gas used during the quarter. How much is her gas bill, if the standing charge is £10.48, and she uses 1335 kilowatt-hours of gas?

5 The volume of a plank of wood is given by the formula $V = l \times w \times h$. Find the volume, in cubic centimetres, of a plank 1.2 m long, 18 cm wide and 10 mm thick.

6 The formula for the volume of an unsharpened pencil is $V = A \times l$, where A is the area of the end of the pencil and l is its length. If $A = 22\ \text{mm}^2$, and $l = 17$ cm, what is the volume of the pencil? Give your answer in cubic centimetres.

7 The Smiths are having a new concrete floor put in their garage. The garage is 7.8 m long and 5.2 m wide. The new floor is to be 15 cm thick. What volume of concrete, in cubic metres, will the Smiths need to order? (Use the same formula as in question 5.)

8 The information given on the wrapping of a pack of toilet rolls is shown. The total area, however, is blurred. What is the total area, in square metres?

Product Information
4 rolls
280 sheets per roll
Sheet size 139 mm × 112 mm
Total area .... sq. m.

4.3 Relationships: number patterns

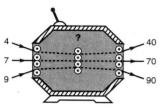

What does this machine do?

It is easy to see that it *multiplies* each number by 10. If 5 is the input, then $5 \times 10 = 50$ will be the output.

The **rule** which changes each input into the corresponding output is:

(input) $\times$ 10 = (output)

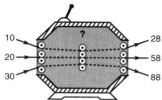

Example   What machine changes 10 into 28, 20 into 58, and 30 into 88?

If we add 2 to each of the second set of numbers, it will become (30, 60, 90), which is 3 times the first set of numbers. The rule is that each number is *multiplied* by 3, then 2 is *subtracted*.

Note: The rule must work for *each* number in turn.

Exercise 6   In each question write, in words, the relationship between the two sets of numbers.

1 (3, 4, 10) and (6, 8, 20)
2 (8, 10, 12) and (7, 9, 11)
3 (2, 9, 14) and (6, 27, 42)
4 (1, 6, 8) and (6, 11, 13)
5 (30, 40, 50) and (3, 4, 5)
6 (4, 12, 18) and (1, 9, 15)
7 (4, 5, 8) and (41, 51, 81)
8 (6, 7, 8) and (13, 15, 17)
9 (5, 8, 9) and (19, 31, 35)
10 (3, 5, 7) and (9, 25, 49)

4.4 Writing formulas for relationships

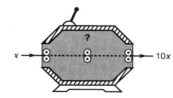

Looking at the example above, where (4, 7, 9) became (40, 70, 90), we can write a **formula**, using letters and numbers, to simplify the relationship, or rule.

Take a number from the first set and call it x.

Take the *matching* number from the second set, and call it y.

Then the formula connecting x and y is:

$y = 10x$

Similarly, for (10, 20, 30) becoming (28, 58, 88), the formula for this relationship is:

$y = 3x - 2$ ***Check that the rule works for each number.***

Exercise 7

Work out the formula for each question in exercise 6.

Example

John wishes to join a cricket club. The annual membership fee is £20, and in addition a fee of £2 is payable for each game John plays. We can write this as a formula for working out how much John will have to pay for the year, depending on the number of games he plays.

If £A is the total amount, then

$$£A = £20 + £(2 \times g)$$

where g is the number of games John plays.
If John plays in four games, the total to pay will be

$$£A = £20 + £(2 \times 4) = £20 + £8 = £28$$

The eleventh-century Persian poet, Omar Khayyám, spent most of his time in the study of algebra. His work on algebra was known throughout Europe, but at that time his now famous poem, 'The Rubaiyat', was not admired.

If he plays in 15 games, the total fees will be

$$£A = £20 + £(2 \times 15) = £20 + £30 = £50$$

Exercise 8

1 Alison's local sports centre charges a membership fee of £12. In addition it costs £1.70 per person for an hour of tennis.

(a) Work out a formula for the cost (£C) of joining the sports centre and playing h hours of tennis.

(b) How much will it cost Alison for joining and playing ten hours of tennis?

2 For using her car to travel to an examination board meeting, Sylvia can claim 40p per mile for the first 30 miles, and then 20p per mile for the rest of the journey.

(a) If the total journey is m miles, write an expression for the distance travelled in which she can claim 20p per mile.

(b) Work out a formula for the total travel claim (£C) for a journey of m miles.

(c) How much can she claim for a journey of 100 miles?

3 Darren wishes to paint his house, and needs to hire some scaffolding from a hire company. The company charges a standard fee of £8.50, and then £1.50 per day.

(a) Write down a formula for the hire charge (£H) if Darren wishes to hire the scaffolding for d days.

(b) If he uses the scaffolding for nine days, what will be the hire charge?

4 Marina knits woolly hats and scarves. She sells the hats for £2.50 each and the scarves for £3.50 each.

(a) Write down a formula for the amount of money (£*M*) she will take if she sells *h* hats and *s* scarves.

(b) How much will she take if she sells six hats and five scarves?

5 A car salesman is paid £240 per week, plus a commission of £45 for every car that he sells.

(a) Write down a formula for his weekly pay (£*P*) if he sells *c* cars in a week.

(b) How much will he be paid for a week in which he sells eight cars?

4.5 Use of calculators

Although calculators do 'number-crunching' very well, not all operate in exactly the same way. You will need to be aware of which buttons to press, in which order, on *your* calculator, so that you become proficient at knowing how to use it most effectively.

First of all, we shall look at the four main functions: +, −, × and ÷.

Example   A grocer sells Cheshire cheese for £1.10 per kilogram. How much will it cost for a piece weighing 1.8 kg?

Check, by working out $\dfrac{1.98}{1.8}$*,*

Cost = 1.10 × 1.8 = £1.98   *which is 1.10.*

Example   A train travels from Edinburgh to London, a distance of 660 km, in a time of $5\frac{1}{2}$ hours.
What is its average speed for the journey?

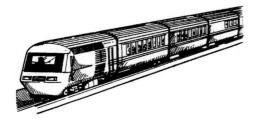

$$\text{average speed} = \frac{\text{total distance travelled}}{\text{total time taken}}$$

$$= \frac{660}{5.5}$$

Check, by working out 120×5.5*, which is 660.*

$$= 120 \text{ km/h}$$

Example   A publishing company sells a text book for £9.95.

  (a) Write down a formula for working out the cost (£C) of *n* of these books.

  (b) What is the cost of (i) 3 (ii) 28 (iii) 60 of these text books?

  (a) $£C = £9.95 \times n$
         $= £(9.95)n$

  When the number has a decimal point, it is usual either to leave in the '×' sign or to put in a bracket: £(9.95)n.

  (b)   (i) $£C = £9.95 \times 3 = £29.85$
         (ii) $£C = £9.95 \times 28 = £278.60$
         (iii) $£C = £9.95 \times 60 = £597$

  Remember that, when you are working in £'s, 278.6 means £278.60.

Example   I receive a telephone bill every three months. The last four bills were £93.65, £105.04, £87.63 and £94.20. Next year, instead of paying each bill when it arrives, I would prefer to pay 12 equal amounts, one each month. What would this monthly payment have been last year, in order to pay the total of the four bills?

Total amount = £93.65 + £105.04 + £87.63 + £94.20 = £380.52
Monthly payment = £380.52 ÷ 12 = £31.71

Note: It is always worth checking your answer by doing the 'opposite' or 'inverse' process. In this case, check that your answer of £31.71, when multiplied by 12, does give £380.52.
It is also worth adding the four amounts in a different order, just in case you entered a mistake, e.g. £78.63 instead of £87.63. Although it takes an extra few seconds, it is always worth doing.

Exercise 9

In this exercise, do not worry about units. Work out the numerical value of these formulas, and check your answer by performing the 'inverse' process.

1 $G = 3h$, when $h = 15.8$

2 $m = 14.8 \times L$, when $L = 3.87$

3 $r = \dfrac{c}{6.28}$, when $c = 28.26$

4 $Y = 29.6 - 2d$, when $d = 12.4$

5 $h = 5p + 0.585$, when $p = 0.379$

6 $J = \dfrac{K}{16}$, when $K = 1024$

7 $A = l \times b$, when $l = 19.3$ and $b = 14.4$

8 $t = \dfrac{6.28}{w}$, when $w = 15.7$

9 $d = 2M + 3N$, when $M = 85.6$ and $N = 50.5$

10 $x = \dfrac{10}{y}$, when $y = 2.63$

4.6 Use of memory

Most calculators have a **memory**, in which you can store a particular number until you need to use it.

The memory is most helpful in two main situations:

(i) when a number is used repeatedly,

(ii) when a long number in the display has to be divided into some other number.

Example In an examination, the mark scored on Paper 1 is multiplied by 0.65. This reduced mark is then used in working out the final grade. Work out the reduced marks for these actual Paper 1 marks: 83, 50, 69, 27, 47, 39, and 66.

First of all, enter 0.65 into your calculator, and transfer it to the memory (follow the instructions for *your* calculator).
Then follow these steps:

(i) Enter 83 into your calculator.

(ii) Press $\boxed{\times}$ followed by the $\boxed{\text{read memory}}$ button followed by $\boxed{=}$. The answer of 53.95 should appear.

Now repeat steps (i) and (ii), for each of the scores 50, 69, ..., 66.

Example   Work out the value of P, if $P = \dfrac{20}{k}$ and $k = 3.14 \times 4.62$

(i)   Using a calculator, $k = 14.5068$.

(ii) I need the display clear, so that I can enter the number 20. Hence transfer the display of 14.5068 into the memory.

(iii) Now enter 20, and then press $\boxed{\div}$ followed by the $\boxed{\text{read memory}}$ button, followed by $\boxed{=}$.

The answer, 1.3786638, is now in the display. It is sensible to round off such an answer, to either 2 or 3 significant figures, since the original numbers are given to three figures. Hence $P = 1.38$ or 1.4.

Exercise 10

Use your calculator, and the memory where necessary, to work out the values of these formulas. In each question, state (i) the full calculator display (ii) the answer rounded to three significant figures.

1 $T = 5.474 \times k$, when $k = 3.186$ **2** $R = \dfrac{V}{0.831}$, when $V = 240$

3 $w = 38.46 \times a$, when (a) $a = 7$ (b) $a = 6.892$ (c) $a = 17.4$

4 $b = \dfrac{500}{l \times h}$, when $l = 10.5$ and $h = 6.93$

5 $d = 44.3 - (2.7 \times e)$, when (a) $e = 11$ (b) $e = 16.2$ (c) $e = 17$

4.7 Rules of indices

How many grains of rice will there be on the 11th square of a chessboard, if there is 1 grain on square one, 2 grains on square two, 4 grains on square three, 8 grains on square four, etc? (The answer is on page 84)

1 Multiplication

Look at these four equations, all of which mean the same:

(i)	8	$\times$	$4 = 32$
(ii)	$2 \times 2 \times 2 \times 2 \times 2 = 32$		*Writing 8 as $2 \times 2 \times 2$, and 4 as 2×2.*
(iii)	2^3	$\times$	$2^2 = 32$	*Writing $2 \times 2 \times 2$ as 2^3, and 2×2 as 2^2.*
(iv)	2^5		$= 32$

In (iii) the small '3' in 2^3 is called a **power** or **index** (more than one index are called indices).

It refers to the number of 2s that are multiplied together (3 of them).
Again, in (iv), the small '5' in 2^5 means $2 \times 2 \times 2 \times 2 \times 2$ (5 of them).

Comparing (iii) and (iv) we can see that $2^3 \times 2^2 = 2^5$.
When two numbers (in this case 8 and 4) are written as powers of the same number (in this case the number 2), then we can:

multiply them by **adding** the powers

For example $3^2 \times 3^3 = 3^5$ *Check: $9 \times 27 = 243$.*
        and $5^3 \times 5 = 5^4$ $5^1 = 5$

Using algebra, we can write:

$x^3 \times x^4 = x^7$

$a^5 \times a = a^6$ $a = a^1$

$r^4 \times r^2 \times r^3 = r^9$

Exercise 11   Simplify these expressions:

1 $2^4 \times 2^2$	**2** $x^2 \times x^6$	**3** $y^3 \times y^3$
4 $a \times a^4$	**5** $4^2 \times 4^3$	**6** $2^5 \times 2^5$
7 $t^2 \times t^2 \times t^2$	**8** $10^6 \times 10^3$	**9** $m^2 \times m \times m^2$
10 $10^2 \times 10^2 \times 10$	**11** $b^3 \times b^4 \times b^5$	**12** $x \times x^3 \times x^6 \times x^{10}$

Example   Simplify
(a) $5p^3 \times 4p^2 \times p$ (b) $(3t^2)^2$ (c) $7a^2 \times 2ab$
(d) $10m^3n \times 6mn^3$

(a)   This is the same as
$5 \times p^3 \times 4 \times p^2 \times p$
$= 5 \times 4 \times p^3 \times p^2 \times p^1$
$= 20 \times p^6$
$= 20p^6$

(b) $(3t^2)^2 = (3 \times t^2) \times (3 \times t^2)$
$= 3 \times 3 \times t^2 \times t^2$
$= 9 \times t^4$
$= 9t^4$

(c) $7a^2 \times 2ab$
$= 7 \times a^2 \times 2 \times a \times b$
$= 7 \times 2 \times a^2 \times a \times b$
$= 14 \times a^3 \times b$
$= 14a^3b$

(d) $10m^3n \times 6mn^3$
$= 10 \times m^3 \times n \times 6 \times m \times n^3$
$= 10 \times 6 \times m^3 \times m \times n \times n^3$
$= 60 \times m^4 \times n^4$
$= 60m^4n^4$

Exercise 12   Simplify these expressions:

1 $3a \times 2a$ **2** $5t \times 6t$ **3** $7y \times y^3$
4 $6z^2 \times 2z^3$ **5** $(4b^3)^2$ **6** $2p^2q \times 4pq$
7 $7s \times 4s^2t$ **8** $10xy^3 \times 8x^3y \times 2x^2y$ **9** $(2ab)^2 \times 2ab$
10 $(m^2n^2)^3$ **11** $(2c^2d)^5$ **12** $4 \times 10^3 \times 2.5 \times 10^2$
13 $(2 \times 10^3) \times (3 \times 10^4)$ **14** $5a \times 8b \times 2a^2b$ **15** $(3xy)^3 \times 2x^2y \times xy^2$

2 *Division*

Look again at the four equations under 'multiplication'.

From (i) we could write: $32 \div 4 = 8$

Using the index notation: $2^5 \div 2^2 = 2^3$

When two numbers (in this case 32 and 4) are written as powers of the
same number (in this case the number 2), then we can:

divide them by **subtracting** the powers

So $3^4 \div 3^1 = 3^3$
$7^5 \div 7^3 = 7^2$
$x^8 \div x^3 = x^5$

Example   Simplify
(a) $m^3 \div m^2$ (b) $18c^5 \div 6c^2$ (c) $q \times 6q^3 \div 3q^2$
(d) $mn^7 \div mn^4$

(a) $m^3 \div m^2 = m$
(b) $18c^5 \div 6c^2 = \frac{18}{6} \times (c^5 \div c^2) = 3c^3$
(c) $q \times 6q^3 \div 3q^2 = 6q^4 \div 3q^2 = \frac{6}{3} \times (q^4 \div q^2) = 2q^2$
(d) $mn^7 \div mn^4 = (m \div m) \times (n^7 \div n^4) = 1 \times n^3 = n^3$

Exercise 13   Simplify these expressions:

1 $4^3 \div 4^2$ **2** $5^3 \div 5$ **3** $r^6 \div r^3$

4 $S^5 \div S$ **5** $12x^8 \div x^3$ **6** $a^3 \times a^2 \div a^1$

7 $20b^4 \div 10b^3$ **8** $p^2q^3 \div p^2q$ **9** $10^2 \times 10^5 \div 10^3$

10 $16z^5 + 2z^3$ **11** $5xy^3 \times 8x^3y + 2x^2y$ **12** $10^7 \times 10^3 + 10^2$

The answer to the problem on page 82 is 1024. By the 21st square there will be over a million grains of rice.

Example   Simplify $a^3 \div a^5$.

This is the same as $\dfrac{a \times a \times a}{a \times a \times a \times a \times a}$

Since $\dfrac{a}{a} = 1$, the fraction can be written as:

$\dfrac{1}{a \times a} = \dfrac{1}{a^2}$

In general, if the higher power of a is in the denominator, then the fraction can be simplified to

$$\dfrac{1}{\text{difference between the powers}}.$$

Example   Simplify (a) $a^3b^2 \div a^5b$ (b) $6m^2n^2 \div 3m^4n^4$
(c) $5yz^3 \div 20y^3z^3$ (d) $4ab^2c^3 \div 6a^3b^2c$

(a) $a^3b^2 \div a^5b = \dfrac{a \times a \times a \times b \times b}{a \times a \times a \times a \times a \times b}$

$= \dfrac{b}{a^2}$

When terms are multiplied or divided, we consider each letter in turn, after any numbers.

(b) $6m^2n^2 \div 3m^4n^4 = \dfrac{6 \times m^2 \times n^2}{3 \times m^4 \times n^4} = \dfrac{2}{m^2n^2}$

(c) $5yz^3 \div 20y^3z^3 = \dfrac{5 \times y \times z^3}{20 \times y^3 \times z^3} = \dfrac{1}{4y^2}$ $z^3 \div z^3 = 1$

(d) $4ab^2c^3 \div 6a^3b^2c = \dfrac{4 \times a \times b^2 \times c^3}{6 \times a^3 \times b^2 \times c} = \dfrac{2c^2}{3a^2}$

Exercise 14   Simplify these expressions:

1 $\dfrac{y^2}{y^5}$ **2** $\dfrac{5a^3}{a^5}$ **3** $\dfrac{a^3b^2}{a^2b^3}$ **4** $\dfrac{10x^3y}{2x^2y^4}$

5 $\dfrac{3pq}{9p^2q^2}$ **6** $\dfrac{2m^3n^3}{m^2n^2}$ **7** $\dfrac{12xy}{4xy^2}$ **8** $\dfrac{c^2d}{c^3}$

9 $\dfrac{5yz^3}{2y^2z}$ **10** $\dfrac{(4ab)^2}{8a^5b^2}$ **11** $\dfrac{24xy^3}{(6xy)^2}$ **12** $\dfrac{2000p^6q^9}{(10p^2q^3)^3}$

4.8 Simplifying algebraic expressions

There are many opportunities for errors when simplifying algebraic expressions. Care must be taken to follow the various rules for combining terms. There are two main approaches that can help:

(i)   plenty of practice!

(ii) substituting simple numbers in place of the letters in the original expression and in your simplified expression to see if they give the same answers.

Example   Simplify these expressions:
(a) $3p - p + 4p$ (b) $2j - k + 5j - 3k$ (c) $12m - 5 - 4m$

(a) $3p - p + 4p$
   $= 3p + 4p - p$ **Taking the '+' terms first.**
   $= 7p - p$
   $= 6p$

Check: take $p = 2$, $3p - p + 4p = 6 - 2 + 8 = 12$.

Our answer is $6p$, which *is* 12 when $p = 2$.

Group terms with the same letters.

(b) $2j - k + 5j - 3k$ (c) $12m - 5 - 4m$
   $= 2j + 5j - k - 3k$ $= 12m - 4m - 5$
   $= 7j - 4k$ $= 8m - 5$

Exercise 15

You can check your answers by substituting a number for each letter, and seeing if your solution gives the same answer as the original question.

Simplify these expressions:

1 $4x - 3x + 7x$ **2** $5 - 3y + 4y$
3 $a + 6b - 3a$ **4** $4w + 2w - 3w$
5 $6g - 7h - 5g + 3g + 3h$ **6** $3c + 5 - 2c - 4$
7 $8a - 5b - 2a + 3b$ **8** $5p + 3p - q - 4p$
9 $x + x + x + 3 - 2x$ **10** $3y - 5z + y + 2z - 4y + 3z$
11 $12h - 4k + 3h - 4k$ **12** $2p - 4p + 5q + 9q + 2p$
13 $2a - 6b - 5a + 18a + 2$ **14** $7x + 14y - z + 9x - 12x$

Example   Simplify $4c^2 \times 5c$

You may make a slip and write down $20c^2$ as your answer.

Trying $c = 3$, say, the original expression will be
   $(4 \times 3 \times 3) \times (5 \times 3) = (36 \times 15) = 540$

Putting $c = 3$ into your simplified answer will give $20 \times 3 \times 3 = 180$.

Clearly there is a mistake: you have forgotton that $c^2 \times c = c^3$ and your answer should therefore be $20c^3$ ($20 \times 27 = 540$).

Example   Simplify
(a) $3a^3 + 5a^3$ (b) $7a^2 - 2a^2$ (c) $3a^3 + 7a^2$

(a) There are 3 'lots' of a^3 and 5 'lots' of a^3: altogether there are 8 'lots' of a^3.
Hence $3a^3 + 5a^3 = 8a^3$

(b) Here there are 7 'lots' of a^2, from which are taken 2 'lots' of a^2 leaving 5 'lots' of a^2.
Hence $7a^2 - 2a^2 = 5a^2$

(c) We cannot simplify this expression any further — you *cannot add* (or subtract) different powers of a number — you can only multiply (or divide) them.

An expression such as $x^3 + 5x^2 - 3x - 4$ cannot be simplified further, as the terms cannot be combined.
If, however, we have $x^3 + 5x^2 - 3x^2 - 4$, then we *can* simplify this a little, to $x^3 + 2x^2 - 4$, because $5x^2 - 3x^2 = 2x^2$.

Exercise 16

Simplify these expressions, if possible.

1 $c + 2c + 3c + c$ **2** $4m + 5 - m + 3$ **3** $6x + 2x + 2x - 5x$

4 $3v - 5 - v - 1$ **5** $11a + 2a - 3 + 5a$ **6** $11 + 2a^2 - 3 - 5a^2$

7 $6k^3 - 4 - 5k^3 + 4$ **8** $p + 2q^2 + 3p + 4q^2$ **9** $3x - 7y + 7x - 3y$

10 $3x + 7y - 7x - 3y$ **11** $d^4 + 3d^4$ **12** $4r^3 - 3r + r^3 + r$

13 $3ab^2 + 2a^2b$ **14** $2t^2 \times 3t + 5t^3$ **15** $p^2 + 5pq - 3pq - 15$

16 $6w^2 - \dfrac{10w^5}{5w^3}$ **17** $\dfrac{(3a)^2}{a}$ **18** $x^4 - \dfrac{x^7}{x^3}$

4.9 Brackets

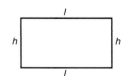

The perimeter of this rectangle is $l + l + h + h$ or $l + h + l + h$

We can write these as $2l + 2h$ or $2 \times (l + h) = 2(l + h)$

We use the **bracket** to show that $(l + h)$ is worked out first, and the answer then doubled.

As both ways of writing the perimeter are the same,

$$2(l + h) = 2l + 2h$$

Example   Write these expressions without brackets:
(a) $2 \times (h + 3)$ (b) $3(a - 8)$ (c) $4(2v^3 + w)$ (d) $20(3 - 2y)$

(a) $2 \times (h + 3) = (2 \times h) + (2 \times 3) = 2h + 6$

(b) $3(a - 8) = 3a - (3 \times 8) = 3a - 24$

(c) $4(2v^3 + w) = (4 \times 2v^3) + (4 \times w) = 8v^3 + 4w$

(d) $20(3 - 2y) = (20 \times 3) - (20 \times 2y) = 60 - 40y$

Exercise 17   Write these expressions without brackets:

1 $4(c + 5)$ 2 $5(a - 2)$ 3 $3(4x + 1)$

4 $6(3k - 2h)$ 5 $10(5 + 6f)$ 6 $5(7x - y)$

7 $2(r^2 + r - 6)$ 8 $8(7 - 3h)$ 9 $3(x^3 + 2x)$

10 $3(5y^3 + 4y^2 + 3y)$ 11 $4(2 + 7j) + 3(5 - 8j)$ 12 $8(2p - 3q) - 5(3p)$

13 $10(3t + 10)$ 14 $3(a + 2) + 2(2a - 1)$ 15 $4(y + 3) - 2(2y)$

The same rule holds if there is a letter in front of the bracket.

Example   Write these expressions without brackets:
   (a) $a(a + 2)$ (b) $p(3p - 2q)$ (c) $5c^3(c + 3d)$

(a) $a(a + 2) = a^2 + 2a$

(b) $p(3p - 2q) = 3p^2 - 2pq$

(c) $5c^3(c + 3d) = 5c^4 + 15c^3d$

In an expression it is usual to write the numbers first, then the letters. For example, in (b) we could have written p3p – p2q. This is not wrong, but not as useful for further work.

Exercise 18   Write these expressions without brackets:

1 $b(b - 5)$ 2 $t(t + 3)$ 3 $y(y^2 - 3y)$

4 $p(5p + 8)$ 5 $z(1 + 2z - 3z^2 + 4z^3)$ 6 $m(m^2 + 4m)$

7 $h(8h - 9)$ 8 $3d(d + 7)$ 9 $6x(x - 10)$

10 $(5x^2)^2 + 5x^2$ 11 $4v^2(v^2 - 3v + 1)$ 12 $2pr(r + h)$

13 $3xy(5x - 2y)$ 14 $2ab(a^2 + 4ab)$ 15 $5x^2(2x + 3xy - 5y^2)$

When brackets appear, they are dealt with first, before simplifying.

Example   Simplify:
   (a) $5x + 2(x - 3y)$ (b) $p(r + s) - r(p + q)$ (c) $20 - 3(4x - 3)$

(a) $2(x - 3y) = 2x - 6y$

   Hence $5x + 2(x - 3y) = 5x + 2x - 6y$

                    $= 7x - 6y$

First expand the brackets. Then add like terms.

(b) $p(r + s) = pr + ps$

             $-r(p + q) = -rp - rq$

   $p(r + s) - r(p + q) = pr + ps - rp - rq$

             $pr - rp = pr - pr = 0$

   Hence $p(r + s) - r(p + q) = ps - rq$

Expanding the first bracket. Expanding the second bracket. Taking both brackets together. As rp = pr.

(c) $-3(4x - 3) = -12x + 9$ *Removing the bracket.*

   Hence $20 - 3(4x - 3) = 20 - 12x + 9 = 29 - 12x$

Remember: '–' × '–' = '+'.

Exercise 19 Simplify these expressions:

1 $3(x + 2y) + 4x$ **2** $5(c - d) - 2c + 3d$

3 $3a + 4(5a - 6)$ **4** $4(2p - 6q) - 3p + q$

5 $5(a^3 + b) + 2(a^3 - b)$ **6** $a(b - 2c) + 2b(a + c)$

7 $16 - 3(x^2 + 4)$ **8** $a(bc - 2) - b(ac - 3)$

9 $12 - 6(x^3 - 8) + 5x$ **10** $p(4p + 7) - (2p^2 + 9)$

4.10 Multiplying brackets

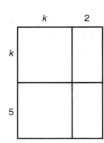

What is the area of this rectangle?

The area is $(k + 2)$ multiplied by $(k + 5)$.

Also, from the four rectangular shapes, the area is $k^2 + 5k + 2k + 10$.

Hence $(k + 2) \times (k + 5) = k^2 + 5k + 2k + 10$
$$= k^2 + 7k + 10$$

We can obtain the right-hand side by:

(i)   multiplying *each* term in the second bracket by k,

(ii)   multiplying *each* term in the second bracket by 2,

(iii)   adding the answers.

Example   Write these expressions without brackets:
       (a) $(x + 6)(x - 2)$ (b) $(2n + 3)(3n + 4)$ (c) $(f - 8)(3f - 5)$.

(a) $(x + 6)(x - 2) = x^2 - 2x + 6x - 12$ *This is x(x − 2) and 6(x − 2).*
$$= x^2 + 4x - 12$$ *Adding.*

(b) $(2n + 3)(3n + 4) = 6n^2 + 8n + 9n + 12$ *This is 2n(3n + 4) and 3(3n + 4).*
$$= 6n^2 + 17n + 12$$ *Adding.*

(c) $(f - 8)(3f - 5) = 3f^2 - 5f - 24f + 40$ *'−' × '−' = '+'*
$$= 3f^2 - 29f + 40$$

Exercise 20 Multiply these brackets, and simplify the answers.

1 $(x + 1)(x + 2)$ **2** $(x + 6)(x + 5)$

3 $(2x - 1)(x + 4)$ **4** $(a + 3)(a + 3)$

5 $(y - 10)(2y + 3)$ **6** $(x - 1)(x + 1)$

7 $(3t - 5)(2t - 3)$ **8** $(m + 5)(5m + 1)$

9 $(5c + 6)(5c + 6)$ **10** $(10x + 1)(10x - 1)$

4.11 Factorising algebraic expressions

From the section on brackets, we know that

$$x(y - 3z) = xy - 3xz$$

The terms x and $y - 3z$ are the two **factors** of the expression $xy - 3xz$, because when they are multiplied together they are equal to the expression.

How can we find factors of an algebraic expression?

Example   Factorise these expressions:
        (a) $4x + 6y$ (b) $4pq - 3pr$ (c) $r^2 + 2rh$ (d) $3t - 6at^2$

We have to look for factors which are **common** to each term.

(a)   Each term has a factor of 2.
$$4x + 6y = 2 \times 2x + 2 \times 3y$$
$$= 2(2x + 3y)$$ *Putting in a bracket.*

(b) $4pq - 3pr$
$$= p \times 4q - p \times 3r$$
$$= p(4q - 3r).$$ *There is a common factor of p.*

(c) $r^2 + 2rh = r(r + 2h)$ *The common factor is r.*

(d)   There are *two* factors common to both terms: 3 and t.
      We can 'take out' each factor separately:
$$3t - 6at^2 = 3(t - 2at^2)$$ *Taking out the 3 first.*
$$= 3t(1 - 2at)$$ *Then taking out the t.*

Or:

$$3t - 6at^2 = t(3 - 6at)$$ *Taking out the t first.*
$$= 3t(1 - 2at)$$ *Then taking out the 3.*

In either case, the answer is the same as when both factors are taken out together: $3t - 6at^2 = 3t(1 - 2at)$.

Note: It is as well to check, by multiplying out the brackets, that the original expression is obtained.

Exercise 21   Factorise each of these expressions completely (i.e. take out *all* the common factors).

1 $2a + 4b$	**2** $6p - 2q$	**3** $100x - 10y$
4 $3a + 4ab$	**5** $pqr + rst$	**6** $mn - 4n$
7 $8gt + 12ht$	**8** $3ab - 4ac + 5ad$	**9** $2xy - 3xz$
10 $ut + 5t^2$	**11** $c^2d - cd^2$	**12** $2ab^2 - 6ab + a$
13 $5s^3 + 20$	**14** $x^2yz + xy^2z + xyz^2$	**15** $36d^3 - 12d^2$
16 $2ap + ap^3$	**17** $a^2x + ax^2$	**18** $3y - 2y^3$
19 $a^4bc - a^3b^2c$	**20** $2\pi r^2 + 2\pi rh$	

4.12 Sequences

Example Work out the next two numbers in each of these sequences:

(a) 3, 6, 9, 12, 15, …, …

(b) 11, 15, 19, 23, 27, …, …

(c) 90, 83, 76, 69, 62, …, …

(d) 5, 10, 20, 40, …, …

(a) This is simply the 3-times table; the next two numbers are 18 and 21.

(b) Each number is 4 greater than the previous number; so the next two numbers are 31 and 35.

(c) Here the numbers are getting smaller, by 7 each time. The next two are, therefore, 55 and 48.

(d) This sequence is different from the other three. Instead of *adding* or *subtracting* a fixed number each time, we *multiply* by 2 to get the next number; the next two will be 80 and 160.

Exercise 22

The Babylonians were the first to use arithmetic about 4000 years ago. They counted in sixties. The Hindus invented the system we now use, called Arabic numerals because the Arabs brought them to Europe.

For each sequence: (a) work out the next two numbers
(b) write down in words how you worked out your answers.

1 13, 18, 23, 28, 33, 38, …, …

2 67, 64, 61, 58, 55, …, …

3 2, 6, 18, 54, …, …

4 96, 48, 24, 12, …, …

5 4, 5, 7, 10, 14, 19, …, …

6 2, 6, 12, 20, 30, 42, …, …

7 100, 91, 82, 73, 64, …, …

8 1, 1, 2, 3, 5, 8, 13, 21, …, …

9 8, 20, 9, 18, 10, 16, 11, 14, …, …

10 8, 13, 20, 29, 40, …, …

4.13 Methods of generating sequences

There are two main ways of generating a sequence:

1   Working out how to obtain the next term from the previous term(s).

2   Finding a rule for writing down any term.

In the previous examples we used method 1. We looked at how each term compared with the previous term.
For example, in the sequence 14, 20, 26, 32, …, we can see that 6 is added to each term to give the next one.

Method 1:

This method can be described as the **difference method**, because we write down the difference between each term and the previous term. The difference is 6 each time, so the next term will be 32 + 6 = 38, and the following will be 38 + 6 = 44.

Sequence: 14   20   26   32   **38**   **44** ⟵ *New terms.*
Difference: +6   +6   +6   **+6**   **+6**

If we try this method with example (d) on page 90, then we obtain:

Sequence: 5   10   20   40   **80**   *Next term.*
Difference: +5 +10 +20 **+40**   *Next difference.*

In fact the set of differences is the same as the sequence. So 40 will be the next difference making the next number in the sequence 80.
The next difference will be 80, which will make the next number in the sequence 160, and so on.

Exercise 23

Use the difference method to work out the next two numbers in each sequence.

1 7, 10, 13, 16, 19, …, …
2 7, 10, 14, 19, 25, …, …
3 3, 10, 17, 24, 31, …, …
4 9, 10, 12, 15, 19, …, …
5 50, 46, 42, 38, 34, …, …
6 2, 2, 4, 6, 10, 16, 26, …, …
7 8, 12, 18, 26, 36, 48, …, …
8 9, 12, 13, 16, 17, 20, 21, …, …
9 10, 20, 35, 55, 80, 110, …, …
10 16, 26, 38, 52, 68, 86, …, …

Method 2:

This method needs to have each term connected to its position along the sequence. The process is helped by writing down each term underneath its **position** in the sequence.

Example   Work out a rule for calculating *any* term (say the nth) in the sequence 4, 8, 12, 16, 20, …

We write down each term underneath its position in the sequence.

Position (n)	1	2	3	4	5	6	7
Term	4	8	12	16	20	?	?

Here, each term is equal to 4 times its position.
So the 6th term will be $4 \times 6 = 24$, the 7th term will be $4 \times 7 = 28$, the 8th term will be $4 \times 8 = 32$, and so on.

What will be the 20th term, the 25th term and 200th term?

The 20th term will be $4 \times 20 = 80$, the 25th term will be $4 \times 25 = 100$, and the 200th term will be $4 \times 200 = 800$.

In this method, we can easily work out any term, however far along the sequence it is. The difference method would take a while to reach the 20th term, never mind the 200th!

We say that the rule for calculating the nth term is $4 \times n$ or $4n$.

Example   Work out the rule for the nth term of the sequence
8, 11, 14, 17, 20, …

Writing down each term underneath its position in the sequence.

Position (n)	1	2	3	4	5
Term	8	11	14	17	20

Using the difference method, each term is 3 greater than the previous term: so we write down the sequence $3n$:

Position (n)	1	2	3	4	5
$3n$	3	6	9	12	15
Term	8	11	14	17	20

Now we can see that each term in the given sequence is 5 greater than the $3n$ sequence: the rule for calculating the nth term is therefore $3n + 5$.
For example, the next (6th) term is $(3 \times 6) + 5 = 23$.

Exercise 24   For each sequence (a) work out the rule for calculating the nth term
(b) work out the 7th and the 50th term.

1 3, 5, 7, 9, 11, …   **2** 4, 9, 14, 19, 24, …   **3** 12, 15, 18, 21, 24, …
4 5, 6, 7, 8, 9, 10, …   **5** 7, 17, 27, 37, 47, …   **6** 6, 10, 14, 18, 22, …
7 10, 12, 14, 16, 18, …   **8** 0.5, 1, 1.5, 2, 2.5, …   **9** −2, −1, 0, 1, 2, 3, …

4.14   Further sequences

Example   For the sequence   1, 4, 9, 16, 25, 36, …:
(a) What are the next two terms?
(b) What is the rule for calculating the nth term?

(a)   The difference method will give:

Sequence:	1		4		9		16		25		36		**49**		**64**
Difference:		+3		+5		+7		+9		+11		**+13**		**+15**	

The next two differences are 13 and 15 (the next two odd numbers); this means that we can work out the next two numbers in the sequence.

(b)   To work out the rule, we begin by writing down each term underneath its position in the sequence:

Position (n)	1	2	3	4	5	6
Term	1	4	9	16	25	36

Each term is the square of n, its position: the rule for calculating the nth term is therefore n^2.

Example   Find (a) the next term (b) the nth term, of the sequence
2, 6, 12, 20, 30, 42.

It is helpful, as in the previous example, to write each number underneath
its position in the sequence

Position (n)	1	2	3	4	5	6
Term (sequence)	2	6	12	20	30	42
Difference		+4	+6	+8	+10	+12

(a)   The next difference will be +14; the next term will therefore be
42 + 14 = 56

(b)   If we work out the differences of this new 'difference' sequence,
we will obtain +2 each time

First difference	+4	+6	+8	+10	+12
Second difference		+2	+2	+2	+2

This confirms that the nth term of the sequence will have an n^2 term in it
(and possibly an n term, and possibly a number term).
Writing down the n^2 sequence will usually enable the nth term to be spotted.

Position (n)	1	2	3	4	5	6
n^2	1	4	9	16	25	36
Term (sequence)	2	6	12	20	30	42

It is clear to see that if we add the numbers in the position (n) row and the
n^2 row, we obtain the bottom row, which is the nth term in the sequence.
Hence, the nth term is $n^2 + n$ or, factorised, $n(n + 1)$.

Exercise 25   For each sequence, work out (a) the next two terms (b) the rule for the nth
term.

Hint: In each case, the rule contains the term n^2. Write down the sequence n^2, underneath the position sequence n.

1 2, 5, 10, 17, 26, 37, ...   **2** 2, 8, 18, 32, 50, ...
3 0, 3, 8, 15, 24, ...   **4** 4, 16, 36, 64, 100, ...
5 5, 11, 21, 35, 53, ...   **6** 3, 6, 11, 18, 27, ...
7 0, 3, 8, 15, 24, ...   **8** 3, 7, 13, 21, 31, ...
9 5, 8, 13, 20, 29, ...   **10** 7, 10, 15, 22, 31, ...

Example   For the sequence $\frac{2}{3}, \frac{3}{4}, \frac{4}{5}, \frac{5}{6}, \frac{6}{7}, \dots$ work out (a) the next two
terms (b) the rule for the nth term.

(a)   The next two terms are clearly $\frac{7}{8}$ and $\frac{8}{9}$.

(b)   It is usual to consider the numerators as one sequence, and the
denominators as another sequence.

Position (n)	1	2	3	4	5
Numerators	2	3	4	5	6
Denominators	3	4	5	6	7

The nth term of the numerators is $n + 1$.

The nth term of the denominators is $n + 2$.

The nth term is therefore $\dfrac{n + 1}{n + 2}$.

Exercise 26

Blaise Pascal, a seventeenth-century French mathematician, made the first mechanical calculator when he was only 20 years old.

Work out (a) the next two terms (b) the rule for the nth term.

1 $\frac{1}{2}, \frac{1}{3}, \frac{1}{4}, \frac{1}{5}, \frac{1}{6}, \cdots$

2 $\frac{1}{2}, \frac{1}{4}, \frac{1}{6}, \frac{1}{8}, \frac{1}{10}, \cdots$

3 $\frac{2}{5}, \frac{3}{6}, \frac{4}{7}, \frac{5}{8}, \frac{6}{9}, \cdots$

4 $\frac{1}{3}, \frac{3}{5}, \frac{5}{7}, \frac{7}{9}, \frac{9}{11}, \cdots$

5 $\frac{3}{8}, \frac{4}{10}, \frac{5}{12}, \frac{6}{14}, \frac{7}{16}, \cdots$

6 $\frac{1}{2}, \frac{3}{4}, \frac{5}{6}, \frac{7}{8}, \frac{9}{10}, \cdots$

7 $\frac{1}{4}, \frac{2}{6}, \frac{3}{8}, \frac{4}{10}, \frac{5}{12}, \cdots$

8 $\frac{1}{2}, \frac{2}{5}, \frac{3}{8}, \frac{4}{11}, \frac{5}{14}, \cdots$

9 $\frac{4}{7}, \frac{5}{8}, \frac{6}{9}, \frac{7}{10}, \frac{8}{11}, \cdots$

10 $\frac{2}{3}, \frac{5}{6}, \frac{8}{9}, \frac{11}{12}, \frac{14}{15}, \cdots$

Example Find the next two terms in the sequence:
1, 1, 2, 3, 5, 8, 13, 21, …, …,

(a) Using the difference method:

```
1    1    2    3    5    8    13    21
  0    1    1    2    3    5    8    13    21
```

The two sequences are identical (except for the '0' at the start). The next difference will therefore be 13, and the next 21, which makes the next two numbers 21 + 13 = 34 and 34 + 21 = 55. The sequence will continue:

```
1    1    2    3    5    8    13    21    34    55    89    144    233 …
  0    1    1    2    3    5    8    13    21    34    55    89 …
```

(b) Another way to look at this sequence is to take any *two* consecutive numbers, and add them: e.g. 2 + 3 = 5, 13 + 21 = 34. Any term is therefore equal to the sum of the two previous terms.

This is a Fibonacci series, named after an Italian mathematician.

Other sequences can be formed by adding the previous three terms, or by adding the first term to twice the second term to obtain the next term, or by adding the two previous terms and then adding 1. There are other ways in which previous terms can be combined to give the next term.

Exercise 27

Work out the next three terms in each of these sequences. Write down the rule in each case.

1 3, 3, 6, 9, 15, 24, 39, …, …, …

2 1, 3, 4, 7, 11, 18, 29, …, …, …

3 1, 1, 2, 4, 7, 13, 24, 44, …, …, …

4 1, 3, 5, 9, 17, 31, 57, …, …, …

5 1, 2, 6, 16, 44, 120, 328, …, …, …

6 3, 5, 9, 15, 25, 41, 67, …, …, …

Review

Exercise 28

1 The charge, £C, for hiring a cement-mixer from an industrial hire firm is given by the formula $C = 12 + 4.5d$, where d is the number of days that the cement-mixer is hired.
How much will it cost to hire the cement-mixer for (a) 2 days (b) 5 days (c) a fortnight?

2 The sum of the first n counting numbers is given by the formula:

$$S = \frac{n(n+1)}{2}.$$

Use the formula to work out (a) $1 + 2 + 3 + 4 + 5$ (b) $1 + 2 + \ldots + 20$
(c) $1 + 2 + \ldots + 99 + 100$

3 The cost of entry (£M) to a theme park is given by $M = 9X + 6Y$, where X is the number of adults and Y is the number of children in the party. What is the entrance fee to the theme park for (a) 2 adults and 3 children (b) 4 adults and 7 children (c) a party of 8 adults and 30 children?

Work out the value of each of these formulas:

4 $K = 3H - 16.8$, when (a) $H = 7$ (b) $H = 27.4$ (c) $H = 5.6$

5 $B = 100 - 13.4z$, when (a) $z = 5$ (b) $z = 6.76$

6 $m = 3n + 7p$, when (a) $n = 8$ and $p = 6$ (b) $n = 7.83$ and $p = 6.08$

Simplify these expressions by collecting like terms together:

7 $3x + y + x + 4y$　　　　　　　　　　**8** $p + 7 + 5p - 3$
9 $x - 2x - 3y + 4x + 5y$　　　　　　**10** $12 - 3x + 5 - 2x$

Write these expressions without brackets:

11 $5(x + 3)$　　　　　　　　　　　　**12** $4(x - 8) + 3(x + 4)$
13 $5x + 3(x - 4)$　　　　　　　　　**14** $5(x - 3) + 2(x + 1)$
15 $3(4x + 5y) - 2(5x - 2y)$　　　　**16** $2(3x^2 + 4x - 5) + x^2 + 3(x - 7)$
17 $(x + 3)(x + 2)$　　　　　　　　　**18** $(2x - 3)(x + 5)$
19 $(x - 10)(x - 10)$　　　　　　　　**20** $(x - 10)(x + 10)$

Work out the next two terms in each sequence:

21 $3, 6, 11, 18, 27, 38, \ldots, \ldots$　　　**22** $400, 200, 100, 50, \ldots, \ldots$
23 $x^2, 2x^3, 3x^4, 4x^5, \ldots, \ldots$　　　**24** $5, 7, 11, 19, 35, \ldots, \ldots$
25 $100, 88, 77, 67, 58, \ldots, \ldots$

Exercise 29

The following questions are all taken from GCSE papers.

1 (a) Evaluate

　　(i)　3^{-4}　　　　　　　　　　　　　*(2 marks)*
　　(ii)　9^0　　　　　　　　　　　　　*(1 mark)*

　(b) Simplify

$$\frac{4a^3c \times 3ab^3}{6a^2b}$$

　　　　　　　　　　　　　　　　　(3 marks)

[AQA/NEAB]

2 Complete this mapping.

Squares		Circles
1	⟶	3
2	⟶	8
3	⟶	15
4	⟶	?
10	⟶	?
n	⟶	?

(3 marks)
[SEG]

3 The diagrams show patterns made out of sticks.

Pattern number   1   2   3

(a) Draw a diagram to show pattern number 4. *(1 mark)*

The table below can be used to show the number of sticks needed for a pattern.

Pattern number	1	2	3	4	5	6	7
Number of sticks	3	5					

(b) Complete the table. *(2 marks)*

(c) (i) Work out the number of sticks needed for pattern number 15.
    (ii) Explain how you obtained your answer. *(4 marks)*

(d) Write down a formula which can be used to calculate the number of sticks, S, in terms of the pattern number, n. *(2 marks)*
[EDEXCEL]

4 A shop sells two types of Lollipops.

The shop sells Big lollipops at 80p each and Small lollipops at 60p each. Henry buys x Big lollipops.

(a) Write down an expression, in terms of x, for the cost of Henry's lollipops. *(1 mark)*

Lucy buys r Big lollipops and t Small lollipops.

(b) Write down an expression, in terms of r and t, for the total cost of Lucy's lollipops. *(1 mark)*

The cost of g Big lollipops and 2 Small lollipops is £10.80

(c) Write this as an equation in terms of g. *(2 marks)*
[EDEXCEL]

The Big lollipop   80p

The Small lollipop   60p

5 (a) (i) Write down the next two terms of the sequence:

17, 14, 11, 8, 5, ...

(ii) Explain how you worked out your answers. (*3 marks*)

(b) Find, in terms of n, an expression for the nth term of the sequence. (*2 marks*)

(c) Find the 50th term of the sequence. (*1 mark*)
[EDEXCEL]

6 (a) Multiply out

(i) $q \times 3q^2$, (*1 mark*)
(ii) $4(2x - 7)$. (*1 mark*)

(b) Multiply out and simplify

$5a(3a + 2b) - 4a(2a - 3b)$. (*3 marks*)
[OCR]

7 (a) Write down (i) the 8th term and (ii) the nth term of this sequence:

1   5   9   13   17   ... (*2 marks*)

(b) Use your answer to (a) to write down the nth term of this sequence:

1   25   81   169   289   ... (*1 mark*)
[OCR]

Ideas for investigations

1 In the sequence of square numbers 1, 4, 9, 16, 25, ..., we can write down the **differences** between each term and the previous one:

Terms in the sequence: 1   4   9   16   25   36   ...
Differences: 3   5   7   9   11   ...

Repeating the process to find **second** differences will give:

Terms in the sequence: 1   4   9   16   25   36   ...
1st difference: 3   5   7   9   11   ...
2nd difference: 2   2   2   2   ...

What will be the **third** differences?
What will be the **fourth** differences? Continue finding the differences in this way.

Investigate the first, second, third, etc. differences in these sequences.

(a) 6, 7, 9, 12, 16, 21, 27, ...
(b) 2, 8, 18, 32, 50, 72, 98, ...
(c) 1, 8, 27, 64, 125, 216, 343, 512, 729, 1000, ...
(d) 2, 2, 4, 6, 10, 16, 26, 42, 68, 110, 178, ...
(e) 2, 3, 5, 9, 17, 33, 65, 129, 257, 513, ...

Can you suggest any general rules that apply to this method of differences?

Further work

Can you use the 'difference' method to work out the next two terms in each of the sequences above?

2 *Fibonacci sequence*

Each term in a 'Fibonacci sequence' is worked out by adding together the two previous terms. Starting with 1 and 1, the sequence will be:

1, 1, 2, 3, 5, 8, 13, 21, 34, 55, 89, 144, 233, ...

A   1   Take any *three* consecutive numbers in the sequence (e.g. 8, 13, 21).
    2   Multiply the first and third together. $(8 \times 21 = 168)$
    3   Find the square of the middle number. $(13 \times 13 = 169)$

Repeat steps 1, 2 and 3 for *any* set of three consecutive numbers. What do you notice? Write down your conclusions.

B   Make a new sequence, by *dividing* each term by the previous one

Sequence:	1	1	2	3	5	8	13	21	34	55	89	...
Divisions:		1	2	1.5	1.67	1.6	1.625	...				

Continue for another few terms. What do you notice?
Write down your conclusions.

Now repeat, but this time divide each term by the *next* one.
What do you notice?
Compare both 'division' sequences.

FORMULAS, EQUATIONS AND INEQUALITIES

'I'm very well acquainted, too, with matters mathematical
I understand equations, both the simple and quadratical!'

W. S. Gilbert, the Pirates of Penzance

5.1 Simple equations

Example   Joe receives 8p change when he hands over 80p for two
'Choco' bars. How much does one 'Choco' bar cost?

The process of working out the answer — quite simple in this case — can
be made into a problem where we have to **solve an equation**.

We can write this as:

Cost of two bars = 80p – 8p
                 = 72p
Cost of one bar = 72p ÷ 2
                 = 36p

An equation has an 'equals' sign
between the two sides, which must
balance

Exercise 1   Answer these questions. Most of them can be done in your head, but write
down all the steps in your thinking, as in the examples above, to show the
processes you have gone through (e.g. subtracting, dividing by 2, etc.).

1 Mike has read 53 pages of a book. There are 174 pages altogether in
   the book. How many more pages has he to read?

2 How much will be made from ticket sales for a college Gala night, if
   138 tickets are sold at £3.00 each?

3 Barbara buys three oranges. She receives 16p change from a £1 coin.
   How much does one orange cost?

4 There are 60 houses in a street. Elsie delivers milk to 24 houses on one
   side of the street, and to 19 houses on the other side. How many
   houses does Elsie *not* deliver to?

5 Brian has a £15 book token. He would like to buy three books, which
   cost £4.99, £6.50 and £5.25. How much extra money will Brian need
   in order to buy the books?

6 Shafiul buys two sandwiches and a can of lemonade at lunchtime. He
   receives 28p change from £2. If each sandwich costs 73p, how much
   is the can of lemonade?

7 Joan is using the photocopier to make five copies of an examination
   paper. There are nine pages on the paper. If the counter on the
   photocopier reads 487 when Joan starts, what will be the reading after
   she has made the five copies?

5.2 Using letters

By using single letters instead of words, we can reduce the amount of writing that is necessary in order to solve equations.

Looking at the example, if the cost of a bar of 'Choco' is b pence then we can write: $2 \times b = 80 - 8$

or $\quad 2b = 72$

Hence $\quad b = \frac{72}{2}$

$$b = 36$$

Less writing is needed but the same mathematical steps are shown. We have solved an algebraic equation: we have worked out the value of a letter representing a quantity, which in this example is money.

An effective way of solving equations is, to imagine a balance with two scale pans. To maintain the balance, whatever we do to one side we must do to the other.

For example if we add 3 to one side we must add 3 to the other.

If we divide one side by 4 we must divide the other side by 4.

Example   Solve these equations: (a) $x + 8 = 12$ (b) $t - 3 = 11$ (c) $3m = 15$.

(a) If we *subtract* 8 from each pan, we will be left with x on one pan, and $12 - 8 = 4$ on the other. So $x = 4$.

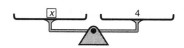

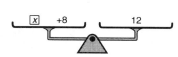

We can write this algebraically as:
$$x + 8 = 12$$
$$x + 8 - 8 = 12 - 8$$
$$x = 4$$

(b) $\quad t - 3 = 11$
$\quad t - 3 + 3 = 11 + 3$
$\quad t = 14$

Adding 3 to each pan to get t by itself.

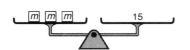

(c) $\quad 3m = 15$
$\quad \dfrac{3m}{3} = \dfrac{15}{3}$
$\quad m = 5$

Dividing each side by 3 to get just one m.

Exercise 2 Solve these equations. Draw a balance if you wish.

1 $x + 5 = 8$ **2** $k + 14 = 20$ **3** $5 + t = 27$

4 $12 + y = 22$ **5** $x - 5 = 11$ **6** $r - 16 = 4$

7 $y - 1 = 7$ **8** $p + 25 = 80$ **9** $z + 8 = 8$

10 $20 + v = 100$ **11** $t - 17 = 23$ **12** $t + 17 = 23$

Example Solve the equation $\dfrac{c}{4} = 6$.

On one pan we have $\dfrac{c}{4}$, or a quarter of c.

We need to *multiply* each side by 4, in order to get c by itself.

$\quad \dfrac{c}{4} \times 4 = 6 \times 4$

$\quad c = 24$

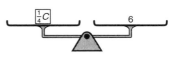

Exercise 3 Solve these equations:

1 $\dfrac{x}{2} = 8$ **2** $\dfrac{y}{3} = 10$ **3** $\dfrac{t}{6} = 3$ **4** $\dfrac{p}{4} = 4$ **5** $\dfrac{m}{2} = 100$

6 $\dfrac{s}{7} = 2$ **7** $\dfrac{x}{10} = 9$ **8** $\dfrac{t}{8} = 8$ **9** $\dfrac{s}{2} = 12.5$ **10** $\dfrac{v}{5} = 1$

11 $\dfrac{x}{20} = 40$ **12** $\dfrac{z}{50} = 2$ **13** $\dfrac{d}{4} = 0$ **14** $\dfrac{x}{5} = 6$

In exercises 2 and 3 there has been only *one* operation to perform, addition, subtraction, multiplication or division. When there is more than one operation, the 'scale pan' approach can often help to decide the strategy for solving the equation.

Example Solve the equation $3x + 5 = 17$

The aim is to arrive at an equation with just x on one side.
If we firstly remove the 5, then we will have $3x$, which we know how to deal with (divide both sides by 3).

Writing this algebraically:

$$3x + 5 = 17$$

$$3x + 5 - 5 = 17 - 5$$

Subtracting 5 from both sides.

$$3x = 12$$

$$x = \frac{12}{3}$$

Dividing both sides by 3.

$$x = 4$$

Check in the original equation:
$(3 \times 4) + 5 = 12 + 5 = 17$

Example   Solve the equation $\frac{t}{5} - 6 = 2$.

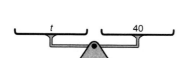

$$\frac{t}{5} - 6 = 2$$

$$\frac{t}{5} - 6 + 6 = 2 + 6$$

Adding 6 to each side.

$$\frac{t}{5} = 8$$

$$\frac{t}{5} \times 5 = 8 \times 5$$

Multiplying both sides by 5.

$$t = 40$$

Example   Find k, if $\frac{5k}{8} = 10$.

There is nothing to add or subtract.

$$\frac{5k}{8} = 10$$

$$\frac{5k}{8} \times 8 = 10 \times 8$$

Multiplying both sides by 8.

$$5k = 80$$

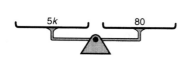

$$\frac{5k}{5} = \frac{80}{5}$$

Dividing both sides by 5.

$$k = 16$$

Exercise 4   Solve these equations. Draw scale pans if you wish.

1 $2x + 1 = 5$ **2** $3k + 4 = 19$ **3** $5 + 4t = 21$

4 $9 + 2y = 33$ **5** $10y + 8 = 98$ **6** $6p + 2 = 50$

7 $\frac{2x}{3} = 4$ **8** $\frac{3y}{5} = 6$ **9** $\frac{4t}{7} = 8$

$\frac{7d}{2}$ *is the same as* $\frac{7}{2}d.$ **10** $\frac{7}{2}d = 21$ **11** $\frac{3d}{4} = 45$ **12** $\frac{4s}{5} = 0$

5.3 Further equations

An equal mixture of water (freezing point 0 °C) and ethanediol (freezing point −13 °C) produces an antifreeze with a freezing point of about −37 °C.

Example   Solve the equation $x + 2 = 8 - x$

As we said in an earlier example. 'The aim is to arrive at an equation with just x on one side.'

When there is a letter on each side, we can add or subtract the letter. We will not upset the balance, as long as we do the *same* to each side. Here we can *add* an x to each side:

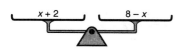

$$x + 2 = 8 - x$$

$$x + x + 2 = 8 - x + x$$

$$2x + 2 = 8$$

We now have an equation with the letter on *one* side as before.

$$2x + 2 - 2 = 8 - 2$$

$$2x = 6$$

$$x = 3$$

Check in original: $x + 2 = 3 + 2 = 5$, and $8 - x = 8 - 3 = 5$

Example   Find z, if $5z - 11 = 3z + 5$.

$$5z - 11 = 3z + 5$$

$$5z - 11 - 3z = 3z + 5 - 3z$$ **Subtracting $3z$ from both sides.**

$$2z - 11 = 5$$ **The z terms are now on one side.**

$$2z - 11 + 11 = 5 + 11$$ **Proceeding as in the previous example.**

$$2z = 16$$

$$z = \frac{16}{2}$$ **Check in original:**
$(5 \times 8) - 11 = 40 - 11 = 29$,
$$z = 8$$ **and $(3 \times 8) + 5 = 24 + 5 = 29$**

Exercise 5

Solve these equations:

1   $2x + 3 = 5 + x$ 2 $3k + 1 = 2k + 4$ 3 $5 + t = 7 - t$

4   $6 + 4y = 2y + 16$ 5 $3x - 6 = 14 + x$ 6 $2r - 7 = 5 - r$

7   $10y - 1 = 89$ 8 $8p + 2 = 50$ 9 $5x - 20 = 80$

10 $12 + v = 14 - v$ 11 $6t - 16 = 14$ 12 $9x + 17 = 71$

13 $16 + 3y = 30 + y$ 14 $4a - 11 = 13$ 15 $5b + 8 = 43 - 2b$

5.4 Useful tips in solving equations

A   An equation can be written with the sides exchanged.

For example $3d - 6 = 1 - 4d$ is the same as $1 - 4d = 3d - 6$, and $12 = 5z + 2$ is the same as $5z + 2 = 12$.

B   When there are terms containing the same letter on *both* sides, ensure that when you remove one of these terms from one side, then the remaining term is *positive*. If it is not, then you should have removed the term from the other side.

For example, in solving the, equation, $11 - 3x = 5 - x$ we could *add* x to each side.

$$11 - 3x = 5 - x$$

$$11 - 3x + x = 5 - x - x$$

$$11 - 2x = 5$$

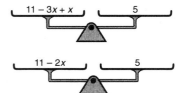

This has given us a '$-2x$' term.

Although we can still work with negative terms, it is better (especially when we come to inequalities later in the chapter) to have **positive** algebraic terms. To achieve this, we should have *added* $3x$ to each side.

$$11 - 3x = 5 - x$$

$$11 - 3x + 3x = 5 - x + 3x$$

$$11 = 5 + 2x$$

$$5 + 2x = 11 \qquad \textbf{\textit{Using tip A.}}$$

$$2x = 11 - 5 \qquad \textbf{\textit{Subtracting 5 from each side.}}$$

$$2x = 6$$

$$x = 3$$

C   If the equation has a *negative* algebraic term, then *add* this term to each side.

For example, if we are given

$$30 - 4x = 2,$$

then we can add $4x$ to each side:

$$30 - 4x + 4x = 2 + 4x$$

Whatever x is, then −4x will be cancelled out by +4x.

$$30 = 2 = 4x$$

Using tip A.

$$2 + 4x = 30$$

$$4x = 30 - 2$$

$$4x = 28$$

$$x = \frac{28}{4}$$

$$x = 7$$

Check that your answer satisfies the *original* equation. For example, in C above, put $x = 7$, and work out

$$30 - (4 \times 7) = 30 - 28, \text{ which } does \text{ equal } 2$$

So far, all answers have been positive whole numbers.

5.5 Negative and fractional solutions

Example Solve the equations (a) $3v + 7 = 1$ (b) $4s = 11$.

(a) $\quad 3v + 7 = 1$

$$3v + 7 - 7 = 1 - 7$$

$$3v = -6$$

Subtracting 7 from both sides.

$$v = \frac{-6}{3}$$

Dividing by 3.

$$v = -2$$

(b) $\quad 4s = 11$

$$\frac{4s}{4} = \frac{11}{4} = 2\frac{3}{4}$$

Dividing by 4.

$$s = 2\frac{3}{4}$$

Exercise 6 Solve these equations; answers may be negative or fractional (or both!).

1 $x + 7 = 4$ **2** $k + 14 = 10$ **3** $5 + 2t = 4$

4 $12 - y = 5$ **5** $6 - 5x = 21$ **6** $3r - 16 = 4$

7 $2y - 1 = 7$ **8** $8p + 25 = -7$ **9** $6x + 30 = 0$

10 $4z + 13 = 3$ **11** $b + 5 = 8 - b$ **12** $5 - 2c = 11 + c$

13 $60 - 3h = 2h + 10$ **14** $2y + 3 = 4y + 5$ **15** $23 = 3 - 3m$

16 $6 + r = 4 - 4r$ **17** $0 = 2 - 3t$ **18** $41 = 21 + 2g$

19 $4c - 7 = 11$ **20** $x = 33 + 4x$

5.6 Brackets

The only temperature which is the same on the Celsius scale and the Fahrenheit scale is −40.

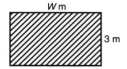

A room is w metres long and 3 metres wide. We can write its perimeter in two ways:

Either $2(w + 3)$ or $w + 3 + w + 3$, which is $2w + 6$.

As these are the same,

$2(w + 3) = 2w + 6$.

If the perimeter is 18 m, then:

$2(w + 3) = 18$, or
$2w + 6 = 18$

We have removed the bracket, multiplying each term by 2: we now have an equation which we know how to solve.

$2w + 6 = 18$

$2w + 6 - 6 = 18 - 6$

$2w = 12$

$w = 6$

The length of the room is 6 metres.

Example   Solve the equation $2(4x + 1) = 3x + 12$.

$2(4x + 1) = 3x + 12$ ***Multiplying each term inside the bracket by 2.***

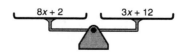

$8x + 2 = 3x + 12$

$5x + 2 = 12$ ***Subtracting 3x from each side.***

$5x = 12 - 2$

$5x = 10$

$x = \frac{10}{5}$

$x = 2$

Exercise 7

Solve these equations. Remove any brackets by multiplication. Check your answers in the original equations. Some answers are negative and/or fractions.

1 $2(t - 3) = 8$

2 $5(H + 3) = 20$

3 $3(n + 5) - 14 = 25$

4 $2(2c - 1) - 7 = 11$

5 $16 + 3(x - 4) = 28$

6 $10(2x + 3) = 10$

7 $5(2s + 7) = 15$

8 $9x + 2(x + 7) = 36$

9 $5(3b - 4) = 8b + 1$

10 $4(w + 3) - 2 = 2$

11 $6(2r - 7) = 0$

12 $1 - z = z - 1$

13 $3 - 5x = 2(2x - 3)$

14 $4(4y + 1) = 3(5y + 4)$

15 $6x + 5 = 2(2x + 1)$

16 $2(3k - 5) + 3(3k + 4) = 17$

17 $5(3p - 1) - 9 = 16$

18 $9(v + 1) = 4(2v + 3)$

19 $3(6g - 3) = 4(5g - 4)$

20 $t - 1 = 3(5 - t)$

5.7 Problems

Example   Mike has £6.30 more than Jim. Together the boys have £21.10. How much does each boy have?

In this case we might go on guessing for a while before we hit on the answer.
By writing an **equation** we can solve the problem.
We need to use a letter: let us say that Mike has £A.
Then Jim will have £A – £6.30.
Together this comes to £A + £A – 6.30, or £2A – 6.30.
As we are told this is £21.10, we can write an equation:

£2A – 6.30 = £21.10

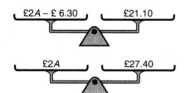

£2A = £21.10 + £6.30   *Adding £6.30 to each side.*

£2A = £27.40

£A = £13.70

Hence Mike has £13.70 and Jim has £7.40, which together make £21.10.

Exercise 9

Form an equation, and solve the problem.

1 Jack and Jill have £50 together. Jill has £12 more than Jack.

(a)   Let Jack have £X. How much has Jill?

(b)   Write an expression, containing X, for the amount they have together.

(c)   Write an equation, and solve it. Write down how much each has.

2 A bill of £177.50 can be paid by a deposit of £20, plus nine equal payments. How much is each of these payments?

3 Charles is one year younger than Betty. Their ages add up to 37. How old is Charles? (Let Charles be c years old.)

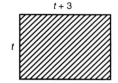

4 The perimeter of this rectangle is 46 cm.

    (a)   Write an expression, containing t, for the perimeter of the rectangle.

    (b)   Write an equation, and solve it, to find the length of the rectangle.

5 An apple weighs twice as much as a banana, and an orange weighs 23 g more than a banana. If all three weigh 143 g, how much does each weigh? (Let the banana weigh b grams.)

6 Mr and Mrs Hardy and their daughter Judith have picked raspberries at a 'pick-your-own' raspberry farm. At the weighing counter, Judith's basket weighs only one third of Mr Hardy's basket. Mrs Hardy's basket weighs the same as Mr Hardy's. Altogether they have picked 14 kg of raspberries. How much has each picked? (Let Judith's basket weigh j kilograms.)

7 Edwina wants to make a triangular flower bed in her garden. She wants the two long sides to be equal in length, and twice as long as the short side. If she has 30 m of plastic edging, what will be the lengths of the three sides? (Let the short side be s metres.)

8 For her new triangular flower bed, Edwina went to the local garden centre and bought some tulip bulbs at 60p each, and twice as many daffodil bulbs at 40p each. If she received 20p change from a £10 note, how many of each bulb did she buy? (Let the number of tulip bulbs she bought be t.)

5.8   Solving equations by 'trial and improvement'

This square has an area of 9 cm^2.
What is the length of a side?

We are in fact solving the equation $x^2 = 9$.
The solution we require is $x = 3$. ($x = -3$ is also a solution, since $-3 \times -3 = +9$, but, as we are finding a length, we can ignore any negative solutions.)

What is the length of the side of this square, which has an area of 10 cm^2?

10 cm^2

Let us guess at 3.1 cm.
   Now $3.1 \times 3.1 = (3.1)^2 = 9.61$.
So 3.1 cm is a little short for the length of the side of this square.
   Trying 3.2 cm: $(3.2)^2 = 10.24$; so 3.2 cm is rather too long. It would seem reasonable to try 3.15 cm, as a better guess.
   Trying 3.15: $(3.15)^2 = 9.9225$, which is near to 10, but *just* too short.
   Trying 3.16: $(3.16)^2 = 9.9856$, the nearest so far.
   Trying 3.17: $(3.17)^2 = 10.0489$, just too long.
A better answer will be between 3.16 and 3.17; try 3.165.
   Trying 3.165: $(3.165)^2 = 10.017225$, just too long.
   Trying 3.163: $(3.163)^2 = 10.004569$, very near.
   Trying 3.162: $(3.162)^2 = 9.998244$, just too short.

We could go on trying numbers between 3.162 and 3.163 until we arrived at the accuracy we needed. However, if we need an answer to 2 decimal places, then 3.16 will be the nearest that we can get.
Hence the side of the square will be 3.16 cm, to 2 decimal places.

In an adult the skin covers an area of about 1.7 square metres, and weighs about 3 kilograms.

Many equations which are non-linear (i.e. other than those which can be arranged into the form $ax + b = c$) can be solved as accurately as is needed, by starting with a reasonable 'guess', and then improving on that guess, as we have done to solve $x^2 = 10$ above.

Example   Solve the equation $x^2 + 2x = 7$.

   Trying $x = 1$: $1^2 + (2 \times 1) = 3$
   Trying $x = 2$: $2^2 + (2 \times 2) = 8$
A solution seems to be between $x = 1$ and $x = 2$, probably nearer 2.
   Trying $x = 1.8$: $(1.8)^2 + (2 \times 1.8) = 6.84$, too small.
   Trying $x = 1.9$: $(1.9)^2 + (2 \times 1.9) = 7.41$, too big.
As 6.84 is 0.16 below 7, and 7.41 is 0.41 above 7, it would seem reasonable to try a number nearer to 1.8 than 1.9, say 1.83.
   Trying $x = 1.83$: $(1.83)^2 + (2 \times 1.83) = 7.0089$, very close.
   Trying $x = 1.82$: $(1.82)^2 + (2 \times 1.82) = 6.9524$, too small.
Hence a solution of the equation $x^2 + 2x = 7$ is: $x = 1.83$ to 2 decimal places

Exercise 10

Solve these equations, to 2 decimal places, using the 'trial and improvement' process. Check your answer by trying the numbers 0.01 above and 0.01 below your answer.

1 $x^2 = 30$ **2** $2x^2 = 100$ **3** $x^3 + 1 = 14$ **4** $x^3 = 60$

5 $2x^2 + x = 25$ **6** $\dfrac{50}{x} = x$ **7** $\dfrac{x}{x+1} = 0.7$ **8** $x(x - 2) = 300$

5.9 Simultaneous equations

If $2x + y = 12$, then there are many possible values for x and y that would satisfy the equation. For example $x = 3$ and $y = 6$ would satisfy the equation.

Also, $x = 4$ and $y = 4$ would work,

as would $x = 0$ and $y = 12$.

(2 × 3) + 6 = 6 + 6 = 12
(2 × 4) + 4 = 8 + 4 = 12
(2 × 0) + 12 = 0 + 12 = 12

If, however, as well as satisfying $2x + y = 12$, we *also* had to have $x + y = 7$, then the only values that satisfy *both* equations simultaneously are $x = 0$ and $y = 2$.

(Check: $(2 \times 5) + 2 = 10 + 2 = 12$ and $5 + 2 = 7$.)

The process of finding the values of x and y when they have to satisfy *two* equations simultaneously, is called **solving simultaneous equations**.

Example   Solve the equations $4v + 5w = 33$ and $2v + 5w = 19$.

$4v + 5w = 33$
$2v + 5w = 19$

Writing one equation under the other.

$2v = 14$

Subtracting the second equation from the first one; the '5w' terms cancel each other.

Hence $v = \frac{14}{2} = 7$

To find w, substitute the value of v ($= 7$) into the first equation.

$(4 \times 7) + 5w = 33$

$28 + 5w = 33$

We know how to solve this linear equation.

$5w = 33 - 28$

$5w = 5$

$w = 1$

Check in the second equation:
(2 × 7) + (5 × 1) = 14 + 5 = 19,
which is correct.

Exercise 11   Solve these equations simultaneously.

1 $x + 2y = 5, x + y = 3$

2 $3a + 2b = 22, 2a + 2b = 16$

3 $3p + 4q = 19, 3p + 2q = 17$

4 $3x + y = 13, 6x + y = 19$

5 $m + n = 14, 5m + n = 38$

6 $4s + 4t = 24, 4s + t = 15$

7 $8a + 3b = 47, 3a + 3b = 27$

8 $2x + 3y = 23, 5x + 3y = 53$

9 $m + 3n = 13, 3m + 3n = 21$

10 $6y + z = 6, 2y + z = 2$

Example   Solve equations $4x + y = 17$ and $2x + 3y = 21$ simultaneously.

There is a different number of xs and ys in each equation. If we multiply the first equation by 3, then we will have a '$3y$' term in each. We could then take one away from the other.

$$12x + 3y = 51$$ ***Equation 1 multiplied by 3.***
$$2x + 3y = 21$$ ***Equation 2.***
$$12x - 2x = 51 - 21$$ ***Subtract equation 2.***
$$10x = 30$$
$$x = 3$$

To find y, substitute this value of x into one of the *original* equations:

$$(4 \times 3) + y = 17$$
$$12 + y = 17$$
$$y = 17 - 12$$ ***Check in the other equation:***
$$y = 5$$ ***$(2 \times 3) + (3 \times 5) = 6 + 15 = 21$.***

Exercise 12

Solve these equations simultaneously: multiply one equation by a number, so that the *same* term appears in each equation, and then subtract.

We can multiply an equation by any number we like:
e.g. $3x + 2y = 8$
is the same as
$6x + 4y = 16$, or
$30x + 20y = 80$.

1 $2x + y = 14$
  $x + 3y = 22$

2 $3a + 2b = 7$
  $a + 4b = 9$

3 $p + 5q = 20$
  $2p + 3q = 19$

4 $u + 2v = 16$
  $2u + 3v = 29$

5 $4x + 3y = 31$
  $2x + 7y = 21$

6 $c + d = 7$
  $3c + 5d = 27$

7 $3x + y = 14$
  $2x + 3y = 28$

8 $5p + 3q = 14$
  $4p + q = 7$

9 $2s + 3t = 25$
  $s + 4t = 25$

The process is similar if there are negative signs in one or other of the equations.

Example   Solve simultaneously $2x + y = 13$, $3x - y = 7$.

$$2x + y = 13$$ ***Writing the equations one under the other.***
$$3x - y = 7$$

If we now *add* these equations, then the '$+y$' term and the '$-y$' term will cancel each other out. This will leave:

$$2x + 3x = 13 + 7$$
$$5x = 20$$
Hence $x = 4$
$$(2 \times 4) + y = 13$$ ***Substituting in the first equation.***
$$8 + y = 13$$ ***Check in the other equation:***
$$y = 5$$ ***$(3 \times 4) - 5 = 12 - 5 = 7$.***

Example   Solve simultaneously $2x - 3y = 7$, $3x + y = 27$.

$2 - 3y = 7$ ***Writing the equations one under the other.***
$3x + y = 27$

Multiplying the second equation by 3 will mean that we have a '$-3y$' in the first equation, and a '$+3y$' in the second; adding will cancel these out.

$2x - 3y = 7$
$9x + 3y = 81$
$11x = 88$ ***Adding the equations.***
$x = \frac{88}{11} = 8$

$(2 \times 8) - 3y = 7$ ***Substituting in the first equation.***
$16 - 3y = 7$
$16 = 7 + 3y$ ***Using tip C.***
$7 + 3y = 16$ ***Using tip A.***
$3y = 16 - 7$
$3y = 9$ ***Check in the other equation:***
$y = 3$ ***$(3 \times 8) + 3 = 24 + 3 = 27$.***

Exercise 13   Solve these equations simultaneously.

1 $4d + e = 13$ 2 $x - 2y = 2$ 3 $3p + 2q = 33$
   $3d - e = 1$ $3x + 2y = 38$ $p - q = 1$
4 $2x - 3y = 0$ 5 $a + b = 20$ 6 $2u - v = 3$
   $2x + 3y = 48$ $a - b = 6$ $2u + v = 13$
7 $5a - 3b = 3$ 8 $4s - t = 5$ 9 $2x + y = 99$
   $2a + b = 10$ $2s + 3t = 13$ $x - y = 48$

Example   Solve the equations $5x + 2y = 26$, $4x - 3y = 7$ simultaneously.

$5x + 2y = 26$ ***Writing the equations one under the other.***
$4x - 3y = 7$

Whatever we multiply one equation by, we cannot make the same number of either xs or ys. In these cases we have to multiply *each* equation by a *different* number.

$15x + 6y = 78$ ***Multiplying the first equation by 3.***
$8x - 6y = 14$ ***Multiplying the second equation by 2.***
$23x = 92$ ***Adding the equations.***
$x = \frac{92}{23}$
$x = 4$

$$(5 \times 4) + 2y = 26 \qquad \textit{Substituting in the first equation.}$$
$$20 + 2y = 26$$
$$2y = 26 - 20$$
$$2y = 6 \qquad \textit{Check in the other equation:}$$
$$y = 3 \qquad \textit{(4} \times \textit{4)} - \textit{(3} \times \textit{3)} = \textit{16} - \textit{9} = \textit{7.}$$

Exercise 14

Solve these equations simultaneously.

1 $x + 3y = 7$
   $3x + 4y = 11$

2 $5a - 2b = 1$
   $2a + 3b = 27$

3 $4p - q = 29$
   $p - q = 2$

4 $a + 6b = 15$
   $4a - 5b = 2$

5 $4u - 3v = 1$
   $5u - 2v = 10$

6 $2y + 5z = 23$
   $3y + 2z = 29$

7 $6d + e = 50$
   $2d + 5e = 26$

8 $4x - 3y = 2$
   $3x + 4y = 14$

9 $2x - 3y = 10$
   $2x + y = 10$

Exercise 15

In these equations, the values of x and y can be positive, negative, whole numbers or fractions. Make sure that your answers satisfy both equations.

1 $2x + 3y = 14$
   $2x + y = 10$

2 $3x - 4y = 7$
   $x + 2y = 9$

3 $x - 3y = 6$
   $x + 2y = 1$

4 $x - 3y = 1$
   $2x + y = 16$

5 $4x - y = 18$
   $2x + y = 6$

6 $5x + 3y = 5$
   $2x + y = 1$

7 $x + 2y = 13$
   $7x - y = 1$

8 $2x - 3y = 13$
   $x - 4y = 14$

9 $2x - 3y = 5$
   $3x + 2y = 40$

10 $x + y = 1$
   $x - y = 9$

11 $2x + y = 5$
   $4x + 3y = 14$

12 $2x - 5y = 25$
   $x + y = 23$

13 $x - 2y = 0$
   $3x + 4y = 15$

14 $5x + 2y = 0$
   $3x + y = 1$

15 $4x + 2y = 8$
   $2x - 5y = 10$

5.10 Use in problems

Example   Two T-shirts and a pair of jeans cost Carl £28. Five T-shirts and a pair of the same jeans cost Carla £43. How much is a T-shirt? How much is a pair of jeans?

We can simplify the writing by letting £t = cost of a T-shirt, and £j = cost of a pair of jeans. We can then write:

$$2t + j = 28 \text{ for Carl}$$
$$\text{and } 5t + j = 43 \text{ for Carla}$$

$$5t + j = 43 \qquad \textit{Writing the first equation under the second.}$$
$$2t + j = 28$$
$$3t = 15 \qquad \textit{Subtracting}$$
$$t = \tfrac{15}{3}$$
$$t = 5$$

So a T-shirt costs £5.

Going back to Carl's clothes, we can now work out the cost of a pair of jeans:

$$2t + j = 28$$
$$(2 \times 5) + j = 28 \qquad \textit{Substituting}$$
$$10 + j = 28$$
$$j = 18$$

So the jeans must cost £18.

Checking with Carla's clothes: $5t + j = (5 \times 5) + £18 = £25 + £18 = £43$, which is correct.

Exercise 16

1 Fred buys three buns and a scone for 27p, and Freda buys a bun and two scones for 24p. How much does a bun cost? How much does a scone cost? (Let a bun cost b pence and a scone cost s pence.)

2 Four nails and a screw weigh 28 g, and two nails and three screws weigh 34 g. What does one nail weigh? What does one screw weigh? (Let a nail weigh n g and a screw weigh s g.)

3 Joanne needs 30 cm of wooden beading for a model she is making. The shop sells either type A or type B beading. Four pieces of type A and three of type B come to 30 cm. Also, three of type A and six of type B come to 30 cm. How long is a type A piece, and how long is a type B piece?

4 Five copies of book X and four of book Y cost £46 altogether. If two copies of book X cost the same as three copies of book Y, how much does each book cost?

5 Three apples and two oranges cost 88p, and an apple and three oranges cost 76p. How much does one apple cost?

5.11 Manipulating formulas

In the formula $P = Q + 12$, we can work out the value of P, if we are given a value of Q. For example, if $Q = 3$, then $P = 3 + 12 = 15$.

How can we find Q, however, if we are told that $P = 20$?

One way is to rearrange the formula to give $Q = \ldots$.

Using the 'balance' idea that we used when solving equations, we can see that, in order to get Q by itself on one side, we need to subtract 12 from each side.

$$P = Q + 12$$
$$P - 12 = Q$$
$$Q = P - 12 \qquad \textbf{\textit{Using tip A.}}$$
$$\text{When } P = 20, \text{ then } Q = 20 - 12$$
$$Q = 8$$

Example   Rearrange the formula $s = ut$, into the form $t = \ldots$.

On the balance, we need to divide each side by u:

$$s = ut$$

$$\frac{s}{u} = t$$

$$t = \frac{s}{u} \qquad \textbf{\textit{Using tip A.}}$$

Exercise 17   Rearrange these formulas, to make the letter in brackets the subject of the formula. If 't' is the letter in brackets the answer should be '$t = \ldots$'.

1 $c = d + 5$ (d) **2** $3m = 12 + n$ (n)

3 $y = x - 2$ (x) **4** $4r = 10 - s$ (s)

5 $t = 2p$ (p) **6** $5g = 3h$ (h)

7 $m = 2p - 5$ (p) **8** $a = 4 + 3k$ (k)

9 $P = \dfrac{k}{V}$ (V) **10** $x = mz$ (z)

11 $f = \dfrac{330}{v}$ (v) **12** $\dfrac{w}{3} = 2d$ (d)

Example Write a formula for working out R, if $e = v + 2R$

$e = v + 2R$

$e - v = 2R$ ***Subtracting v from each side.***

$2R = e - v$ ***Using tip A.***

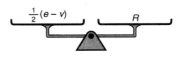

$R = \frac{1}{2}(e - v)$ or $\dfrac{e - v}{2}$

Exercise 18   Rearrange these formulas to give an expression for the letter stated.

Temperature falls by about 6°C for every 1000 metres of altitude. Hence the top of Mt. Kilimanjaro in Tanzania, in the tropics, is covered in snow all the year round.

1 $V = IR : R = \ldots$

2 $d = 3a + b : b = \ldots$

3 $p = \dfrac{3q}{2} : q = \ldots$

4 $C = 2\pi r : r = \ldots$

5 $y = mx + c : m = \ldots$

6 $z = 2x + 3 : x = \ldots$

7 $a = \dfrac{v - u}{t} : v = \ldots$

8 $x = 3(d - 4) : d = \ldots$

9 $F = \dfrac{9C}{5} + 32 : C = \ldots$

10 $k = \dfrac{PV}{T} : V = \ldots$

5.12 Evaluating formulas

Example   In the formula $A = 3x + y$, find x when $A = 40$ and $y = 4$.

There are two main ways of tackling this type of problem:

1. Substitute the numbers into the formula, and then solve the resulting equation.
2. Rearrange the formula, as in exercise 18, then substitute the numbers.

Method 1 $40 = 3x + 4$

$36 = 3x$

$12 = x$

Method 2 $A = 3x + y$

$A - y = 3x$

$x = \dfrac{A - y}{3}$

$x = \dfrac{40 - 4}{3}$

$x = \frac{36}{3}$

$x = 12$

Exercise 19   Find the value of the letter stated in these formulas. Use whichever method you prefer.

1 $B = 2(t - 12)$; find t when $B = 56$

2 $3y = x + 2.4$; find x when $y = 0.6$

3 $v = u + 10t$; find u when $t = 5$ and $v = 70$

4 $2a = 3b + 4c$; find b when $a = 20$ and $c = 5.5$

5 $l = 3p + 17$; find p when $l = 50$

6 $y = mx + c$; find m when $y = 5$, $x = 2$ and $c = -3$

7 $c = 4p - 3q$; find p when $c = 16$ and $q = 4$

8 $C = 16 - 2k$; find C when $k = 3\frac{3}{4}$

9 $y = a + 4x$; find y when $a = -3\frac{1}{2}$ and $x = 2\frac{1}{4}$

10 $M = 6(p - 2q)$; find M when $p = 11\frac{1}{3}$ and $q = 5\frac{1}{3}$

11 $8w = 4x + 10y$; find w when $x = 9\frac{1}{4}$ and $y = \frac{7}{10}$

12 $F = 1.8C + 32$; find C when $F = 50$

13 $w = 6(3c + 4)$; find c when $w = 69$

14 $s = ut + 5t$; find u when $s = 100$ and $t = 4$

5.13 Inequalities

We have looked at solving simple equations, for example $4x - 5 = 7$.

$$4x - 5 = 7$$
$$4x = 7 + 5 = 12$$
$$x = 3$$

Cobalt in vitamin B12 protects against anaemia, but only 0.000 002 g per day is needed by the human body.

If, however, we need a value which does *not* satisfy this equation, we need a value of x which is *not* equal to 3. This means that either x is less than 3 or x is greater than 3.

We write x less than 3 as $\boldsymbol{x < 3}$ and x greater than 3 as $\boldsymbol{x > 3}$ (the wider end of the 'arrowhead' points to the greater side), and these are called **inequalities**. The process of solving inequalities is very similar to that of solving equations.

Example   Solve the inequality $3x + 4 < 19$.

As with equations, we can add or subtract the same value from each side. However we can multiply or divide by *positive* values only.

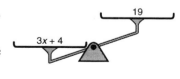

$3x < 19 - 4$ ***Subtract 4 from each side.***

$3x < 15$

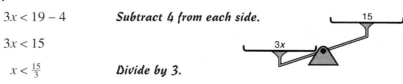

$x < \frac{15}{3}$ ***Divide by 3.***

$x < 5$ ***Check: if x < 5, 3x < 15 and 3x + 4 < 19.***

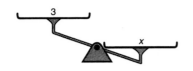

Note: We CANNOT use tip A in inequalities: if x is less than 3 ($x < 3$) then 3 must be *greater* than x ($3 > x$). If we change over the sides of an inequality, we must change the sign (from < to > or from > to <).

Example   Solve the inequality $23 - 4x > 7$.

Looking back at the method used for negative terms in equations, we have:

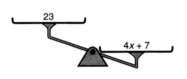

$23 > 4x + 7$ ***Adding 4x to each side.***

$23 - 7 > 4x$ ***Subtracting 7.***

$16 > 4x$

$4 > x$

So, $x < 4$ ***Look at the note above.***

So if x is less than 4, then $23 - 4x$ will be greater than 7.

Exercise 20   Solve these inequalities.

1 $x + 3 > 5$	**2** $k - 14 < 20$	**3** $5 + 2t > 23$
4 $12 - y < 5$	**5** $8 + 5x < 43$	**6** $3r - 16 > 14$
7 $2y - 6 < 7$	**8** $8p + 25 > -15$	**9** $4z + 13 < 0$

Example   Solve the inequality $12 - x > 3x - 5$.

As with equations, we need to have the 'x' term positive, and on one side.

$12 > 4x - 5$ ***Adding x to each side.***

$17 > 4x$ ***Adding 5 to each side.***

$\frac{17}{4} > x$ ***Dividing each side by 4.***

$4\frac{1}{4} > x$, i.e. $x < 4\frac{1}{4}$

Exercise 21   Solve these inequalities.

1 $x + 8 > 5 + 2x$	**2** $2k - 14 < 5 + k$	**3** $4 + 3t > 22 - 3t$
4 $9 - y < 15 + y$	**5** $4 - 2x < 12 - 3x$	**6** $4 + 7y < 7 + 4y$
7 $20 - 2n > 3n + 5$	**8** $6x + 20 < 3x$	**9** $2 + 6z < 100 - z$

5.14 Two conditions

'Think of a number between 3 and 12.' This sort of request is asked for when you are trying a riddle on a friend.

If we let the number be n, then we can write $n > 3$ and $n < 12$.

If we write the first condition the other way round, remembering to change the sign, we will have $3 < n$ and $n < 12$.

These two inequalities can be combined into one 'double' condition:

$3 < n < 12$: n has to be *greater* than 3 but *less* than 12.
So $n = 4, 5, 6, 7, 8, 9, 10$ or 11

$\leqslant$ *means 'less than or equal to'.*

Example List the possible values of n, where n is a whole number, if

$1 < n \leqslant 7$.

The only possible values of n are: $n = 2, 3, 4, 5, 6$ or 7

Example List the values of x, if x is a whole number, such that
$-3 < 2x < 16$.

We must first get x by itself:

$-\frac{3}{2} < x < 8$ **Dividing by 2.**

If x has to be a whole number, then: $x = -1, 0, 1, 2, 3, 4, 5, 6$ or 7

Exercise 22

List the values which satisfy each inequality, assuming in all cases that answers are whole numbers.

1 $4 < t < 10$	**2** $0 < x \leqslant 9$	**3** $-5 < s < 2$
4 $6 \leqslant 3n \leqslant 30$	**5** $1 \leqslant 4x \leqslant 20$	**6** $-10 < 3t < 10$
7 $-20 < 2x < -4$	**8** $100 < 10m \leqslant 200$	**9** $-6 < 6n < 60$

Example Solve the inequality $2n^2 \leqslant 32$

$n^2 \leqslant 16$ **Dividing by 2.**

Because $n \times n = n^2$ and $(-n) \times (-n) = n^2$, we will have *two* inequalities:

$n \leqslant 4$ and $-n \leqslant 4$

Taking the second inequality:

$0 \leqslant n + 4$ **Adding n to each side.**

$-4 \leqslant n$ **Then subtracting 4.**

So $-4 \leqslant n \leqslant 4$ **Writing both inequalities together.**

So if $2n^2 \leqslant 32$, then the value of n lies between -4 and 4.

Exercise 23 Solve these inequalities. There should be two conditions in each case.

1 $x^2 < 9$ **2** $c^2 - 20 < 5$ **3** $72 \geqslant 2s^2$ **4** $\dfrac{x^2}{2} < 32$

5 $98 > 2x^2$ **6** $25k^2 < 100$ **7** $4x^2 \leqslant 9$ **8** $100 \geqslant \dfrac{n^2}{4}$

9 $d^2 < \frac{1}{4}$ **10** $x^2 \leqslant 0.01$

Review

Exercise 24 Solve these equations:

1 $x + 3 = 8$ **2** $x - 6 = 7$ **3** $2x + 5 = 21$

4 $5x - 2 = 28$ **5** $3(x - 3) = 12$ **6** $4(x + 9) = 80$

7 $3x - 4 = 2x + 6$ **8** $2x + 17 = 4x - 1$ **9** $5(x + 2) = 7x$

10 $25 - 3x = 1$ **11** $2x + 8 = 0$ **12** $2x + 3 = x - 5$

13 $x + 2x + 3x = 4x + 5$ **14** $\dfrac{x}{5} = \dfrac{1}{4}$ **15** $\dfrac{x}{4} + 6 = 6\frac{1}{2}$

Solve these equations, correct to two decimal places, using a 'trial and improvement' process:

16 $x^3 = 13$ **17** $x^3 + x = 75$ **18** $x^3 - 2x = 100$

19 $x^3 = 200$ **20** $x^2(x + 5) = 100$ **21** $\dfrac{x^3}{(1 + x)} = 50$

22 $3x^3 = 70$ **23** $\dfrac{100}{x} = x^2$

Solve these simultaneous equations:

24 $x + y = 12; x - y = 2$ **25** $2x + y = 27; x + y = 17$

26 $x + 2y = 8; x + 5y = 17$ **27** $2x - y = 14; x + 3y = 14$

28 $x - y = 5; 2x + 3y = 15$ **29** $3x - 2y = 19; x + 4y = 18$

30 $x + 3y = 1; x - y = 9$ **31** $x + y = 1; x = 2y$

Rearrange these formulas to make the given letter the subject:

32 $x = 4y: y$ **33** $3h = k - 5: k$ **34** $h = 3k - 5: k$

35 $h = 3(k - 5): k$ **36** $m = \dfrac{n}{3} + 2p; n$ **37** $C = \frac{5}{9}(F - 32); F$

38 $s = 10t^2: t$ **39** $v^2 = u^2 + 2as: u$

Solve these inequalities:

40 $x + 5 > 12$ **41** $x - 3 < 2$ **42** $2x - 3 < 35$

43 $3x + 10 > 100$ **44** $x + 5 < 2x + 1$ **45** $5(x + 4) > 2(x + 16)$

46 $20 - 3x < 5x$ **47** $x < 2(x - 1)$ **48** $2x^2 < 288$

Exercise 25

49 $(x - 8)^2 < 9$

The following questions are all taken from GCSE papers.

1 (a)   Solve the equation $2x = 10$.

(*1 mark*)

(b)   Solve the equation $6y + 1 = 25$.

(*2 marks*)

(c)   Solve the equation $8p - 3 = 3p + 13$.

(*2 marks*)

(d)   Solve the equation $4x + 3 = 2(x - 3)$.

(*3 marks*)

(e)   Solve the inequality $2x + 3 \leqslant 8$.

(*2 marks*)
[EDEXCEL]

2   Use trial and improvement to find a solution of the equation $x^3 = 22$.
Start with $x = 2$ and show your trials in the table. Give your answer

x	x^3
2	

correct to one decimal place.

(*3 marks*)
[SEG]

3 (a)   Solve the simultaneous equations

$$3x + 2y = 7$$
$$5x - 4y = 8.$$

(*3 marks*)

(b)   List all the integer values of n for which this inequality is true.

$$n^2 < 10$$

(*2 marks*)
[SEG]

4 (a) Solve the equation $\frac{1}{3}x = 2$.

(*1 mark*)

(b) Solve the simultaneous equations

$$x + 3y = 5$$
$$x - y = 3.$$

You must show all your working.

(*3 marks*)

(c) List the values of n, where n is an integer, such that

$$1 \leqslant 2n - 3 < 5.$$

(*3 marks*)

(d) Solve the equation $x^2 - 5x + 6 = 0$.

(*2 marks*)
[AQA/SEG]

5 A solution of the equation

$$x^3 + x^2 = 4$$

lies between $x = 1$ and 2.

Use the method of trial and improvement to find this solution. Give your answer to one decimal place. You must show all your trials.

(*3 marks*)
[AQA/SEG]

6

3x + 2

2x

The diagram shows a rectangle with length $3x + 2$ and width $2x$. All measurements are given in centimetres. The perimeter of the rectangle is P centimetres, the area of the rectangle is A square centimetres.

(a) Write down an expression in its simplest form, in terms of x, for

(i) P,
(ii) A.

(*3 marks*)

$P = 44$.

(b) Work out the value of A.

(*3 marks*)
[EDEXCEL]

7 Using trial and improvement, or otherwise, solve the equation

$$t^3 + t = 17.$$

Show *all* your working and give your answer correct to 2 decimal places.

(4 marks)
[EDEXCEL]

8 Solve

(a) $4a + 3 = 9$

(2 marks)

(b) $5b - 7 = 2b + 5$

(2 marks)

(c) $3(c - 6) = 10 - 2c$

(2 marks)
[EDEXCEL]

9 (a) Find the values of the integer n if

$$-4 < n \leqslant 3 \qquad \text{and} \qquad n \geqslant -2.$$

(2 marks)

(b) Solve the inequality

$$5 - 2x < 11.$$

(3 marks)
[OCR]

10 (a) Factorise completely.

$$3x^2 - 6x$$

(2 marks)

(b) Expand and simplify.

$$(3x + 2)(x - 4)$$

(3 marks)

(c) Make t the subject of the formula.

$$W = \frac{5t + 3}{4}$$

(3 marks)
[NEAB]

11 Solve the equations

(a) $x + 13 = 18$, *(1 mark)*

(b) $6x = 75$, *(1 mark)*

(c) $\dfrac{x}{2} = 12$, *(1 mark)*

(d) $5x - 18 = 2x + 6$. *(2 marks)*
[OCR]

12 Solve the simultaneous equations below by an algebraic (not graphical) method. Show all your working.

$$3x + 4y = -6$$
$$5x + 3y = 1$$

(4 marks)
[WJEC]

13 (a) Remove the brackets from the expression. Give your answer in its simplest form.

$$5(2x + 4) - 3(8 - x)$$

(2 marks)

(b) Solve the inequalities

(i) $7 - 4y \leqslant 15$, *(3 marks)*

(ii) $x^2 \geqslant 25$. *(2 marks)*
[MEG]

14 All lengths in this question are in metres. A rectangular garden has a square patio of side x metres in one corner. The remainder of the garden is a lawn.

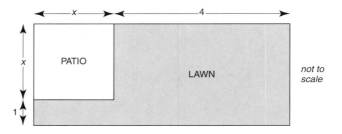

(a) Write down an expression, in terms of x, for the longest side of the lawn. *(1 mark)*

(b) Find an expression, in terms of x, for the perimeter of the lawn. *(1 mark)*

(c) The perimeter of the lawn is 34 metres.
Find the value of x. *(2 marks)*
[MEG]

15 The angles of a triangle are $(2x - 3)°$, $(x + 4)°$ and $(x + 19)°$.

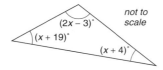

(a) Write an expression, in terms of x, for the sum of the angles.
Write your answer in its simplest form. *(2 marks)*

The sum of the angles is 180°.

(b) (i)   Write down an equation in x.   *(1 mark)*

   (ii)   Solve your equation to find the size of the smallest angle in the triangle.   *(3 marks)*

   [SEG]

16 (a)   Solve the equations:

   (i) $2x + 3 = 15 - x$,   *(2 marks)*

   (ii) $(x + 3)(x - 4) = 0$.   *(2 marks)*

(b)   Solve the simultaneous equations

$$2x + y = 9$$
$$x - 2y = 7.$$

You must show all your working.   *(3 marks)*

(c)   List the values of n, where n is an integer, such that

$$3 \leqslant n + 4 < 6.$$

   (2 marks)

   [SEG]

Ideas for investigations

1   **A** We know that, if $-x = 3$, then $x = -3$.
But if $-x < 3$, then $x > -3$.

Investigate the rules that apply when inequalities are:

(a) multiplied by (i) a positive number (ii) a negative number,
(b) divided by (i) a positive number (ii) a negative number.

B We know that, if $\dfrac{1}{x} = 3$ then $x = \frac{1}{3}$.

But if $\dfrac{1}{x} < 3$, then $x > \frac{1}{3}$.

Investigate the rules that apply when we are given an inequality with x on the denominator.

Extension work

Investigate the situation when both of the above occur
(e.g. $\dfrac{-3}{x} > 12$, find an inequality for x).

GRAPHICAL REPRESENTATION

6.1 Coordinates

As a reminder, the first coordinate is the distance across from the origin 0. The second coordinate is the distance up from 0.

The first coordinate is called the x-coordinate, and the second coordinate is called the y-coordinate.

Example   The point A has coordinates (3, 5).
What are the coordinates of the other points?

A is 3 units across, and 5 units up; its coordinates are, therefore, (3, 5).

B is the point (1, 4).

C is the point (4, 0).

D is the point (0, 5).

E is the point (−3, 6).

F is the point (5, −2).

G is the point (−4, −3).

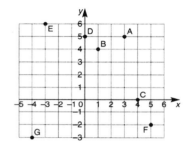

Exercise 1

1 Copy and complete these statements:

(a) Point H has coordinates (−2,).   (b) Point I has coordinates (, −3).

(c) Point J has coordinates (,).   (d) Point K has coordinates (,).

(e) Point L has coordinates (,).

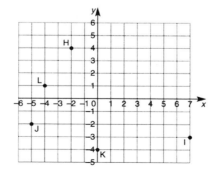

These are called Cartesian coordinates, after a French mathematician of the seventeenth century, René Descartes.

2 Make a copy of the grid on squared paper. Mark these points on your grid.

A = (−5, 2), B = (4, −1), C = (−4, 1), D = (−1, −4), E = (3, −2), F = (−3, 2)

Exercise 2

In these questions you will need to draw a pair of axes on squared paper.

1 Draw a pair of axes, where $-2 \leqslant x \leqslant 5$, and $-3 \leqslant y \leqslant 4$. (See the end of chapter 5 for the meaning of '$\leqslant$'.)

(a) Plot the points $(4, 1)$, $(1, 3)$ and $(-1, 0)$.

(b) A fourth point is added to make a square. What are its coordinates?

2 Draw a pair of axes, where both x and y have values from -6 to $+8$.

(a) Plot the points $(7, 1)$, $(6, 2)$, $(4, 4)$, $(2, 6)$ and $(0, 8)$.

(b) What is common to all these points? Draw in the line, and write down the coordinates of any other points on the line.

3 Draw a pair of axes, where $-10 \leqslant x \leqslant 8$, and $-3 \leqslant y \leqslant 5$. Join these five sets of points, in order:

(a) $(-6, 2)$, $(-6, 3)$, $(-9, 3)$, $(-9, -1)$, $(-6, -1)$, $(-6, 1)$, $(-7, 1)$, $(-7, 0)$

(b) $(-2, 2)$, $(-2, 3)$, $(-5, 3)$, $(-5, -1)$, $(-2, -1)$, $(-2, 0)$

(c) $(2, 2)$, $(2, 3)$, $(-1, 3)$, $(-1, 1)$, $(2, 1)$, $(2, -1)$, $(-1, -1)$, $(-1, 0)$

(d) $(6, 3)$, $(3, 3)$, $(3, -1)$, $(6, -1)$

(e) $(3, 1)$, $(6, 1)$

Let's hope you improve your grade!

The most deadly poison produced by an animal comes from the skin of the Kokoi frog that lives in Colombia, South America. About 0.00001 grams is enough to kill a human.

6.2 Mappings and plotting graphs

A simple 'function machine' takes one number and **maps** it on to another number. For example, the '-2' machine will take the number 5 and map it on to 3.

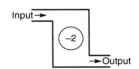

We can make a list of inputs, and the corresponding outputs, in a table.

INPUT		OUTPUT
5	$\rightarrow$	3
6	$\rightarrow$	4
10	$\rightarrow$	8
12	$\rightarrow$	10
x	$\rightarrow$	$x - 2$

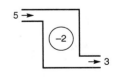

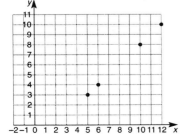

If we call the input x, then the output will be $x - 2$. We can represent this mapping on a graph. Let x be the input and y the output. This means that the output y is equal to $x - 2$.

$$y = x - 2$$

The diagram shows the four points in the table.

The mapping
$x \rightarrow x - 2$
means the same as the function
$y = x - 2$, *since we are mapping x onto y.*

Example Draw a graph of the mapping $x \rightarrow x + 3$, for values of x from $x = 0$ to $x = 6$.

First, make a table of x values from 0 to 6; underneath each x value write down its value after the mapping:

x	0	1	2	3	4	5	6
$y = x + 3$	3	4	5	6	7	8	9

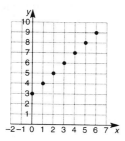

Plot these values on a graph: clearly the y values range from 3 to 9.
We can join the points with a straight line.
This enables us to do two further things:

(i) we can find what $x = 3.5$ maps on to,

(ii) we can extend the line to show x values that are greater than 6 or less than 0.

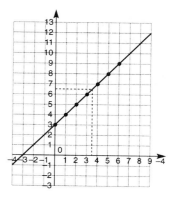

In simple cases, a function is the same as a mapping.

Example Plot the graph of the function $y = 2x - 1$. Take x values from -3 to 5.

As before, make a table of x values from -3 to 5:

Initially, it is easier to work out y values for positive values of x.
When $x = 5$, $2x - 1 = (2 \times 5) - 1 = 9$
When $x = 4$, $2x - 1 = (2 \times 4) - 1 = 7$
When $x = 3$, $2x - 1 = (2 \times 3) - 1 = 5$, etc.
Take care with negatives: $(2 \times -2) - 1 = -4 - 1 = -5$.

The table looks like this:

x	-3	-2	-1	0	1	2	3	4	5
$y = 2x - 1$	-7	-5	-3	-1	1	3	5	7	9

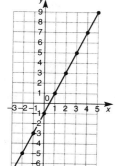

Plot the points, and join them with a straight line.

Exercise 3

Make up a table for these mappings, and plot the graphs. Unless stated otherwise, take values of x from $x = -3$ to $x = 4$.

1 $x \rightarrow x + 2$ **2** $x \rightarrow x - 1$

3 $x \rightarrow 2x + 5$ **4** $x \rightarrow 5 - x$

5 $x \rightarrow 3x - 5$ **6** $x \rightarrow \frac{x}{2} + 7$

7 $x \rightarrow \frac{x}{2} - 1$ **8** $x \rightarrow 15 - 2x, 0 \leqslant x \leqslant 8$

9 $x \rightarrow 10 - x, 0 \leqslant x \leqslant 12$ **10** $x \rightarrow 2x - 2$

Example   Plot the graph of $2x + y = 15$, where $0 \leqslant x \leqslant 10$.

We can rearrange the equation so that we have '$y = \dots$', i.e. where y is expressed as a function of x.
Looking back to chapter 5, we need to subtract $2x$ from each side:

$$2x + y = 15$$

$$y = 15 - 2x$$

In making up the table, an extra line ($2x$) can be added, to help in calculating the values for y.

x	0	1	2	3	4	5	6	7	8	9	10
$2x$	0	2	4	6	8	10	12	14	16	18	20
$y = 15 - 2x$	15	13	11	9	7	5	3	1	-1	-3	-5

Now plot the points.

Exercise 4

Rearrange these equations into '$y = \dots$', then make up a table and draw their graphs.

1 $x + y = 8$ **2** $y + 3 = 2x$

3 $y - 2 = x$ **4** $x + y = 12$

5 $x = y - 4$ **6** $2x + 3 = y - 1$

7 $2y + 3 = 4x + 8$ **8** $y - 2x = 3$

9 $3y = 6x - 2$ **10** $2y - x = 8$

6.3 Drawing a line from points lying on it

The speed of sound in air is about 331 m/s.

If you can find *any two* points which lie on a line, then you can join the points to form the line you require. You must be sure that you have worked out the two points correctly, and it is as well to check with a third point, just to make sure that you have not made a slip.

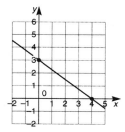

Example   Draw the graph of the line given by $3x + 4y = 12$.
One way of finding a point on the line is to make $x = 0$:

$$(3 \times 0) + 4y = 12$$
$$4y = 12$$
$$y = 3$$

The point $(0, 3)$ must lie on the line.
Now try making $y = 0$:

$$3x + (4 \times 0) = 12$$
$$3x = 12$$
$$x = 4$$

The point $(4, 0)$ must lie on the line.
This line passes through the point $(2, 1.5)$. Check to ensure that $(2, 1.5)$ satisfies the equation: $(3 \times 2) + (4 \times 1.5) = 6 + 6 = 12$.

Example   Draw the graph of the line given by $5y = 2x - 3$.

If we let $x = 0$, then $5y = -3$
    and $y = \frac{-3}{5}$

This is not very easy to plot. We may be able to find easier points.

Let $y = 0$: $0 = 2x - 3$
        $3 = 2x$ *Adding 3 to each side.*
        $x = 1.5$ *Dividing by 2.*

The point $(1.5, 0)$ is easy to plot. To find another 'easy' point, try $x = 1$, then $x = 2$, etc. until $2x - 3$ is divisible by 5.

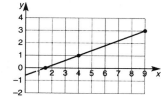

When $x = 4$
        $2x - 3 = 8 - 3 = 5$
Hence $5y = (2 \times 4) - 3 = 5$
So $y = 1$

The point $(4, 1)$ lies on the line. We can now draw the line.
The point $(9, 3)$ lies on this line. Check that it satisfies the equation:
$5y = 5 \times 3 = 15$, and $2x - 3 = (2 \times 9) - 3 = 18 - 3 = 15$.

Exercise 5

By working out two points which satisfy the equation, draw the graph of the line. Check with a third point.

1 $y = x + 3$ **2** $y = 2x - 1$ **3** $x = y - 2$

4 $x = 3y + 1$ **5** $2y = x + 8$ **6** $3x - 1 = y$

7 $x = 12 - y$ **8** $\frac{y}{2} = x + 1$ **9** $x - y = 4$

10 $x + y = 10$ **11** $2y = x - 4$ **12** $2x + y = 16$

13 $x + 3y = 9$ **14** $24 - 2x = 3y$ **15** $4x - y = 16$

6.4 The straight line equation $y = mx + c$

A 'light year', the distance travelled by light in a year, is equivalent to 9 460 528 405 000 kilometres.

Example   Where do the lines
(a) $y = x + 3$
(b) $y = 2x + 5$
(c) $y = 3x - 2$ cut the y-axis?

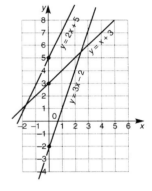

From the graph
$y = x + 3$ cuts the y-axis at $(0, \mathbf{3})$,
$y = 2x + 5$ cuts the y-axis at $(0, \mathbf{5})$,
$y = 3x - 2$ cuts the y-axis at $(0, \mathbf{-2})$.

Any straight line, written in the form
$y = mx + c$, cuts the y-axis at the point $(0, \mathbf{c})$.

Example   Find the coordinates of the point where the line $2y = 3x + 6$ cuts the y-axis.

The answer is *not* $(0, 6)$, because we have not made the equation into $y = $ (something).
We must have y by itself:

$$2y = 3x + 6$$

$$y = \frac{3x}{2} + 3. \qquad \textit{Dividing each side by 2.}$$

This line will cut the y-axis at $(0, 3)$.

Exercise 6

Find the coordinates of the point where each of these lines cuts the y-axis.

1 $y = 4x + 1$ **2** $y = 3x - 4$ **3** $y = 5x - 3$

4 $y = x + 5$ **5** $2y = x - 4$ **6** $3y = 2x + 9$

7 $y = -3x - 1$ **8** $4y = x + 3$ **9** $2y = 5x + 1$

The distance up (or down) from the origin where the line cuts the *y*-axis is called the **intercept** on the *y*-axis. It is the *y*-coordinate of the point where the line cuts the *y*-axis.

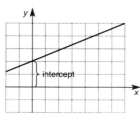

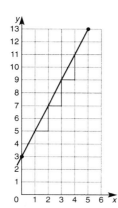

The line $y = 2x + 3$ is drawn. The steepness, or **gradient**, of the line is measured by working out how many units the line rises up, for each unit across.

In this case, the line rises 2 units up for each unit across (in the positive direction).
The gradient of the line $y = 2x + 3$ is 2.

In any equation of the form $y = mx + c$, the **gradient** is **m**: it is the number of *x*s that there are, (i.e. the **coefficient** of *x*).

As with the intercept, the line must be expressed in the form $y = $ (something). For example, the line $2y = 4x - 7$ does not have a gradient of 4. $2y = 4x - 7$ is the same as $y = 2x - 3.5$: the gradient is 2 and the intercept is −3.5.

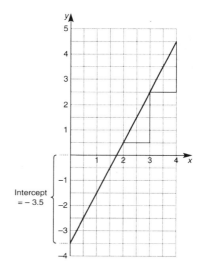

Exercise 7

For each line find (a) the gradient (b) the intercept on the *y*-axis. Remember to write the equation in the form '$y = mx + c$'.

1 $y = 2x - 1$ **2** $y = 3x + 4$ **3** $y = 5x + 2$

4 $y = x - 7$ **5** $2y = x + 4$ **6** $3y = 2x - 6$

7 $x + y = 3$ **8** $2x + y = 0$ **9** $y = 10 - 3x$

Exercise 8   Work out the gradient, and the intercept on the *y*-axis for each line. Hence write down an equation for each line.

1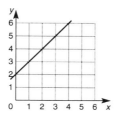

2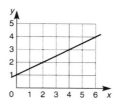

3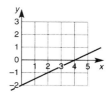

4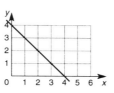

5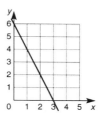

6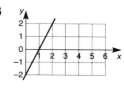

6.5 Solving simultaneous equations graphically

If we draw two non-parallel lines on the same graph grid, the lines will cross. At the point of intersection, the *x* and *y* values will satisfy the equations of *both* lines; the *x*- and *y*-coordinates of the point therefore represent the solution when the equations are solved simultaneously.

Example   By drawing their graphs, solve the equations
$x + y = 8$ and $x = y + 2$ simultaneously.

Two points on the line
$x + y = 8$ are $(8, 0)$ and $(0, 8)$.
(Check: $(4, 4)$ is a third point.)

Two points on the line
$x = y + 2$ are $(2, 0)$ and $(7, 5)$.
(Check: $(4, 2)$ is a third point.)

From the graph we can see
that the lines meet at the point
$(5, 3)$. (Check in each equation:
$x + y = 5 + 3 = 8$ and
$x = y + 2 : 5 = 3 + 2$.)

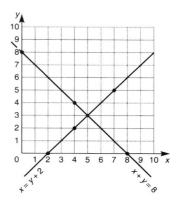

Exercise 9   Find the solution of these pairs of simultaneous equations from the graph. Check that your solution 'works' in both equations.

1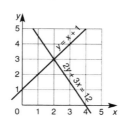

2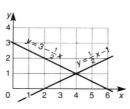

3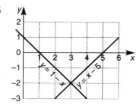

4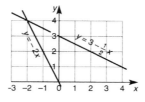

5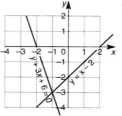

6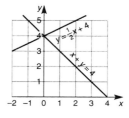

Exercise 10   By drawing each pair of lines, find graphically the solution of each pair of simultaneous equations.

The Egyptians used geometry for land surveys and for building in about 3000 BC.

1 $x + y = 4$
   $y = x - 2$

2 $x + 2y = 6$
   $y = x$

3 $y = 2x - 5$
   $y = \frac{x}{2} + 1$

4 $x + y = 1$
   $y = 2x + 4$

5 $y = x + 5$
   $x + y = 5$

6 $x + y = 0$
   $y = 2x - 6$

6.6   Curves (1): the quadratic function

Example   Draw the graph of the equation $y = x^2$, for values of x from $x = -4$ to $x = +4$.

The table will be:

x	-4	-3	-2	-1	0	1	2	3	4
$y = x^2$	16	9	4	1	0	1	4	9	16

The graph will look like this:

Remember that
$(-4) \times (-4) = +16.$

This is called a **quadratic curve**. Any curve of the form $y = ax^2 + bx + c$ will have this shape.

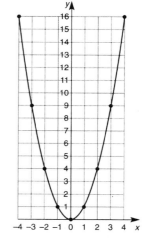

Here are three quadratic curves:

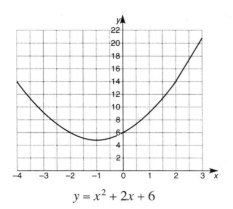

$y = x^2 + 2x + 6$

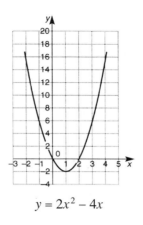

$y = 2x^2 - 4x$

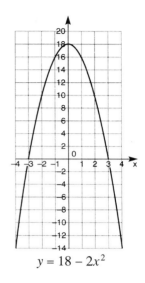

$y = 18 - 2x^2$

Car headlights and theatre spotlights are in the shape of a quadratic curve, because the light source can be placed at a particular point (the focus) to produce a beam of parallel rays.

All quadratic curves have a symmetry line, which passes through the lowest (or highest) point and is parallel to the y-axis.

All quadratic curves can be transformed into the basic quadratic curve $y = x^2$.

Example Use the graph of $y = x^2$ to solve
(a) the equation $x^2 = 4$ (b) the inequality $x^2 < 9$.

(a) From the graph you can see that there are *two* values of x for which $x^2 = 4$:

$x = 2$ and $x = -2$

(Similarly, if $x^2 = 64$, $x = 8$ and $x = -8$.

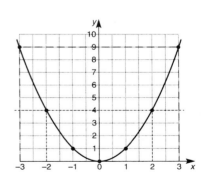

(b) From the graph, if $x^2 = 9$, then the two solutions are $x = 3$ and $x = -3$. Hence, if $x^2 < 9$, then

$x > -3$ and $x < 3$

We can write this more conveniently as $-3 < x < 3$.

6.7 Curves (2): the cubic function

Example Draw the graph of the function $y = x^3$ for $-3 \leqslant x \leqslant 3$.

x	-3	-2	-1	0	1	2	3
$y = x^3$	-27	-8	-1	0	1	8	27

If $x = 4$ then $y^3 = (4)^3 = 64$;
the graph rises quite rapidly as x
increases (e.g. when $x = 10$,
$y = (10)^3 = 1000$). Similarly,
when $x = -10$, $y = -1000$.

Cubic graphs have the general shape
of an 's'.

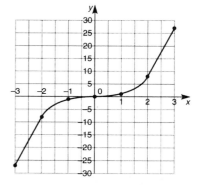

Here are some cubic curves:

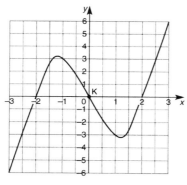

$y = x^3 - 4x$

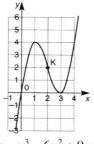

$y = x^3 - 6x^2 + 9x$

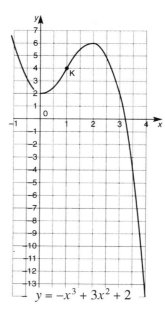

$y = -x^3 + 3x^2 + 2$

Imagine a piece of string in the shape of the first cubic curve. The others
can be obtained by 'pulling' each end of the string. Cubic curves have
'half-turn' rotational symmetry about the point marked K.

6.8 Curves (3): the reciprocal function

Example   Plot the graph of $y = \frac{24}{x}$, for $1 \times x \leqslant 6$.

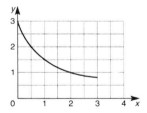

x	1	2	3	4	5	6
$y = \frac{24}{x}$	24	12	8	6	4.8	4

The graph of this **reciprocal** function is a curve which approaches the x-axis more closely as values of x become larger, and which approaches the y-axis for small values of x.

The lines which are approached by a reciprocal function are called **asymptotes**.

Here are some reciprocal curves:

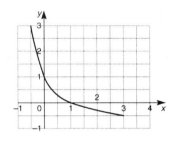

$$y = \frac{3}{x + 1}$$

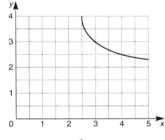

$$y = \frac{1 - x}{1 + x}$$

$$y = \frac{1}{x - 2} + 2$$

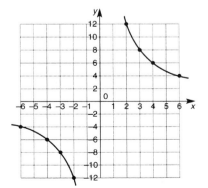

To be absolutely correct, the curve $y = \frac{24}{x}$ has *two* branches; if we look at negative x values, then the table will be:

x	-1	-2	-3	-4	-5	-6
$y = \frac{24}{x}$	-24	-12	-8	-6	-4.8	-4

Three complete reciprocal curves are drawn below:

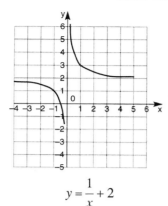

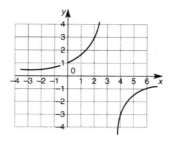

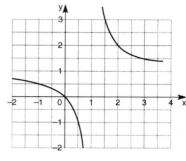

$$y = \frac{1}{x} + 2 \qquad\qquad y = \frac{3}{3 - x} \qquad\qquad y = \frac{1}{x - 1} + 1$$

As with cubic curves, reciprocal curves have half-turn rotational symmetry.

6.9 Plotting simple quadratic functions

The graph of the function $y = x^2$ was drawn earlier:

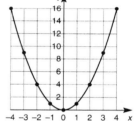

Example Draw the graph of the function
(a) $y = x^2 + 2$ (b) $y = 2x^2$ for values of x from $x = -4$ to $x = 4$.

(a)

x				-4	-3	-2	-1	0	1	2	3	4
x^2				16	9	4	1	0	1	4	9	16
$y = x^2 + 2$				18	11	6	3	2	3	6	11	18

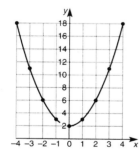

(b)

x				-4	-3	-2	-1	0	1	2	3	4
x^2				16	9	4	1	0	1	4	9	16
$y = 2x^2$				32	18	8	2	0	2	8	18	32

We could have sketched the graphs without the need to make up a table.
Graph (a) is $y = x^2$ moved up 2 units, and graph (b) is $y = x^2$ 'stretched' up the y-axis.

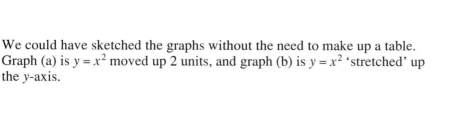

Exercise 11   Make a sketch of these quadratic graphs. See if you can draw them without having to make up a full table of values.

1 $y = x^2 - 3$ **2** $y = x^2 + 4$ **3** $y = x^2 + 6$

4 $y = x^2 - 1$ **5** $y = 2x^2 + 3$ **6** $y = 2x^2 - 5$

7 $y = 3x^2 - 3$ **8** $y = \frac{x^2}{2} + 4$ **9** $y = x^2 - 4x$

6.10   Using quadratic graphs to solve equations

Once we have drawn a quadratic graph, we can use it to solve other quadratic equations which are similar to the one drawn, without the need to draw another quadratic graph.

Example   Use the graph of $y = x^2$ to solve the equations
(a) $x^2 = 4$ (b) $x^2 = 12$

(a)   The given curve is $y = x^2$. If we want $x^2 = 4$, then we need to find where $y = 4$ on this curve. If, therefore, we draw the line $y = 4$ on the graph, then where this line cuts the curve will be where $x^2 = 4$. Following the dotted lines on the diagram, the solutions are $x = -2$ and $x = 2$.

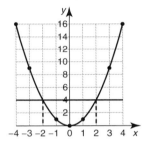

(b)   Similarly, where the line $y = 12$ meets the curve $y = x^2$ will enable us to read off the solutions of the equation $y = x^2$. From the graph the solutions are $x = -3.5$ and $x = 3.5$ (approx).

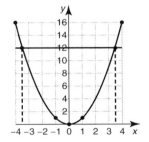

Example   Use the graph of $y = x^2 + 2$ to solve the equations (a) $x^2 = 6$
(b) $x^2 - 8 = 0$.

(a)   If we are to use the given graph, then we must rearrange the equation to be solved, so that the left hand side is exactly the equation of the curve. Hence, from $x^2 = 6$, we can add 2 to each side, which gives $x^2 + 2 = 8$. By the technique used in the first example, the required solutions will be where the line $y = 8$ meets the curve $y = x^2 + 2$. From the graph, the solutions are $x = -2.5$ and $x = 2.5$ (approx).

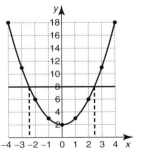

(b) As in (a), we need to rearrange the
equation $x^2 - 8 = 0$ so that the left hand
side is $x^2 + 2$. So, rearranging $x^2 - 8 = 0$,

$$x^2 = 8 \qquad \textit{adding 8}$$
$$x^2 + 2 = 10 \qquad \textit{adding 2}$$

Drawing the line $y = 10$ on the diagram
will give the solution of the required
equation, i.e. $x^2 - 8 = 0$, by reading off
the x-values.
Hence the solutions are $x = -2.8$ and
$x = 2.8$

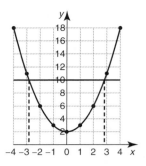

Exercise 12

1 Draw the graph of the equation $y = x^2$, and use it to solve the equations
(a) $x^2 - 8 = 0$ (b) $2x^2 = 11$.

2 Draw the graph of the equation $y = x^2 - 4$, and use it to solve the
equations (a) $x^2 - 4 = 0$ (b) $x^2 - 11 = 0$.

3 Draw the graph of the equation $y = x^2 - x - 6$, and use it to solve the
equations (a) $x^2 - x - 6 = 0$ (b) $x^2 - x - 10 = 0$ (c) $x^2 - x = 8$.

4 Draw the graph of the equation $y = 4 + 3x - x^2$, and use it to solve the
equations (a) $4 + 3x - x^2 = 0$ (b) $1 + 3x - x^2 = 0$.

5 Draw the graph of the equation $y = 2x^2 - x - 10$, and use it to solve the
equations (a) $2x^2 - x - 10 = 0$ (b) $2x^2 - x - 3 = 0$.

6 Draw the graph of the equation $y = 2x^2 - 6x + 7$, and use it to solve the
equations (a) $2x^2 - 6x + 7 = 12$ (b) $2x^2 - 6x - 5 = 0$.

6.11 Regions

Example Draw two axes, each going from 0 to
7, and shade in the region where $x > 3$.

All points which have an x-coordinate *greater*
than 3 will be in the required region. The
boundary of the region is the line $x = 3$.

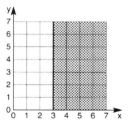

Example On the same grid, shade in the region
where $y < 4$.

All points with a y-coordinate *less* than 4 will be
in the required region. The boundary of this
region is the line $y = 4$. Any point in the region
with *both* types of shading satisfies *both*
inequalities.

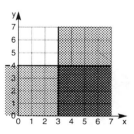

Exercise 13

Drawing both axes from 0 to 10, (a) shade in both regions (b) write down the coordinates of *any* point which satisfies *both* inequalities.

1 $x < 6, y < 4$ **2** $x < 3, y > 7$ **3** $x > 5, y > 5$

4 $x > 8, y < 3$ **5** $x < 2, y < 1$ **6** $x > 7, y > 1$

7 $x > 0, y > 8$ **8** $x < 10, y > 7,$ **9** $x < 4, y < 6$

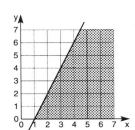

Example   Draw two axes, each ranging from 0 to 7, and shade in the region where $y < 2x - 2$.

Begin by drawing the boundary line $y = 2x - 2$.

Any point *below* the line will have a y value *less* than $2x - 2$. (Also, any point above the line will have a y value greater than $2x - 2$.)

Originally, a metre was defined as a ten-millionth of the distance between the North Pole and the Equator.

Example   On a grid, shade in the region which satisfies the three inequalities $y < 12 - x$, $x > 2$, and $y > 5$. (Take both x- and y-axes from 0 to 12.)

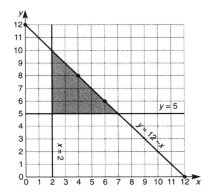

Begin by working out some points on the boundary line $y = 12 - x$ (e.g. (0, 12), (4, 8) (6, 6) (12, 0), and then draw the line.

Now draw the lines $x = 2$ and $y = 5$, and shade in the required region.

Exercise 14

Drawing both axes from 0 to 10, (a) shade in the required regions (b) write down the coordinates of *any* point which satisfies *all* of the inequalities.

1 $x > 5, x < 8, y < 4$ **2** $x > 6, x < 7, y < 10$

3 $x < 8, x > 3, y > 6$ **4** $x > 4, x < 7, y > 1, y < 5$

5 $x + y < 10, y < 7$ **6** $y < \frac{x}{2} + 6, x < 7$

7 $y > x, y < 8, y > 5$ **8** $y < x + 3, x > 6, x < 8$

Note: In the exercises on regions, we have restricted answers to the positive quadrant, i.e. where $x > 0$ and $y > 0$. The same principles apply in all four quadrants.

6.12 Travel graphs

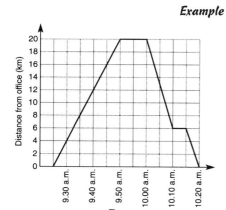

Example John rides a motorbike, and delivers parcels for a small delivery firm. He has to deliver a package to Mrs Holmes, who lives 20 km away from the firm's main office. The graph represents John's journey to Mrs Holmes's house and back to the office.

(a)   At what time did he leave the office?

(b)   When did he arrive at Mrs Holmes'?

(c)   How long did he stay?

(d)   How long did it take him to return?

(e)   What was his average speed for the outward journey?

(f)   What was his average speed for the return journey?

Horizontally each square represents 5 minutes.

(a)   John leaves the office at 9.25.

(b)   He arrives at Mrs Holmes' at 9.50.

(c)   He stays for 10 minutes.

(d)   It takes him 20 minutes to return.

(e)   Average speed for outward journey

If you drove towards a red traffic light at a speed of 60 000 km/s, the light would appear green.

$$= \frac{\text{total distance}}{\text{total line}}$$

$= 20 \div \left(\frac{25}{60}\right)$ ◄——— *Divide by 60 to convert minutes to hours.*

$= 48$ km/h

(f)   Average speed for the return journey

$= 20 \div \left(\frac{20}{60}\right)$

$= 60$ km/h

Exercise 15

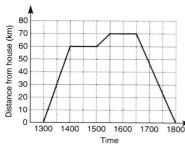

1   Alison leaves home at 1300 and drives to the supermarket, which is 60 km away. After shopping, she continues to her aunt's house for a cup of tea. Then she drives back home.

(a)   At what time did Alison arrive at the supermarket?

(b)   What was her average speed for this journey?

(c)   How long did she spend at the supermarket?

(d)   How far is it from the supermarket to her aunt's house?

(e)   How long did she stay at her aunt's?

(f)   How long did it take her to drive home?

(g)   What was her average speed for this part of the journey?

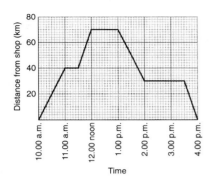

2 An electrician is sent out in a van to do three repairs. The travel graph represents the journey made.

(a) At what time did he set out?

(b) He arrived to do the first repair at 11.00 a.m. How long did the repair take?

(c) How far from the shop was the second place that required a repair?

(d) How long did it take to travel from the second to the third repair?

(e) Which repair took longest?

(f) What was the van's average speed from finishing the third repair to arriving back at the shop?

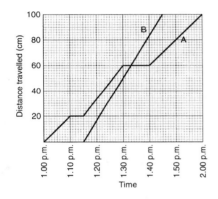

3 Snail A started at 1.00 p.m. to travel across a garden. Snail B started a little later.

(a) How far had A moved before it stopped at 1.10 p.m.?

(b) At what time did B start?

(c) What was B's average speed in crossing the 100 cm garden?

(d) Between which two times did A move fastest?

(e) What was this fastest speed of A?

(f) At what time did B pass A?

(g) How many minutes did A rest, altogether?

(h) Work out A's average speed for the 100-cm trip.

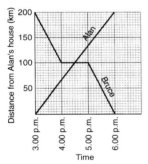

4 Alan leaves home at 3.00 p.m. for Bruce's house, 200 km away, and drives straight there. At the same time Bruce leaves his house for Alan's, but stops for an hour on the way.

(a) What is Alan's average speed?

(b) What is Bruce's average speed for the first part of his journey?

(c) At what time does Alan pass Bruce?

(d) If Bruce had not stopped, but continued at the same speed, at what time would he have arrived at Alan's?

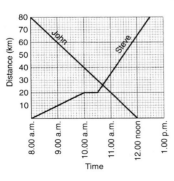

5 Steve and John, who live 80 km apart, leave at 8.00 a.m. for each other's house. At 10.00 a.m. Steve pulled into a garage and had a fault on his car fixed.

(a) How long did it take to fix his car?

(b) At what time did he stop at the garage?

(c) How far had John travelled when Steve left the garage?

(d) At what time did they pass each other?

(e) Which car went the faster, after Steve's had been fixed?

(f) Steve rang his own house immediately he arrived at John's. How long had John been at Steve's house when he answered the telephone?

Review

1   The points P(−3, 2) and Q(5, 2) are two corners of a square. What are the coordinates of the other two corners, if:

   (a)   the square is drawn *above* the side PQ,

   (b)   the square is drawn *below* the side PQ,

   (c)   PQ is a diagonal of the square?

2   (a)   Draw the line $y + 3x = 12$ on a graph, for $0 \leqslant x \leqslant 4$.

   (b)   On the same axes, draw the line $y = 3x + 12$, for $-4 \leqslant x \leqslant 0$.

   (c)   What is the area of the triangle formed by these two lines and the x-axis?

3   Draw the lines $x + y = 16$ and $x + 2y = 20$ on the same graph. (Take both axes from 0 to 20, and make up a table if you wish.)
From your graph, state the coordinates of the points where:

   (a)   line $x + y = 16$ cuts each axis,

   (b)   line $x + 2y = 20$ cuts each axis,

   (c)   the lines meet.

4   On a graph, draw the square ABCD, where A is (0, 6), B is (−6, 0), C is (0, −6), and D is (6, 0).
By looking at the coordinates of points on each side, work out the equation of each of the four sides of the square. (Extend each of the sides of the square if you wish.)

5   By making up a table, or otherwise, draw the graph of the equation $y = x^2 + 4$, for $-4 \leqslant x \leqslant 4$.

   (a)   What is the least value that y can take?

   (b)   For what range of values of x is $y < 13$?

6   Make a table of values (take x from 0 to 8), and draw the graph of the equation $y = \frac{30}{x+2}$. Use your graph to find:

   (a)   the value of y when x is 5.5

   (b)   the value of x when y is 5.5

   (c)   the value of y when $x = 298$.

What happens to the value of y as x becomes larger and larger?
Will the value of y ever be zero?

7   Draw axes, where $0 < x < 12$ and $0 < y < 20$.
Draw these four inequalities on your grid:
(i) $2x + y > 10$ (ii) $y < x + 10$ (iii) $x + y < 20$ (iv) $y < 2x - 10$.
What shape is formed by all the points which satisfy these four inequalities?

Exercise 17   The following questions are all taken from GCSE papers.

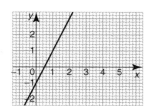

1   A graph shows the line $y - 2x = -1$.
By drawing another line, use the graph to solve the simultaneous equations

$$y - 2x = -1$$
$$x + 2y = 4.$$

(3 marks)
[SEG]

2   (a)   Complete this table of values for $y = 2x + 3$.

x	-3	-2	-1	0	1	2
y		-1				

(2 marks)

    (b)   Draw the graph of $y = 2x + 3$ on the grid.

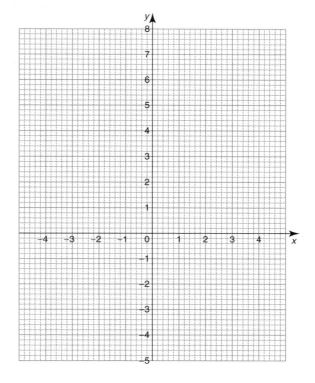

(2 marks)

    (c)   Use your graph to find

       (i)   the value of y when $x = 1.5$,
       (ii)   the value of x when $y = -0.5$.

(2 marks)
[EDEXCEL]

3 (a) Draw the graph of $y = x^2 - x - 4$. Use values of x between -2 and $+3$

(4 marks)

(b) Use your graph to write down an estimate for
   (i) the minimum value of y
   (ii) the solutions of the equation $x^2 - x - 4 = 0$. *(3 marks)*

[EDEXCEL]

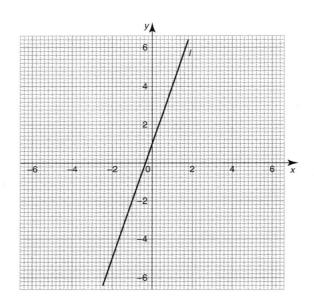

4 The shaded region of a graph can be defined by three inequalities. One of these is $x \geqslant 1$.

Write down the other two inequalities. *(2 marks)*

[OCR]

5

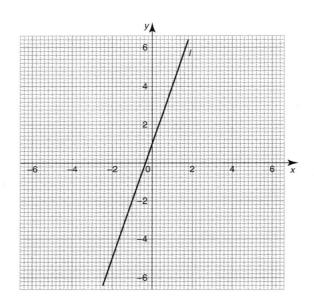

(a) Find the gradient of the line l. *(2 marks)*
(b) Find the equation of the line l. *(2 marks)*

[OCR]

6 (a) Complete the table below for $y = x^3 - 2x + 4$.

x	-3	-2	-1	0	1	2	3
y	-17		5			8	

(b) Draw the graph of $y = x^3 - 2x + 4$.

(3 marks)

(c) Use your graph to solve $x^3 - 2x + 4 = 4$. *(2 marks)*

[OCR]

7

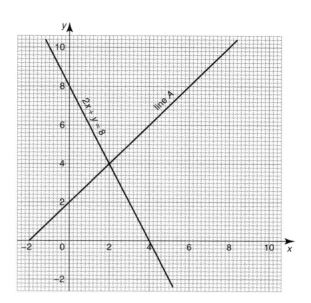

(a) What is the equation of the line A drawn on the grid? (*2 marks*)

(b) Draw the line $x + 2y = 6$ on the grid. (*2 marks*)

(c) Hence solve the simultaneous equations

$$2x + y = 8$$
$$x + 2y = 6.$$

(*2 marks*)
[OCR]

8 (a) Complete the following table which gives the values of $y = 2x^2 - 6x + 5$ for values of x from -2 to 4.

x	-2	-1	0	1	2	3	4
$y = 2x^2 - 6x + 5$	25		5	1		5	13

(*2 marks*)

(b) Draw the graph of $y = 2x^2 - 6x + 5$ for values of x from -2 to 4.
(*3 marks*)

(c) Draw the line $y = 10$ on the same graph paper and write down the x-values of the points where your two graphs intersect.
(*2 marks*)

(d) Write down the equation in x whose solutions are the x-values you found in (c). (*1 mark*)
[WJEC]

9 (a) On a grid, plot the points (1, 1), (0, 3), (−1, 5) and (2, −1) and join them up with a straight line. *(2 marks)*

These points lie on the straight line with the equation $y = 3 − 2x$.

(b) By drawing another straight line on the grid, solve the simultaneous equations

$$y = 3x − 1$$
$$y = 3 − 2x.$$

(4 marks)
[MEG]

10 (a) On a graph draw and label the following lines.

$$y = 2x \quad \text{and} \quad x + y = 5$$

(4 marks)

(b) Explain how to use your graph to solve the equation $2x = 5 − x$
(1 mark)

(c) Show clearly the single region that is satisfied by all of these inequalities.

$$x + y \leqslant 5 \qquad y \geqslant 2x \qquad x \geqslant 0$$

Label this region R. *(1 mark)*
[SEG]

11 A graph of the equation $y = ax + b$ is shown.

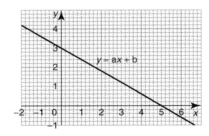

Find the values of a and b. *(3 marks)*
[SEG]

12 (a) Complete the table of values for $y = x^2 − 2x − 2$.

x	−2	−1	0	1	2	3	4
y	6		−2			1	

(2 marks)

(b) Draw the graph of $y = x^2 − 2x − 2$ for values of x from −2 to 4.

(2 marks)

(c) Use your graph to solve the equation $x^2 − 2x − 2 = 0$. *(2 marks)*
[SEG]

13 The diagram shows a sketch of the line $2y = x - 2$.

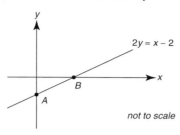

(a) Find the coordinates of points A and B.

(*2 marks*)

(b) Find the gradient of the line $2y = x - 2$.

(*1 mark*)

(c) Explain why the simultaneous equations $2y = x - 2$ and $2y = x - 3$ have no solution.

(*1 mark*)

(d) Another line passes through B and through the point $(0, 2)$. Find the equation of this line.

(*3 marks*)

[SEG]

14 In the diagrams below there are six sketches of graphs labelled (a), (b), (c), (d), (e) and (f).

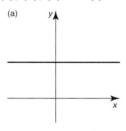
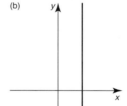
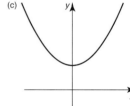
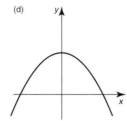
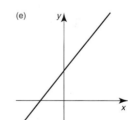
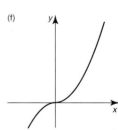

Three of the above are sketches of the graphs of the following functions. Write down the letter denoting the graph for the appropriate function.

(i) $y = -x^2 + 2$

(ii) $y = 2$

(iii) $y = x^3$

(*3 marks*)

[WJEC]

Ideas for investigations

1 Make up a table of values for the graphs of:
(i) $y = x^2$ (ii) $y = x^2 + 3$ (iii) $y = x^2 - 7$

Draw the three graphs on the same grid.

What do you notice?

On your graph, sketch the curve $y = x^2 - 4$, without making up a table.

What can you say about any graph of the form $y = x^2 + c$ where c is a constant number, positive or negative?

Extension work

Make up tables of values for;
(i) $y = (x + 1)^2$ (ii) $y = (x + 3)^2$ (iii) $y = (x - 7)^2$.

Draw the graphs. What do you notice?
What general principles can you deduce?

2 (a) Draw a grid, with $0 < x < 300$ and $0 < y < 300$.

(b) Draw the line $x + y = 100$.

(c) Choosing another suitable line, shade in the region where $100 < x + y < 200$.

Draw the line $x + y = 250$.
What can you say about all lines of the form $x + y =$ (some number)?

Extension work

On a grid, as before, draw a line whose equation is of the form $2x + y = K$, where K is any number (say 100).

Now choose some further values for K, and draw the lines.

What happens to the lines, as the value of K increases?
What happens if $K = 0$?

Repeat the process for the equations:
(i) $x + 2y = K$ (ii) $3x + 2y = K$.

MEASURES 7

7.1 Metric units

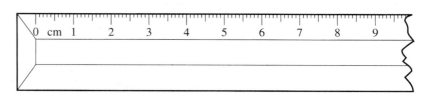

Smaller

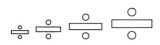

Bigger

1 kilometre (km) = 1000 metres (m)

1 metre (m) = 100 centimetres (cm)

1 metre (m) = 1000 millimetres (mm)

1 centimetre (cm) = 10 millimetres (mm)

1 kilogram (kg) = 1000 grams (g)

1 gram (g) = 1000 milligrams (mg)

1 tonne (t) = 1000 kilograms (kg)

1 litre (*l*) = 100 centilitres (cl)

1 litre (*l*) = 1000 millilitres (ml)

1 centilitre (cl) = 10 millilitres (ml)

To change from one unit into a smaller unit we multiply.

To change from one unit into a larger unit we divide.

Example Change (a) 2.46 kg into grams (b) 42 cm into metres.

(a) 2.46 kg × 1000 = 2460 g *kg → g: smaller units so multiply.*

(b) 42 cm ÷ 100 = 0.42 m *cm → m: larger units so divide.*

Exercise 1

The smallest measure of length is the ångström, where 1 millimetre is 10 000 000 ångströms.

Change the following:

1 7 cm into mm	**2** 4 m into cm	**3** 43 m into km
4 62.5 mm into cm	**5** 1250 g into kg	**6** 0.31 *l* into ml
7 1.37 kg into g	**8** 1300 ml into cl	**9** 3 km into m
10 351 cm into m	**11** 0.03 *l* into ml	**12** 2 t into kg
13 200 mg into g	**14** 40 cl into *l*	**15** 700 kg into t
16 3000 mg into kg	**17** 0.498 m into cm	**18** 0.07 *l* into ml
19 11.32 cm into mm	**20** 9.63 m into cm	

Exercise 2

1 A bottle of orange juice is used to fill six cups, each of which holds 175 ml. How many litres of orange juice are in the bottle?

2 A man is running a 5 km race. He has already run 2450 m. How many metres has he yet to run?

3 A lorry load of 3 tonnes of potatoes is to be shovelled into 2 kg bags. How many bags can be filled from this load?

4 A man weighs himself. The scales show 49.5 kg. He then takes off his boots, which weigh 900 g. What weight will now be shown on the scales?

5 How many 30 g servings of breakfast cereal are there in a box containing 0.75 kg?

6 Bobby has used 200 g of flour in making a cake, and 75 g in making buns. How much flour will be left, if he started with a 5 kg bag?

7 If 350 g of minced beef are used in a pie, how many kilograms of minced beef would be needed for 30 pies?

Write each set of measurements in order of size, starting with the smallest:

8 750 mm, 0.4 km, 78 m, 0.072 km, 1.5 km. 550 m, 35 m, 0.3 km

9 400 cl, 0.14 *l*, 750 cl, 0.012 *l*, 270 cl, 0.02 *l*, 1.3 *l*, 600 cl

10 300 kg, 0.2 t, 875 kg, 0.85 t, 1.4 t, 1500 kg, 112 kg, 0.8 t

7.2 Imperial units

Occasionally you will see the old-fashioned signs " for inches and ' for feet.

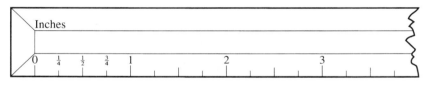

1 mile = 1760 yards (yd)	1 ton = 20 hundredweight (cwt)
1 yard (yd) = 3 feet (ft)	1 hundredweight (cwt) = 112 pounds (lb)
1 foot (ft) = 12 inches (in)	1 pound (lb) = 16 ounces (oz)
1 gallon (gal) = 8 pints (pt)	1 stone (st) = 14 pounds (lb)
1 pint (pt) = 20 fluid ounces (fl. oz)	

The longest unit of measure is the parsec, a stellar distance that is equivalent to 30 856 776 000 000 km, or 19 173 511 000 000 miles.

Example Change (a) 1 ft 3 in into inches (b) 50 in into feet and inches (c) $4\frac{1}{2}$ yd into feet (d) 13 ft into yards and feet

(a) 1 ft 3 in = $(1 \times 12) + 3 = 15$ inches

(b) 50 in = $(4 \times 12) + 2 = 4$ ft 2 in

(c) $4\frac{1}{2}$ yd = $(4\frac{1}{2} \times 3) = 13\frac{1}{2}$ ft

(d) 13 ft = 12 + 1 = $(4 \times 3) + 1 = 4$ yd 1 ft

Exercise 3

The earliest known measure of weight is the beqa, which was used by the Egyptians about 3800 BC.

Change the following:

1 $83\frac{1}{2}$ in into ft and in
2 $1\frac{3}{4}$ gal into pints
3 125 lb into st and lb
4 $\frac{3}{4}$ lb into oz
5 65 in into ft and in
6 $\frac{5}{8}$ mile into yd
7 2 yd 4 ft into feet
8 2 lb 3 oz into oz
9 22 ft into yd and ft
10 $\frac{1}{4}$ pt into fl. oz
11 52 st into cwt
12 $31\frac{1}{4}$ in into ft and in

Exercise 4

1 A man is 5 ft $7\frac{1}{2}$ in tall. His daughter is 4 ft $10\frac{1}{2}$ in tall. Find the difference in their heights, in inches.

2 A length of curtain measures 6 ft 8 in. It also has a folded hem of 6 inches. What is its total length?

3 A petrol tank is filled to a capacity of 10 gallons. How many gallons and pints will be left in the tank, if 3 gallons 3 pints of petrol are then used in a journey?

4 A furlong is $\frac{1}{8}$ of a mile. A horse has run 3 furlongs. How many yards is this?

5 A bag of coal weighs 1 cwt. If 35 bags are loaded onto a lorry, what is the weight of the load in tons and cwt?

6 An athlete drinks $1\frac{1}{2}$ pints of milk each day. How many gallons will the athlete drink in 10 weeks?

7 A man weighs $12\frac{1}{2}$ stone. He loses 21 lb whilst on a diet. How much will he now weigh?

8 A heavyweight boxer weighs 224 lb. How many stones is this?

9 A block of cheese, which weighs 3 lb 9 oz, is to be divided into twelve equal portions. How many ounces will each portion weigh?

10 How many pint bottles of milk can be filled from a 5-gallon milk churn?

85 million years ago a year was 370 days long; 600 million years ago it was as long as 425 days.

7.3 Approximate equivalents

5 miles ≈ 8 kilometres	1 yard ≈ 1 metre	1 foot ≈ 30 centimetres
1 inch ≈ 2.5 centimetres	1 kilogram ≈ 2.2 pounds	1 litre ≈ 1.75 pints

Example Change (a) 30 miles into kilometres (b) 64 km into miles

(a) 30 miles $\approx 30 \times \frac{8}{5} = \frac{240}{5} = 48$ km

Changing miles → km: 1 mile is the same as $\frac{8}{5}$ km.

(b) 64 km $\approx 64 \times \frac{5}{8} = \frac{320}{8} = 40$ miles

Changing km → miles: 1 km is the same as $\frac{5}{8}$ miles.

Exercise 5

Change the following into their approximate equivalents:

1 10 kg into lb   **2** 6 in into cm   **3** 15 miles into km

4 15.4 lb into kg   **5** $2\frac{1}{4}$ gal into litres   **6** 54 km into miles

7 4 litres into pt   **8** 44 lb into kg   **9** 2 ft into cm

10 25 miles into km   **11** 95 in into cm   **12** 2 lb 10 oz into kg

13 $4\frac{1}{2}$ yd into metres   **14** 1.2 m into ft   **15** 96 km into miles

Exercise 6

Work out the approximate answers to these questions.

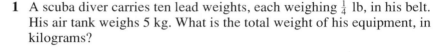

1 A scuba diver carries ten lead weights, each weighing $\frac{1}{4}$ lb, in his belt. His air tank weighs 5 kg. What is the total weight of his equipment, in kilograms?

2 A pair of trousers has a waist measurement of 34 inches. What is this in centimetres?

3 Whilst on holiday a family drive 332 km in a day. How many miles is this?

4 In a shop they are selling 3 kg of potatoes for 80p. In another shop they are selling a 5 lb bag for the same price. Which is the better buy?

5 A recipe requires 0.4 kg of flour. How many ounces is this?

6 A roll of carpet is 12 yd long. What is this in metres?

7 A driver buys 30 litres of petrol. Approximately how many gallons is this?

8 A Christmas hamper weighs 8 kg. What is its weight in pounds?

9 A house is estimated to be 24 ft high. Approximately how high is this in metres?

10 A man is 1.8 metres tall. What is his height in feet?

The length of a day is becoming increasingly irregular owing to the moon's tidal drag. Atomic clocks are so accurate they have to be adjusted to fit in with the earth's irregular movements!

7.4 Using units

When measuring, it is important to choose the correct measure for the purpose. For example, it would be no use trying to measure the length of a train with a 30 cm ruler!

Exercise 7   Which *metric* unit would you use use to measure the following:

1   The heaviest weight lifted by a man.

2   The longest fingernail grown by a human.

3   The farthest distance travelled by car on 1 litre of petrol.

4   The diameter of the largest bubble-gum bubble.

5   The largest petrol tank of a family car.

6   The length of the largest crystal grown in a week in a chemistry laboratory.

7   The widest head in your class of students.

8   The capacity of an egg cup.

9   A bottle of wine.

10   The longest oil-pipeline.

11   A medicine bottle in common use.

12   The thinnest slice of cucumber.

The longest measure of time is the kalpa in Hindu chronology, equivalent to 4320 million years.

7.5 Perimeter

The **perimeter** is the distance all around a shape.

Example   Find the perimeters:

(a)
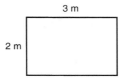

(b)

(a) $2 + 3 + 2 + 3 = 10$ m   (b) $2 + 2 + 1 + 1 + 1 + 1 = 8$ m

7.6 Area

The space contained within a shape is its **area**.
Area is measured in square units: cm^2, m^2, km^2.

Area of a **rectangle** = length × breadth

Area of a **triangle** = $\frac{1}{2}$ base × height

Example   Find the area of each shape:

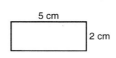

$$\text{Area} = 5 \times 2 = 10 \text{ cm}^2 \qquad \text{Area} = \tfrac{1}{2} \times 4 \times 5 = 10 \text{ cm}^2$$

We can find the area of **combined** shapes by dividing them into separate shapes that we recognise, and then adding them.

Example   Find the area:

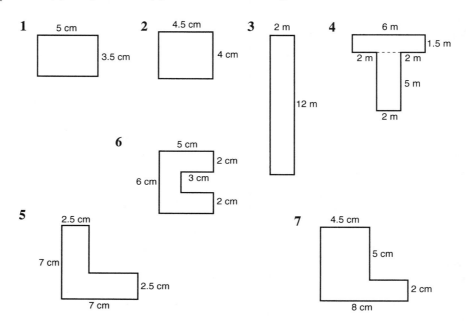

Divide the shape into two separate rectangles.

The UK has an area of 244 103 km², or 94 249 square miles.

$3 \times 2 = 6 \text{ cm}^2$
$5 \times 1 = 5 \text{ cm}^2$
Total area $= 11 \text{ cm}^2$

Exercise 8   Find (a) the perimeter (b) the area of each shape:

1   5 cm
3.5 cm

2   4.5 cm
4 cm

3   2 m
12 m

4   6 m
1.5 m
2 m   2 m
5 m
2 m

6   5 cm
2 cm
6 cm   3 cm
2 cm

5   2.5 cm
7 cm
2.5 cm
7 cm

7   4.5 cm
5 cm
2 cm
8 cm

Exercise 9

Find the area of each shape:

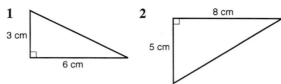

The surface area of the earth is 510 065 600 km², 196 937 400 square miles.

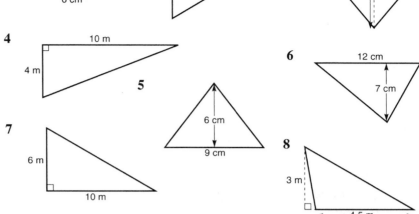

Exercise 10

Copy and complete the tables.

Rectangles			
Length	Breadth	Area	Perimeter
1 3 m		6 m²	
2 9 m		45 m²	
3 4 cm			14 cm
4		24 cm²	20 cm
5 10 m			35 m
6 18 cm		81 cm²	
7	12.5 cm		105 cm
8	25 cm	750 cm²	

Triangles		
Base	Height	Area
9 4 m		6 m²
10	14 m	70 m²
11 18 cm	12.5 cm	
12	16 cm	192 cm²

157

To find the areas of other shapes we use simple formulas:

Area of a **parallelogram** = length of base × vertical height

Area of a **trapezium** = $\frac{1}{2}h(a + b)$,
where a and b are the lengths of the two parallel sides, and h the perpendicular distance between them.

Example   Find the area of each shape:

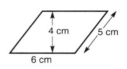

70.92% of the surface of the earth is covered by water.

Area = $6 \times 4 = 24$ cm^2

Area = $\frac{1}{2} \times 3 \times (7 + 10)$
     = $0.5 \times 3 \times 17 = 25.5$ cm^2

Exercise 11

Find the area of each shape:

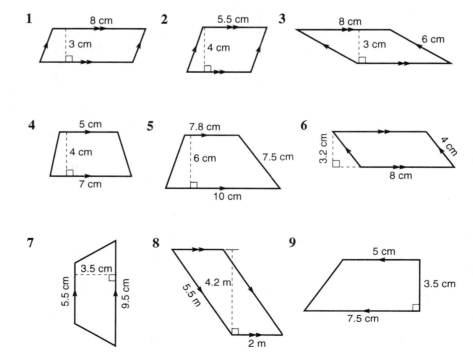

1   8 cm   3 cm

2   5.5 cm   4 cm

3   8 cm   3 cm   6 cm

4   5 cm   4 cm   7 cm

5   7.8 cm   6 cm   7.5 cm   10 cm

6   3.2 cm   8 cm   4 cm

7   3.5 cm   5.5 cm   9.5 cm

8   4.2 m   5.5 m   2 m

9   5 cm   3.5 cm   7.5 cm

7.7 The circle

In 1989, in the USA, the greatest number of decimal places to which π has been calculated was 1 011 196 691.

The radius of a circle is half the diameter.
The circumference of a circle is found by using the formula:
$$C = \pi \times \text{diameter}$$
Some calculators will provide a value for π.
If your calculator does not have a π button, use the value $\pi = 3.14$.

Example   Find the circumference of each shape:

$$C = \pi \times \text{diameter}$$
$$= 3.14 \times 8 \text{ cm}$$
$$= 25.12 \text{ cm}$$

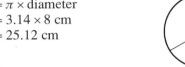

$$C = \pi \times \text{diameter}$$
$$= \pi \times (3 \times 2) \text{ cm}$$
$$= 3.14 \times 6$$
$$= 18.84 \text{ cm}$$

diameter = 2 × radius

Example   Find the radius of a circle if the circumference is 35 cm.

$$C = \pi \times d$$
$$35 = \pi \times d$$
$$\text{So } d = 35 \div \pi = 35 \div 3.14 = 11.14 \text{ cm (to 2 d.p.)}$$
$$\text{So radius} = d \div 2 = 5.57 \text{ cm}$$

Exercise 12   Find the circumference.

1
12 cm

2
22 cm

3
4 cm

4
13 cm

5
1.5 cm

6
5.5 cm

Find the circumference of the circle with:

7 $r = 26$ cm   **8** $d = 10$ cm   **9** $r = 3.8$ m
10 $r = 14$ cm

Find the radius of the circle with circumference:

11 40 cm   **12** 85 m   **13** 240 m

Find the diameter of the circle with circumference:

14 150 mm   **15** 90 cm   **16** 63 m

Exercise 13

1 A wheel has a diameter of 60 cm. What is the distance around the rim?

2 The radius of a coin is 5.5 mm. What is the length of the circumference?

3 A mountain bike has a wheel with a diameter of 65 cm. What is its circumference?

4 The radius of the earth is approximately 6370 km. What is the approximate distance around the earth?

5 A gardener wants to put a fence around a circular pond of radius 150 cm. What length of fence is needed?

6 A lighthouse lower floor has an internal diameter of 6.8 metres. What is the distance around the walls of the lower floor?

In 1897 the General Assembly of Indiana stated that π was 'nearly 4'.

The area of a circle is found by using the formula:

$$A = \pi r^2 \quad \text{or} \quad \text{Area} = \pi \times \text{radius} \times \text{radius}$$

Example   Find the area of each shape:

$A = \pi r^2$
$\quad = 3.14 \times 3 \times 3$
$\quad = 28.26 \text{ cm}^2$

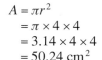

3 cm

$A = \pi r^2$
$\quad = \pi \times 4 \times 4$
$\quad = 3.14 \times 4 \times 4$
$\quad = 50.24 \text{ cm}^2$

radius* = $\frac{1}{2}$ *diameter

8 cm

Example   Find the radius of a circle if the area is 80 cm^2.

$A = \pi r^2$
$80 = \pi r^2$
$r^2 = 80 \div \pi = 80 \div 3.14 = 25.48 \text{ cm}$

So $r = \sqrt{25.48} \text{ cm} = 5.05 \text{ cm}$

Exercise 14

Find the area:

1

2

3

4

5

6

Find the area of each circle with:

7 $d = 4.9$ cm   **8** $r = 3.8$ cm   **9** $r = 4$ m   **10** $d = 10$ cm

Find the radius of each circle with the following area:

11 65 cm^2 **12** 100 m^2 **13** 180 mm^2
14 94 cm^2 **15** 20 m^2

Exercise 15

1 A horse is tied to a stake in a field with a rope 8 m long. What area of the field can be grazed by the horse?

2 A discothèque has a circular dance floor with a diameter of 12 metres. What area is the dance floor?

3 A circular pond has a diameter of 3.5 m. What area of netting is needed to cover the pond?

4 A circular ring has a radius of 1.2 m. What is the area of the ring?

5 A circular pine table has a top with an area of 8 m^2. What is the radius of the top of the table?

6 A circular pond has an area of 16.6 m^2. What is the diameter of the pond?

Find the area:

7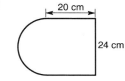

8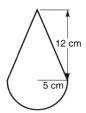

9

10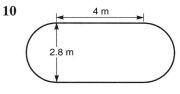

7.8 Volume

The building with the largest cubic capacity in the world is the Boeing assembly plant in USA, completed in 1968, with a capacity of 5.6 million m³.

Volume is a measure of the space occupied by a solid shape.
Volume is measured in cubic units: cm³, m³, km³.

Example Find the volume of the cuboid.

Volume of a **cuboid** = length × breadth × height

Volume = $5 \times 7.8 \times 4.5 = 175.5$ cm³

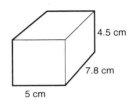

Example Find the volume of the prism.

Volume of a **prism** = area of cross-section × length

Area of cross-section = $\frac{1}{2} \times 4 \times 5$ ***The cross-section is a triangle.***

$= 10$ m²

Volume = area of cross-section × length

$= 10 \times 8 = 80$ m³

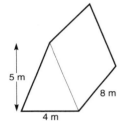

The most capacious scientific building is the Vehicle Assembly Building at Cape Kennedy, with a capacity of 3.6 million m³.

Example Find the volume of the cylinder.

Volume of a **cylinder** = $\pi r^2 h$ ***The cross-section is a circle.***

$= \pi \times$ radius × radius × height

Volume = $\pi \times 3 \times 3 \times 5$

$= 3.14 \times 3 \times 3 \times 5 = 141.3$ cm³

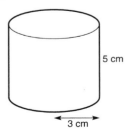

Exercise 16   Find the volume of each of the following solids:

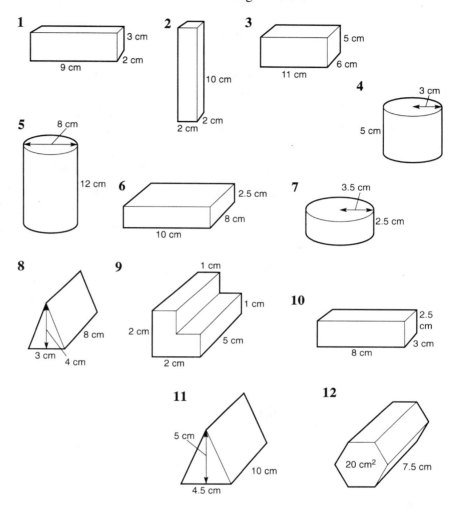

Example   The volume of a box is 24 cm³. Its height is 4 cm, and its width is 3 cm. What is its length?

Volume = length × breadth × height
$24 = 4 \times 3 \times h$
So $h = 24 \div (4 \times 3) = 24 \div 12 = 2$ cm

Example   The volume of a cylinder is 62 cm³. Its diameter is 4 cm. What is the height of the cylinder?

Volume = $\pi r^2 h$ **radius = half diameter**
$62 = \pi \times 2 \times 2 \times h$ **= d ÷ 2 = 4 ÷ 2 = 2**
So $h = 62 \div (3.14 \times 2 \times 2) = 62 \div 12.56 = 4.94$ cm

Exercise 17

1 A box has a volume of 50 cm^3. It has a length of 8 cm, and a height of 2.5 cm. What is its width?

2 A cylinder has a volume of 100 cm^3. Its height is 10 cm. What is its radius?

3 A box has a height of 3 m, and width of 4 m. Find its length if the volume of the box is 85 m^3.

4 A cylinder has a radius of 4 mm, and a volume of 230 mm^3. Find the height of the cylinder.

5 A tank in the shape of a cylinder has a height of 4 m. It has a volume of 50 m^3. Find the diameter of the tank.

6 A lorry with a skip in the shape of a cuboid contains 7 m^3 of sand. The load is 2 m wide and 1 m high. How long is it?

7 A box has a volume of 192 cm^3. It is 16 cm long and 4 cm high. What is its width?

8 A cylindrical tank is designed to hold 1000 litres of water. The diameter of the tank is to be 0.5 m. What height will the tank have to be? (1 m^3 = 1000 litres.)

7.9 Surface area

The surface area of a solid is the total area of all of its faces.

The combined surface area of all the alveoli inside the human lungs is equivalent to the area of a tennis court.

Example   Find the surface area of each shape:

Each face of each block has an area of 1 cm^2.
Top: 5 faces = 5 cm^2
Around the sides: 12 faces = 12 cm^2
Base: 5 faces = 5 cm^2
Total surface area = 5 + 12 + 5 = 22 cm^2

1 cm cubes

The Forth Bridge is the bridge in the UK which has the greatest surface area requiring painting. Once the team of painters have worked their way to one end, they have to start again at the other!

Top face: 5×7 = 35 cm^2
Base face: 5×7 = 35 cm^2
Left face: 5×2 = 10 cm^2
Right face: 5×2 = 10 cm^2
Front face: 7×2 = 14 cm^2
Back face: 7×2 = 14 cm^2
Total surface area = 118 cm^2

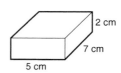

Exercise 18 Find the surface area of these solids:

1
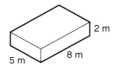
2 m
5 m 8 m

2
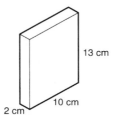
13 cm
2 cm 10 cm

3

1 cm³ cubes

4

1 cm³ cubes

5

10 cm
6 cm 6 cm

6
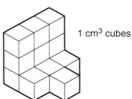
3 cm 5 cm
4 cm 6 cm

7
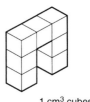
1 cm³ cubes

8
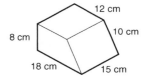
1 cm³ cubes

9
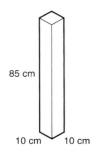
85 cm
10 cm 10 cm

10
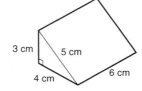
12 cm
10 cm 15 cm

11

30 cm
10 cm 8 cm

12
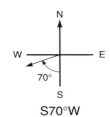
12 cm
8 cm 10 cm
18 cm 15 cm

7.10 Direction

There are two common ways of giving a direction:

The earliest navigators at sea used familiar landmarks on the shoreline – this meant they could never sail out of sight of land.

1 Compass directions. Face North or South, and turn clockwise or anticlockwise, measuring the angle.

W — E N 40° S
S40°E

W — E N 35° S
N35°E

W — E N 70° S
S70°W

2 3-figure bearings. Face North and turn only clockwise, measuring the angle, and giving the answer as a 3-figure number.

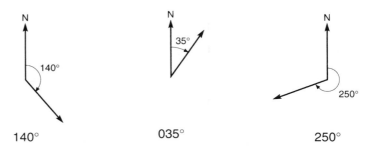

140°   035°   250°

Write the following compass directions as 3-figure bearings:

1 N30°E	**2** N60°W	**3** N50°W	**4** S70°E
5 S45°W	**6** N25°E	**7** S65°E	

Write the following 3-figure bearings as compass directions:

8 160°	**9** 185°	**10** 330°	**11** 158°
12 025°	**13** 075°	**14** 295°	**15** 110°

Can you *draw* directions? Select several compass directions, and several 3-figure bearings from the exercise above. Use your protractor to draw a diagram for each of the chosen directions. Clearly label each diagram.

Unless otherwise stated, direction is normally given as a 3-figure bearing.

Example   Find the bearing (a) of Heywood *from* Radcliffe (b) of Radcliffe *from* Prestwich.

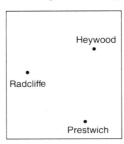

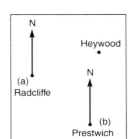

The word *from* tells you where you are standing when you measure the bearing. Always draw a North line at this point.

Then draw in the route. These are the lines you need to use to measure the bearings.

The bearing at (a): Heywood *from* Radcliffe is 070°.

The bearing at (b): Radcliffe *from* Prestwich is 312°.

Measure these bearings on the diagram for yourself.

In giving a **location**, we not only need the **direction**, but also the **distance**. On maps and diagrams we use a scale.

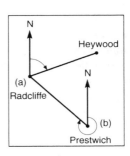

Example   Using the given scale, find the actual distance represented by
(a) 3.5 cm (b) 5.8 cm.

(a) 0   1   2   3   4   km   1 cm → 1 km so 3.5 cm → 3.5 km

A scale of 1 cm to 1 km.

(b) 0 10 20 30 40 50 60 70 80 km   2 cm → 40 km
                                          5.8 cm → 5.8 × 20 = 116 km

A scale of 1 cm to 20 km.

Exercise 21

Today's navigation satellites can give ships, aircraft and mobile stations their exact location on the globe to an accuracy of 6 metres.

In each question give the actual distance for each distance on the map.

1   0   40   80   120   160 km

(a) 2.5 cm   (b) 3.3 cm   (c) 6.9 cm   (d) 7.2 cm

2   0   5   10   15   20 km

(a) 1.5 cm   (b) 2.8 cm   (c) 8.3 cm   (d) 8.4 cm

3   0   25   50   75   100 km

(a) 3.5 cm   (b) 1.2 cm   (c) 9.7 cm   (d) 6.7 cm

4   0   6   12   18   24 km

(a) 0.5 cm   (b) 1.4 cm   (c) 10.1 cm   (d) 12.1 cm

5   0   70   140   210   280 km

(a) 2.5 cm   (b) 0.6 cm   (c) 7.6 cm   (d) 8.8 cm

Exercise 22

Use the map of the Isle of Man to find (a) the 3-figure bearing (b) the direct distance (in km) in each case. All the places are on the coast.

1 From Castletown to Ramsey   **2** From Ramsey to The Cronk

3 From The Cronk to Point of Ayre   **4** From Point of Ayre to Ramsey

5 From Ramsey to Peel   **6** From Peel to Ramsey

7 From Ramsey to Castletown   **8** From Castletown to Peel

9 From Peel to Maughold Head   **10** From Maughold Head to Port

11 From Port Erin to Peel   Erin

12 From Peel to Castletown

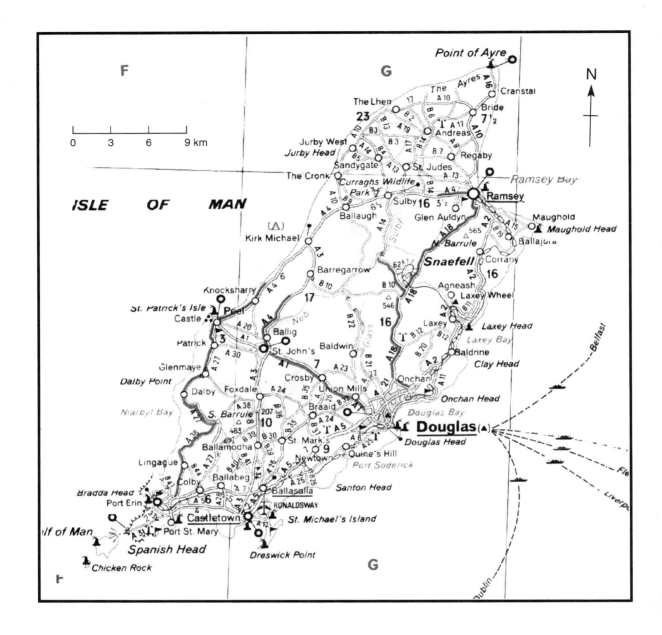

7.11 A final word on units

When map scales are given as a ratio, we need to change units to find what 1 centimetre actually represents on the map.

Remember:

10 mm = 1 cm
100 cm = 1 m
1000 m = 1 km

Example   What does 1 cm represent using a map scale of 1 : 50 000?

1 : 50 000 = 1 cm : 50 000 cm = 1 cm : 500 m = 1 cm : 0.5 km

The oldest map is an Iraqi clay tablet dated about 2250 BC, showing part of the river Euphrates.

Example   What does 3.8 cm represent using a map scale of 1 : 300 000?

1 : 300 000 = 1 cm : 300 000 cm = 1 cm : 3000 m = 1 cm : 3 km
so 3.8 cm represents 3.8 × 3 km = 11.4 km

Exercise 23

The first printed map of Britain was Ptolemy's outline printed in Italy in 1477. The earliest maps had no scale, as they were merely sketches.

In each question find what the actual distance will be, using the given map scale. Give your answer in an appropriate unit.

1 1 cm using 1 : 3000   **2** 1 cm using 1 : 500 000
3 1 cm using 1 : 20 000   **4** 1 cm using 1 : 40 000
5 2.5 cm using 1 : 50 000   **6** 3.5 cm using 1 : 250 000
7 12.5 cm using 1 : 10 000   **8** 7.5 cm using 1 : 8000
9 3.2 cm using 1 : 150 000   **10** 8.7 cm using 1 : 25 000

We have to be clear about the **accuracy** of any measurement. This is because measurements you are given have often been rounded off.

Example   You are told a car has travelled 10 km. What is the maximum and minimum distance it might have travelled?

It might have been rounded to the nearest 1 km, so it would lie between 9.5 km and 10.5 km:

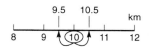

Example   You are told a snail has travelled a distance of 6.5 cm. What range of distances might it have travelled?

It might have been rounded to the first decimal place, so it could lie between 6.45 and 6.55 cm.

Exercise 24

For each measurement given below, give the minimum and maximum measurements between which it could actually lie.

1 1.7 cm   **2** 8.3 m   **3** 10.4 km
4 9.1 cm   **5** 4.5 m   **6** 8.0 m
7 3.0 cm   **8** 4.85 cm   **9** 2.13 mm
10 7.25 cm   **11** 8.95 cm   **12** 2.1 mm
13 14.51 m   **14** 8.39 m   **15** 7.12 cm

Review

Change the following:

1 5 cm into mm   **2** 0.04 *l* into ml   **3** 3.5 t into kg

4 2000 mg into kg   **5** 7.52 m into cm   **6** 700 mm into m

7 How many lengths of wood, each 200 mm in length, can be cut from a piece 3.7 m in length?

8 If 4500 g of potatoes are used in a guest-house kitchen each day, how many kilograms will be needed over a ten-day period?

9 Change $3\frac{3}{4}$ gallons into pints (8 pints = 1 gallon).

10 Change 12 feet into yards (3 ft = 1 yd).

11 What is $1\frac{1}{2}$ lb in ounces (16 oz = 1 lb)?

12 Change 56 in into feet and inches (12 in = 1 ft).

Change the following into their approximate equivalents:

13 36 inches into cm (1 in ≈ 2.5 cm)

14 10 pints into litres (1 litre ≈ 1.75 pints)

15 40 miles into km (5 miles ≈ 8 km)

Calculate (a) the perimeter (b) the area:

16 4.5 cm 3.2 cm   **17** 2 cm 6.5 cm 4.5 cm 7 cm   **18** 12 cm 4 cm 4 cm 4 cm 4 cm 4 cm

Calculate the area:

19 8 cm 10 cm   **20** 6 cm 7 cm 10 cm   **21** 6 cm 4 cm 8 cm   **22** 2.5 cm 7 cm

Calculate (a) the circumference (b) the area of each of these circles:

23 5 cm   **24** 12 cm   **25** 1.5 cm   **26** 7 cm

Calculate the volume:

27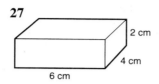

28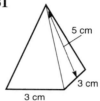

Volume = πr²h

29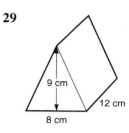

Calculate the surface area:

30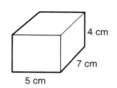

31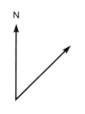

32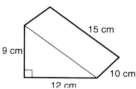

Write each of these directions (a) as a compass direction (b) as a 3-figure bearing:

33   **34**   N   **35**   **35** N

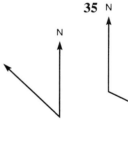

Exercise 26   The following questions are all taken from GCSE papers.

1 (a) Chris is 13 cm taller than Steven. Their heights add up to 307 cm.
             How tall is Steven?   (*2 marks*)

Sarah is 122 cm tall.

(b) (i) Sarah's height has been given to the nearest centimetre.
             What is the minimum height she could be?   (*1 mark*)

     (ii) Estimate Sarah's height in feet. Give your answer to the
             nearest foot.   (*2 marks*)
                                                                    [AQA/SEG]

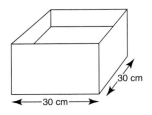

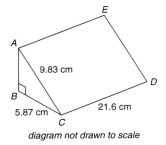

diagram not drawn to scale

2 Water is stored in a tank in the shape of a cuboid with a square base. The sides of the base are 30 cm long. The depth of the water is 20 cm.

(a) Work out the volume of the water. *(2 marks)*

More water is put in the tank. The depth of the water rises to 21.6 cm.

(b) Calculate the percentage increase in the volume of the water in the tank. *(3 marks)*

[EDEXCEL]

3 The diagram shows a glass prism. The uniform cross-section of the prism is a right-angled triangle with a hypotenuse of 9.83 cm and a base of 5.87 cm. The length of the prism is 21.6 cm.

(a) Calculate the length of *AB*. *(3 marks)*

(b) Calculate the volume of the prism, giving your answer correct to one significant figure. *(3 marks)*

[WJEC]

4 Mary has some cubes of side 1 centimetre.  *not drawn to scale*

(a) 24 of Mary's cubes just fill this box.

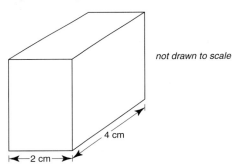

not drawn to scale

What is the height of the box *(1 mark)*

(b) Here is another box.

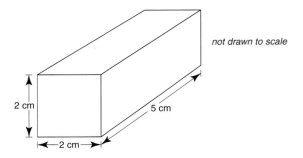

not drawn to scale

Will 24 of Mary's cubes fit into it? Give a reason for your answer. *(2 marks)*

[AQA/NEAB]

5 A skip is in the shape of a prism with cross-section *ABCD*.
AD = 2.3 m, *DC* = 1.3 m and *BC* = 1.7 m. The width of the skip is
1.5 m.

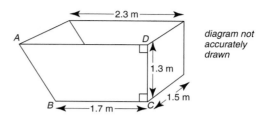

diagram not
accurately
drawn

(a) Calculate the area of the shape *ABCD*. (*2 marks*)

(b) Calculate the volume of the skip. (*2 marks*)

The weight of an empty skip is 650 kg. The skip is full to the top with
sand. 1 m³ of sand weighs 4300 kg.

(c) Calculate the total weight of the skip and the sand. (*3 marks*)
[EDEXCEL]

6

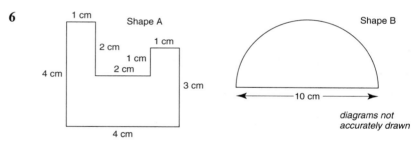

diagrams not
accurately drawn

(a) Work out the area of Shape A. (*2 marks*)

(b) (i) Work out the perimeter of the semicircle, Shape B.
(*3 marks*)

(ii) Work out the area of the semicircle, Shape B. (*2 marks*)
[EDEXCEL]

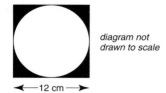

diagram not
drawn to scale

7 A circular mirror is mounted on a square wooden frame of side 12 cm
so that it touches the sides of the frame as shown in the diagram.
Calculate the area of the wooden frame not covered by the mirror (the
shaded part of the diagram).

(*3 marks*)
[WJEC]

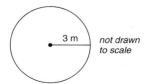

not drawn
to scale

8 (a) A circular pond has a radius of 3 metres.
Calculate the circumference of the pond. (*2 marks*)

(b) Calculate the area of the pond. (*2 marks*)
[AQA/NEAB]

9 Karen has a pencil that has a length of 10 centimetres, correct to the nearest centimetre.

Write down
(i)   the minimum length the pencil could be
(ii) the maximum length the pencil could be.

(*2 marks*)
[EDEXCEL]

10 The cylinder is 20 cm high and holds 1000 cm³ of water.

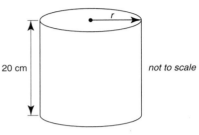

20 cm

not to scale

Find the radius of the cylinder.

(*4 marks*)
[AQA/SEG]

THE SENATE

Petrol consumption:
9 litres per 100 km.

11 1 km = $\frac{5}{8}$ mile. 1 gallon = 4.54 litre.

Change 9 litres per 100 km into miles per gallon.

(*4 marks*)
[EDEXCEL]

12 The diagram shows the cross-section, *ABCDEF*, of a metal block. *AB* and *ED* are parallel, with *AB* = 12.1 cm and *ED* = 6.3 cm. *AF* and *BC* are perpendicular to *AB* and are each 5.3 cm. The perpendicular distance between *ED* and *AB* is 8.7 cm.

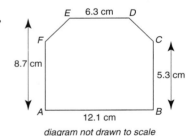

E   6.3 cm   D

F

8.7 cm

C

5.3 cm

A

12.1 cm

B

diagram not drawn to scale

Calculate the area of cross-section of the metal block.

(*3 marks*)
[WJEC]

13 Ice cream is sold in a box that is the shape of a prism. The ends are parallelograms. The size of the prism is shown in the diagram. The length of the prism is 12 cm.

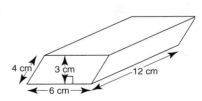

4 cm   3 cm   12 cm

6 cm

Calculate the volume of the ice cream in the box.

(*4 marks*)
[AQA/NEAB]

14

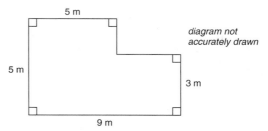

This diagram shows the floor plan of a room.

Work out the area of the floor. Give the units with your answer.

(*4 marks*)
[EDEXCEL]

15 Calculate the area of this trapezium

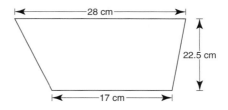

(*3 marks*)
[AQA/NEAB]

Ideas for investigations

1 There have been several attempts throughout history to discover an accurate value for π.

1700 BC (Greece): $256 \div 81$
250 BC (Greece): a maximum of $273 \div 71$, and a minimum of $22 \div 7$
AD 100 (China): the square root of 10
AD 300 (China): $142 \div 45$
AD 500 (China): $355 \div 113$

How accurate are these ways of finding π? Use values of 3.142, or the π button on your calculator. Find the percentage error in the above methods. Which are the most accurate?

2 Netting is needed to make a 3-sided guinea-pig enclosure. The enclosure needs to be as large as possible, that is, with the largest area.

(a) The total length of the netting is 16 feet. What length and width would give you the maximum area?

(b) Repeat part (a) a number of times, using other lengths of fencing. Can you arrive at an easy way of working out the length and width that will give you the maximum area (that is, a rule)? Can you give the maximum area in terms of a length of fencing of x feet?

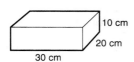

3 (a) The volume of the cuboid is $10 \times 20 \times 30 = 6000$ cm^3.
What happens when we increase the dimensions by 10%? The
volume will become $11 \times 22 \times 33 = 7986$ cm^3. The change in
volume is 1986 cm^3. The percentage increase in volume is given
by the calculation $\frac{1986}{6000} \times 100 = 33.1\%$.

(b) Try increasing by 10% the volume of cuboids with other dimensions. Find the effect this has on the volume. Do the new
volumes have anything in common?

(c) What happens if you *double* the dimensions instead of increasing
them by 10%? Investigate other ways of increasing the
dimensions, and the effect this has on the volume.

GEOMETRY AND 8 TRIGONOMETRY

8.1 Congruence

Two shapes are **congruent** if they are identical in every way.

Example Decide whether each pair of shapes is congruent or not congruent.

 Although these triangles are in different positions, they have exactly the same angles, and the same lengths of sides.
They are congruent.

 One rectangle is slightly larger than the other.
They are *not* congruent.

Exercise 1 Write down whether each pair of shapes is congruent, or not congruent.

1  2   3   4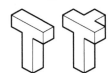

5   6 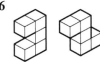 7

Identify the two shapes in each question which are congruent:

8 A   B   C   D   9 A   B   C   D   10 A   B   C   D

11 A   B   C   D   12 A   B   C   D   13 A   B   C   D

14 A   B   C   D   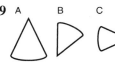 15 A   B   C   D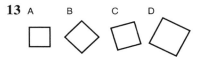

8.2 Angles

There are four main types of angle: acute, right, obtuse and reflex.

Acute angles are less than 90°.
Right angles are exactly 90°.
Obtuse angles are between 90° and 180°.
Reflex angles are more than 180°.

Angles which make a full circle add up to 360°.

Angles on a straight line, that is in a half circle, add up to 180°.

These angles are vertically opposite angles. They are equal in size.

Exercise 2

In each case, (a) find the missing angles indicated by the letters (b) write down which type of angle it is.

1 a 123° 135°

2 b 141°

3 c 82°

4 d 75°

The mathematician who worked most on geometry was Euclid of Alexandria, who lived around 300 BC in Egypt.

5 e 146° 146°

6 81° 60° f

7  g 64° 80° 74°

8 h 150°

9 120° 120° i

10 q 70° 85°

11 44° 40° 48° r

12 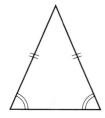 40° 42° s

8.3 Triangles

There are four main types of triangle: scalene, right-angled, isosceles, and equilateral.

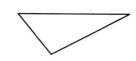

Scalene
All sides different

Isosceles
Two sides the same length. Two angles the same size.

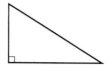

Equilateral
All sides the same
length. All angles the
same size (60°).

Right-angled
One 90 ° angle.

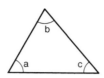

The angles of *any* triangle add up to 180°.
$a + b + c = 180°$

Exercise 3   In each question find the missing angles indicated by the letter x.

1 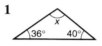   **2**   **3**   **4**

5   **6**   **7**   **8**

Exercise 4   In each question
(a) find the missing angle indicated by the letter x
(b) name the type of triangle.

1 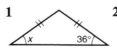   **2**   **3**   **4**

5   **6**   **7**   **8**

Exercise 5   In each question find the missing angle indicated by a letter.

1   2   3   4

5   6   7   8

8.4   Parallel lines

Parallel lines are lines which will never meet:

Any line which crosses a pair of parallel lines
is called a transversal.
The transversal forms angles, some of which
have special names:

Alternate angles   Corresponding angles

Alternate angles are the   Corresponding angles are the
same size.   same size.

Exercise 6   Copy each diagram, writing in all the angles:

1   2   3   4

In each question find the missing angle indicated by a letter:

5

6

7

8

9

10

11

12

8.5 Quadrilaterals

The angles of any quadrilateral add up to 360°.

Exercise 7 Copy and complete each diagram, writing in the missing angles.

1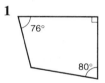

2

3

4

There are several different types of quadrilateral. They are listed, each with their properties.

Square
Four sides of equal length.
Opposite sides parallel.
Four right angles.

Rectangle
Opposite sides of equal length.
Opposite sides parallel.
Four right angles.

Trapezium
One pair of opposite sides parallel.

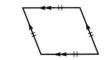

Parallelogram
Opposite sides parallel.
Opposite sides of equal length.
Opposite angles equal.

Rhombus
Opposite sides parallel.
All sides of equal length.
Opposite angles equal.

If we also include the **diagonals** of these quadrilaterals, we can say:

The diagonals bisect each other (square, rectangle and parallelogram).
The diagonals bisect each other at right angles (square and rhombus).

Exercise 8   Write down the name(s) of the quadrilateral(s) to which each statement can be applied.

1   All the sides are of equal length.
2   Only one pair of parallel sides.
3   Diagonals bisect at right angles, and angles are all 90°.
4   The diagonals are of equal length.
5   Both pairs of opposite angles are equal, and are not 90°.
6   None of the angles are equal.
7   Another shape which has all the properties of a parallelogram.
8   Does not have two pairs of sides of equal length.
9   Another shape which has all the properties of a rectangle.
10 Another shape which has all the properties of a rhombus.

8.6   Solids

There are several different types of solids. They are listed below, with some of their properties. Solids have vertices (corners), faces (sides), and edges.

The largest pyramid is the Quetzalcóatl, near Mexico City, which has a volume of 3.3 million m³, compared with 2.5 m³ for the pyramid of Cheops in Egypt.

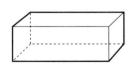

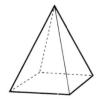

Cube
All edges the
same length.

Cuboid
Opposite edges the
same length.

Pyramid
Square or
rectangular base.

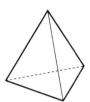

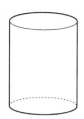

Tetrahedron
Triangular base.

Cylinder
One curved, two
flat surfaces.

Cone
One curved, one
flat surface.

Sphere
One curved surface.

Ellipsoid
One curved surface.

There are also many different types of prisms:

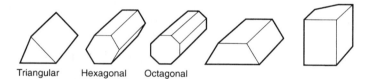

Triangular   Hexagonal   Octagonal

A **prism** is a solid with a constant cross-section.

Exercise 9

1 For each of the solids (but not prisms or spheres) write down how
many (a) faces (b) vertices (c) edges they each have.

2 There is a relationship between faces, vertices and edges for any solid.
The relationship is known as Euler's relationship. Can you find it?

3 What is another name for (a) a rectangular prism (b) a square prism
(c) a prism with a circular cross-section?

8.7 Nets

A net is a flat shape which can be cut out and folded
to make a solid. It is a 2-D representation of a solid.

The simplest net is that of a cube:

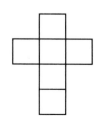

Nets can be drawn to a certain size:

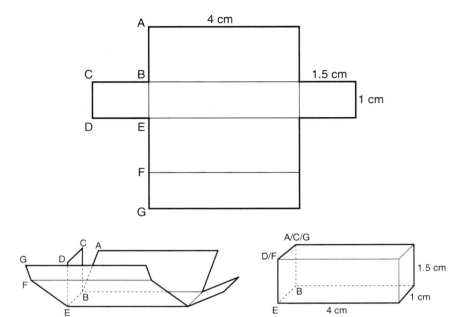

These diagrams show how the various points on the net come together to make the vertices of the solid.

Example   Of which solid is this the net?

A pyramid

Exercise 10   Which solids can be made from the nets below?

1   **2**   **3**

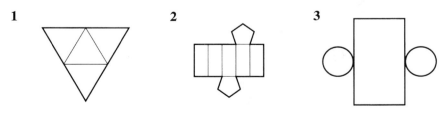

Draw a sketch of the net for each of the following:

    4 A triangular prism   **5** An octagonal prism
    6 A cone

Draw nets of the cuboids for which the dimensions are given below. Write the lengths on all the sides of your nets.

7 5 cm × 6 cm × 7 cm   **8** 3.5 cm × 5 cm × 7 cm   **9** 4 cm × 7 cm × 10 cm

Draw a sketch of the net for these solids:

10

11

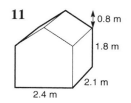

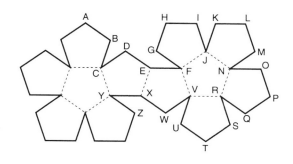

12 Which letters will come together to form the vertices of the solid from this net?

8.8 Accurate drawings

To make accurate drawings we need the correct equipment:

Ruler, protractor, a pair of compasses, a sharp pencil, and a rubber.

Exercise 11

Draw the following accurately, using your mathematical instruments.

The largest drawings in the world are the ground figures drawn in the Nazca Desert, Peru. Drawn some time between 100 BC and AD 600, they are up to seven miles in length.

1
2
3

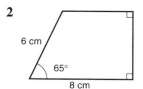

4
5

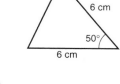

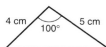

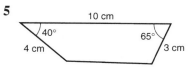

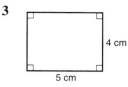

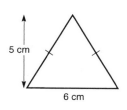

6 A rectangle with sides of length 6 cm and 4.5 cm.

7 A square of sides 7 cm.

8 An isosceles triangle with base 6 cm and vertical height 5 cm.

9 A right-angled triangle with sides 3 cm, 4 cm and 5 cm.

10 An isosceles triangle with base 5.5 cm, and sides at angles of 35 ° to the base.

8.9 Scale drawings

In practical problems it is useful to make a drawing. However, the lengths may actually be in metres, but the drawing cannot be in metres (it would be too big). We need to make a scale drawing in centimetres or millimetres.

Example   A room 12 m by 8 m is to have a 1 m work-surface built along a short side. Show this on a scale diagram, using a scale of 1 cm to 2 m.

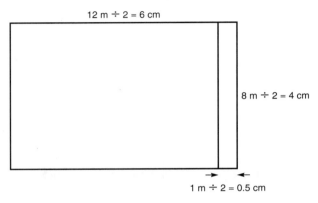

12 m ÷ 2 = 6 cm

8 m ÷ 2 = 4 cm

1 m ÷ 2 = 0.5 cm

Exercise 12   Draw the following scale diagrams, to the scale stated in each question.

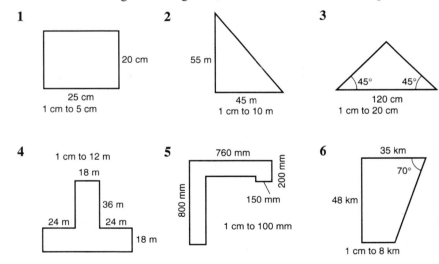

1

20 cm
25 cm
1 cm to 5 cm

2

55 m
45 m
1 cm to 10 m

3

45°   45°
120 cm
1 cm to 20 cm

4

1 cm to 12 m
18 m
36 m
24 m   24 m
18 m

5

760 mm
200 mm
150 mm
800 mm
1 cm to 100 mm

6

35 km
70°
48 km
1 cm to 8 km

8.10 Loci

A locus (plural loci) is the set of all points which satisfy a rule. When we trace the path made by joining such a set of points, this path is called the **locus** of the points.

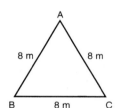

Example   Draw the following:

(a)   The locus of points 1 cm from point E.
The locus of points at a given distance from a fixed point is actually a **circle**.

(b)   The locus of points 1 cm from line AD.
The locus of points at a given distance from a fixed line is two lines **parallel to the first line**.

(c)   The locus of points which are the same distance from AD and DC.
The locus of points which are the same distance from two lines is the **bisector of the angle between these two lines**.

(d)   The locus of points which are the same distance from B and C.
The locus of points of equal distance from two points is a **line which is at right angles to, and bisects, the line joining the two points**.

Exercise 13

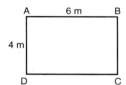

1   Copy the diagram to scale.

(a)   A light at A illuminates all points up to a distance of 3 m from the light. Shade the area lit up inside the rectangle.
(b)   Draw the locus of points which are at equal distances from AB and BC.
(c)   An extension lead is laid across the floor so that it lies an equal distance from corners D and C. Draw the extension lead in the diagram.

2   Copy the diagram to scale.
(a)   Draw the locus of points 5 m from B.
(b)   Draw the locus of points 6 m from C.
(c)   Shade the region where all points are within 5 m from B *and* 6 cm from C.
(d)   Draw the locus of all points which are at equal distances from A and C.

3   Mark a point on your page. Draw the locus of points which are all 3 cm from the point.

4   Draw a square of side 4 cm. Draw the locus of points which are all 1 cm from the sides of the square.

5   Mark any two points A and B on your page. Draw the locus of points which are of equal distance from A and B.

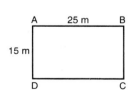

6   ABCD represents a school yard. Lights at points A and B can illuminate objects 10 m away. Another light at D can illuminate objects 5 m away. An illuminated notice board along DC casts light for a distance of 5 m. Draw a scale diagram of the yard, and shade those parts of the yard which are *not* illuminated.

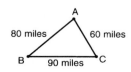

7   Three television transmitters are positioned as shown. The transmitters have a range as follows: A 50 miles, B 55 miles, and C 40 miles. Make a scale drawing and shade the part of the diagram where signals from all three transmitters can be received.

8.11 Pythagoras' theorem

Pythagoras followed the teaching of Buddha, and was also a vegetarian. He was the founder of a private school for mathematics at Crotone, Italy.

Pythagoras was a Greek mathematician who is said to have discovered a rule we can use with right-angled triangles.

In any right-angled triangle

$$c^2 = a^2 + b^2$$

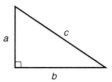

The **hypotenuse** is the longest side in a right-angled triangle.

Example   Find x.

Using Pythagoras' theorem: $x^2 = 4.7^2 + 5.3^2$ *The hypotenuse is on the left hand side.*

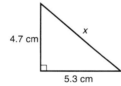

$$= 22.09 + 28.09$$

$$= 50.18$$

so $x = \sqrt{50.18} = 7.08 \approx 7.1$ cm

Example   Find x.

Using Pythagoras' theorem: $7.8^2 = x^2 + 5.2^2$ *Put the hypotenuse on the left hand side..*

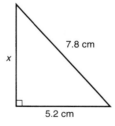

so $x^2 = 7.8^2 - 5.2^2$

$$= 60.84 - 27.04$$

$$= 33.8$$

so $x = \sqrt{33.8} = 5.8$ cm

When we are *finding* the hypotenuse, we add the square of the other two sides. When we are *given* the hypotenuse, we subtract the square of one of the other two sides.

Note: Pythagoras' theorem is a method of *calculation*. These problems can also be done by accurate/scale drawing. Draw a right-angled triangle to represent that shown in the first example above. Measure the missing side x. Is your measurement as accurate as 7.1 cm?

Which will generally be the more accurate method: calculation, or scale drawing?

Exercise 14 Find the missing sides in each of the following triangles. Give your answers to one decimal place.

1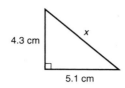

2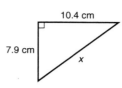

3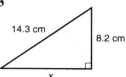

4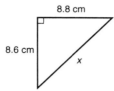

5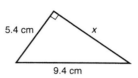

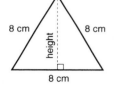

6 A BT pole 6.8 m high is held firm by a wire which is fixed to the top of the pole and to a point in the ground 5.9 m horizontally from the foot of the pole. How long is the wire?

7 Calculate the length of a diagonal of a rectangle with dimensions 5.75 m by 6.05 m.

8 A ladder leans against a wall. Its upper end is 3.6 m off the ground. Its lower end is 3.2 m from the foot of the wall. How long is the ladder?

9 Calculate the height of an equilateral triangle with sides 8 cm long.

10 Calculate the length of a diagonal of a square with sides 4.6 m.

8.12 Trigonometry

In any right-angled triangle:

$$\sin x = \frac{\text{opposite side}}{\text{hypotenuse}}$$

The opposite side is the side opposite the angle.

$$\cos x = \frac{\text{adjacent side}}{\text{hypotenuse}}$$

The adjacent side is the side next to the angle.

$$\tan x = \frac{\text{opposite side}}{\text{adjacent side}}$$

Sin x means the sine of angle x, cos x the cosine of angle x, and tan x the tangent of angle x.

In solving problems a decision has to be made: which one of the three trigonometrical ratios will be used in the solution?

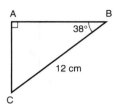

Example Find AB.

$$\cos 38° = \frac{AB}{12}$$

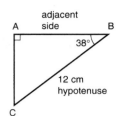

To find AB we need to use the adjacent side and the hypotenuse: we will therefore need cosine.

$$12 \times \cos 38° = AB$$

$$12 \times 0.7880 = AB$$

Press 38 and cos on your calculator to change cos 38° into a decimal.

So AB = 9.46 cm (to 3 s.f.)

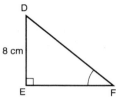

Example Find EF

$$\tan 40° = \frac{8}{EF}$$

It is difficult to solve the equation when the missing side is on the bottom of the fraction.

$$\tan 50° = \frac{EF}{8}$$

Change the problem by using the other angle.

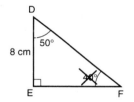

$$8 \times \tan 50° = EF$$

$$8 \times 1.192 = EF$$

So EF = 9.53 cm (to 3 s.f.)

Exercise 15

In this exercise give your answers to 3 significant figures.

Find the missing side labelled *x*:

1

2

3

4

5

6

7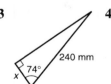

8

9

10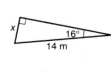

11 A ladder 6 metres long lies against the wall of a house so that it is inclined to the horizontal at an angle of 68°. How far does it reach up the wall?

12 A square has a diagonal of length 8.5 cm. How long is one of its sides?

13 A road is inclined at 15° to the horizontal. A woman walks 100 m up the road. What distance will she have risen *vertically?*

14 A boy looks up to the top of a tree, and estimates the top is inclined at an angle of 30° from where he is standing, 10 m from the foot of the tree. How high is the tree?

15 A diagonal of a rectangle is 10 m long, and is inclined at an angle of 38° to the longer side. Find the length and width of the rectangle.

Trigonometry can also be used to find the missing angles in triangles.

Example Find the angle x

Use inverse tan on the calculator:
$0.5357 \rightarrow 28.2°$

$$\tan x = \frac{1.5}{2.8} = 0.5357$$

$x = 28.2°$ (to 1 d.p.)

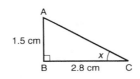

The two sides that have been given are the opposite side and the adjacent side, so this is a tangent problem.

Note: Some calculators have different ways of finding the inverse of trigonometrical functions: $\tan^{-1}$, 2nd Fct TAN, INV TAN.

Exercise 16 Find the missing angles labelled x. Give your angles to 1 decimal place.

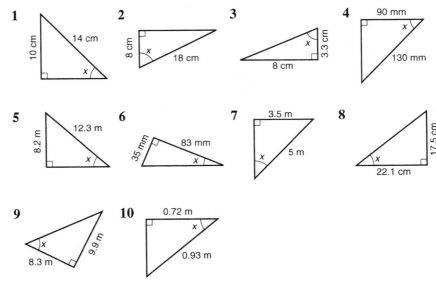

11 A ladder which is 12 m long leans against the wall of a house. The top of the ladder is 9 m off the ground. What angle does the ladder make with the ground?

12 A pipe from a reservoir is 3000 metres long. One end is 100 m higher than the other. At what angle (to the horizontal) is the pipe inclined?

13 A road is 2000 m long, and it climbs 700 m. What is the angle of inclination of the road?

14 The sloping roof of a shed is 4.5 m long. One side of the roof is 2.5 m higher than the other. Find the angle of inclination of the roof.

15 A rectangle has dimensions 12 cm × 8 cm. What are the angles between the diagonals?

Example   Find the hypotenuse AC.

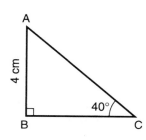

Either:

$$\sin 40° = \frac{4}{AC}$$

$$0.6428 = \frac{4}{AC}$$

$$\frac{1}{0.6428} = \frac{AC}{4}$$

So $AC = \dfrac{4}{0.6428}$

$$AC = 6.22 \text{ cm}$$

Or:

$$\tan 50° = \frac{BC}{4} \quad \textbf{\textit{Find BC first.}}$$

$$BC = 4 \times \tan 50° = 4.767 \text{ cm}$$

$$AC = \sqrt{4^2 + 4.767^2}$$

$$= \sqrt{38.72} \quad \textbf{\textit{Then find AC}}$$
$$\textbf{\textit{using Pythagoras'}}$$
$$AC = 6.22 \text{ cm} \quad \textbf{\textit{Theorem.}}$$

Exercise 17   Find the missing hypotenuse labelled *x*. Give your answers to 3 significant figures.

1
28°
5 cm

2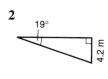
19°
4.2 m

3
35°
200 mm

4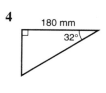
180 mm
32°

5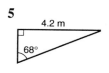
4.2 m
68°

6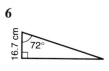
16.7 cm
72°

7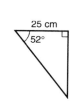
25 cm
52°

8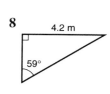
4.2 m
59°

Review

Exercise 18   Find the missing angles indicated by a letter:

1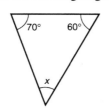

2

3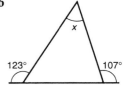

4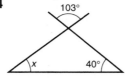

5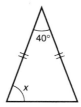

6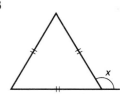

7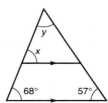

8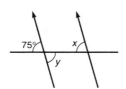

9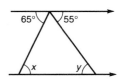

10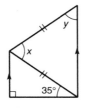

11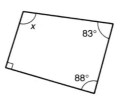

12   How many edges has a hexagonal prism?

13   Which quadrilateral has only *one* pair of parallel sides?

14   Which quadrilaterals have four sides of equal length?

15   Which solid has just *two* flat surfaces?

16   Which solid has just *one* flat surface?

17   Draw a net for a square-based pyramid.

18   Draw the accurate net for a cuboid with length 4 cm, width 2 cm, and height 1.5 cm.

19   This is the net for a solid. Write down the name of the solid.

Draw these shapes to the scale given:

20   **21**   **22**

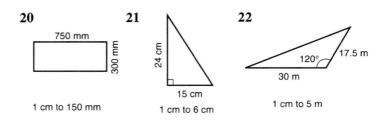

20 750 mm / 300 mm / 1 cm to 150 mm

21 24 cm / 15 cm / 1 cm to 6 cm

22 120° / 17.5 m / 30 m / 1 cm to 5 m

23 Draw this rectangle to the exact dimensions shown. Draw the locus of points which are

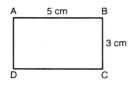

A   5 cm   B
3 cm
D   C

   (a)   2 cm from A

   (b)   of equal distance from sides AB and BC

   (c)   2 cm from side DC

   (d)   of equal distance from corners D and C.

Find the missing side or angle labelled. Give lengths to 3 significant figures, and angles to 1 decimal place.

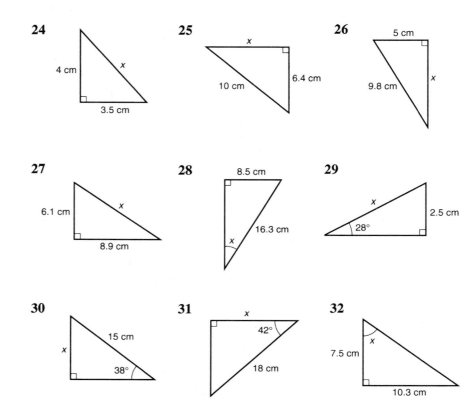

24 4 cm / x / 3.5 cm

25 x / 10 cm / 6.4 cm

26 5 cm / 9.8 cm / x

27 6.1 cm / x / 8.9 cm

28 8.5 cm / 16.3 cm / x

29 x / 28° / 2.5 cm

30 15 cm / x / 38°

31 x / 42° / 18 cm

32 7.5 cm / x / 10.3 cm

Exercise 19

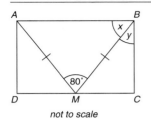

not to scale

The following questions are all taken from past GCSE papers.

1 (a) The diagram shows a rectangle *ABCD*. *M* is the mid-point of *DC*, angle *AMB* = 80°, *AM* = *MB*.
Work out the sizes of angles *x* and *y*. *(2 marks)*

(b) The diagram shows a quadrilateral *PQRS*. *PQ* = *QR* and *PS* = *SR*.

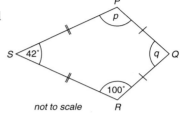

not to scale

(i) Which of the following correctly describes the quadrilateral *PQRS*?

Diamond   Kite   Rhombus   Parallelogram
Trapezium *(1 mark)*

(ii) Angle *PSR* = 42° and angle *QRS* = 100°. Work out the sizes of angles *p* and *q*. *(2 marks)*
[AQA/SEG]

2 The diagram is drawn accurately. It shows part of the net of a triangular prism. Two of the faces are missing.

(a) By taking suitable measurements, calculate the volume of the prism. State clearly the units of your answer. *(4 marks)*

(b) Complete the net by drawing the two missing faces in the correct places accurately. *(3 marks)*
[WJEC]

3 Draw the locus of all points which are 3 cm away from the line *AB*. *(3 marks)*
[EDEXCEL]

$\vdash\!\!\!-\!\!\!-\!\!\!-\!\!\!-\!\!\!-\!\!\!-\!\!\!-\!\!\!\dashv$
A   *B*

4 The diagram represents the positions of Wigan and Manchester.

(a) Measure and write down the bearing of Manchester from Wigan.
(1 mark)

(b) Find the bearing of Wigan from Manchester. *(2 marks)*
[EDEXCEL]

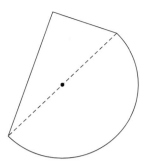

5 The diagram shows a penguin pool at a zoo. It consists of a right-angled triangle and a semi-circle. The scale is 1 cm to 2 m. A safety fence is put up around the pool. The fence is always 2 m from the pool. Draw accurately the position of the fence on the diagram.

(*4 marks*)

[AQA/SEG]

6

diagram not accurately drawn

Simone made a scale model of a 'hot rod' car on a scale of 1 to 12.5. The height of the model car is 10 cm.

(a) Work out the height of the real car. (*1 mark*)

The length of the real car is 5 m.

(b) Work out the length of the model car. Give your answer in centimetres. (*1 mark*)

The angle the windscreen made with the bonnet on the real car is 140°.

(c) What is the angle the windscreen makes with the bonnet on the model car? (*1 mark*)

The width of the windscreen in the real car is 119 cm correct to the nearest centimetre.

(d) Write down the smallest length this measurement could be. (*1 mark*)

[EDEXCEL]

7 (a) Write down th size of the angle marked x in each of the following diagrams.

(i)

(*1 mark*)

(ii)

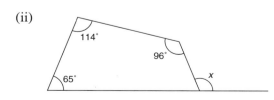

(*1 mark*)

(b)

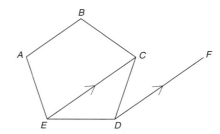

The above diagram shows a regular pentagon *ABCDE*, a diagonal *EC* and a line *DF* which is parallel to *EC*.

(i)   Calculate the size of $E\hat{D}C$.   (*2 marks*)

(ii) Calculate the size of $E\hat{C}D$.   (*2 marks*)

(iii) Calculate the size of $C\hat{D}F$.   (*1 mark*)

[WJEC]

8 The diagram shows two points *P* and *Q*.

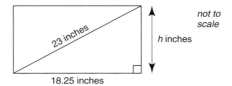

On the diagram shade the region which contains all the points that satisfy both the following

the distance from *P* is less than 3 cm,
the distance from *P* is greater than the distance from *Q*.   (*3 marks*)

[EDEXCEL]

9 The size of a television (TV) is given by the length of the diagonal of the screen. A 23 inch TV, therefore, has a screen diagonal length of 23 inches.

(a) The width of the screen of a 23 inch TV is 18.25 inches. Calculate the height, *h* inches, of the screen.

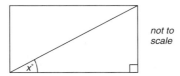

(b) A cinema screen is mathematically similar to the television screen in part (a).
Calculate the angle, $x°$, that the diagonal of the screen makes with the width.

(*3 marks*)

[OCR]

10.

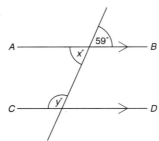

diagram not accurately drawn

AB is parallel to *CD*.

(a) Write down the size of the angle marked $x°$. Give a reason for your answer. *(2 marks)*

(b) Work out the size of the angle marked $y°$. Explain how you worked out your answer. *(2 marks)*

[EDEXCEL]

11 This diagram shows a vertical pole, *AB*, standing on horizontal ground *DBC*. The pole is held by two wires *AC* and *AD*. The wire *AC* is 16 m long and makes an angle of 54° with the ground.

(a) Calculate the length of the pole *AB*. *(3 marks)*

(b) The distance *CD* is 25 m. Calculate the angle the wire *AD* makes with the ground *(4 marks)*

[WJEC]

diagram not drawn to scale

12 In a triangle *ABC*, *BC* = 8 cm, angle *CBA* = 24°, *AB* = 10 cm.

(a) Use the information to draw triangle *ABC*. *(2 marks)*

(b) (i) Measure the size of angle *BAC* *(1 mark)*

(ii) What mathematical name is given to angle *BAC*? *(1 mark)*

[EDEXCEL]

13 The sketch map shows the positions of Poolbridge (*P*), Rosegrove (*R*) and Beacon Point (*B*). Beacon Point is 10 km due North of Poolbridge. Rosegrove is 7 km from Poolbridge on a bearing of 056°.

(a) (i) Construct triangle *PBR* using a scale of 1 cm to represent 1 km. *(2 marks)*

(ii) Use your diagram to find the distance of Rosegrove from Beacon Point. *(1 mark)*

(iii) Use your diagram to find the bearing of Rosegrove from Beacon Point. *(2 marks)*

[OCR/MEG]

• Beacon Point

• Rosegrove

• Poolbridge

(b) A town, Seton (*S*), is 3.5 km due West of Beacon Point.

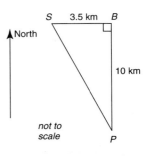

    (i)   Calculate the distance from Poolbridge to Seton.
             (*3 marks*)

    (ii) Calculate the bearing of Seton from Poolbridge.
             (*4 marks*)

[OCR/MEG]

14 The diagram is drawn using a scale 1 cm to 2 km. It shows two roads *AB* and *AC*. A radio mast has to be built so that it satisfies the following conditions.

It must be closer to *A* than to *B*.
It must be closer to *AB* than to *AC*.
It must not be nearer than 2 km to *A*.

On the diagram, shade the area where the radio mast can be built.

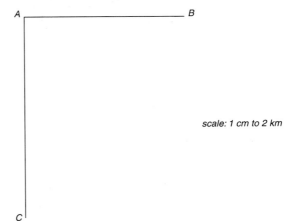

scale: 1 cm to 2 km

(*4 marks*)
[WJEC]

15

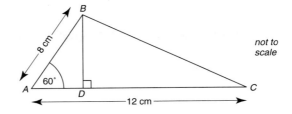

(a) Calculate the area of the triangle *ABC*.   (*5 marks*)
(b) Calculate the length *DC*.   (*3 marks*)
[OCR/MEG]

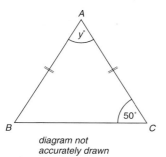

diagram not
accurately drawn

16 In triangle *ABC*, *AB* = *AC* and angle *C* = 50°.

    (a) Write down the special name for triangle *ABC*.   *(1 mark)*

    (b) Work out the value of *y*.   *(2 marks)*

                                                      [EDEXCEL]

17 A ladder, 2.75 m long, leans against a wall. The bottom of the ladder is 1.80 m from the wall, on level ground. Calculate how far the ladder reaches up the wall. Give your answer to an appropriate degree of accuracy.   *(4 marks)*

                                                 [AQA/NEAB]

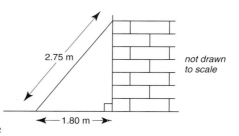

2.75 m

not drawn
to scale

1.80 m

18 In the diagram *AB* is parallel to *ED*. Angle *CED* = 54° and angle *BCD* = 100°.

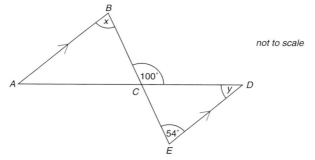

not to scale

    (i) Write down the size of angle *x*.   *(1 mark)*

    (ii) Find the size of angle *y*.   *(2 marks)*

                                                   [AQA/SEG]

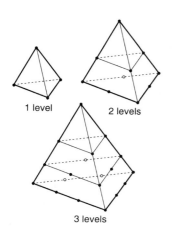

1 level   2 levels

3 levels

Ideas for investigations

1 A model can be built up using several rods and interconnectors.

Diagram:	1	2
Number of interconnectors:	4	10

How many interconnectors will be needed in the (a) 5th diagram (b) 10th diagram?

2 The numbers 3, 4, 5 form a Pythagorean triple, since they can be used to make the dimensions of a right-angled triangle: $3^2 + 4^2 = 5^2$
There are many other Pythagorean triples: 6, 8, 10; 5, 12, 13.
How many Pythagorean triples can you find? Make sure you explain the strategy you use.

3 Copy one of the diagrams. Draw straight lines that join pairs of points which total 13, for example, 3 and 10, 4 and 9, etc. The shape you get is called an envelope. You can vary the type of envelope you get by changing the total you use (e.g. use 11, 9, etc.). You can also change the shape of grid you use. Investigate the various shapes of envelopes you can get by changing the total number and the shape of grid you use.

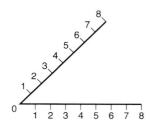

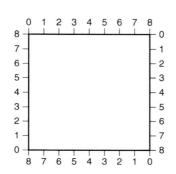

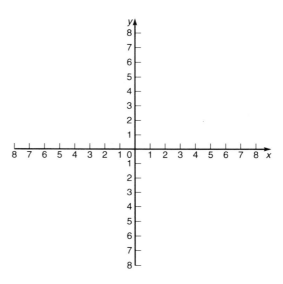

SYMMETRY 9

9.1 Reflection

The first primitive geometrical designs have been dated at around 25000 BC.

A **reflection** is a type of transformation. The complete shape has line symmetry, and the dotted line is called a **line of symmetry** or mirror line.

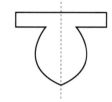

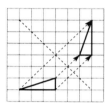

This shape has been reflected in the dotted line, which is also the line of symmetry, or mirror line.

Exercise 1

In each question copy and complete the diagram, and draw the reflection of the shape in the line of symmetry.

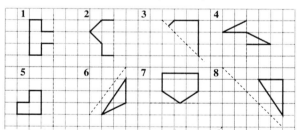

Exercise 2

Copy each shape and draw in *all* possible lines of symmetry. For each question write down the number of lines of symmetry you have found.

1   2   3   4   5

    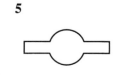

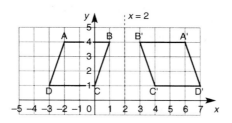

Lines on coordinate grids can be used as lines of symmetry:

Shape ABCD has been reflected in the line $x = 2$ to give the reflected shape A′B′C′D′

In each question copy the diagram, and draw the reflections of the shapes as requested.

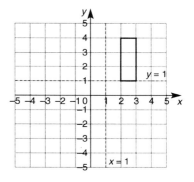

1 (a) reflected in the x-axis.

   (b) reflected in the line $x = 1$

   (c) reflected in the line $y = 1$

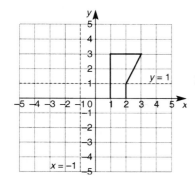

2 (a) reflected in the y-axis

   (b) reflected in the line $y = 1$

   (c) reflected in the line $x = -1$

3 (a) reflected in the y-axis

   (b) reflected in the line $y = x$

   (c) reflected in the line $y = -x$

   (d) reflected in the line $y = -1$

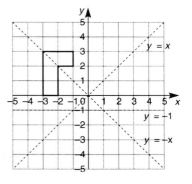

The largest mirror is 6 m, or $19\frac{1}{2}$ ft, in diameter, which is included in a reflector telescope on Mount Semirodriki in the Caucasus Mountains, USSR.

Note: When describing a transformation which is a reflection, always note down in which **line** it is reflected.

9.2 Planes of symmetry

The cube has been divided into two symmetrical halves by a **plane** of symmetry.

This shape has been divided into two by a plane, but the two halves are not symmetrical. The plane is not a plane of symmetry.

Exercise 4   Each solid is shown with one plane of symmetry. How many planes of symmetry does each solid have (including the one shown)?

1

2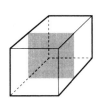

3

4

5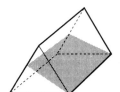

6

7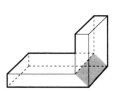

8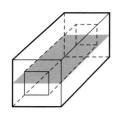

9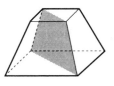

9.3 Rotation

A **rotation** is another type of transformation.
As a shape rotates about a point it will fit on top of itself in certain positions. The number of times it does this in one revolution is called the **order** of rotational symmetry.

Tracing paper is a useful aid when finding rotational symmetry.

1   Trace the shape onto tracing paper.
2   Place your pen on the centre of rotation.
3   Rotate the tracing paper around the point, and through one full turn (360°). As you do, count the number of times the shapes line up exactly.
4   Your count is the order of symmetry.

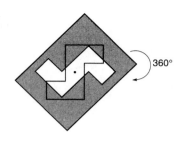

Example   Find the order of rotational symmetry.

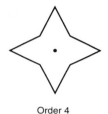

Order 4   Order 2

Exercise 5   For each shape give the order of rotational symmetry.

1   **2**   **3**   **4**

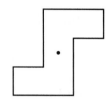

5   **6**   **7**   **8**

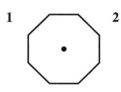      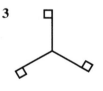   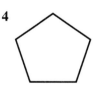

Use the shape given to draw a diagram which has rotational symmetry of the order stated, using the marked point as centre.

9   **10**   **11**   **12**

Order 2   Order 6   Order 4   Order 3

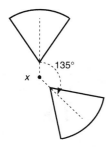

Shapes can also be rotated through a given angle about a point. This shape has been rotated 135° clockwise about point X.

Tracing paper is a useful aid when rotating shapes:

1   Trace the shape onto tracing paper.
2   Place your pen on the centre of rotation.
3   Turn the tracing paper around by the required angle, clockwise or anticlockwise.
4   Trace the shape into its new position.

Note: When describing a transformation which is a rotation, always note down the **angle** (degrees), the **direction** (anticlockwise/clockwise), and the **centre** of rotation.

Exercise 6

The highest man-made rotational speed ever achieved is 7250 km/h at Birmingham University in 1975.

Each shape A has been moved to a new position A'. Describe the rotation using the point marked x as the centre.

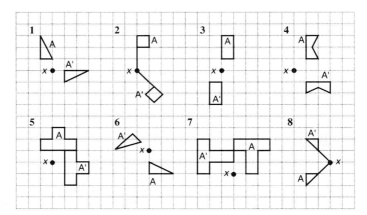

Exercise 7

Draw each shape A. Rotate the shape about the centre point x, through the given angle. Label the new position A'.

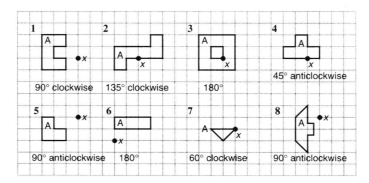

9.4 Enlargement

A third type of transformation is an **enlargement**.
Enlargement is a term used frequently in photography.

Shape A′ has sides that are twice as long as A: an enlargement of **scale factor** 2.

Shape A″ has sides that are three times longer than A: an enlargement of scale factor 3.

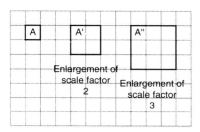

Exercise 8

Draw an enlargement of each diagram to the scale factor indicated.

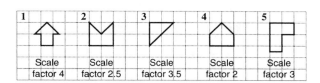

Shape A has been enlarged to become shape A′. In each question write down the scale factor of the enlargement.

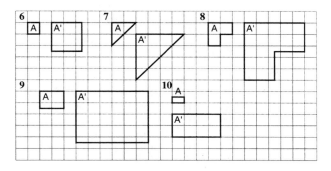

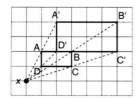

A transformation which is an enlargement has a point from which the shape is enlarged, called the **centre of enlargement**.

ABCD has been enlarged by a scale factor of 2: the distance of each point of the shape from the centre of enlargement x has been increased by a factor of 2, ABCD becomes A'B'C'D'.

ABC has been enlarged by a scale factor of 3. A'B'C' is the enlargement of ABC with the origin $(0, 0)$ as centre. A"B"C" is the enlargement of ABC with the point $(-3, 1)$ as centre.

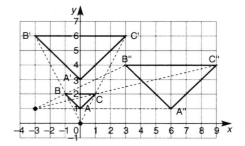

Note: When describing a transformation which is an enlargement always write down two things: the **scale factor**, and the **centre of enlargement**.

Exercise 9

Describe each of the enlargements which transform shape A to shape A', stating the scale factor and the centre of enlargement.

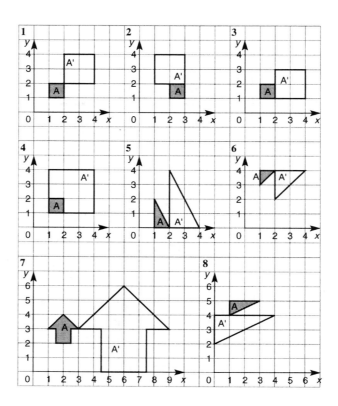

Copy the diagram and draw the enlargement by the given scale factor, from the centre of enlargement. You may need to extend the axes.

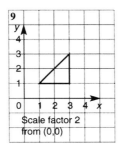

9 Scale factor 2
from (0,0)

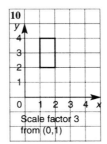

10 Scale factor 3
from (0,1)

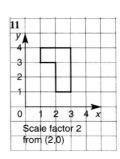

11 Scale factor 2
from (2,0)

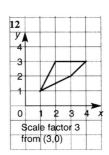

12 Scale factor 3
from (3,0)

9.5 Regular polygons

Triangle   Square   Pentagon   Hexagon   Heptagon   Octagon

Regular polygons are polygons with sides of equal length, and angles of equal size. There are two angles which are useful in calculations involving polygons: the exterior angle and the interior angle.

There are two angle properties which you must know:

Interior angle + Exterior angle = 180° at any vertex of the polygon.

Sum of the Exterior angles = 360°.

Example   The interior angle of a polygon is 120°. How many sides has the polygon?

Interior angle = 120°, so exterior angle = 180° − 120° = 60°.

Sum of all exterior angles is 360°,

so the number of angles = number of sides = 360° ÷ 60° = 6 sides.

Example   The sum of the interior angles of a regular polygon is 1260°. How many sides has the polygon?

Sum of exterior angles is 360°,

so sum of interior angles + sum of exterior angles is 1260° + 360° = 1620°.

But 1 exterior + 1 interior angle = 180°,

so the number of sides is 1620° ÷ 180° = 9 sides.

The mathematician Gauss, who died in 1814, wanted a 17-sided polygon drawn on his tombstone, but it too closely resembled a circle for the stonemaster to carve.

Example A regular polygon has 30 sides. What is the sum of the interior angles?

Each exterior angle is $360° \div 30 = 12°$. ◄——— *As the sum of exterior angles is 360°.*

So interior angle $= 180° - 12° = 168°$, ◄——— *As interior angle + exterior angle is 180°.*

so 30 interior angles $= 168° \times 30 = 5040°$

Exercise 10

Find the number of sides of each regular polygon given the following information:

1 Interior angle 135°   **2** Interior angle 108°

3 Exterior angle 40°   **4** Exterior angle 30°

5 Interior angle 144°   **6** Exterior angle 24°

7 Sum of interior angles is 3240°   **8** Sum of interior angles is 2880°

Find the sum of the interior angles of regular polygons with:

9 16 sides   **10** 25 sides   **11** 32 sides   **12** 36 sides

13 Can a regular polygon be drawn, such that each exterior angle is
(a) 20° (b) 16° (c) 15°? If so, state the number of sides,

14 Can a regular polygon be drawn, such that each interior angle is
(a) 144° (b) 140° (c) 130°? If so, state the number of sides.

The US Defense Department Building, the Pentagon, has the largest ground area covered by any office building: 604 000 m², and 27 km of corridors.

Exercise 11

Use your results from Exercise 10 to help you copy and complete this table:

Regular polygon	Number of sides	Sum of all interior angles	Size of one interior angle	Size of one exterior angle
Triangle (equilateral)				
Quadrilateral (square)				
Pentagon				
Hexagon				
Heptagon				
Octagon				
Nonagon				
Decagon				
Undecagon				
Dodecagon				

9.6 Tessellations

Shapes **tessellate** when they fit together exactly, without any gaps.

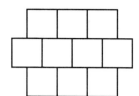 

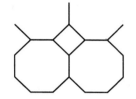

Squares tessellate; circles do not tessellate.

We can also have tessellations made up of more than one shape. This tessellation is made using squares and regular octagons.

Exercise 12

1 Show, by drawing a diagram, which of the regular polygons can tessellate.

2 Show, by drawing a diagram, which of these shapes tessellate:

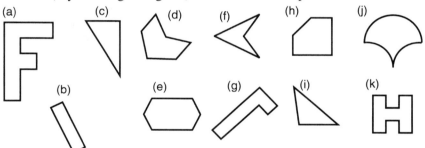

9.7 Moving shapes: translation

A **translation** is another type of transformation. A translation is a way of describing how a shape has been moved by sliding. In the diagrams, shape ABCD has been moved to a new position A'B'C'D'. Look at the point C: it has moved 4 spaces across to the right, and 1 space up, to C'. All the points have moved the same amount: A → A', B → B', C → C', D → D'.

ABCD → A'B'C'D' is described by the translation $\begin{pmatrix} 4 \\ 1 \end{pmatrix}$

From C to C" is 2 to the left and 1 down.

ABCD → A"B"C"D" is described by the translation $\begin{pmatrix} -2 \\ -1 \end{pmatrix}$

So a translation is described by: $\begin{pmatrix} \text{moves to the right} \\ \text{moves upwards} \end{pmatrix}$

Exercise 13   Describe the translations which map:

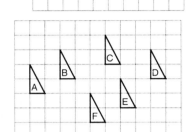

1 A onto C   2 A onto B

3 B onto A   4 B onto C

5 C onto A   6 C onto B

Describe the translations which map:

7 A onto C   8 B onto A

9 D onto B   10 D onto F

11 F onto D   12 E onto B

13 F onto C   14 D onto A

15   Draw this shape on a square grid.
Draw and label the translations of this shape as follows:

(a) A $\begin{pmatrix} 1 \\ 2 \end{pmatrix}$ (b) B $\begin{pmatrix} 3 \\ -2 \end{pmatrix}$ (c) C $\begin{pmatrix} 4 \\ 1 \end{pmatrix}$ (d) D $\begin{pmatrix} -2 \\ -3 \end{pmatrix}$

16   Draw this shape on a square grid.
Draw and label the translations of this shape as follows:

(a) A $\begin{pmatrix} -3 \\ -2 \end{pmatrix}$ (b) B $\begin{pmatrix} 4 \\ 0 \end{pmatrix}$ (c) C $\begin{pmatrix} 3 \\ -2 \end{pmatrix}$ (d) D $\begin{pmatrix} -3 \\ 0 \end{pmatrix}$

9.8 **Transformation combinations**

A transformation **combination** occurs when we perform a transformation on a shape, and then follow this by a further transformation.
The combination of two transformations can frequently be replaced by a single transformation.

Example   Carry out the two transformations detailed.

(a) Reflect triangle D in the y axis to become triangle E

(b) Reflect triangle E in the line $y = x$ to become triangle F.

(c) Find the **single** transformation that would map triangle D on to triangle F.

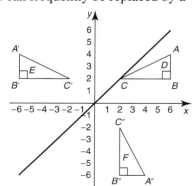

The single transformation from D to F is a rotation of 90° clockwise about the origin O. This single transformation has the same effect as the two combined transformations.

Exercise 14

In each question carry out the two transformations on triangle D above, and find the single transformation that would have the same effect as the two combined transformations.

1 (a) A reflection in the line $y = x$ (b) a reflection in the y-axis

2 (a) A reflection in the x-axis   (b) a rotation of 90° clockwise about the origin O.

3 (a) A reflection in the x-axis   (b) a reflection in the y-axis.

4 (a) A translation of $\begin{pmatrix} 4 \\ 3 \end{pmatrix}$ (b) a reflection in the x-axis.

5 (a) A reflection in the y-axis   (b) a rotation of 90° clockwise about the origin O.

6 (a) A reflection in the x-axis   (b) a reflection in the line $y = x$.

7 (a) A reflection in the x-axis   (b) a rotation of 180° about the origin O.

8 (a) A rotation of 90° clockwise about the origin O   (b) a reflection in the line $y = -x$.

Review

Exercise 15

1 Reflect this shape in the dotted line.

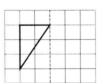

2 Reflect this shape in the dotted line.

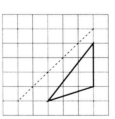

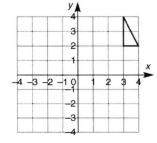

3 Reflect the triangle as follows:

(a) in the x-axis, and label it A

(b) in the y-axis, and label it B

(c) in the line $y = 1$, and label it C

(d) in the line $y = -x$, and label it D.

4 How many planes of symmetry have each of these solids?

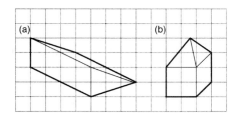

5 Write down the order of rotational symmetry:

(a)   (b)   (c)   (d)

Copy the shape and complete the rotation about the marked point as centre.

6   **7** 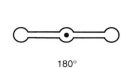   **8**

135° clockwise   180°   45° anticlockwise

9 Enlarge the shape using (0, 1) as centre, and using a scale factor of 3.

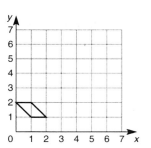

10 Can a regular polygon be found such that the interior angle is 136°?

11 A regular polygon has an interior angle of 165°. How many sides has it?

12 A regular polygon has an exterior angle of 45°. How many sides has it?

13 Describe the translation which maps:

(a) A → C   (b) C → D
(c) D → B   (d) B → A

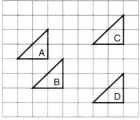

Exercise 16   The following questions are all taken from GCSE papers.

1 (a)   Draw in all the lines of symmetry for a rectangle.

(2 marks)

   (b)   On a grid, show how this kite
          will tessellate. You should draw
          at least 6 kites.

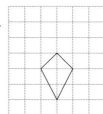

(2 marks)
[EDEXCEL]

2

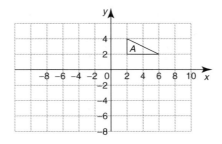

   (a)   Rotate the shape A through 90° clockwise with centre (−2, 0).
          Label the image B.   *(2 marks)*
   (b)   Reflect the shape A in the line $y = x$. Label the image C. *(1 mark)*
[WJEC]

3 The diagram shows shapes Q and R which are transformations of
   shape P.

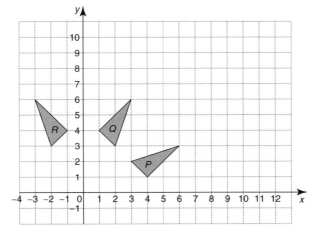

   (a)   Describe fully the single transformation which takes P onto R.

(3 marks)

(b)   Describe fully the single transformation which takes *P* onto *Q*.
(2 marks)

(c)   On a diagram draw an enlargement of shape *P* with scale factor 2, centre (3, 2).   *(2 marks)*
[AQA/SEG]

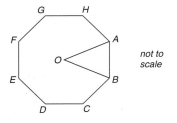

4 (a)   *ABCDEFGH* is a regular octagon with centre *O*.

(i)   Calculate angle *AOB*. Show your working clearly. *(2 marks)*

(ii)   Calculate angle *ABC*. Show your working clearly. *(2 marks)*

(b)   The diagram shows the top of a table which is covered by four identical regular octagonal tiles and sixteen identical triangular tiles.

Explain why the quadrilateral formed in the centre of the table top is a square.   *(2 marks)*

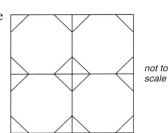

not to scale

[OCR/MEG]

5 (a)   Triangle *A* is a reflection of the shaded triangle.

Draw the mirror line for this reflection on the diagram.   *(1 mark)*

(b)   Describe fully the transformation that maps the shaded triangle onto triangle *B*.   *(3 marks)*

[AQA/NEAB]

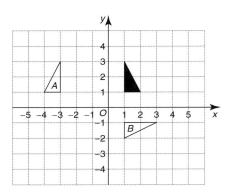

6 The diagram represents two photographs.

(a)   Work out the area of the small photograph.   *(2 marks)*

The photograph is to be enlarged by scale factor 3.

(b)   Write down the measurements of the enlarged photograph.   *(2 marks)*

(c)   How many times bigger is the area of the enlarged photograph than the area of the small photograph?   *(2 marks)*
[EDEXCEL]

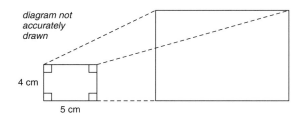

diagram not accurately drawn

4 cm

5 cm

7 *ABCDEF* is a regular hexagon.

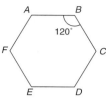

(a)   Show how you can calculate that angle *ABC* is 120°.   (*1 mark*)

Squares are placed on each side of the hexagon. The polygon
OPQRSTUVWXYZ is formed by joining the outer corners of the
squares, as shown in the diagram.

(b)   (i)   Calculate the size of angle
            QBR (*b* in the diagram).
                                (*2 marks*)
      (ii) Calculate the size of angle
            PQR (*q* in the diagram).
                                (*1 mark*)

(c)   What type of triangle is *QBR*?
                                (*1 mark*)
                          [AQA/NEAB]

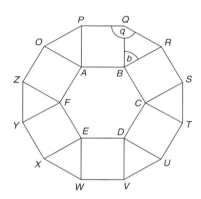

8 (a)   Reflect the 'L' shape in the *x*-axis.   (*1 mark*)

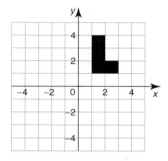

(b)   Rotate the 'L' shape 90° anti-clockwise, centre (0, 0).   (*2 marks*)

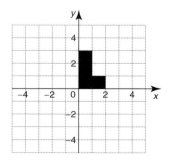

(c)   Translate the 'L' shape 3 units to the right and 2 units up.

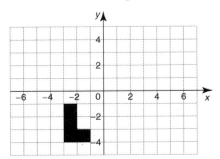

(1 mark)
[OCR/MEG]

9

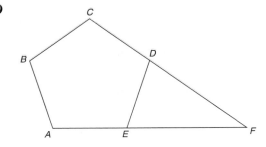

ABCDE is a regular polygon. *CDF* and *AEF* are straight lines.

(a)   Write down the name given to a polygon with 5 sides.   *(1 mark)*

(b)   Calculate the size of an interior angle of the polygon *ABCDE*.

(3 marks)

(c)   (i)   Explain why triangle *EDF* is isosceles.   *(1 mark)*

(ii)   Calculate the size of angle *EFD*.   *(2 marks)*
[OCR]

10   The diagram shows shape *A*.

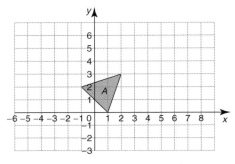

(a)   Reflect shape *A* in the line $x = 3$. Label its new position *B*.

(2 marks)

(b) Rotate shape *A* through 90° anticlockwise about centre (1, 0). Label its new position *C*. *(2 marks)*

(c) Another triangle, *D*, has vertices (−3, 3), (−5, 5) and (−2, 6). Describe fully the single transformation which will take *A* onto *D*. *(3 marks)*

[AQA/SEG]

11 Triangles A, C and D have been drawn on the grid.

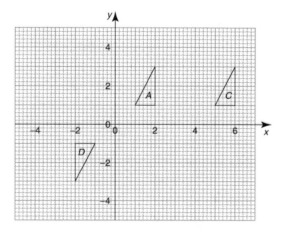

(a) Draw the reflection of triangle A in the *y*-axis. Label the new triangle B. *(1 mark)*

(b) (i) Describe the single transformation which maps triangle A onto triangle C. *(2 marks)*

(ii) Describe the single transformation which maps triangle C onto your triangle B. *(2 marks)*

(c) Describe the single transformation which maps triangle A onto triangle D. *(2 marks)*

[OCR/MEG]

Ideas for investigations

1 ——   ————   ——————————

The first line has been enlarged by a scale factor of 2, and 3.

The dimensions of the first square have been enlarged by a scale factor of 2, and 3. By what factors has the area been enlarged?

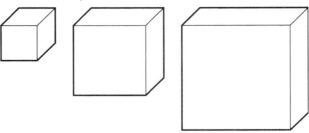

The dimensions of the first cube have been enlarged by a scale factor of 2, and 3. By what factors has the volume been enlarged?

Can you describe a rule connecting scale factor of enlargement of distances (lengths), scale factor of enlargement of areas, and scale factor of enlargement of volumes?

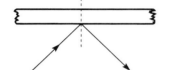

2 In snooker a ball hits the cushion and rebounds. The second part of its path is a reflection of the first part of its path. Draw a scale diagram of a snooker table, 6 ft × 3 ft, and use this idea of reflections to plot the path of snooker balls as they rebound off the cushion.

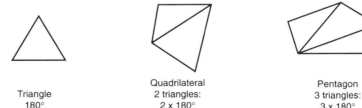

Try a few examples with the ball starting in different places on the table.

3

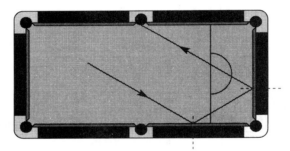

Triangle
180°

Quadrilateral
2 triangles:
2 x 180°

Pentagon
3 triangles:
3 x 180°

The diagram shows how polygons can be divided up into triangles to help find the total of all the interior angles.
Total for a triangle (3 sides) = 180°.
Total for a quadrilateral (4 sides) = 180° × 2 = 360°.
Total for a pentagon (5 sides) = 180° × 3 = 540°.
Can you use this method to help find a rule linking the number of sides of the polygon with the total of the interior angles?

COLLECTING AND PROCESSING

The heaviest rainstorm recorded occurred in 1952 on the Island of Reunion in the Indian Ocean: 1870 millimetres of rain fell in 24 hours.

Statistical information required for processing can be gathered in a number of ways of which two of the more common ones are:

(1) from data collecting sheets (e.g. questionnaires),
(2) from tables and lists (e.g. train timetables).

In the next chapter we shall look more closely at representing and interpreting information, but in this chapter we will concentrate on the collection and processing of information.

10.1 Data collecting sheets

Example
A hot-drinks machine in a college canteen sells tea, coffee, chocolate, tomato soup and vegetable soup.
As part of a survey, information has been collected on the data sheet shown.

Copy and complete the 'Total' column.

(a) How many coffees were sold?
(b) How many soups?
(c) If one of the drinks had to be withdrawn, which one would you choose? Why?

(a) There were 26 coffees sold.
(b) There were 16 + 23 = 39 soups sold.
(c) Based only on the survey information, you would choose tomato soup, because it had fewest sales.

With further information from other days and from other times in the day, your choice may be different.

A good data collecting sheet:
(1) has a clear heading, with dates, times where necessary,
(2) is clear in what it is asking for,
(3) is easy to complete, with ticks or simple numbers.

Survey Sheet
HOT DRINKS

Start: 10.30 a.m.   Finish: 12.30 p.m.

DRINK	TALLY	TOTAL
Tea	~~HHH~~ ~~HHH~~ ~~HHH~~ ~~HHH~~ ///	23
Coffee	~~HHH~~ ~~HHH~~ ~~HHH~~ ~~HHH~~ ~~HHH~~ /	
Chocolate	~~HHH~~ ~~HHH~~ ~~HHH~~ ~~HHH~~ ~~HHH~~ ~~HHH~~ //	
Tomato soup	~~HHH~~ ~~HHH~~ ~~HHH~~ /	
Vegetable soup	~~HHH~~ ~~HHH~~ ~~HHH~~ ~~HHH~~ ///	
	Total	

Exercise 1

The purpose of each data sheet is given. Say what aspects of each of these data collecting sheets you think could be improved. Write down your improvements in each case.

Lunch survey
Date:

Customer	Meal	Cost
1.	Pizza + chips	1.20
2.	Baked potato	0.85
3.		
4.		
5.		
6.		
7.		
8.		
9.		
10.		

Cars

Car No.	No. of passengers
1	
2	
3	
4	
5	
6	
7	
8	
9	
10	

1 To see how many occupants there are in cars travelling into a town in the morning, as part of a survey into public transport facilities.

2 To survey the lunches provided in a canteen, with a view to improving the meals service.

Newspaper Survey
Date:

From 9.30 – 10.30 a.m.

Paper	No. bought	Total
Mirror		
Express		
Mail		
Sun		
Today		
Times		
Guardian		
Telegraph		
Independent		

Car parking
Date:

Time	Empty spaces
13.00	
13.15	
13.30	
13.45	
14.00	
14.15	
14.30	
14.45	
15.00	

3 To look into which morning newspapers are the most popular with students by surveying the papers bought at the college bookshop in a morning.

4 To look into the car parking provision in a supermarket car park by checking the number of vacant spaces.

As with data collecting sheets, questionnaires need to be carefully worded, otherwise the information collected could be confusing or biased.

Exercise 2

The following questionnaires attempt to gather information for the purpose stated. Criticise each of these questionnaires, and rewrite them so as to remove as much of the confusion or bias as you can.

Lecturer questionnaire

Please rate the lecturers in order of preference, entering a number from 1 to 5 in the box beside the name

Mr N. James
Mr B. Anderson
Mrs K. Robson
Mr M. Islam
Mrs L. Oates

Signed (if desired): ....

1 To ascertain the effectiveness of the five college lecturers who teach on a mathematics course.

2 To look into making the menu in the college canteen more acceptable to students.

Canteen Questionnaire

(a) Which of these meals do you eat?

Sausage	Vegetarian
Pizza	Baked potato
Stir-fry	Hamburger
Roast meat	Other

(b) Which meal would you prefer to eat?

Name: ....
(not compulsory)

3 To investigate foreign holidays.

4 To look into destinations, having completed a one-year course.

Where do you go on holiday? Are you male/female?
Please indicate your holiday destination last year.
France   Germany Spain   Greece Belgium   U.S.A Other – please name
Signed: ....

Leavers' destinations Date: _____	
Which course have you recently completed?	What are you Intending to do?
Male/female	16 19 22 over Age: 17 20 23 24 18 21 24

10.2 Information from tables and lists

There are more than 12 000 different species in the 'pea' family (leguminosae).

Example A holiday company makes a charge if a previously booked holiday is cancelled. The charge depends on how many days' notice is given, before the holiday is due to begin. The rates are shown in the table.

Holidays of 1–3 nights	Holidays of 4 nights or more	Charge
2–14 days	2–14 days	60%
15–21 days	15–28 days	45%
22–28 days	29–42 days	30%
28+ days in advance	42+ days in advance	deposit only

Find the charge for cancelling a holiday which should have lasted:

(a) 6 nights, costing £300, with 25 days' notice,
(b) 1 night, costing £55, with 3 days' notice,
(c) 8 nights, costing £840, with 32 days' notice.

(a) The charge is 45% of £300, which is £135.
(b) The charge is 60% of £54, which is £32.40.
(c) The charge is 30% of £840, which is £252.

Exercise 3 Use the information in the tables or lists to answer the questions.

Element	Density (g/cm^3)	Melting point (°C)	Boiling point (°C)
Aluminium	2.7	660	2470
Copper	8.9	1084	2570
Gold	19.3	1064	3080
Iron	7.9	1540	2750
Lead	11.3	180	1340
Magnesium	1.7	650	1110
Silver	10.5	961	2212
Tin	7.3	232	2270
Zinc	7.1	419	907

1 The table gives the density, melting point and boiling point of some metallic elements.

(a) What is the melting point of silver?
(b) What is the boiling point of copper?
(c) Which metals are denser than iron?
(d) Which is the least dense metal?
(e) Which metal has the highest boiling point?
(f) Brass consists of 60% copper and 40% zinc. Will its density be more than, or less than, 8 g/cm^3?

INTERCITY
Newcastle–London Mondays to Fridays

	Newcastle depart	King's Cross arrive
	1500	1808
	1535	1840
	1600	1918
(P)	1622	1903
	1700	2015
	1730	2045
	1845	2159
	1905	2222
	2039	0023

2 The train times for travelling between Newcastle upon Tyne and London are shown, from 3.00 p.m. onwards.

(a) At what time does the 1700 arrive at King's Cross?

(b) If I arrive in London just after 7.15 p.m., at what time did the train leave Newcastle?

(c) How long is the journey on the 1730?

(d) The fastest train is the First Class Pullman service (P). How long is this journey?

(e) At what time does the last train arrive at King's Cross?

3 The monthly repayments for personal loans from an insurance company are shown in the table.

	Number of payments		
Amount	12	24	36
£7500	713.98	396.66	292.93
£5000	475.98	264.44	194.61
£3000	286.25	159.34	117.45
£2000	190.83	106.22	78.30
£1000	95.42	53.11	39.15
£500	47.71	26.56	19.58

(a) What is the premium for a loan of £3000 over 24 payments?

(b) I wish to borrow £5000 over three years. What are the monthly repayments?

(c) What loan can I have, if I can afford to pay up to £80 a month for three years?

(d) What would the premium be for a loan of £1500 over 12 payments?

4 A table of continental quilts from a mail-order catalogue shows the size, catalogue number, price, and weekly payments over 20 weeks.

Size	Cat. No.	Price	20 weeks
54 × 78	MQ 23 56	£49.99	£2.50
54 × 78	MQ 23 59	£59.99	£3.00
78 × 78	MQ 23 57	£69.99	£3.50
78 × 78	MQ 23 60	£84.99	£4.25
90 × 86	MQ 23 58	£79.99	£4.00
90 × 86	MQ 23 61	£94.99	£4.75

(a) What is the price of the quilt MQ 23 59?

(b) What is the weekly payment for quilt MQ 23 58?

(c) What size is the quilt which is priced at £84.99?

(d) I buy two of the large MQ 23 61 quilts. What will be my weekly payments?

(e) I would like one each of the two 54 × 78 quilts. What will be the weekly payments for these two quilts?

10.3 Ordering data

When information is collected, by whatever means (questionnaires, data collection sheets, set of test results, etc.), it needs to be put into some sort of **order**, if further work is to be done.

WALKER'S GARAGE

Repairs, MOT, service.
Phone: 729 401

brown red red blue
white blue blue green
red brown red green
red yellow red white
blue green red red red
blue blue brown grey
red yellow blue green
yellow brown

Example A garage worker was asked to note the colours of cars passing through the garage over a period of half an hour. From his figures he was asked to work out:

(a) the most popular colour,

(b) the least popular colour,

(c) the total number of cars seen,

(d) the percentage of cars of the most popular colour.

From his sheet, it is not clear what the answers are to any of the questions. We need to rearrange the information into some order.

Firstly, make a list of all the colours seen. Now count how many of each colour there were. The safest way to ensure that you do not miss any out is to go through the list of colours one by one, making a **tally mark** under the appropriate colour.

The complete **tally table** looks like this:

brown	red	blue	white	green	yellow	grey
////	//////	//////	//	////	///	/
	//////	//				

Note: We usually draw the fifth tally mark *across* the previous four marks, to help us to count in 5s, especially when there are many tally marks to add up. We can now answer questions (a) and (b) easily: the most popular colour was red and the least popular colour was grey.

To answer (c) we can add up the tally marks for each colour:

brown   red   blue   white   green   yellow   grey
$$4 + 10 + 7 + 2 + 4 + 3 + 1 = 31$$

(d) The percentage of red cars is $\frac{10}{31} \times 100 = 32\%$, approximately.

WALKER'S GARAGE

Repairs, MOT, service.
Phone: 729 401

Colour	Tally	Frequency
brown	////	4
red	////// //////	10
blue	////// //	7
white	//	2
green	////	4
yellow	///	3
grey	/	1
	Total	31

It would have been much more convenient if the garage worker had planned his data collecting sheet rather more carefully in the first instance. This sheet would have been much better; he does not need to write down each colour, only a tally mark.

225

Exercise 4

For each of these sets of data, make up a suitable tally table, and complete it, showing the totals in the 'Frequency' column.

1 A set of 40 marks obtained by students in a test, with a maximum score of 10.

3	6	7	2	8	5	9	6	4	8
0	9	5	7	10	3	5	6	0	7
6	4	8	2	6	9	2	10	1	4
7	8	4	9	6	7	3	0	6	8

The column headings should be: Mark, Tally, Frequency.

2 A survey on the favourite fruit eaten by a group of students.

apple	apple	grape	melon	orange	orange
apple	banana	apple	orange	pear	grape
pear	apple	kiwi	banana	melon	apple
orange	pear	apple	apple	orange	melon

The column headings should be: Fruit, Tally, Frequency.

3 The number of minutes a local train is late, over a period of 35 weekdays.

3	0	0	8	5	1	1	2	0	4	0	0
1	4	0	0	2	2	9	3	0	1	2	1
0	5	7	0	0	3	1	4	4	0	2	

4 The National Curriculum level in mathematics attained by students wishing to follow a science course at a college.

The strongest surface wind was 372 km/h recorded at Mt. Washington in the USA in 1934.

8	6	9	7	6	6	7	6	5	9	7	7	6
7	5	9	8	8	6	7	6	6	7	6	5	8
7	8	6	7	6	5	7	8	7	6	7	7	7
6	7	6	5	6	7	6	6	9	6	8		

10.4 Grouping data

Example

The marks scored by 28 students in a test (marked out of 100) are given.

(a) Make up a tally table.

To reach grade B a score of 60 was needed.

To reach grade A a score of 80 was needed.

(b) How many grade As were there?

(c) How many grade Bs were there?

43	47	88	76
52	66	49	68
92	77	37	65
49	71	91	62
83	74	71	70
57	19	37	90
50	85	66	75

(a) A tally table would be tedious to produce for these figures as they stand, as the mark range is from 19 to 92, and most scores occur only once. A more useful method would be to **group** the scores, into tens.

Mark	Tally	Frequency
0–9		0
10–19	/	1
20–29		0
30–39	//	2
40–49	////	4
50–59	///	5
60–69	ᵗᴴᴸ	5
70–79	ᵗᴴᴸ //	7
80–89	///	3
90–100	///	3
Total		28

We can represent this information in a diagram – there are more examples in the next chapter.

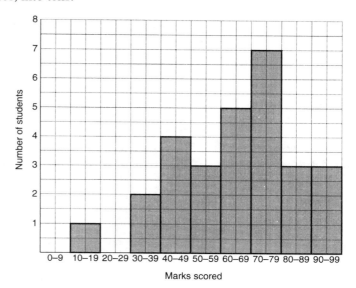

(b) From the table, there were 3 + 3 = 6 grade As.
(c) From the table, there were 5 + 7 = 12 grade Bs.

Exercise 5

For each set of data, make up a tally table, using the groupings suggested, and complete the frequency column.

1 The number of tomatoes picked from 24 tomato plants:

18	31	25	16	21	20	34	7
19	18	24	26	30	21	26	18
28	31	11	25	33	23	17	24

0–4, 5–9, 10–14, 15–19, ...

2 The number of words in each line of a page in a book:

12	8	9	15	2	14	10	9
7	15	9	11	13	12	5	14
7	10	11	1	11	13	9	3
8	10	8	11	12	11	3	11
10	8	8	6	14	12	10	4

0–2, 3–5, 6–8, 9–11, 12–14, 15–17, ...

How many lines altogether are there on this page?

3 The number of books on 27 of the shelves in a college library:

35	42	43	31	27	39	30	45	37
33	36	26	30	29	38	36	34	43
23	35	43	34	30	26	37	44	37

21–25, 26–30, 31–35, 36–40, ...

10.5 Discrete and continuous data

So far we have considered numbers of objects: items which can be **counted**, e.g. test marks, tomatoes, words, and books. If data has been counted, then the values are **discrete** — they can be only whole numbers. (In the examples above, there are no half-marks, and no half-tomatoes!)

The groupings are quite arbitrary: it is normal to have between six and ten groups. In question 3 of exercise 5 we could just as easily have chosen our groups as 20–23, 24–27, 28–31, ...

discrete = countable
continuous = measurable

If, however, the information has been **measured**, then there must have been some degree of approximation, depending on the accuracy of the measuring instrument, whether it be a stopwatch, a set of weighing scales or a ruler. If data has been measured, then the values are **continuous** — they can have *any* values (within a certain range).

Example The ages of people taking out a policy with an insurance company is shown. Make up a suitable grouped frequency table.

34	42	19	26	30	23	18	20	53	38
23	27	49	29	34	36	19	22	45	31
20	20	28	29	22	24	19	26	40	38

Firstly, we need to identify exactly what each figure represents. The range of ages for anyone aged '34' will be any age from the day of their 34th birthday up to the day before their 35th birthday. We can use inequality signs to help us here:

$34 \leqslant \text{age} < 35$ will mean anyone aged 34.

We can now choose groupings (between about 6 and 10 is suitable).

Age (y)	$15 \leqslant y < 20$	$20 \leqslant y < 25$	$25 \leqslant y < 30$	$30 \leqslant y < 35$
Tally	IIII	⊬⊬ III	⊬⊬ I	IIII
Frequency	4	8	6	4

Age (y)	$35 \leqslant y < 40$	$40 \leqslant y < 45$	$45 \leqslant y < 50$	$50 \leqslant y < 55$
Tally	III	II	II	I
Frequency	3	2	2	1

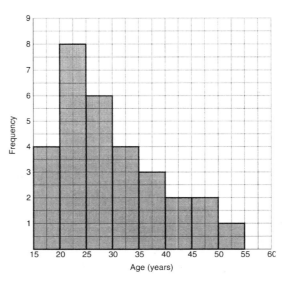

Along the horizontal axis the scale is continuous, so we can mark it quite easily.

Exercise 6 For each set of data, decide on your groupings, make up a tally table, and complete the frequency column. State whether or not the information is discrete or continuous. (A possible grouping is suggested for question 1.)

1 The amount £A spent in a supermarket by customers passing through a particular till.

£15.76	£52.63	£24.53	£8.92	£16.02	£10.70	£33.57	£19.46
£12.72	£21.80	£40.52	£28.88	£36.63	£13.29	£2.99	£18.49
£38.62	£42.73	£31.74	£11.24	£14.80	£20.66	£17.04	£36.29
£10.63	£18.20	£6.46	£16.33	£29.05	£25.81	£58.31	£22.77
£45.62	£38.01	£10.42	£18.62	£33.38	£28.01	£5.74	£44.77

£0 ≤ A < £10, £10 ≤ A < £20, £20 ≤ A < £30, ...

2 The weights, in kilograms, of baskets of raspberries picked at a 'pick-your-own' fruit farm.

2.32	0.67	1.62	1.95	0.79	1.21	2.31	1.98
1.58	1.53	1.83	1.42	2.70	1.20	1.58	1.87
2.88	1.03	1.16	0.80	1.44	1.35	2.20	2.35
1.79	1.76	1.09	1.59	0.82	2.34	2.67	1.92
0.83	1.43	1.71	1.18	1.22	1.88	2.61	1.43

3 The duration of films, in minutes, on video from a video-hire shop.

93	106	104	89	92	90	115	89
111	126	96	98	100	102	120	114
100	91	123	110	81	87	102	93
96	105	85	91	109	99	100	86
90	128	116	97	92	119	113	88

10.6 Mode and median

In the year 1583, Pope Gregory instructed that 5th October should become 15th October, thus losing ten days.

The mode and the median of a set of numerical data are measures of a single average value. They are usually, but not always, central values, i.e. somewhere in the middle of the range of numbers.

The **mode** is easiest to work out — it is the most popular, or frequently occurring value in the set of data.

The **median** requires the figures to be written in order — it is the middle value when the figures are written in order of size.

Example   In its first eleven games in a season, a rugby team scored these points: 15, 12, 20, 8, 12, 16, 14, 17, 23, 16, 12. What is (a) the mode (or modal number of points) (b) the median?

(a)   We can see, by merely looking at the figures, that the mode is 12 points, because 12 occurs more often than any other number of points (12 occurs three times).

If there is an even number of figures, then the median is halfway between the middle two numbers.

(b)   To find the median, we first put the numbers in order:

     8, 12, 12, 12, 14, 15, 16, 16, 17, 20, 23

The median is 15 points, because it is the middle value.

Exercise 7

In questions 1 to 7, work out the mode, and the median, of each set of figures.

1   3, 4, 4, 4, 5, 6, 6, 8, 9

2   13, 15, 20, 13, 16, 15, 18, 13, 12

3   8, 5, 6, 6, 4, 7, 7, 4, 7, 5, 6, 7

4   52, 51, 53, 66, 55, 46, 51, 52, 51

5   4, 8, 5, 8, 8, 5, 6, 8, 6

6   24, 24, 24, 27, 29, 29, 32, 35

7   4, 7, 8, 8, 11, 11, 11, 14, 15

8   Students were asked to estimate the height of the college sports hall, in metres. Their guesses were:

     14, 13, 11, 13, 16, 15, 15, 12, 13, 12, 16, 14, 14, 15, 13

(a) What is the modal guess at the height?

(b) Work out the median guess at the height.

9   In a test out of 20, the marks for a class of 22 students were:

     8, 15, 14, 17, 10, 6, 9, 16, 16, 15, 20,
     10, 15, 18, 3, 12, 16, 17, 12, 19, 9, 16.

Find (a) the modal mark (b) the median mark.

10   A student says that she has solved the problem of writing down seven whole numbers, from 3 to 9 inclusive, which have a mode of 4 and a median of 6. Work out her seven numbers.

10.7 Mode and median for grouped data

Example The mass of apples produced by each tree in an orchard is recorded. The table shows the result for 50 apple trees:

Weight of apples (kg)	0–9.9	10–19.9	20–29.9	30–39.9	40–49.9
Number of trees	4	11	18	10	7

(a) What is the modal mass?   (b) Work out the median mass.

(a) We cannot say exactly what the mode is here, because we have a **range** of masses for each group, and do not have the mass of apples produced by each individual tree. What we can say is that the **modal group** is the most popular, which is the 20 – 29.9 kg group.

(b) As there are 50 trees, the median mass will be midway between the mass of apples produced by the 25th and 26th trees, when put in order. There is a broad 'order' already — the lightest 15 masses are under 20 kg (4 + 11). As with the mode, we do not know the mass of apples produced by any individual tree; all we can say for certain is that the median mass is between 20 kg and 29.99 kg.

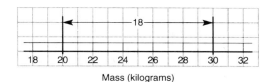

Mass (kilograms)

However, we can make an assumption that the 18 trees in the 20–29.9 kg group are more or less evenly distributed throughout this range.

Hence the mass increase per tree = $\frac{10}{18}$ ⟵ *Mass in range 20–29.9.*
   ⟵ *Number of trees in range.*

As we need the mass halfway between the 25th and 26th mass, and as there are 15 masses below 20 kg, we need

$\frac{10}{18} \times 10.5$ ⟵ *25.5 – 15*

= 5.8 kg approximately

We can estimate, therefore, that the median mass is about 25.8 kg. Bear in mind, however, that this is only an approximation to the median mass.

Exercise 8   State the modal group, and estimate the median value, in each case.

1 The heights of 35 saplings in a market garden nursery.

Height of samplings (mm)	0–99	100–199	200–299	300–399	400–499
Number of saplings	2	10	12	9	2

2 The lengths of cable bought in a DIY shop.

Length of cable (m)	0–1.99	2–3.99	4–5.99	6–7.99	8–9.99
Number bought	12	15	8	5	3

3 The points scored by a snooker player in the 11 frames in a competition.

Score	0–19	20–39	40–59	60–79	80–99	100–119
Number of frames	3	0	2	4	1	1

4 The amount of money taken daily (Monday–Friday) over the counter in a college bookshop during a period of six weeks.

Money taken	£0–£29.99	£30–£59.99	£60–£89.99	£90–£119.99	£120–£149.99
Number of days	3	6	10	7	4

10.8 Bar graphs

The highest recorded temperature in the shade was 58 °C, in Libya in 1922.

A **bar graph**, or **block graph**, gives a picture of a set of data which has been collected. It does not matter whether or not there is a gap between the blocks.

Example   Draw a bar graph for the colours of cars in Walker's Garage (see the example in section 10.3).

Colour	Brown	Red	Blue	White	Green	Yellow	Grey
Number of cars	4	10	7	2	4	3	1

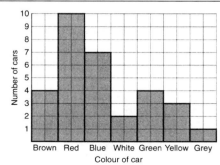

The diagram gives a clearer picture of the information than the figures in the table. Sometimes it is more convenient to draw a block graph 'on its side'.

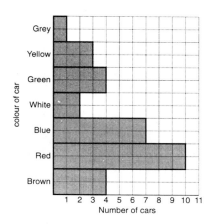

Exercise 9   Draw a block graph for the data in each question. Choose a suitable scale, and decide which way you wish to draw the diagram.

1 The number of horses, dairy cattle, beef cattle and sheep on a large collection of Russian farms.

Animal	Horses	Dairy cattle	Beef cattle	Sheep
Number	500	1100	1600	4600

2 The daily takings, over a week, on a stall in a market (taken to the nearest £).

Day	Monday	Tuesday	Wednesday	Thursday	Friday	Saturday
Takings	£45	£76	£26	£68	£88	£136

How much money did the stall take in the week?

3 The number of players in different sections of an orchestra.

Section	String	Brass	Woodwind	Percussion
Number of players	40	12	18	6

How many players are there in the orchestra?

4 The results of an assignment given to a group of students.

Result	Distinction	Credit	Pass	Fail
Number of students	8	19	15	6

How many students did not fail?

5 The annual sulphur dioxide emissions from factories and power stations during the 1980s (in millions of tonnes).

Country	UK	Spain	West Germany	Italy	France	Belgium
SO_2 emission	3.9	2.5	2.2	2.1	1.5	0.6

10.9 Frequency diagrams for discrete data

A **frequency diagram** is a particular type of bar graph. The vertical scale shows the **frequency** with which each value occurs.

Example Draw a frequency diagram of scores when two dice are thrown 100 times.

Score	2	3	4	5	6	7	8	9	10	11	12
Frequency	3	7	5	8	13	24	16	13	6	3	2

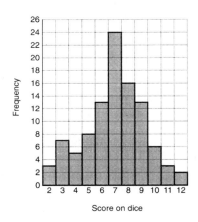

Score on dice

The mode is very easy to see from a frequency diagram — it is the highest bar. In this case the mode is 7, as 7 occurs more often than any other score.

The median is obtained by working out the average of the 50th and 51st score when placed in order. Adding the frequencies, there are 36 $(3 + 7 + 5 + 8 + 13)$ scores of 6 or below. The 50th and 51st scores are both 7, as there are 24 scores of 7 — hence the median is 7.

Exercise 10

Draw a bar graph of the information. Work out the mode and the median in each case.

1 The number of hits on a target by 39 marksmen each firing six shots.

Number of hits	0	1	2	3	4	5	6
Frequency	1	3	4	10	8	9	4

2 The number of no-score draws during a football season of 41 weeks.

Number of no-score draws	3	4	5	6	7	8
Frequency	7	13	8	5	6	2

3 The number of faulty packets per minute produced by a packaging machine, in a one-hour period.

Number of faulty packs per minute	0	1	2	3	4	5	6	7
Frequency	23	2	9	6	10	6	3	1

4 The number of GCSEs gained by students beginning a course of further education.

Number of GCSEs	4	5	6	7	8	9	10	11
Number of students	2	5	8	16	19	11	7	1

10.10 Frequency diagrams for grouped data

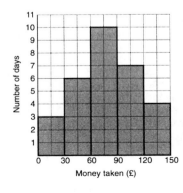

Example Draw a frequency diagram for the information in exercise 8, question 4.

Money taken	£0–£29.99	£30–£59.99	£60–£89.99	£90–£119.99	£120–£149.99
Number of days	3	6	10	7	4

There is no problem in deciding where to draw the bars, as the information is given to the nearest penny (i.e. the fourth or fifth significant figure). The mode or modal group is the £60–£89.99 group. The median can be calculated in the same way as before.

Example   The times (to the nearest minute) taken by students to complete a piece of homework is given in the table. Draw a frequency diagram.

Time taken (min)	5–9	10–14	15–19	20–24	25–29	30–34
No. of students	2	5	6	5	5	1

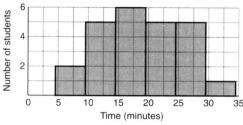

Every snowflake is hexagonal in form.

In this case the bars are drawn at 9.5 min, 14.5 min, 19.5 min, etc. because the two students in the 5–9 min column could have taken up to 9.5 minutes. Similarly, the 5 students in the 10–14 min column could have taken any time between 9.5 and 14.5 minutes.

Exercise 11   Draw a frequency diagram for each of questions 1, 2 and 3 of exercise 8.

10.11   Frequency polygons

A frequency polygon is made by joining the **centre points** of the top of the columns in a frequency diagram with straight lines. The frequency polygon is useful for seeing changes between adjoining bars, as well as for giving a general picture of how the frequencies vary.

Example   Draw a frequency polygon for the data in the table, showing the number of heads appearing when five coins are thrown 100 times.

Number of heads	0	1	2	3	4	5
Frequency	4	12	36	30	15	3

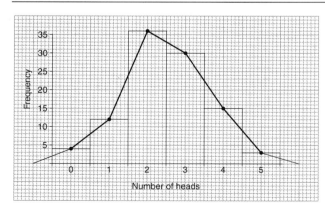

In order to show how to draw the frequency polygon, the columns have been drawn in but they are not essential. It is usual to start the frequency polygon at the centre point of the first column. The frequency polygon is, in fact not a polygon, because a polygon is a closed, straight sided figure. (In fact, to complete an actual polygon, we would need to join the first point to the x-axis at $x = -1$, the last point to the x-axis at $x = 6$, and then include the x-axis between these points.)

Exercise 12   Draw a frequency polygon for each of the four questions in exercise 10.

10.12   Mean value

The mode and median provide a simple type of average measure for a set of data. However neither take into account all of the data. The mode looks at the most popular value, and the median looks at the middle one, when put in order.

When people talk about the 'average value' of a set of numerical data, they are usually referring to the **mean** value (more correctly, the arithmetic mean).

The **mean** value of a set of N numbers is calculated by *adding* the numbers, and *dividing* this total by N.

Example   Find the mean value of
(a) 3, 6, 7, 8   (b) 24, 25   (c) 2, 4, 4, 5, 5, 6, 7, 9.

(a)   mean value is $(3 + 6 + 7 + 8) \div 4 = \frac{24}{4} = 6$
(b)   mean value is $(24 + 25) \div 2 = 24.5$
(c)   mean value is $(2 + 4 + 4 + 5 + 5 + 6 + 7 + 9) \div 8 = \frac{42}{8} = 5.25$

Example   Two dice were thrown, and the higher score noted (if both dice showed the same number, then that number was noted).
The frequency table shows the results of 100 throws of the two dice. What was the mean score?

Score	1	2	3	4	5	6
Frequency	4	7	14	22	25	28

The frequency table shows that there were 4 ones, 7 twos, 14 threes, 22 fours, 25 fives and 28 sixes.

The total of the 100 scores was

$(4 \times 1) + (7 \times 2) + (14 \times 3) + (22 \times 4) + (25 \times 5) + (28 \times 6)$
$= 4 + 14 + 42 + 88 + 125 + 168 = 441$

The mean score is therefore $\frac{441}{100} = 4.41$.

In general, to work out the mean value from a frequency table:

1 Multiply each score by its frequency.
2 Add these numbers.
3 Divide this total by the sum of the frequencies.

Exercise 13

1 My gas bills for the last four quarters were £121.53, £142.74, £85.39 and £124.06. What was my average quarterly bill?

2 The eight forwards in a rugby side weigh 103 kg, 104 kg, 96 kg, 88 kg, 98 kg, 104 kg, 98 kg and 107 kg. What is the mean weight?

3 Sandra sat six tests and Tracey sat seven tests. Their percentage scores were:

| Sandra | 64 | 72 | 66 | 38 | 49 | 60 | |
| Tracey | 47 | 49 | 86 | 71 | 36 | 50 | 56 |

Who has the higher mean score?

4 An office thermometer was read at 9.00 a.m. each day for a week.
'The temperatures, in °C, were 16, 19, 14, 14, 10, 13, 12.'
'What was the mean temperature over the week?'

5 The number of winning horses backed by a gambler each day, over a period of 24 days, is shown.
Calculate the mean number of winners per day.

Number of winners	0	1	2	3	4	5
Number of days	8	7	6	2	0	1

6 Mrs Hunter noted the number of minutes that the 0745 train was late in arriving at the station, over a period of 20 days. She claimed that the train was over three minutes late every day, on average.

Minutes late	0	1	2	3	4	5	6
Number of days	6	3	2	0	1	5	3

(a) Calculate the mean number of minutes late per day.
(b) Was Mrs Hunter correct in her claim?

7 A pigeon fanciers' club has 23 members. The frequency table shows the number of pigeons that these members have.

Number of pigeons	9	10	14	15	16	17	18	20	21
Number of members	3	2	3	5	1	2	3	2	2

What is the mean number of pigeons per member?

8 The table shows the number of students enrolled in science classes at a college.

Number of students in class	12	13	14	15	16	17	18
Number of classes	2	3	2	5	4	3	1

Work out the mean class size (average number of students per class).

10.13   Mean value of grouped data

Example   Find the mean daily takings at the college bookshop in exercise 8, question 4.

Money taken	£0–£29.99	£30–59.99	£60–89.99	£90–119.99	£120–£149.99
Number of days	3	6	10	7	4

The frequency diagram is drawn in the first example of section 10.10. We can only *estimate* the mean value, because we do not know each value; we only know the limits within which each value lies. The only reasonable assumption to make is that each value is in the *centre* of its range; in this case these central values are £15, £45, £75, £105 and £135.
These **mid-interval** values can be shown in an extra row in the table:

Money taken	£0–£29.99	£30–£59.99	£60–£89.99	£90–£119.99	£120–£149.99
Mid value	£15	£45	£75	£105	£135
Number of days	3	6	10	7	4

The best estimate of the mean value is:

$[(3 \times £15) + (6 \times £45) + (10 \times £75) + (7 \times £105) + (4 \times £135)] \div 30$
$= (£45 + £270 + £750 + £735 + £540) \div 30$
$= £2340 \div 30 = £78$

Exercise 14   Find the best estimate of the mean value for these grouped data.

1   The lengths of cable bought in an electrical wholesale shop.

Length (m)	0–4.99	5–9.99	10–14.99	15–19.99	20–24.99
Mid value (m)	2.5	7.5	12.5	17.5	22.5
Frequency	3	6	12	4	5

2   The number of free-range eggs laid by a farmer's hens.

Number of eggs	10–14	15–19	20–24	25–29	30–34
Mid value	12	17	22	27	32
Number of hens	4	7	6	9	7

3   The points scored by a snooker player in the eleven frames of a competition.

Score	0–9	10–19	20–29	30–39	40–49	50–59	60–69
Mid value	4.5	14.5	24.5	34.5	44.5	54.5	64.5
Number of frames	3	1	0	3	1	2	1

4   The number of faulty components in each batch of 100.

Number of faulty components	0–1	2–3	4–5	6–7	8–9	10–11
Mid value	0.5	2.5	4.5	6.5	8.5	10.5
Number of batches	8	5	0	1	1	2

10.14 Range

The **range** of a set of figures is: (highest value) − (lowest value). For example, when two dice are thrown and the highest score is 12 and the lowest is 2, then the range of scores is 12 − 2 = 10.

If a machine is filling cans with lemonade, the manufacturer will want the range to be as small as possible, so that (a) there is the stated volume in the can (440 ml, say) but (b) there is as little extra as possible.

Exercise 15   These questions require you to understand the mean and the range of a set of numerical information.

1   My first three telephone bills this year were £89.67, £95.62 and £107.94. If I want my mean telephone bill for the year to be under £100, what is the maximum amount that I can allow my fourth bill to be?

2 Dean's scores in his last ten innings were: 68, 2, 19, 126, 51, 88, 5, 17, 62, and 103. Ian's last seven innings were: 46, 27, 1, 133, 94, 50 and 74.

  (a) What is the range of each batsman's scores?

  (b) Which batsman had the better average (i.e. mean score per innings)?
      (*Note*: Both batsmen were 'out' in every innings.)

3 In her last six rounds of golf, Betty's scores were 81, 83, 84, 79, 77, and 82. Moira has played eight rounds recently, with scores of 74, 73, 92, 81, 74, 93, 88 and 73.

  (a) Work out the mean score per round for each lady.

  (b) What is the range for each lady?

  (c) Which lady is the more consistent?

  (d) The golf club has one place left in the team to play in a tournament. Which lady would you choose? Why?

4 The average (mean) attendance for the first five days of a six-day tennis tournament was 743. The average attendance for the whole six days was 750. How many people attended the tournament on the last day?

5 Edwin ran a market stall on Monday, Tuesday and Wednesday, and Edwina took over the stall for Thursday and Friday. Edwin's mean takings were £45.62 per day, and Edwina's mean takings were £52.32 per day.

  (a) How much did Edwin take altogether?

  (b) Work out the mean takings for the five days.

  (c) They both work on the stall on Saturday. How much, at least, will they have to take, in order to make the mean daily takings for the six days come to over £55?

Review

Exercise 16

1 The tally table shows the number of marks scored in a test that was taken by 40 students. Copy and complete the table, showing the frequencies of each mark scored.

  (a) What was the modal mark?

  (b) The 'pass' mark was 7. How many passed the test?

  (c) If you scored 3 or fewer marks, you had to resit the test. How many students had to resit?

Mark	Tally	Frequency
0	I	1
1	III	3
2	I	
3	III	
4	TTH II	
5	TTH IIII	
6	TTH II	
7	IIII	
8	II	
9		
10	III	
	Total	

Mark	Tally	Frequency
1–10	﬌ /	6
11–20	﬌ ///	
21–30	﬌ ﬌ //	
31–40	﬌ ﬌ /	
41–50	﬌ ///	
	Total	

2 For a teacher-assessed piece of coursework the marks (out of 50) for a group of students are shown in the tally table.

Copy and complete the frequency column.

(a) Draw a bar chart of this information.

(b) A score of more than 30 marks was considered satisfactory. For how many students was the coursework satisfactory?

(c) A score of 15 marks or fewer was considered 'ungraded'. Estimate the number of 'ungraded' students.

3 The registration letters of 30 cars entering a seaside car park were noted.
Make up a tally chart and frequency table. Draw a bar chart from this information.

H	K	A	T	D	D	E	G	Y	C
G	H	B	B	D	F	K	F	X	J
E	J	F	D	D	A	D	G	Y	H

(a) What was the modal registration letter?

(b) What was the registration letter of the oldest car?

(c) How many cars were older than 'G' registrations?

4 The opening bowler in a cricket team noted the number of wickets he had taken in each game throughout the season:

3 6 3 4 1 5 2 8 6 4 2 0
1 3 4 4 6 3 1 7 4 3 4 5
4 2 0 4 6 5 4 6 3 4 2

Make up a tally chart, and frequency table. Draw a bar chart.

(a) In how many games did he take no wickets?

(b) What was his modal number of wickets taken per game?

(c) In how many games did he take five or more wickets?

(d) How many wickets did he take all season?

(e) What was his mean number of wickets per game?

Work out the mode, the median, the mean, and the range, for each of the sets of figures in questions 5, 6 and 7.

5 5, 7, 9, 9

6 28, 30, 30, 30, 30, 31, 34, 34, 35, 38, 43

7 14, 16, 17, 17, 18, 18, 18, 23, 30

8 Estimate the mean height of these students from the grouped frequency table. Use mid-interval values of 155 cm, 165 cm, etc.

Height (cm)	150–159.99	160–169.99	170–179.99	180–189.99	190–199.99
Frequency	5	8	20	16	11

9 After applying a certain fertiliser, a fruit grower measured the total weight of apples collected from each tree in his orchard.

Weight of apples (kg)	2–3.99	4–5.99	6–7.99	8–9.99	10–11.99	12–13.99	14–15.99	16–17.99
Number of trees	4	3	6	10	10	5	6	2

(a) Draw a frequency diagram.
(b) How many apple trees were in the orchard?
(c) How many trees yielded at least 12 kilograms of apples?
(d) Using mid-interval values of 3 kg, 5 kg, etc., estimate the mean weight of apples per tree.

10 A new process for manufacturing long-life batteries was being evaluated. Sixty of these new batteries were tested for continual use, and the number of hours that each lasted is shown in the table.

Life (hours)	0–9.99	10–19.99	20–29.99	30–39.99	40–49.99	50–59.99
Number of batteries (frequency)	12	2	4	12	20	10

(a) Draw a frequency diagram.
(b) What was the modal frequency?
(c) Estimate the median life, to the nearest hour.
(d) Using mid-interval values of 5 h, 15 h …, estimate the mean life of a battery.

Exercise 17

The following questions are all taken from GCSE papers.

1 All the mothers at a 'baby and toddler' club were asked to complete a questionnaire.

(a) Information was collected about the birth weights, in kilograms, of their children.
Some of the weights are given.

3.26   2.95   4.08   3.63   3.04   3.20   2.76   3.02   2.50   3.86

Complete the grouped frequency table for these weights.

Birth weight w kg	Tally	Frequency
$2.00 \leqslant w < 2.50$		
$2.50 \leqslant w < 3.00$		
$3.00 \leqslant w < 3.50$		
$3.50 \leqslant w < 4.00$		
$4.00 \leqslant w < 4.50$		

(2 marks)

(b) The two-way table shows information collected about the numbers of boys and girls in each family.

Number of boys in family						
4	1					
3						
2			2	1	1	
1		6	4	2		
0			3		1	
		0	1	2	3	4

Number of girls in family

(i)   How many families have three children?   (*1 mark*)

(ii) How many children are in the largest family?   (*1 mark*)

(iii) What is the modal number of children per family? (*1 mark*)

[SEG]

2 Mrs Wright marks the English essays of a large number of boys and girls. She finds that she has the following grouped frequency distribution of marks.

Mark	1–5	6–10	11–15	16–20	21–25
Number of Essays	0	27	52	29	7

(a)   Calculate an estimate of the mean mark.   (*4 marks*)

The frequency polygon shows the distribution of marks for the boys.

(b) (i)   On the same axes, draw the frequency polygon for the distribution of marks for the girls.

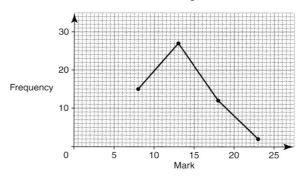

(*2 marks*)

(ii) Use the frequency polygons to compare the means and ranges of the two distributions. *(1 mark)*
[SEG]

3 The table shows the annual wages of the employees of Manoj's firm.

Wages (£ x thousands)	$10 \leqslant x < 15$	$15 \leqslant x < 20$	$20 \leqslant x < 30$	$30 \leqslant x < 40$	$40 \leqslant x < 50$
Number of employees	20	60	13	0	6

Manoj calculates that the mean wage is £19 140.

(a) Calculate an estimate of the median wage. *(2 marks)*

(b) Manoj claims that wages at his firm are too low. In order to support this claim he quotes the average wage.
Should he quote the mean or the median? Explain your answer. *(2 marks)*
[SEG]

4 A class took a test. The mean mark of the 20 boys in the class was 17.4. The mean mark of the 10 girls in the class was 13.8.

(a) Calculate the mean mark for the whole class. *(2 marks)*

5 pupils in another class took the test. Their marks, written in order, were 1, 2, 3, 4 and x. The mean of these 5 marks is equal to twice the median of these 5 marks.

(b) Calculate the value of x. *(3 marks)*
[EDEXCEL]

5 A company has two machines which should pack about 300 matches into a matchbox. The frequency polygon shows the number of matches in 50 boxes from machine A.

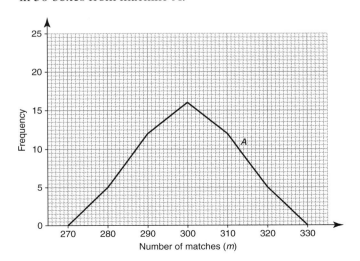

The table shows the number of matches in 50 boxes from machine B.

Number of matches (m)	$265 \leqslant m < 275$	$275 \leqslant m < 285$	$285 \leqslant m < 295$	$295 \leqslant m < 305$	$305 \leqslant m < 315$	$315 \leqslant m < 325$
Frequency	4	10	20	8	4	4

(a) On the same diagram, draw a frequency polygon of the data for machine B. *(2 marks)*

(b) (i) Find the maximum possible range for machine B. *(1 mark)*

(ii) Compare the output of machine A with that of machine B. *(2 marks)*

[OCR]

6 The weights, in kilograms, of the 11 boys in a class are

58.3 48.1 60.3 55.4 61.7 72.5
48.6 51.4 50.6 57.9 54.7

(a) Calculate the mean weight. Give your answer to an appropriate degree of accuracy. *(3 marks)*

(b) The mean weight of the 13 girls in the class is 53.1 kg.

(i) Calculate the total weight of the 13 girls. *(1 mark)*

(ii) Calculate the mean weight of the 24 pupils in the class. *(2 marks)*

[OCR]

7 Some students took a mental arithmetic test. Information about their marks is shown in the frequency table.

Mark	Frequency
4	2
5	1
6	2
7	4
8	7
9	10
10	3

(a) Work out how many students took the test. *(1 mark)*

(b) Write down the modal mark. *(1 mark)*

24 students had a higher mark than Caroline.

(c) Work out Caroline's mark. *(1 mark)*

(d) Find the median mark. *(2 marks)*

(e) Work out the range of the marks. *(2 marks)*

[EDEXCEL]

8 A manufacturer claims that the flavour of Megagum chewing gum lasts three times as long as any other gum.
One hundred teenagers chew other brands of gum. The mean time that the flavour lasts is calculated to be 2.08 hours.
The same 100 teenagers then chew Megagum. The time that they each think the flavour lasts is shown in the grouped frequency table below.

Time (t hours)	Frequency
$5.8 < t \leqslant 5.9$	2
$5.9 < t \leqslant 6.0$	15
$6.0 < t \leqslant 6.1$	47
$6.1 < t \leqslant 6.2$	34
$6.2 < t \leqslant 6.3$	2

(a) Calculate an estimate of the mean time that the flavour of Megagum lasts. (*4 marks*)

(b) Is the manufacturer's claim correct? Support your answer by calculation. (*2 marks*)
[OCR]

9 The label on a jar of honey states that it contains 454 grams of honey. The actual weight of honey in each of 20 jars was checked. The results are shown in the table below.

Weight (g)	Number of jars
454	0
455	1
456	6
457	7
458	3
459	1
460	2

(a) Work out the range of the weights in the table. (*1 mark*)

(b) Calculate the mean weight of honey per jar. (*3 marks*)
[OCR]

10

Sita plays in the school netball team. After 8 games her mean score is 6.5 goals.

(a) What is the total number of goals that Sita has scored in these 8 games? *(2 marks)*

(b) Selection for the County team is made after 9 games have been played. Sita will be chosen for the County team if her mean score is 7 goals or more.

What is the smallest number of goals she must score in the ninth game in order to be chosen? *(2 marks)*

(c) In the ninth game she actually scores 10 goals.
Does her mean score of goals increase or decrease? Explain your answer. *(2 marks)*

[NEAB]

11 A sample of 100 cartons of cottage cheese was taken from a production line. The cartons were weighed. The weights were recorded to the nearest 5 grams. The results are displayed in this frequency polygon.

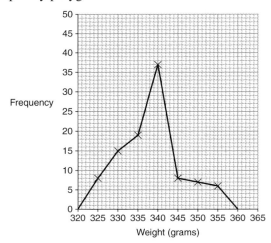

(a) How many of these cartons were recorded as less than 340 g? *(1 mark)*

A second sample was taken. The results are given in the table below.

Weight	Number of cartons
325	3
330	9
335	19
340	43
345	21
350	4
355	1

(b) Draw a frequency polygon for the second sample on the same grid as the first sample. *(2 marks)*

(c) Work out the mean of the second sample. Give your answer to the nearest gram. (You may use the extra column in the table.) *(3 marks)*

The mean of the first sample is 338 g to the nearest gram.

(d) Compare the two samples. Make two comparisons. *(2 marks)*
[MEG]

12 (a) The heights of 11 members of the Rovers football team were measured. The results, in centimetres, were:

190, 179, 181, 184, 186, 174, 171, 174, 184, 183, 174.

For these heights, find

(i) the mode, *(1 mark)*

(ii) the mean, *(2 marks)*

(iii) the range. *(1 mark)*

(b) The heights of the 11 players in the City team were also measured. Their mean was 176 cm and the range was 7 cm. Compare the heights of the two teams. *(2 marks)*
[MEG]

13 Some women walked one mile. The time taken by each was recorded. The results are as follows.

Time t minutes	$12 \leqslant t < 16$	$16 \leqslant t < 20$	$20 \leqslant t < 24$	$24 \leqslant t < 28$	$28 \leqslant t < 32$
Number of women	1	9	43	22	5

(a) (i) What is the modal class for the time taken? *(1 mark)*

(ii) Calculate an estimate of the mean time taken. *(4 marks)*

One mile is approximately 1.6 km.

(b)   Use the data to calculate an estimate of the mean time taken by these women to walk one kilometre. *(2 marks)*

[SEG]

14   The police measure the speeds, correct to the nearest mile per hour, of 100 cars passing a radar trap. The table below shows the results.

Speed (mph)	16 to 20	21 to 25	26 to 30	31 to 35	36 to 40	41 to 45	46 to 50
Frequency	2	20	32	28	8	6	4
Mid-point							

(a)   Complete the mid-point row. *(1 mark)*

(b)   Calculate, in miles per hour, an estimate of the mean speed of the cars. *(3 marks)*

(c)   On the grid, draw a frequency polygon to show the distribution of the speeds. *(2 marks)*

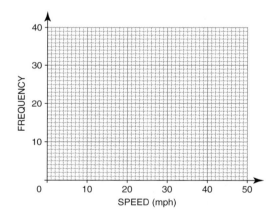

[WJEC]

15   A nurseryman measures the heights of some shrubs correct to the nearest centimetre. This table shows his results.

Height (cm)	1 to 10	11 to 20	21 to 30	31 to 40	41 to 50
Frequency	2	3	9	12	4

(a)   On a grid, draw a grouped frequency diagram to show these results. *(2 marks)*

(b)   One shrub is selected at random. What is the probability that its height, correct to the nearest cm, is between 11 cm and 20 cm? *(2 marks)*

This grouped frequency diagram shows the distribution of the heights of a different sample of shrubs.

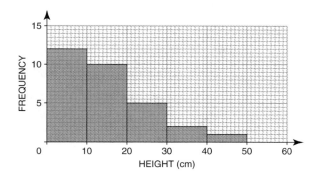

(c) Which sample of shrubs, the first or the second, was taller on average? You must give a reason for your answer. *(2 marks)*

[WJEC]

16 A supermarket collects information about the apples supplied by two different orchards. The information is displayed in the following table.

	Mean weight (g)	Modal weight (g)	Median weight (g)	Range (g)
Orchard A	110	113	112	24
Orchard B	104	100	102	12

(a) Calculate the approximate total weight, in kilograms, of 1000 apples from orchard A. You must show all your working.

(2 marks)

(b) The supermarket wants all the apples it sells to be roughly the same weight as each other.
Which orchard should it use? You must give a reason for your answer. *(2 marks)*

[WJEC]

Ideas for investigations

1 When there are quite a large number of results (e.g. the marks scored in a test by 70 students, say), we have usually grouped the marks into ranges: 1 to 9, 10 to 19, 20 to 29, etc.

Choose a set of results (from one of the questions in the chapter, if you wish).

Investigate what differences occur in (a) the estimated mean value (b) the bar chart, when you change the groupings, for example, from 1 to 6, 7 to 12, 13 to 18, 19 to 24, etc. or from 1 to 8, 9 to 16, 17 to 24, etc.

2 For a set of results, there is an approximate rule which states that:

mean − mode = 3(mean − median)

Choose four or five sets of results, and investigate the accuracy of this 'rule'.

REPRESENTING AND INTERPRETING

11.1 Line graphs

Example   A patient's temperature is taken every two hours.

Time	0600	0800	1000	1200	1400	1600	1800	2000	2200
Temperature (°C)	39.4	39.8	37.6	38.1	37.4	37.4	37.1	36.9	36.9

(a) Plot the points on a graph.

(b) Draw a line graph.

(c) Estimate the patient's temperature at 1100 and at 1700.

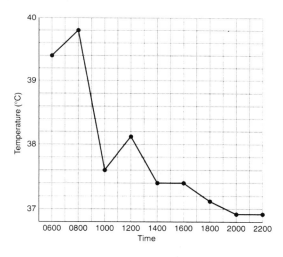

It is reasonable to join the points and complete the line graph, because the patient's temperature at intermediate times can be estimated.

(c) The patient's temperature at 1100 is estimated at 37.9° and at 1700 is 37.3 °C.

In some line graphs, values along the lines themselves have no meaning; they can, however, show a trend.

Example   The profits of a company are issued every three months in the company's quarterly account statement. The table shows the figures for a two-year period during 1990 and 1991.

Date	Mar 90	Jun 90	Sept 90	Dec 90	Mar 91	Jun 91	Sept 91	Dec 91
Profit (£M)	18	21	16	14	18	15	10	2

(a) Plot the points and join them to make a line graph.

(b) What can you say about the company's prospects?

(a)

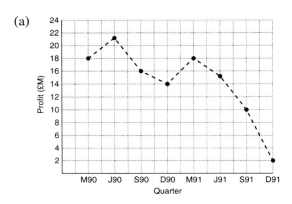

(b) Any values *along* the line graph are meaningless, because the points represent profits over a three-month period, not at any one time. The June 1990 figure of £21M could mean £7M in April, £9M in May and £5M in June, for example. The **trend** however, can be seen more easily from the line graph than from either the table or just plotting the points. For example, the rate of profit over the last year has declined more and more steeply during each quarter; it would appear that the company will make a **loss** in the next quarter.

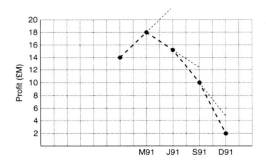

Exercise 1

1 The value of a share index at the end of trading on each day of one week is given in the table.

Day	Monday	Tuesday	Wednesday	Thursday	Friday
Share index	1788	1800	1806	1794	1790

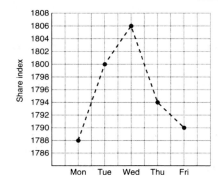

Use the graph to answer these questions;

(a) What was the lowest index? On which day?

(b) On which day was the rise from the previous day the greatest?

(c) What was the greatest fall, from one day to the next?

(d) Work out the mean index for the week.

2 The number of customers who visited 'X & Y Superstore' each day is given in the table.

Day	Mon	Tue	Wed	Thu	Fri	Sat
Number of customers	107	143	68	206	153	294

Plot these figures on a graph (similar to question 1) and join the points to form a line graph (dotted).

(a) The superstore was closed for one half-day during the week, and stayed open until 9.00 on one week night. Which was the half-day, and which night did it stay open?

(b) Why do you think Saturday had most customers?

(c) Work out the mean number of customers per *hour*, given that the store is open for 52 hours per week.

3 The temperature in a garden centre greenhouse was taken at hourly intervals, as shown in the table.

Time	0700	0800	0900	1000	1100	1200	1300	1400	1500	1600	1700	1800
Temperature (°C)	21.5	21.7	22.6	23.4	25.9	26.6	23.3	23.5	24.2	23.0	22.2	21.8

(a) Draw a line graph of the temperature through the day.

(b) Between which two times was the fall in temperature greatest?

(c) At what time, approximately, was the temperature 25 °C and rising?

(d) Estimate for how long the temperature was above 25 °C.

4 Andrea's savings account balance at the end of each month is given in the table.

Month	Jan	Feb	Mar	Apr	May	June	July	Aug	Sept	Oct	Nov	Dec
Balance (£)	120	91	84	101	160	252	326	69	75	195	211	72

Draw a line graph of the balance on Andrea's account.

(a) During which month did she withdraw most money?

(b) What was the increase in the balance from the end of February until the end of May?

(c) During which months did she spend more than she saved?

11.2 Conversion graphs

If we know that 5 miles is the same distance as 8 kilometres, then we can convert any distance, given in miles, into kilometres, (and vice-versa) by a calculation. For example, 35.6 km = 35.6 × 5 ÷ 8 = 22.25 miles. If we have a number of these conversions to do, then a useful aid is a **conversion graph**.

To make a conversion graph between miles and kilometres, mark the point P, corresponding to 8 km and 5 miles on the graph, join it to the origin, and extend it over the range of the graph paper.

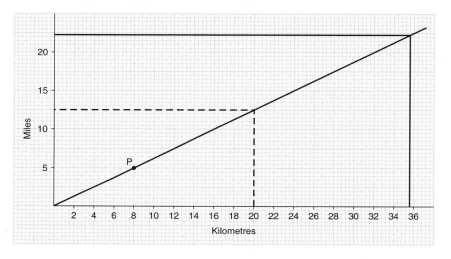

We can then read off the distance in miles corresponding to any distance given in kilometres (and vice versa). For example, the dotted lines on the graph show that 20 km is the same distance as $12\frac{1}{2}$ miles.

Exercise 2

1 If 1 kg = 2.2 lb, draw a conversion graph. Take the 'kilograms' axis from 0 kg to 6 kg. Use your graph to estimate a weight of (a) $3\frac{1}{2}$ kg in pounds (b) 10 lb in kg.

2 Assume that $1\frac{1}{2}$ Euros are equivalent to £1. Draw a conversion graph (up to £20), and estimate the value of (a) £8.75 in Euros (b) 24.5 Euros in £.

3 A gallon of water weighs about 4.5 kg. Use a conversion graph to estimate (a) the weight of 6.3 gallons of water (b) the number of gallons of water that weigh 100 kg.

4 One litre is equivalent to 1.76 pints. Draw a conversion graph, and use it to convert (a) 5 pints into litres (b) 2.75 litres into pints.

5 I can walk at an average rate of $3\frac{1}{2}$ miles in an hour. Draw a graph, and use it to estimate (a) how far I could walk in $5\frac{3}{4}$ hours (b) how long it would take to walk a distance of 10 miles.

6 If the exchange rate is 8.8 French francs to £1, (a) calculate how many French francs there are in £1000 (b) draw a conversion graph, and hence estimate (c) the cost in £ of a holiday costing 5860 French francs (d) the cost in French francs of weekend break costing £350.

7 A salmon, weighing 11.7 kg, cost £14.39 in a fishmongers. By drawing a suitable graph, estimate (a) the cost of a piece of salmon weighing 4.75 kg (b) the weight of a piece of salmon costing £8.50.

8 0 °C is the same as 32 °F and 100 °C is the same as 212 °F. Taking the Celsius axis (horizontally) from 0 to 100, mark the points (0, 32) and (100, 212) on a graph. Join these points with a straight line. From this line, estimate a temperature of (a) 70 °C in °F (b) 100 °F in °C.

9 By extending your graph in question 8 to temperatures below freezing point, estimate the temperature that is the same in both Celsius and Fahrenheit.

11.3 Pie charts

There are deep underground streams beneath some parts of the Sahara desert. People digging for fresh water have been known to catch live fish.

Example Michael has recently started to collect stamps from France, Germany, Spain and the UK. The table shows how many stamps he has. Represent this information in a pie chart.

Country	France	Germany	Spain	UK
Number of stamps	33	49	31	67

In a **pie chart**, the 'slices' of the 'pie' are in proportion to the numbers of stamps.

Michael has 180 stamps altogether. As there are 360° in one revolution, each stamp will be represented by 2°, and we can add another row to the table:

Country	France	Germany	Spain	UK
Number of stamps	33	49	31	67
Angle of sector	66°	98°	62°	134°

The pie chart can now be drawn. The order in which the sectors are drawn does not matter.

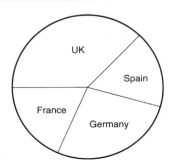

The following example shows how to work out the angles in a pie chart.

Example The students in a flower-arranging class were asked to state the colour of their favourite rose. Their replies are given in the table.

Colour	Red	White	Yellow	Pink
Number of replies	8	5	3	4

(a) Calculate the angles required for a pie chart.

(b) Draw a pie chart of the colours.

(a) $8 + 5 + 3 + 4 = 20$ *Finding the total number of replies.*

$\frac{360}{20} = 18$ *Dividing 360 by this total.*

Angle of sector for red   *Multiplying each value by this number*

$= 18° \times 8$ *to give the required angle.*

$= 144°$

Colour	Red	White	Yellow	Pink
Number of replies	8	5	3	4
Angle of sector	144°	90°	54°	72°

Check: total = 360°

(b) The pie chart can now be drawn

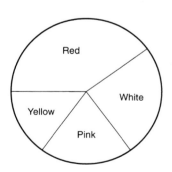

Exercise 3 For each question, calculate the required sector angles, and then draw a pie chart of the information.

1 The number of times the letters E, A, S and T occur in a paragraph from a book.

Letter	E	A	S	T
Number of occurrences	38	23	19	10

2 The number of items that are sold with chips in a fish and chip shop.

Item	Fish	Sausage	Pie	Fishcake	Spring roll
Number sold	24	26	17	32	21

3 The amount from £10 000 that is allocated to three projects and the administration in a charity.

Project	A	B	C	Administration
Money allocated	£5000	£3000	£1500	£500

4 A shop sold 90 packets of crisps in each of two weeks. The pie charts show the sales of four types of crisps for these two weeks.

(a) Which was the most popular flavour over the fortnight?

(b) Which flavours had a reduction in sales?

(c) By measuring angles in the diagrams, estimate the number of packets of plain crisps that were sold each week.

5 The pie chart shows which TV channel was watched by 600 people one evening. Estimate, by measuring angles in the pie chart, the number of people who watched each channel.

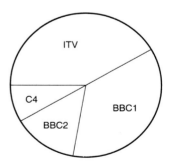

6 The number of various makes of car sold by a second-hand car dealer in a week is given in the table. Draw a pie chart of the information.

Make of car	Ford	BL	Renault	Vauxhall	Others
Number of cars sold	10	8	4	3	5

259

7 Stainless steel is made of 72% Iron, 19% Chromiun, 8% Nickel and 1% Carbon. Draw a pie chart to represent the proportions of each element in stainless steel.

8 A pie chart has four sectors. Three are equal, and the fourth is 50% larger than each of the other three.

(a) What are the angles of the sectors?

(b) Draw the pie chart.

11.4 Scatter graphs

If it is claimed that two *separate*, *variable* quantities are connected, then one way of testing the claim is to plot a **scatter graph**.

Example The scores of 12 students in a numeracy test and a literacy test are given in the table.

Student	A	B	C	D	E	F	G	H	I	J	K	L
Numeracy score	26	18	20	17	16	10	12	22	19	19	23	18
Literacy score	18	14	15	12	10	12	7	17	14	12	15	16

Draw a scatter diagram, and from the diagram decide whether there is a connection between numeracy score and literacy score.

To draw a scatter graph, we take the two scores for each student as **coordinates**. (The points are identified by the letter corresponding to each student.)

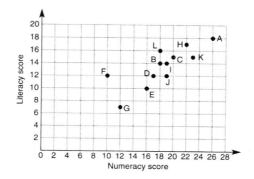

As higher numeracy scores tend to match with higher literacy scores, there seems to be some evidence to suggest that there *is* a **correlation** between these two scores.

The first electronic computer, built in 1945, weighed 30 tonnes, filled a hall of 140 square metres, and contained over 18 000 valves.

Example   A non-golfer borrows his friend's iron clubs, from a 3-iron to a 9-iron, and hits a golf ball with each of the seven clubs. The distance travelled by the ball after each hit is measured.

Iron club used	3	4	5	6	7	8	9
Distance (metres)	85	72	90	46	26	35	28

(a)   Plot the points on a scatter graph.

(b)   Is there a connection between the number of the club, and the distance the ball travelled?

(a)

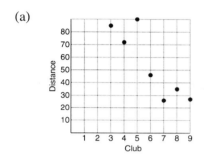

(b)   From the graph, there appears to be a trend that the *higher* the number of the club used, the *shorter* the distance travelled by the ball.

There are three general types of scatter graph; they are shown below.

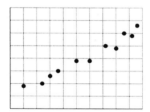

Positive correlation

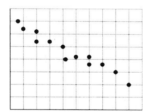

Negative correlation

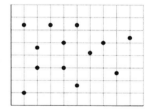

No correlation

Exercise 4   **1**   The table shows the handicap, and the score for a round of golf, for eight golfers in a competition. Plot a scatter diagram.

Golfer	John	Ann	Matt	Rena	Judy	Henry	Shaidul	Ellen
Handicap	6	7	12	1	6	8	14	6
Score	81	84	90	75	78	77	92	83

Is there a connection between the handicap and the score for a round?

2 Two judges rate eight contestants in a 'knobbly knees' competition from 1 to 8. Plot a scatter graph.

Contestant	A	B	C	D	E	F	G	H
Judge X	1	2	3	4	5	6	7	8
Judge Y	6	2	5	7	8	1	4	3

Do the judges have similar opinions?

3 The table states the marks scored in a science assignment (out of 50) and a technology assignment (out of 40) by 11 students.

Student	A	B	C	D	E	F	G	H	I	J	K
Science	42	28	40	44	30	37	42	38	33	37	45
Technology	33	26	32	29	20	24	26	26	26	30	35

Draw a scatter diagram. Does your diagram suggest that there is a link between science marks and technology marks?

4 The heights and weights of seven junior badminton players are given in the table. Draw a scatter graph.

Player	Amanda	Sally	Jim	Donna	Cliff	Suzy	Harry
Height (cm)	152	144	158	168	150	139	148
Weight (kg)	44	43	48	49	45	40	43

For these players, does taller mean heavier, in general?

11.5 Line of best fit

Look again at the scatter diagram in the previous example.

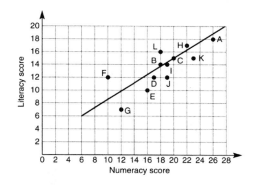

A '**trend**' line is drawn on the graph, so that it passes close to as many points as possible. This is called the **line of best fit**.

We can use the line to help us with further estimates.

Example   A student scored 24 marks in the numeracy test. What mark would the student expect to score in the literacy test?

From the 'line of best fit' we can estimate that the student would score about 18 marks in the literacy test.

Exercise 5

1 The marks scored by ten students in papers 1 and 2 of a mathematics examination are shown.

Student	1	2	3	4	5	6	7	8	9	10
Paper 1	35	56	87	43	52	94	23	35	48	56
Paper 2	43	69	72	62	51	88	24	40	40	60

(a)   Draw a scatter diagram.

(b)   Draw the line of best fit.

(c)   Maria scored 60 marks on paper 1, but was ill for paper 2. What mark might she have been expected to score on paper 2?

(d)   Daniel's paper 1 script is missing. He scored 57 on paper 2. What is his paper 1 mark likely to have been?

2 The mass of eleven paperbacks, and the number of pages in each, is given in the table.

Number of pages	79	90	100	104	116	127	140	140	148	158	166
Mass (g)	158	180	180	202	232	263	265	291	320	330	349

(a)   Draw a scatter diagram and line of best fit.

(b)   A paperback has 135 pages. What is its likely mass?

(c)   Another paperback has a mass of 190 g. How many pages is it likely to have?

3 On Sports Day there were nine competitors who had entered for both the men's 100 m race and the long jump. Their times and distances are given in the table.

100 m (time in seconds)	12.3	12.3	12.5	12.6	12.9	13.4	13.7	13.7	14.3
Long jump (length in metres)	6.03	5.95	5.40	4.93	5.04	4.69	4.66	4.12	3.87

(a)   Draw a scatter diagram and line of best fit.

(b)   Sean ran the 100 m in 13.1 s. If he had entered the long jump, how far might he have been expected to jump?

The Romans built the first known road tunnel in 36 BC. It was near Naples, and was nearly a mile long (about 1600 m).

4 Ten members of 'Weightwatchers' have been following a diet. The number of kilograms lost over various periods of time is shown in the table.

Number of weeks	3	4	5	7	7	8	8	10
Weight loss	6	6	8	9	12	15	14	16

(a) Draw a scatter graph, and the line of best fit.

(b) Does this diet seem useful, if you wish to lose a specific number of kilograms?

(c) About how many weeks would it take Susan to get her weight down from 65 kg to 52 kg?

11.6 Cumulative frequency

Example Make up a cumulative frequency table from the group frequency table, which gives the marks scored by 80 students in an examination, in groups of ten marks.

Mark	0–9	10–19	20–29	30–39	40–49	50–59	60–69	70–79	80–89	90–99
Frequency	2	4	9	13	20	14	8	6	3	1

Cumulative frequency means the frequency of that group **together** with any lower group. It gives the 'running total'. The cumulative frequency for the 10–19 group is therefore 6, as there are 6 (2 + 4) students whose marks were in the 10–19 group or any lower group (i.e. those who scored 19 or fewer). Similarly, there are 15 (2 + 4 + 9) students who scored 29 marks or fewer. The complete cumulative frequency row is added to the bottom of the table:

Mark	0–9	10–19	20–29	30–39	40–49	50–59	60–69	70–79	80–89	90–99
Frequency	2	4	9	13	20 ·	14	8	6	3	1
Cumulative frequency	2	6	15	28	48	62	70	76	79	80

This confirms that there were 80 students who took the examination, because all 80 students scored 99 marks or fewer.

Example From the frequency table, which shows the heights (to the nearest centimetre) of tomato plants in a market garden, (a) make up a cumulative frequency row (b) draw the cumulative frequency diagram.

Height (cm)	0–4	5–9	10–14	15–19	20–24	25–29
Frequency	1	4	10	19	12	4

(a) A row for the cumulative frequency has been added:

Height (cm)	0–4	5–9	10–14	15–19	20–24	25–29
Frequency	1	4	10	19	12	4
Cumulative frequency	1	5	15	34	46	50

(b) The cumulative frequency scale is drawn on the *vertical* axis, as it is in a frequency diagram.

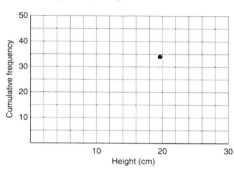

The figure 34 in the cumulative frequency row represents those plants whose heights were in the 15–19 group or any lower group. We can only be sure that the *tallest* of any of these 34 plants is 19 cm, to the nearest centimetre.

On the cumulative frequency diagram, we have to mark the cumulative frequency of 34 at *19.5 cm*, because any plant whose height is *19.5 cm or less* will be included in the figure of 34.

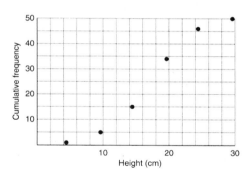

The complete cumulative frequency diagram is drawn.

There are only two types of regular polygon that you can make using rubber bands round the pins on a rectangular pin-board: squares and octagons.

The points can be joined, either by straight lines to make a cumulative frequency polygon, or by a smooth curve to make a **cumulative frequency curve**.

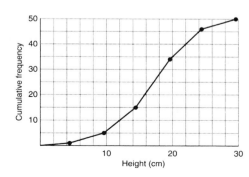

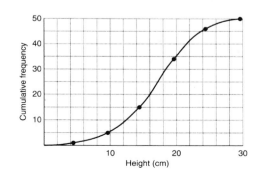

Exercise 6   For each frequency table:

(a) Make a cumulative frequency row.

(b) Draw a cumulative frequency diagram.

(c) State the sum of the frequencies (the last number in the cumulative frequency row).
(The next exercise will require you to extract some information from these cumulative frequency diagrams.)

1 A radar speed detector measured the speeds of 100 cars moving along a road, to the nearest km/h.

Speed	0–9	10–19	20–29	30–39	40–49	50–59	60–69	70–79
Number of cars	1	4	11	27	38	12	4	3

2 A market gardener has Christmas trees for sale. He classifies them by height: less than 4 feet, from 4 to 5 feet, from 5 to 6 feet, etc.

Height (feet)	up to 4	4 to 5	5 to 6	6 to 7	7 to 8	8 to 9
Number of trees	4	8	15	22	18	14

These points will have to be plotted at 4 ft, 5 ft, 6 ft etc. Why?

3 At a 'Guess the weight of the cake' stall at a Fayre, the range of guesses was noted. (Each guess was to the nearest gram.)

Weight (g)	450–499	500–549	550–599	600–649	650–699
Frequency	5	10	22	18	11

Why does it make little difference whether the points are marked at (a) 499.5, 549.5, 599.5, etc. or (b) 500, 550, 600, etc.?

4 The amount spent by a group of students on cassettes, albums or CDs in a month.

Amount	0–£4.99	£5–9.99	£10–£14.99	£15–19.99	£20–24.99	£25–29.99
Frequency	4	7	18	12	7	3

Why does it make little difference whether the points are marked at (a) £4.99. £9.99, £14.99, etc. or (b) £5, £10, £15, etc.?

11.7 Median value from a cumulative frequency diagram

Example   Estimate the median height of tomato plants in the previous example.

The **median value** is the halfway value, when the heights are put in order. In this case it is the height midway between the heights of the 25th and 26th tomato plant. The cumulative frequency scale puts the heights in order, so we can estimate the median by drawing a line across from 25.5 mark on the cumulative frequency scale until it meets the graph, and then read off the value on the horizontal axis.

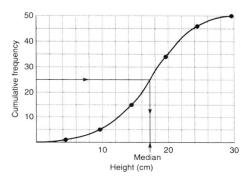

In this case the **median height** is approximately 17 cm.

In many cases, as the values will be approximate, it is reasonable to take the halfway value up the cumulative frequency axis, i.e. 25 in this case.

Exercise 7   From the cumulative frequency diagrams, estimate the median value for questions 1 to 4 in exercise 6.

11.8 Quartiles, interquartile range

Another name for the median value is the **50th percentile**. If the frequency is expressed as a percentage, then the median, or halfway value, will be obtained by taking the reading on the horizontal scale which corresponds to the value that is 50% of the way up the cumulative frequency axis.

The **lower quartile** is the value of the 25th percentile.

Also, the **upper quartile** is the 75th percentile.

Example   What are the upper and lower quartiles of the heights of tomato plants in the previous example?

Drawing lines across from 12.5 ($\frac{1}{4}$ of 50) and 37.5 ($\frac{3}{4}$ of 50), and down to the horizontal scale, the lower quartile is 13 cm approximately, and the upper quartile is about 21 cm.

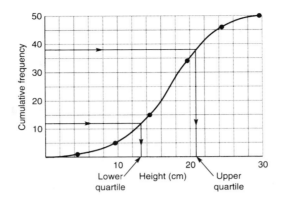

The **interquartile range** is the range between the two quartiles, and is the difference between these two values.

For example, the interquartile range for the tomato plants is
21 cm – 13 cm = 8 cm

Exercise 8   From these cumulative frequency tables and diagrams, estimate the lower and upper quartiles. State the interquartile range in each case. (You will need to draw the cumulative frequency diagrams for questions 4 and 5.)

1   The lengths of metal rods in a batch, measured to the nearest centimetre, was recorded.

Length (cm)	8	9	10	11	12	13	14	15
Cumulative frequency	14	50	105	187	267	328	362	372

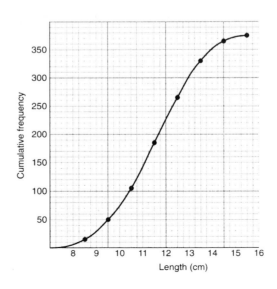

2 The value of each of the houses in a village was estimated by an estate agent, to the nearest £1000.

Value (£1000)	up to 40	40 up to 60	60 up to 80	80 up to 100	100 up to 120	120 up to 140	140 up to 160
Cumulative frequency	6	13	29	43	54	60	64

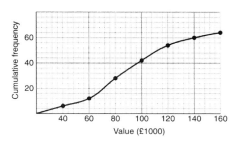

3 A library issued fines for overdue books. The cumulative frequency of each range of fines is given in the table.

Fine (pence)	0–39	40–79	80–119	120–159	160–199	200–239
Cumulative frequency	8	14	25	49	67	76

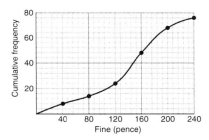

4 The tomatoes collected from each plant in a greenhouse were weighed, to the nearest 0.1 kg. The table shows the cumulative frequency of weights.

Weight (kg)	1.7 up to 1.9	1.9 up to 2.1	2.1 up to 2.3	2.3 up to 2.5	2.5 up to 2.7	2.7 up to 2.9
Cumulative frequency	3	11	21	34	36	37

5 The length of telephone calls from the students' telephone was recorded over a period of a fortnight.

Length (min)	0 up to 1	1 up to 2	2 up to 3	3 up to 4	4 up to 5	5 up to 6	6 up to 7	7 up to 8	8 up to 9	9 up to 10
Cumulative frequency	5	22	54	92	123	147	170	188	197	202

Review

1   The line graph shows the money taken in the college bookshop on each day of a week.

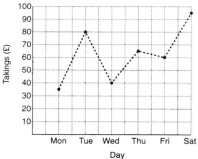

   (a)   On which day were the takings the highest?

   (b)   What were the takings on Friday?

   (c)   On which days were the takings greater than £50?

   (d)   How much was taken altogether in the week?

2   The table shows the number of copies made by a photocopier on each day during a week.

Day	Mon	Tue	Wed	Thu	Fri
Number of copies	138	154	86	208	134

   (a)   Draw a line graph of this information.

   (b)   How many copies were made on Tuesday and Wednesday?

   (c)   On which day was there a fault that prevented the use of the machine for three hours?

   (d)   How many copies were made in the week?

3   The pie chart shows the distribution of the 36 'A' level grades (A,B,C,D and E) gained by a group of students.

   By measuring the angles, estimate the number of each grade obtained.

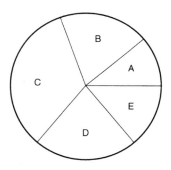

4   A pie chart is to be drawn to show the number of photocopies in question 3. Copy and complete the table which shows the angles for each sector in the pie chart.

Day	Mon	Tue	Wed	Thu	Fri	Total
Number of copies	138	154	86	208	134	
Angle	69°				67°	360°

   Draw the pie chart, labelling each sector (Mon, Tue, etc.).

5 The ages of the 24 members of an under-25 athletics team are shown in the table. Copy and complete the table to show the angles required for each sector of a pie chart.

Age	19	20	21	22	23	24
Number of athletes	6	3	2	4	4	5
Angle	90°					

(a) Draw the pie chart.

(b) What fraction of the students are aged 22 or 23?

6 The height and weight of ten of the athletes in question 6 are shown in the table.

Height (cm)	163	167	170	170	175	178	180	183	185	187
Weight (kg)	65	68	69	73	72	75	79	80	84	88

(a) Draw a scatter graph.

(b) Draw in a line of best fit.

(c) Another athlete joins the team. She is 173 cm tall. Estimate her weight from the graph.

(d) John, a reserve athlete, weighs 82 kg. How tall is he likely to be?

7 The girth (circumference) and height of a set of eight conifer trees is shown.

Girth (cm)	25	26	28	30	32	32	35	36
Height (cm)	220	240	270	275	290	305	320	340

(a) Draw a scatter graph and line of best fit.

(b) Another tree is 300 cm high. What is its likely girth?

(c) How tall will a tree be, which has a girth of 27 cm?

8 The table shows the scores gained by a group of 50 students in a test. Copy the table and complete the cumulative frequency row.

Score	0–10	11–20	21–30	31–40	41–50	51–60	61–70	71–80	81–90	91–100
Frequency	1	3	4	6	10	8	6	5	4	3
Cumulative frequency	1	4	8	?	?	?	?	?	?	?

(a) Draw a cumulative frequency curve.

(b) Estimate the median score.

(c) Estimate the lower and upper quartiles.

9 The weights of boxes of waste paper returned to a pulp mill over a ten-week period are shown in the frequency table.

Weight (kg)	0–20	20–40	40–60	60–80	80–100	100–120	120–140
Frequency	5	18	33	52	42	26	8
Cumulative frequency	5	23	?	?	?	?	?

(a) Draw a cumulative frequency curve.

(b) Estimate the median weight.

(c) Estimate the lower and upper quartiles, and the interquartile range.

Exercise 10

The following questions are all taken from GCSE papers.

1 Jane and Katy predict the finishing positions of all 8 runners in a race. After the race they compare their predictions with the actual positions. This table shows their predictions and the actual positions of the runners.

Actual position of runner	1	2	3	4	5	6	7	8
Jane's predicted position	3	2	6	1	4	5	7	8
Katy's predicted position	2	1	3	4	5	7	8	6

(a) Draw scatter graphs to show Jane and Katy's predictions compared with the actual positions. *(2 marks)*

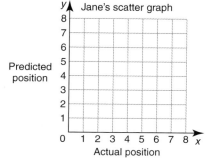

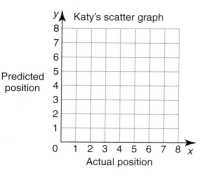

(b) Who makes the better prediction? Use the scatter graphs to explain your answer. *(1 mark)*

[SEG]

2 The graph shows the age distribution of the United Kingdom population in 1995 compared with the predicted age distribution in the year 2035.

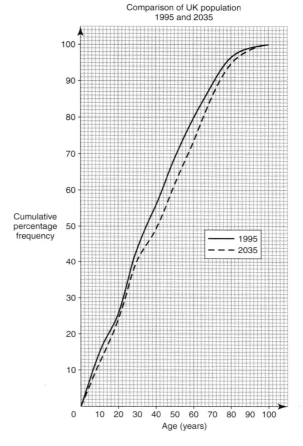

Comparison of UK population
1995 and 2035

(a) (i) What percentage of the population was younger than 50 in 1995? *(1 mark)*

(ii) What percentage of the population is predicted to be older than 70 in 2035? *(1 mark)*

(b) Complete the missing values in this table.
Show any working on the graph.

	Age distribution in 1995	Predicted age distribution in 2035
Median age		40
Upper quartile age		62
Lower quartile age		20
Interquartile range		

(4 marks)

(c) What is expected to happen to the population of the United Kingdom? Use your answers to parts (a) and (b) to explain your answer. *(1 mark)*

[SEG]

3 A number of women do aerobics for one minute. Their ages and pulse rates are shown in the table.

Age (years)	16	17	22	25	38	42	43	50
Pulse rate (per minute)	82	78	83	90	99	97	108	107

(a) Use this information to draw a scatter graph. *(2 marks)*

(b) What type of correlation is there between the ages and pulse rates of these women? *(1 mark)*

(c) Draw a line of best fit. *(1 mark)*

(d) Betty is 35 years old. Estimate her pulse rate after doing aerobics for one minute. *(1 mark)*

[AQA]

4 In a survey, 200 students were asked how many hours of sleep they had during one week. The cumulative frequency graph shows the results.

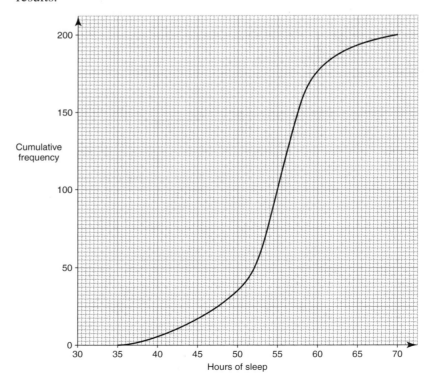

(a) How many students slept 60 hours a week or more? *(1 mark)*

(b) Use the graph to estimate:

    (i) the median; *(1 mark)*

    (ii) the interquartile range. *(2 marks)*

(c) A similar survey of retired people found that they had a median of 55 hours sleep and an interquartile range of 8 hours.

    Use this information to comment on the sleeping habits of retired people compared to students. *(1 mark)*

                                            [AQA/SEG]

5 The table shows the main language used by the people working in one department of the European Parliament.

Main Language	Number ofpeople
French	267
German	57
English	68
Others	27
Total	419

(a) (i) Bernadette was asked to show this information in a pie chart. Calculate the angle of the sector representing German. *(3 marks)*

    (ii) Bernadette started to draw the pie chart for the above data. Draw a complete pie chart. *(2 marks)*

(b) 2700 people work in another department of the European Parliament. The pie chart below shows where these people come from.

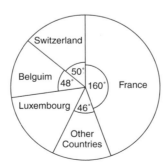

    (i) Calculate the size of the angle for Luxembourg. *(2 marks)*

    (ii) From the information given, calculate how many of the 2700 people come from France. *(2 marks)*

                                            [NEAB]

6 Information is collected about the number of organised firework displays and the number of serious injuries on Bonfire Nights over a period of years. The data is shown in this table.

Number of organised displays	85	169	277	410	432	458	496
Number of serious injuries	58	41	30	28	19	13	11

(a) Plot this data on a grid.   (*2 marks*)

(b) What does the scatter diagram tell you about the connection between the number of organised firework displays and the number of serious injuries?   (*1 mark*)

(c) Draw a line of best fit.   (*1 mark*)

(d) Use your graph to estimate

    (i)   the number of serious injuries if there were 100 organised firework displays,   (*1 mark*)

    (ii) the number of organised firework displays if there were 25 serious injuries.   (*1 mark*)

(e) The table below shows information about the number of organised firework displays on Bonfire Nights over a period of years.

Year	1987	1989	1990	1991	1995	1996	1997
Number of organised displays	85	169	277	410	432	458	496

Use a sketch graph to show how you would estimate the number of organised firework displays on Bonfire Night in 1993.

(*2 marks*)
[NEAB]

7 The ages of 500 people attending a concert are given in the table below.

Age, A, years	Number of people	Cumulative frequency
$0 \leqslant A < 10$	20	
$10 \leqslant A < 20$	130	
$20 \leqslant A < 30$	152	
$30 \leqslant A < 40$	92	
$40 \leqslant A < 60$	86	
$60 \leqslant A < 80$	18	
$80 \leqslant A < 100$	2	

(a) (i) Complete the cumulative frequency column in the table.

(1 mark)

    (ii) Draw a cumulative frequency diagram on a grid. *(3 marks)*

(b) Use your diagram to estimate

    (i) the median age, *(1 mark)*

    (ii) the interquartile range. *(2 marks)*

(c) Use your diagram to estimate the percentage of people at the concert who are under the age of 16 years. *(3 marks)*

[AQA/NEAB]

8 Five friends share the use of a computer. Each week, the computer is used for 40 hours. The table shows how long each of them uses it.

Name	Number of hours
Sue	6
Caroline	7
Richard	9
Michael	8
Diana	10

(a) Draw a labelled pie chart to display the data. *(4 marks)*

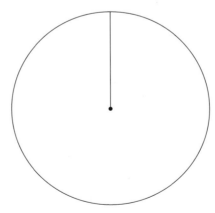

(b) They need a new ink refill for the printer. Each person pays a share of the price in proportion to the time spent on the computer. Caroline pays £4.20.

Calculate how much Richard pays. *(3 marks)*

[OCR]

9 The table below shows a grouped frequency distribution of the ages, in complete years, of the 80 people taking part in a carnival in 1997.

Age in years	0 to 29	30 to 39	40 to 49	50 to 59	60 to 69	70 to 89
Frequency	2	18	27	18	12	3

(a) Complete this cumulative frequency table. *(2 marks)*

Age (less than)	30	40	50	60	70	90
Cumulative frequency						

(b) Draw a cumulative frequency diagram to show these results.

(2 marks)

[WJEC]

10 In a school examination, 96 students each took two maths papers. Each paper was marked out of 100. The results for Paper 1 are given in the table below.

Exam mark (M)	Number of students	Cumulative Frequency
$0 \leqslant M \leqslant 20$	0	
$20 < M \leqslant 30$	2	
$30 < M \leqslant 40$	9	
$40 < M \leqslant 50$	19	
$50 < M \leqslant 60$	25	
$60 < M \leqslant 70$	20	
$70 < M \leqslant 80$	10	
$80 < M \leqslant 90$	8	
$90 < M \leqslant 100$	3	

(a) (i) Complete the cumulative frequency column for the table.
(1 mark)

(ii) Draw a cumulative frequency diagram on a grid. *(3 marks)*

(b) Showing your method clearly, use your diagram to estimate

(i) the median mark, *(1 mark)*

(ii) the interquartile range. *(2 marks)*

(c) The students' results on Paper 2 have a median of 61 marks and an interquartile range of 17 marks.
Which exam paper did the students find easier? Give a reason for your answer. *(1 mark)*

[NEAB]

11 In a survey a researcher asks 72 people to name their favourite types of television programmes. The results are shown in the table below.

Type of programme	Soaps	Drama	Comedy	Sport
Frequency	40	4	10	18

(a) Draw a pie chart to show the distribution of the results. You must show how you calculate the angles of your pie chart. (*4 marks*)

(b) The pie chart below shows the results of a similar survey of 192 people.

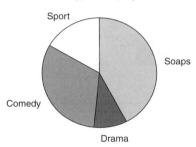

Favourite type of TV programme

Which survey, the first or the second, had the greater number of people whose favourite type of television programme was sport? Show your working below. (*3 marks*)

[WJEC]

12 Year 8 pupils were given a problem to solve. The cumulative frequency curve shows the time taken for the 50 pupils to solve the problem.

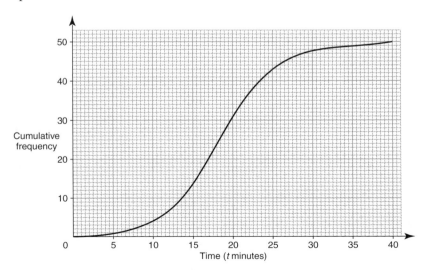

(a) (i) Find the number of pupils who took more than 25 minutes to solve the problem. (*1 mark*)

(ii) Find the number of pupils who took between 15 and 20 minutes to solve the problem. (*1 mark*)

[MEG]

Two years later, the same 50 pupils, who were now in Year 10, solved the problem again. The table shows the time taken for the pupils to solve the problem.

Time (*t* minutes)	$0 < t \leqslant 5$	$5 < t \leqslant 10$	$10 < t \leqslant 15$	$15 < t \leqslant 20$	$20 < t \leqslant 25$	$25 < t \leqslant 30$	$30 < t \leqslant 35$
Number of pupils	4	12	16	9	6	2	1

(b) (i) Complete the cumulative frequency table below. (*1 mark*)

Time (*t* minutes)	$t \leqslant 0$	$t \leqslant 5$	$t \leqslant 10$	$t \leqslant 15$	$t \leqslant 20$	$t \leqslant 25$	$t \leqslant 30$	$t \leqslant 35$
Number of pupils	0	4						50

(ii) Draw the cumulative frequency curve for the Year 10 times on the same grid as the Year 8 curve. (*2 marks*)

(c) (i) Find the median time taken by the Year 10 pupils. (*2 marks*)

(ii) Had the performance of the pupils in solving the problem improved over the two years? Give two comparisons to support your answer. (*2 marks*)

[MEG]

13 The table gives information about the age and mileage of a number of cars. The mileages are given to the nearest thousand miles.

Age (years)	1	3	5	3	5	4	7	$4\frac{1}{2}$
Mileage (nearest 1000)	9 000	26 000	46 000	27 000	41 000	39 000	62 000	40 000

(a) Use this information to draw a scatter graph. (*2 marks*)

(b) What type of correlation is there between the age and mileage of cars? (*1 mark*)

(c) By drawing a line of best fit estimate the age of a car with a mileage of 54 000. (*2 marks*)

[SEG]

14 The length of life of 100 batteries of a certain make was recorded. The table shows the results.

Length of life (hours)	< 10	< 15	< 20	< 25	< 30	< 35	< 40
Cumulative frequency	0	2	9	50	86	96	100

(a) Draw a cumulative frequency graph to illustrate these data.

(2 marks)

(b) How many batteries had a life of more than 32 hours? *(1 mark)*

(c) Use your graph to estimate:

  (i) the median: *(1 mark)*

  (ii) the interquartile range. *(3 marks)*

[SEG]

Ideas for investigations

1 Some people say a bar graph is better than a pie chart for presenting information.

By choosing examples from colour supplements, finance sections, etc. of newspapers and magazines, investigate the advantages and disadvantages of each type of diagram.

2 Investigate ways of improving the 'line of best fit' on a scatter graph, to ensure that the sum of the distances of each point from the line is the least that it can be.

PROBABILITY 12

12.1 Probability scales

How likely is it that these three events will happen?

A: You will find a 20p coin on the ground next week.

B: You will watch more than two hours of television next week.

C: You will buy a cassette next week.

Event A is most unlikely, while B is very likely. Event C will depend on a number of factors, and you just might buy a cassette.
We can put these events in order of likelihood, by marking their positions on a scale.

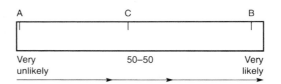

In order to express these likelihoods in mathematical terms, we can give them a number from 0 to 1. The likelihoods are then called **probabilities**.
Event A has a very small probability — possibly 0.01.
Event B has a high probability — it could be 0.95.
Event C could have a probability of between 0.4 and 0.5.

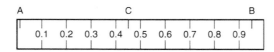

Probabilities can be expressed as percentages as well as decimals, as is shown on this scale.

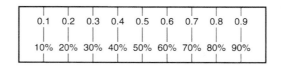

The probability of event A is 1%, the probability of event B is 95%, and the probability of event C could be between 40% and 50%.

Exercise I

For each of the events P, Q, R, S and T,

(a) estimate its probability (as a decimal and as a percentage)

(b) mark its letter in the appropriate place on a probability scale.

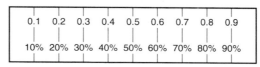

P: a coin land 'tails' when it is spun.
Q: two coins both land 'tails' when they are spun.
R: it will snow next winter somewhere in Great Britain.
S: you will back the winner of the Grand National horse race.
T: the first four cards you are dealt from a pack are all the same suit.

12.2 Certainty, impossibility

An event which is **certain** to occur has a probability of 1 (or 100%).
An event which is **impossible** has a probability of 0 (or 0%).
All other events must have a probability of between 0 and 1.

The number 0.99999...
is equal to 1.

For example, the probability of 'throwing a total of 14 with two dice' is 0, because it is impossible to have a score of 14 with only two dice.

Also, the probability that 'the day of your birthday is a number less than 32' is 1, because it is certain that the day is less than 32, as the longest months have only 31 days.

12.3 Calculating probabilities

Example   Four sweets, coloured red, green, brown and yellow, are wrapped in the same way so that they all look the same. If you pick one sweet, what is the probability that it is green?

On a probability scale, we might guess at between 20% and 30%. We can work out the probability accurately, by a method which uses fractions. Firstly, find out how many possible equally likely outcomes there are. In this example there are *four*, because there are four sweets to pick from. Secondly, work out how many of these are asked for in the question. In this example, we are asked for the probability of a green sweet, and there is only *one* of these.

The probability of picking a green sweet is therefore:

$\frac{1}{4}$ *The number of ways the event can occur.*
     The total number of possible outcomes.

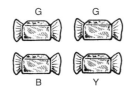

Example   The red sweet is exchanged for a green sweet. Now what is the probability that you pick a green sweet?

There are *two* ways in which the event can occur, out of a total of *four* possible outcomes.

The probability of a green sweet is $\frac{2}{4} = \frac{1}{2}$.   **Simplifying the answer.**

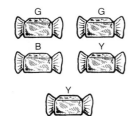

Example   Another yellow sweet is now added. What is the probability of picking (a) a green sweet (b) a brown sweet (c) a black sweet (d) either a yellow or a brown sweet?

(a) The probability of picking a green sweet $= \frac{2}{5}$ *Two green sweets.*
   A total of five sweets.

(b) The probability of picking a brown sweet $= \frac{1}{5}$ *One brown sweet.*
   A total of five sweets.

(c) The probability of picking a black sweet $= 0$ *None of the sweets is black.*

(d) The probability of picking either a yellow or a brown sweet

$= \frac{3}{5}$ *Three sweets are either yellow or brown.*

Exercise 2

1 In his bag, Colin has three similar notebooks. Two are for science and one is for technology. If he picks one notebook from his bag, what is the probability that it is (a) one of the science notebooks (b) the technology notebook?

2 Mandy has seven pieces of paper. She writes 'Monday' on one piece, 'Tuesday' on another, and so on, up to 'Sunday' on the last piece. Each piece is folded up, and then Brenda picks one of them. What is the probability that Brenda picks (a) Wednesday (b) Monday or Thursday (c) neither Saturday nor Sunday?

3 Harriet has two ordinary dice. One falls on to the floor. What is the probability that it lands showing (a) a four (b) either a two or a three (c) an odd number (d) any number except five?

4 There are five blue and seven black pens in a drawer. One pen is picked out. What is the probability that it is (a) blue (b) black (c) red (d) either black or blue?

5 Ian is playing a board game in which there are twelve counters. Three are red, four are white and five are green. He shakes the twelve counters in a cup, and then picks one out. What is the probability that it is (a) green (b) white (c) either green or red (d) not red (e) brown?

6 I buy ten raffle tickets at a village fête. Altogether there are 200 tickets sold.

(a) What is the probability that I have the winning ticket?

(b) Of the 200 tickets, how many would I need to buy to ensure that my probability of winning is greater than $\frac{1}{4}$?

7 There are 37 possible numbers on a roulette wheel (0, 1, 2, …, 36). What is the probability that I win if I bet on:

(a) 8   (b) 12 or 13

(c) 17, 18, 19, or 20   (d) 30 or over

(e) a multiple of 3   (f) an even number?

12.4 Estimating probabilities

In the examples in section 12.3, we have been able to work out probabilities by knowing beforehand all the equally likely possible outcomes. There are some situations, however, where we can only make *estimates* of probabilities based upon experimental results.

Example   A cube has one of the three letters A, B or C on each of the six faces. You do not know how many faces are As, Bs or Cs. The cube is thrown; the results of the first ten throws are: two As, six Bs and two Cs.

(a) What are the **experimental** probabilities of each letter?

(b) How many faces are likely to be As, Bs or Cs?

(a) $p(A) = \frac{2}{10} = \frac{1}{5}$, $p(B) = \frac{6}{10} = \frac{3}{5}$ and $p(C) = \frac{2}{10} = \frac{1}{5}$.

p(A) is a shorthand for 'the probability of the event A occurring'.

(b) As just over half of the results are Bs, it is likely that, based on these ten throws, there are either 3 or 4 faces with a B.
If 3 faces are B, then there must be *either* 2 As and a C or an A and 2 Cs.
If there are 4 Bs, then there is one A and one C.

Clearly the information is not enough to enable you to be reasonably sure how many of each letter is on each face of the cube. With more throws, you should be able to be more accurate in your guesses.

Example   The next 20 throws produce three As, thirteen Bs and four Cs. Looking at all 30 results so far:

(a) *Now* what are the experimental probabilities of each letter?

(b) How many faces are likely to be As, Bs or Cs?

The results so far are five As, nineteen Bs and four Cs.

(a) $p(A) = \frac{5}{30} = \frac{1}{6}$, $p(B) = \frac{19}{30}$ and $p(C) = \frac{6}{30} = \frac{1}{5}$

(b) It would appear that the cube is likely to have one A, four Bs and a C.

1 There are 24 eggs on a tray. 23 are used, of which three are found to have double yolks. What is the probability that the remaining egg is a 'double-yolker'?

2 In her last 30 shots, Judi, a shooter at netball, has scored 22 times. What is the probability that she scores with her next shot?

3 Colin shuffles a pack of playing cards and deals Syeda the first eight cards. She picks one card at random from these eight and makes a note of its suit. She then returns it to the other seven, shuffles the eight cards, and again picks one at random, noting its suit. After 12 turns she has noted a heart six times, a club four times, and a diamond and a spade once each.

(a) What is the probability of a heart?

(b) How many cards of each suit do you think make up Syeda's eight cards?

4 A plastic bottle contains coloured beads. When it is turned upside down, one bead is visible through the bottle top. Brian shakes the bottle, and turns it upside down 20 times, noting the colour of the bead each time.

Colour of bead	White	Red	Black
Frequency	12	3	5

(a) Using these figures, what is the probability that, when Brian again turns the bottle upside down, the bead is (i) red (ii) black (iii) white (iv) blue?

(b) If there are 60 beads in the bottle, how many are likely to be (i) red (ii) black (iii) white (iv) blue?

12.5 Comparing probabilities as decimals, fractions and percentages

In the example in section 12.4, where a cube had the letters A, B and C on its faces, the probabilities after 30 throws were:

$$p(A) = \tfrac{1}{6}, \; p(B) = \tfrac{19}{30} \text{ and } p(C) = \tfrac{1}{5}$$

Changing these fractions into decimals gives,

Dividing the top number by the bottom number.

$p(A) = \tfrac{1}{6}$	$p(B) = \tfrac{19}{30}$	$p(C) = \tfrac{1}{5}$
$= 0.1666\ldots$	$= 0.6333\ldots$	$= 2$
$= 0.167$	$= 0.633$	$= 0.2$

Rounding to three decimal places.

Changing these into percentages gives,

p(A) = 16.7%, p(B) = 63.3% and p(C) = 20%   *Multiplying by 100.*

All probabilities *must* lie between 0 and 1; hence probabilities (other than certainty) expressed as:

- **fractions** must have the numerator *smaller* than the denominator
- **decimals** must begin with '0.' …
- **percentages** must be *less* than 100%

Exercise 4   In each question, write down the probability of each of the two events as a fraction. By converting to a decimal (or a percentage), decide which of the two events is more likely to happen.

1 (i) Choosing a girl from a group of eight girls and twelve boys.
    (ii) Choosing a girl from a group of six girls and eight boys.

2 (i) Picking a green sock from three green and five red socks.
    (ii) Picking a white sock from two white and three black socks.

3 (i) Picking a club from a pack of cards.
    (ii) Picking a red pen from a bag with one red and four blue pens.

4 (i) Choosing a 2p piece from a purse with five 2p pieces and two 10p pieces.
    (ii) Choosing a 5 note from a wallet with three £5 notes and one £10 note.

5 (i) Winning a raffle, if you have bought four of the 100 tickets sold.
    (ii) Winning a raffle, if you have bought fifteen of the 350 tickets sold.

12.6 Combined events

Example   What is the probability of a score of 11 when two dice are thrown?

There are two ways of scoring 11: either 6–5 or 5–6.

The probability that the first die scores a 6 is $\frac{1}{6}$.

The probability that the second die scores a 5 is $\frac{1}{6}$

The probability of this *combined* event is $\frac{1}{6} \times \frac{1}{6} = \frac{1}{36}$.

Similarly, the probability of a 5 on the first die and a 6 on the second is $\frac{1}{6} \times \frac{1}{6} = \frac{1}{36}$.

As these are the only two ways of scoring 11, then the probability of a score of 11 is $\frac{1}{36} + \frac{1}{36} = \frac{2}{36} = \frac{1}{18}$.

With 'two-dice' problems, it is often easier to work out probabilities by showing all 36 possibilities in a 6×6 square.

		second score					
		1	2	3	4	5	6
first score	1	2	3	4	5	6	7
	2	3	4	5	6	7	8
	3	4	5	6	7	8	9
	4	5	6	7	8	9	10
	5	6	7	8	9	10	(11)
	6	7	8	9	10	(11)	12

$$p(11) = \tfrac{2}{36}$$
$$= \tfrac{1}{18}$$

Exercise 5   Find the probability of each event, when two dice are thrown:

1 a score of 6   **2** a score greater than 9

3 an even number   **4** either 3 or 4

5 a score of 13

If the outcomes of two events are **independent**, i.e. the results of one are not affected by the results of the other, then the probability of a **combined event** is obtained by *multiplying* the two separate independent probabilities.

Example   A boy and a girl are chosen from a group of four boys, Alan, Bablus, Colin and Damian, and three girls, Judith, Kathleen and Maureen. What is the probability that the chosen pair are (a) Alan and Kathleen (b) Bablus and not Judith (c) neither Colin nor Maureen?

(a) P(Alan) $= \tfrac{1}{4}$ and p(Kathleen) $= \tfrac{1}{3}$

Hence p(Alan and Kathleen) $= \tfrac{1}{4} \times \tfrac{1}{3} = \tfrac{1}{12}$

(b) (Bablus) $= \tfrac{1}{4}$ and p(not Judith) $= \tfrac{2}{3}$

As 2 of the girls are not Judith.

Hence p(Bablus and not Judith) $= \tfrac{1}{4} \times \tfrac{2}{3}$

$= \tfrac{2}{12} = \tfrac{1}{6}$

(c) P(not Colin) $= \tfrac{3}{4}$ and p(not Maureen) $= \tfrac{2}{3}$

Hence p(neither Colin nor Maureen) $= \tfrac{3}{4} \times \tfrac{2}{3}$

$= \tfrac{6}{12} \times \tfrac{1}{2}$

Exercise 6

1 When I toss two coins, what is the probability that they both land 'heads'?

2 In a game, I have to toss a coin and pick a card from the four aces. If the coin lands 'heads', and I pick the ace of hearts, I win. What is the probability that I win?

3 Pens are packed in boxes of ten, of which eight are black and two are red. Kate picks a pen from a box, and Emma picks a pen from another box. What is the probability that they both pick (a) a black pen (b) a red pen?

4 The probability that the No. 33 bus is late at Harry's bus stop is $\frac{1}{5}$.

   (a)   What is the probability that the next No. 33 is on time?

   (b)   What is the probability that the next two No. 33's are on time?

5 One of the four batteries in Samantha's personal stereo is flat. Also, one of the three batteries in Clive's torch is flat. If two batteries are chosen, one from Samantha and one from Clive, what is the probability that neither is flat?

12.7 Bar graphs

One gram of gold can be drawn out into a wire 2 kilometres long.

In earlier chapters we have drawn bar graphs of the results of experiments. We can make the heights of the bars represent probabilities if we change the scale from frequency to **relative frequency**. This we can easily do by dividing *each* outcome by the *total number* of outcomes.

Relative frequency = estimate of probability

Example   Two dice are thrown 100 times. The table shows the results. Draw a relative frequency diagram. What is the probability that the outcome is (a) 8 (b) less than 5 (c) an odd number?

Score	2	3	4	5	6	7	8	9	10	11	12
Frequency	3	6	7	10	13	18	15	14	8	5	1

The relative frequency row is worked out by *dividing* each frequency by 100:

Score	2	3	4	5	6	7	8	9	10	11	12
Frequency	3	6	7	10	13	18	15	14	8	5	1
Relative frequency	0.03	0.06	0.07	0.1	0.13	0.18	0.15	0.14	0.08	0.05	0.01

The diagram can now be drawn.

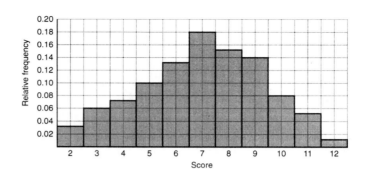

(a) p(8)   = 0.15

(b) p(less than 5)   = 0.03 + 0.06 + 0.07
                       = 0.16

(c) p(odd)   = 0.06 + 0.1 + 0.18 + 0.14 + 0.05
                       = 0.53

Exercise 7

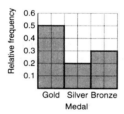

1 The relative frequency of medals awarded at a sports meeting to a college athletic team is shown in the diagram. The ribbon attached to one of the medals is faulty.
What is the probability that the faulty ribbon is attached to a medal which is (a) gold (b) not bronze (c) either silver or bronze?

2 The diagram shows the relative frequency of heights of sunflowers grown by a group of science students. What is the probability that a sunflower was: (a) between 1.6 m and 1.8 m, (b) taller than 1.8 m, (c) shorter than 1.4 m?

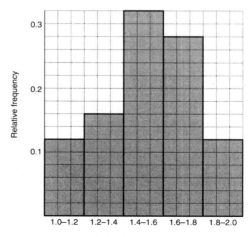

3 A darts player's scores were noted after each throw of three darts. The table shows the relative frequency of scores.

Score	under 20	21–40	41–60	61–80	81–100	over 100
Relative frequency	0.15	0.3	0.25	0.1	0.1	0.1

(a) Draw a relative frequency diagram.

(b) What is the probability that, on the next throw of three darts, the player scores (i) 40 or less (ii) over 80 (iii) more than 60?

4 Fifty students following a statistics course are grouped by age. The table shows the number in each age band.

Age band	under 20	20 to 29	30 to 39	40 to 49	over 50
Number	27	13	6	3	1

(a) Add a relative frequency row, and draw a relative frequency diagram.

(b) If a statistics student is selected at random, what is the probability that the student is (i) under 20 (ii) 30 or over (iii) under 50?

12.8 Adding probabilities

In an experiment, if two outcomes cannot both happen together, then the probability of either result occurring is the *sum* of the probabilities of the two individual outcomes.
You have been using this principle in answering some of the questions in the previous exercise, because the diagrams separate the outcomes into events that cannot occur simultaneously.
Outcomes like this are said to be **mutually exclusive**.

Example   What is the probability of throwing either a 3 or a 5 with an ordinary die?

$p(3) = \frac{1}{6}$ and $p(5) = \frac{1}{6}$.

$p(3 \text{ or } 5) = \frac{1}{6} + \frac{1}{6}$

These outcomes cannot both occur together.

$= \frac{2}{6} = \frac{1}{3} \ (= 0.33 \ ...)$

Example   I have been dealt these eight cards. I ought to have been dealt seven cards, so my partner removes one card from these eight. What is the probability that the card removed is either a 6 or a 7?

$p(6) = \frac{3}{8}$ and $p(7) = \frac{2}{8}$.

$p(6 \text{ or } 7) = \frac{3}{8} + \frac{2}{8}$ **The outcomes are mutually exclusive.**

$= \frac{5}{8}$ ($= 0.625$)

Exercise 8

1   There are three green, four white and five red counters in a jar. One is picked out. What is the probability that it is (a) either red or white (b) either green or red?

2   Barbara has six coins in her purse. Three are 10p pieces, one is a 20p piece and the other two are 2p pieces. She picks one coin out of her purse.
What is the probability that it is (a) either a 2p or a 10p piece (b) either a 10p or a 20p piece?

3   Twelve of Marie's cassettes fall out of their boxes on to the floor. She knows that five are Queen tapes, four are Julian Lennon, two are INXS and one is Simply Red. What is the probability that the first cassette she picks up is (a) either Queen or INXS (b) Julian Lennon or Simply Red?

4   The table shows the handicaps of 16 golfers entering a competition.

Handicap	10	9	8	6	5	3
Number of players	6	4	1	1	3	1

What is the probability that the first person drawn will have a handicap of (a) ten (b) five or six (c) eight or more?

5   Gerald is dealt a hand of thirteen cards, in which five are hearts, four are diamonds, one is a club and three are spades.
He picks a card at random.
What is the probability that the card is (a) a heart or a spade (b) a club or a diamond (c) a red card?

12.9 **P(A) = I − p(not A)**

Example When a die is thrown, what is the probability that the number is (a) a 4 (b) not a 4?

(a) $p(4) = \frac{1}{6}$

(b) This can be worked out in two ways.

Method 1

If the number is *not* a 4 it must be either 1, 2, 3, 5 or 6.

$$p(1, 2, 3, 5 \text{ or } 6) = \frac{1}{6} + \frac{1}{6} + \frac{1}{6} + \frac{1}{6} + \frac{1}{6}$$

$$= \frac{5}{6}$$

Method 2

As the number must be *either* a 4 or not a 4, these two probabilities must add up to 1. Hence

$$p(\text{not a } 4) = 1 - p(4)$$

$$= 1 - \frac{1}{6}$$

$$= \frac{5}{6} \text{ as before.}$$

In this example both methods are quite straightforward.

Example What is the probability that when I am dealt a card, it is (a) an ace (b) not an ace?

(a) $p(\text{ace}) = \frac{4}{52} = \frac{1}{13}$

(b) It is easy to work out p(not an ace):

$$1 - p(\text{ace}) = 1 - \frac{1}{13}$$

$$= \frac{12}{13}$$

Exercise 9

1 Claire is a keen hockey player. The probability that she does not score a goal in any game is 0.3. What is the probability that she scores at least one goal in the next game?

2 When six dice are thrown, the probability that there are no 3s showing is 0.335. What is the probability that there is at least one 3 showing?

3 When four coins are thrown, the probability that all land 'heads' is $\frac{1}{16}$. (a) What is the probability that they all land 'tails'? (b) What is the probability that, in the four coins, there will be at least one 'head' and one 'tail'?

4 A box contains 18 coloured straws: ten are red, five are yellow and three are green. If one straw is selected, what is the probability that it is (a) yellow (b) not green (c) not red?

5 A bag contains a set of snooker balls. There are 15 reds, and one each of the colours white, yellow, green, brown, blue, pink and black. One ball is picked out at random. What is the probability that it is (a) white (b) not white (c) red (d) not red?

12.10 Repetition with replacement

Example   There are five 10p pieces and three 20p pieces in a box.
I select two coins, one after the other.
What is the probability that *both* coins are 20p pieces, if the first coin is replaced before the second selection?

$p(20) = \frac{3}{8}$ *There are 8 coins, 3 of which are 20p.*

For the second selection,

$p(20p) = \frac{3}{8}$ *The same as for the first selection.*

Hence, $p(\text{two } 20p) = \frac{3}{8} \times \frac{3}{8} = \frac{9}{64}$ $(= 0.14...)$

Exercise 10

1 In her cupboard, Jane has six white socks and two blue socks. She takes one sock out, puts it back, then picks another sock. What is the probability that she has picked (a) two white socks (b) two blue socks?

2 Amanda picks a counter from a box which contains two green and two brown counters. She puts the counter back, and then Brenda picks a counter from the box. What is the probability that both counters are green?

3 George has a 'full house' in a game of poker. His five cards are three kings and two sevens. Harry picks one of these cards, returns it, shuffles the five cards and picks another. What is the probability that both cards are kings?

4 A teacher says, 'Choose any letter from the word "seven" and write it down.' What is the probability that both Tim and Jim write down the letter 'e'?

5 There are two dice. Michelle and Tracy each throw one of them. What is the probability that neither of them throws a '6'?

6 In a standard set of 28 dominoes there are seven doubles. Jake turns over one domino, turns it over again and shuffles it with the others, then turns over another domino. What is the probability that neither domino is a double?

7. Angie shuffles together six 'Chance' cards and four 'Community Chest' cards. She picks one card out, then returns it, and shuffles the cards. She does this two more times. Betty says that the probability that Angie picks three 'Chance' cards is 1/6. Is Betty correct?

8 Molly has four blue pens and one red pen in her pencil case. Polly has exactly the same in her pencil case. Each girl picks out a pen at random and puts it on the desk. What is the probability that neither pen is red?

12.11   Tree diagrams

When we are considering two events, whether they are both different events or whether they are a repeat of the same event, a useful way of showing the probabilities is to draw a **tree diagram**.
The most straightforward example is to investigate the outcomes when two coins are thrown.

Example   A 10p and a 50p piece are thrown. Draw a tree diagram to show all of the outcomes and their probabilities.

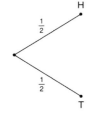

Firstly, the 10p coin has two outcomes: either heads (H) or tails (T). Each outcome has a probability of $\frac{1}{2}$; the first section of the diagram can be drawn:

Along each branch we write the probability of that outcome.

For each outcome (H or T) of the 10p coin, the 50p piece could land heads or tails, each again with a probability of $\frac{1}{2}$. We draw another section on to each of the first set of outcomes.

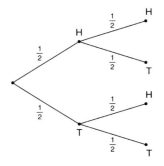

From any starting point, the sum of the probabilities on the branches must add up to 1.

It is convenient to draw an 'outcome/probability' table beside the diagram. In the 'outcome' column we list all the possible outcomes that can be obtained by following all possible branches of the tree diagram.

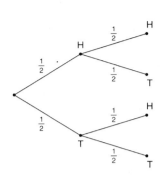

Outcome	Probability
HH	
HT	
TH	
TT	

To work out the probability of each outcome, we *multiply* the probabilities along the branches leading to each outcome. In this example the probability along each branch is $\frac{1}{2}$, so each combined outcome has a probability of $\frac{1}{4}$. The complete tree diagram and table is shown below.

In a random group of 25 people, the probability that two people have the same birthday (for example, 7th February) is better than evens.

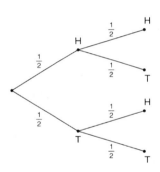

Outcome	Probability
HH	$\frac{1}{2} \times \frac{1}{2} = \frac{1}{4}$
HT	$\frac{1}{2} \times \frac{1}{2} = \frac{1}{4}$
TH	$\frac{1}{2} \times \frac{1}{2} = \frac{1}{4}$
TT	$\frac{1}{2} \times \frac{1}{2} = \frac{1}{4}$

Questions can then be answered, using the information in the table.

Example What is the probability of (a) two heads (b) two tails (c) a head and a tail?

(a) $p(HH) = \frac{1}{4}$

(b) $p(TT) = \frac{1}{4}$

(c) There are two ways of getting a head and a tail: either HT or TH. Each has a probability of $\frac{1}{4}$.

Therefore $p(HT \text{ or } TH) = \frac{1}{4} + \frac{1}{4} = \frac{1}{2}$.

Note: The **sum** of the probabilities in the table *must* be 1, as we have listed *all* the possible outcomes. In this example, $\frac{1}{4} + \frac{1}{4} + \frac{1}{4} + \frac{1}{4} = 1$.

Example   When I throw two dice, what is the probability that I get (a) a double 4 (b) one 4 (c) no 4s?

Although there are six outcomes for each of the dice, for the purposes of this question we are concerned only whether or not we get a 4.

$p(4) = \frac{1}{6}$,

then $p(\text{not } 4) = 1 - \frac{1}{6} = \frac{5}{6}$ *using p(not A) = 1 – p(A).*

(We could have said $p(\text{not } 4) = p(1, 2, 3, 5 \text{ or } 6) = \frac{1}{6} + \frac{1}{6} + \frac{1}{6} + \frac{1}{6} + \frac{1}{6} = \frac{5}{6}$: the first approach is much quicker, however.)

The tree diagram can now be drawn, followed by the table.

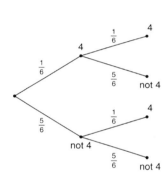

Outcome	Probability
4,4	$\frac{1}{6} \times \frac{1}{6} = \frac{1}{36}$
4, not 4	$\frac{1}{6} \times \frac{5}{6} = \frac{5}{36}$
not 4, 4	$\frac{5}{6} \times \frac{1}{6} = \frac{5}{36}$
not 4, not 4	$\frac{5}{6} \times \frac{5}{6} = \frac{25}{36}$

(a) $p(4 \text{ and } 4) = \frac{1}{36}$

(b) $p(\text{one } 4) = \frac{5}{36} + \frac{5}{36}$ *The middle two outcomes both have one 4 (and one not 4)*

   $= \frac{10}{36} = \frac{5}{18}$

(c) $p(\text{no 4s}) = \frac{25}{36}$

(We can check that, as these are the only possible outcomes, the sum of their probabilities is 1: $\frac{1}{36} + \frac{10}{36} + \frac{25}{36} = \frac{36}{36} = 1$.)

Example   Ivan has five medals for swimming, which he keeps in a drawer. Two are gold and three are silver. He picks two medals out of the drawer. Use a tree diagram to list all the possible outcomes.

(a) What is the probability that both medals are silver?

(b) What is the probability that at least one medal is gold?

In this case we must consider the selection of each medal separately, because Ivan is selecting **without replacement**: the second selection will depend upon the outcome of the first one, because there will be only four medals to choose from, instead of five.

The tree diagram for the first selection is shown.

The probability of picking a gold medal on the *second* selection, assuming the *first* was gold, is $\frac{1}{4}$, as there would then be only one gold medal left out of the remaining four medals. Similarly, the probability that the *second* medal is gold, assuming that the *first* was silver is $\frac{2}{4}$, as there would be two gold medals left out of the remaining four.

The complete diagram, and table, will be:

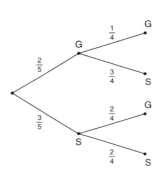

Outcome	Probability
GG	$\frac{2}{5} \times \frac{1}{4} = \frac{2}{20} \left(= \frac{1}{10} \right)$
GS	$\frac{2}{5} \times \frac{3}{4} = \frac{6}{20} \left(= \frac{3}{10} \right)$
SG	$\frac{3}{5} \times \frac{2}{4} = \frac{6}{20} \left(= \frac{3}{10} \right)$
SS	$\frac{3}{5} \times \frac{2}{4} = \frac{6}{20} \left(= \frac{3}{10} \right)$

(a) p(two silver medals) = $\frac{3}{10}$.

(b) For at least one medal to be gold, one of the outcomes GG, GS or SG must happen.

Hence p(at least one G) = $\frac{1}{10} + \frac{3}{10} + \frac{3}{10} = \frac{7}{10}$.

We could have said that any outcome, other than two silver medals, would contain at least one gold medal.

Hence p(at least one G) = 1 − p(no Gs)

$$= 1 - p(SS)$$

$$= 1 - \frac{3}{10}$$

$$= \frac{7}{10}, \text{ as before.}$$

Exercise 11

1   Paul shuffles the four aces from a pack of cards, and asks Robert to pick one card, look at it, and return it to the three other aces. He then asks Gina to do the same. By copying and completing the tree diagram, work out the probability that, of the two aces:

(a)   both are hearts,

(b)   neither is a heart,

(c)   only one is a heart.

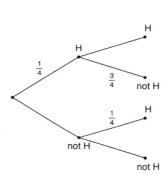

Outcome	Probability
HH	
H, not H	$\frac{1}{4} \times \frac{3}{4} = \frac{3}{16}$
not H not H	

2   On an island during July, the probability that it will rain on any day is 0.2. Copy and complete the tree diagram and table. What is the probability that on two consecutive days:

(a)   it will be dry,

(b)   it will rain on one of the days,

(c)   it will rain on both days?

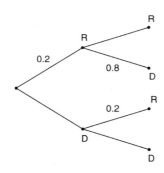

Outcome	Probability
RD	0.2 x 0.8 = 0.16
DD	

3 Robin has a cassette holder which holds eight tapes. Five of these are Queen tapes.
Draw a tree diagram (use 'Q' and 'not Q') and a table.
When Robin picks out two cassettes, what is the probability that:

(a) both are Queen cassettes, (b) one is a Queen cassette,

(c) neither is a Queen cassette?

4 As Tammy cycles to school, she passes through two sets of traffic lights. The probability of having to stop at the first set is 0.4, and at the second is 0.6. Copy and complete the tree diagram. What is the probability that Tammy:

(a) has to stop at both sets of lights,

(b) gets straight through both sets,

(c) has to stop at one set only?

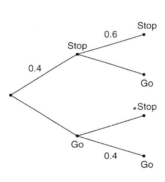

Outcome	Probability
SS	
SG	

5 The probability that Claire beats David at Scrabble is 0.7. They play two games, neither of which ends in a draw.

(a) Draw a tree diagram to show the possible outcomes.

(b) What is the probability that (i) Claire wins both games (ii) David wins at least one game?

6 Sally's spinner has one blue and four red sections. She spins it twice.

(a) Draw a tree diagram to show the possible outcomes.

(b) What is the probability that Sally spins (i) two different colours (ii), either two reds or two blues?

12.12 More than two events

During spawning a female salmon lays 10 000 eggs.

Example Three coins are thrown.

(a) Draw a tree diagram of the possible outcomes.

(b) What is the probability of (i) three heads (ii) one tail (iii) at least one head?

(a) With three events, we continue the tree diagram to show all possibilities, and their probabilities.

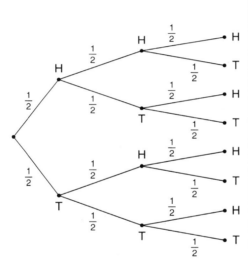

Outcome	Probability
HHH	$\frac{1}{2} \times \frac{1}{2} \times \frac{1}{2} = \frac{1}{8}$
HHT	$\frac{1}{2} \times \frac{1}{2} \times \frac{1}{2} = \frac{1}{8}$
HTH	$\frac{1}{2} \times \frac{1}{2} \times \frac{1}{2} = \frac{1}{8}$
HTT	$\frac{1}{2} \times \frac{1}{2} \times \frac{1}{2} = \frac{1}{8}$
THH	$\frac{1}{2} \times \frac{1}{2} \times \frac{1}{2} = \frac{1}{8}$
THT	$\frac{1}{2} \times \frac{1}{2} \times \frac{1}{2} = \frac{1}{8}$
TTH	$\frac{1}{2} \times \frac{1}{2} \times \frac{1}{2} = \frac{1}{8}$
TTT	$\frac{1}{2} \times \frac{1}{2} \times \frac{1}{2} = \frac{1}{8}$

(b) (i) $\text{p(HHH)} = \frac{1}{8}$

(ii) $\text{p(one T)} = \text{p(HHT + HTH + THH)} = \frac{3}{8}$

(iii) $\text{p(at least one H)} = 1 - \text{p(no H)}$

$$= 1 - \text{p(TTT)}$$

$$= 1 - \frac{1}{8}$$

$$= \frac{7}{8}$$

Exercise 12

1 Using the information from question 2 in exercise 11; the diagram is extended to three days.
What is the probability that the three consecutive days
(a) are all dry (b) have at least two wet days?

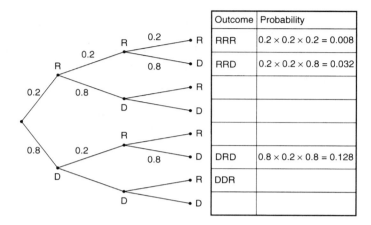

2 From question 3 in exercise 11, extend the tree diagram to show the outcomes if three cassettes are picked.
What is the probability that, of the three cassettes,

(a) all are Queen cassettes   (b) at least one is a Queen cassette

(c) none is a Queen cassette?

3 Looking back at question 5 in exercise 11, Claire and David play three games of Scrabble.

(a) Make up a new tree diagram, and outcome table.

(b) What is the probability that (i) David wins all three games (ii) Sally wins at least two games?

4 Sally spins her spinner three times (see question 6, exercise 11). Use a tree diagram to work out the probability that she spins (a) three reds (b) two reds (c) one red (d) no reds.

5 There are eight sandwiches remaining on a plate. Of these, six are cheese and two are cucumber. Gerald ate three sandwiches.
By making up a tree diagram, what is the probability that Gerald ate

(a) three cheese sandwiches   (b) at least one of each?

Review

Exercise 13

1 I have six batteries for my walkman in a drawer. I know that four are new and two are old. If I pick one battery at random, what is the probability that it is (a) a new one (b) an old one?

2 Ian is in a hurry and grabs a handkerchief from a drawer which contains eight handkerchiefs, five of which are white and three coloured. What is the probability that the handkerchief is (a) white (b) coloured?

3 One person is selected at random from a class of nine girls and seven boys. What is the probability that the person is (a) a girl (b) a boy?

4 Judy has seven scarves on a shelf, three of which are red, two are blue and two are white. She picks one scarf from the shelf, without looking. What is the probability that it is (a) red (b) either white or red (c) not white (d) green?

5 A set of 16 pool balls is made up of seven 'spots', seven 'stripes', a white and a black. One ball drops on to the floor. What is the probability that it is (a) a 'stripe' (b) the black (c) not a 'spot'?

6 In a game of darts, Steve has scored 60 or more seven times in his last 20 throws of three darts. From this information, estimate the probability that his next throw will be 60 or more.

7 The seventh hole on a golf course is surrounded by bunkers. In her last 15 rounds of golf, Karen has landed in one of these bunkers 12 times. Estimate the probability that, during the next round she plays, Karen does *not* land in one of these bunkers.

8 The rules of indoor six-a-side cricket state that a batsman must retire, temporarily, once he has scored 25 runs. In the eight games so far this season, Pete has scored 25 six times, and Les has scored 25 on five occasions. For the next game, estimate the probability that (a) Pete will score 25 runs (b) Les will *not* score 25 runs.

9 A ball is rolled through a maze, and ends up in one of the slots A, B, C D or E. Nathan has rolled the ball 20 times and it has ended up as shown in the table.

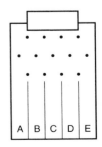

Slot	A	B	C	D	E
Number of times	1	5	9	3	2

From these figures, estimate the probability that the next ball Nathan rolls will end up in (a) slot B (b) either slot D or E (c) *not* slot C.

10 Chloe has a box which contains white, red and green beads. She picks one out, notes its colour, and puts it back. She repeats this ten times, and notes that the bead is white six times, red three times and green once.
What is the probability that the next time she picks a bead it will be
(a) white (b) blue (c) not red?

11 A coin is spun three times.

Use a tree diagram and outcome table to calculate the probability of getting (a) three heads (b) only one head (c) at least two tails.

12 I have six black socks and four white socks in a drawer. I pick out one sock and then another. By drawing a tree diagram, or otherwise, work out the probability that I pick a matching pair of socks.

Exercise 14 The following questions are all taken from GCSE papers.

1 Kerry has eight cards: three hearts and five diamonds.

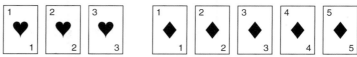

She takes one of the heart cards and one of the diamond cards at random. Kerry then subtracts the numbers on her cards. For example:

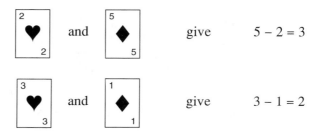

give $5 - 2 = 3$

give $3 - 1 = 2$

(a) Complete this table to show all the possible results. *(2 marks)*

		Diamond card				
		1	2	3	4	5
Heart card	1					
	2					3
	3	2				

(b) Calculate the probability that the result is 3. *(2 marks)*
[SEG]

2 Four dice each have 3 red faces, 2 blue faces and 1 green face. Four students each pick one of these dice and throw it a number of times. Their results are summarised in this table.

Student's name	Number of throws	Frequency		
		Red	Blue	Green
Seema	20	10	7	3
Keith	300	126	84	90
Kelly	160	84	52	24
Bryn	400	195	140	65

(a) Seema says, 'My results prove that my dice is fair'.
Explain why she could be wrong. *(1 mark)*

(b) Which student's dice is most likely to be unfair? Explain your answer. *(1 mark)*
[SEG]

3 Sharon has 12 computer discs. Five of the discs are red. Seven of the discs are black. She keeps all the discs in a box.
Sharon removes one disc at random. She records its colour and replaces it in the box.
Sharon removes a second disc at random, and again records its colour.

(a) Complete the tree diagram. *(2 marks)*

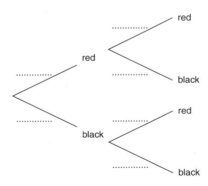

(b) Calculate the probability that the two discs removed

(i) will both be red,

(ii) will be different colours. *(5 marks)*
[EDEXCEL]

4 Lauren and Yasmina each try to score a goal. They each have one attempt.
The probability that Lauren will score a goal is 0.85. The probability that Yasmina will score a goal is 0.6.

(a) Work out the probability that both Lauren and Yasmina will score a goal. *(2 marks)*

(b) Work out the probability that Lauren will score a goal and Yasmina will not score a goal. *(2 marks)*

[EDEXCEL]

5 Martin bought a packet of mixed flower seeds. The seeds produce flowers that are red or blue or white or yellow. The probability of a flower seed producing a flower of a particular colour is:

Colour	Red	Blue	White	Yellow
Probability	0.6	0.15		0.15

(a) Write down the most common colour of a flower. *(1 mark)*

Martin chooses a flower seed at random from the packet.

(b) (i) Work out the probability that the flower produced will be white.

(ii) Write down the probability that the flower produced will be orange. *(3 marks)*

[EDEXCEL]

6 Two fair spinners are used for a game. The score is the difference. For example, the score for these two spinners is 6 − 4 = 2.

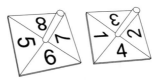

(a) Complete the table to show all the possible scores for the two spinners.

	5	6	7	8
1			6	
2	3			
3				5
4		2		

(2 marks)

(b) What is the probability of the score being an odd number?

(2 marks)

[NEAB]

7 Martin is playing with a biased four sided dice. The four faces are numbered 1, 2, 3 and 4. When Martin throws the dice, his score is the number it lands on. The table shows the probability of his scoring 1, 2 or 3.

Score	1	2	3
Probability	0.4	0.15	0.25

(a) Martin throws the dice once. What is the probability that he scores

    (i) 4, *(1 mark)*

    (ii) 2 or 3? *(1 mark)*

(b) Martin throws the dice twice. Find the probability that he scores

    (i) 3 on each throw, *(2 marks)*

    (ii) a total of 3 on the two throws. *(3 marks)*

                                         [OCR]

8 (a) The bar chart shows the number of pupils in a class playing different sports on a games afternoon.

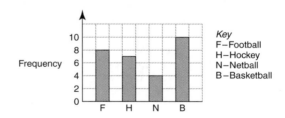

Key
F—Football
H—Hockey
N—Netball
B—Basketball

A pupil is chosen at random from the class.
Find the probability that the pupil plays

    (i) netball, *(2 marks)*

    (ii) hockey or basketball. *(1 mark)*

(b) The probability that Jim scores a goal from a penalty shot in hockey is 0.7. Jim takes two penalty shots.

    (i) Draw a tree diagram to show all the possible outcomes of the two shots. Label the diagram carefully. *(3 marks)*

    (ii) Calculate the probability that Jim scores exactly one goal from the two penalty shots. *(3 marks)*

                                         [OCR]

9 In one turn of a game at a fête, a contestant spins two spinners. Each spinner is numbered 1 to 5 and these numbers are equally likely to occur. A contestant's score is the sum of the two numbers shown on the spinners.

(i) Complete the following table to show the possible outcomes of a contestant's score on one turn.

second spinner						
5	...	...	...	...	...
4	...	...	...	...	...
3	4	...	...	...	...
2	3	4	5	6	7
1	2	3	4	5	6
	1	2	3	4	5

First spinner

(ii) What is the probability of scoring 2 on one turn?

(iii) Contestants win a prize if they score 8 or more. Jennifer has one turn at the game.
What is the probability that she wins a prize?

(iv) At the fête, 200 people each have one turn at the game.
Approximately how many of them will win a prize?

(7 marks)
[WJEC]

10 Andy travels to work by bus on two days. The probability that the bus is late on any day is 0.6

(a) Complete the tree diagram to show the possible outcomes for the two days.

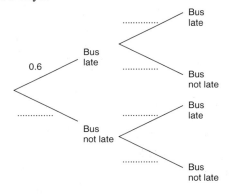

(2 marks)

(b) (i) What is the probability that the bus is 'not late' on both days? *(2 marks)*

(ii) What is the probability that the bus is late on at least one of the two days? *(2 marks)*
[NEAB]

11 (a) A bag contains a large number of sweets which are either mints, toffees, fruits or nut clusters. A sweet is chosen at random.

 (i) Complete the table.

Type of Sweet	Probability of choosing that type of sweet
Mint	0.3
Toffee	0.4
Fruit	0.1
Nut cluster	

(1 mark)

 (ii) What is the probability that the sweet is not a fruit?

(1 mark)

 (iii) What is the probability that the sweet is either a mint or a toffee? *(2 marks)*

 (iv) There were 120 sweets in the bag. How many were toffees? *(2 marks)*

 (b) A large container, which is full of sweets, contains only sherbets and humbugs. Jane takes out 5 sweets and finds that 2 are sherbets and 3 are humbugs. She says, 'The probability of choosing a sherbet from this container is $\frac{2}{5}$.'

 (i) Explain why Jane's statement may not be correct.

(2 marks)

 (ii) Suggest two methods Jane could use to obtain a better estimate of the probability that a sweet chosen at random from the container will be a sherbet. *(2 marks)*

[MEG]

12 Polly has kept records of the weather for five years. She works out that the probability that it will rain on any day in September is 0.2.

 (a)

SEPTEMBER		1998		
	6	13	20	27
	7	14	21	28
1	8	15	22	29
2	9	16	23	30
3	10	17	24	
4	11	18	25	
5	12	19	26	

On how many September days could it be expected to rain?

(2 marks)

(b) Polly has been invited to attend two weddings. The first wedding is on September 5th and the second is on September 19th.

(i) Complete the tree diagram below.

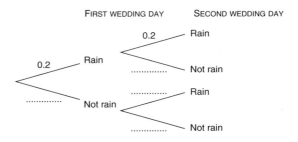

FIRST WEDDING DAY   SECOND WEDDING DAY

0.2 ── Rain

0.2 ── Rain

.... ── Not rain

.... ── Rain

.... ── Not rain

Not rain

(2 marks)

(ii) Find the probability that it will not rain on the day of the first wedding but it will rain on the day of the second wedding.

(2 marks)
[MEG]

Ideas for investigations

1 A pack of cards is shuffled and the cards are dealt out until the first heart appears.
The process is repeated a number of times.
Jack says that the most likely position of a heart is FIRST; Jill says that the most likely position of a heart is THIRD.
By performing the experiment a number of times, decide who you think is correct.
Which do you think is the most likely position for the first heart?

2 At one of the stalls at a village fête, you pay £1 to throw three dice.
If none of the dice show a '6' you lose your £1.
If one of the dice shows a '6' you get your £1 back.
If two of the dice show a '6' you get £2 back.
If all three dice show a '6' you get £10 back.

Investigate whether or not the game is fair.
Suggest how to alter the pay-outs, so that the organisers of the fête make a profit of about £2 for every ten attempts.
(A tree diagram may assist with the calculations.)

ANSWERS

1 Using numbers

Exercise 1

1 20	**2** 35 min	**3** 69	**4** 34	**5** 134 mm
6 £1018	**7** 2	**8** 420		

Exercise 2

1 £120 000	**2** £2000	**3** £20	**4** 300
5 1600 g	**6** 4000	**7** 40 litres	**8** 350

Exercise 3

1 565 mm	**2** 2908	**3** 49	**4** 300	**5** £82
6 4	**7** 15 264	**8** 5856		

Exercise 4

1 £6.20	**2** £101.40	**3** 90	**4** £22
5 £171	**6** £65 200	**7** £590	**8** £121.03

Exercise 5

1 £153 **2** 8th Dec.

3 (a) £9.80 (b) £15.30 (c) £18.70 **4** (a) £83.41 (b) £67.57

5 £3311

Exercise 6

1 100 010	**2** 3 105 400	**3** 1 030 250
4 410 006	**5** 5 002 509	**6** 4 805 078

7 Two hundred and five thousand, one hundred and three.

8 Four million, thirty thousand, one hundred and twenty.

9 Nine hundred and ninety thousand, and nine.

10 Eight million, seven hundred and fifty thousand, and three.

11 Seven million, six thousand, two hundred and seven.

12 Five million, one hundred thousand, five hundred and fifty.

13 605431, 609495, 631427, 649531, 650001, 650547

14 3600005, 3571453, 2837431, 2450401, 2435721, 2404321, 2314373

15 500250	**16** 1 million	**17** 750 000
18 £50 000	**19** £22 750	**20** £35 750 000

Exercise 7

1 81	**2** 256	**3** 8	**4** 0	**5** 125
6 1	**7** 729	**8** 3125	**9** 64	**10** 3375
11 169	**12** 1	**13** 2	**14** 9	**15** 1296

16 16	**17** 6561	**18** 15625	**19** 2401	**20** 1
21 $\frac{1}{8}$	**22** $\frac{1}{6}$	**23** $\frac{1}{81}$	**24** $\frac{1}{1000}$	**25** 1
26 $\frac{1}{49}$	**27** $\frac{1}{243}$	**28** $\frac{1}{64}$	**29** $\frac{1}{27}$	**30** 1
31 3	**32** 3	**33** 6	**34** 3	**35** 5
36 3	**37** 3	**38** 3	**39** 10	**40** 3

Exercise 8

1 64	**2** 16	**3** 256	**4** 72	**5** 16
6 180	**7** 375	**8** 82 944	**9** 13 824	**10** 25

Exercise 9

1 $\frac{5}{8}$	**2** $\frac{9}{12} = \frac{3}{4}$	**3** $\frac{4}{6} = \frac{2}{3}$	**4** $\frac{6}{10} = \frac{3}{5}$
5 $\frac{2}{3} = \frac{6}{9}$	**6** $\frac{2}{5} = \frac{8}{20}$	**7** $\frac{1}{2} = \frac{2}{4}$	**8** $\frac{7}{10} = \frac{70}{100}$
9 $\frac{90}{100} = \frac{9}{10}$	**10** $\frac{15}{9} = \frac{135}{81}$	**11** $\frac{18}{21} = \frac{6}{7}$	**12** $\frac{4}{3} = \frac{16}{12}$
13 $\frac{24}{36} = \frac{6}{9}$	**14** $\frac{3}{8} = \frac{90}{240}$	**15** $\frac{7}{12} = \frac{84}{144}$	**16** $\frac{2}{3} = \frac{16}{24}$

Exercise 10

1 $\frac{11}{6}$	**2** $\frac{20}{3}$	**3** $\frac{47}{6}$	**4** $\frac{13}{6}$	**5** $\frac{41}{5}$
6 $\frac{23}{3}$	**7** $\frac{43}{5}$	**8** $\frac{57}{10}$	**9** $\frac{50}{9}$	**10** $\frac{31}{8}$

Exercise 11

1 $6\frac{1}{8}$	**2** $8\frac{5}{6}$	**3** $3\frac{3}{10}$	**4** $8\frac{5}{9}$	**5** $5\frac{3}{4}$
6 $7\frac{7}{11}$	**7** $5\frac{4}{5}$	**8** $5\frac{5}{11}$	**9** $4\frac{11}{12}$	**10** $5\frac{5}{7}$

Exercise 12

1 $\frac{2}{3}$	**2** $\frac{3}{4}$	**3** $\frac{2}{3}$	**4** $\frac{1}{6}$	**5** $\frac{2}{5}$
6 $\frac{3}{7}$	**7** $\frac{2}{3}$	**8** $\frac{3}{4}$	**9** $\frac{5}{8}$	**10** $\frac{2}{5}$

Exercise 13

1 $\frac{2}{3}$	**2** $\frac{1}{5}$	**3** $1\frac{1}{5}$	**4** $\frac{1}{4}$
5 $1\frac{3}{5}$	**6** $1\frac{3}{7}$	**7** $\frac{3}{16}$	**8** $\frac{1}{4}$
9 $\frac{3}{16}$	**10** $1\frac{1}{12}$	**11** $1\frac{1}{8}$	**12** $\frac{11}{16}$
13 $8\frac{1}{12}$	**14** $3\frac{1}{8}$	**15** $7\frac{7}{16}$	**16** $7\frac{9}{16}$

Exercise 14

1 $\frac{1}{10}$	**2** $\frac{5}{8}$	**3** $\frac{1}{15}$	**4** $\frac{4}{15}$
5 $\frac{1}{20}$	**6** $\frac{1}{16}$	**7** $\frac{4}{7}$	**8** $\frac{2}{7}$
9 $2\frac{4}{5}$	**10** $1\frac{1}{5}$	**11** $\frac{3}{4}$	**12** 30

Exercise 15

1 $\frac{3}{4}$	**2** $1\frac{1}{2}$	**3** $1\frac{1}{5}$	**4** $\frac{5}{6}$
5 $6\frac{2}{3}$	**6** $4\frac{2}{3}$	**7** $17\frac{1}{3}$	**8** $1\frac{5}{6}$
9 $3\frac{3}{20}$	**10** $1\frac{7}{8}$	**11** $1\frac{2}{7}$	**12** $3\frac{1}{5}$

Exercise 16

1 15   **2** 20   **3** (a) £9   (b) £6

4 $\frac{3}{5}$ of 18 kg   **5** $\frac{1}{9}$ **6** 120   **7** £82.80   **8** 85

Exercise 17

1 $7\frac{5}{8}$ ft   **2** 27   **3** $15\frac{1}{2}$ in

4 25   **5** $4\frac{11}{16}$ in   **6** $4\frac{3}{8}$ hands

7 $7\frac{1}{2}$ **8** $18\frac{2}{3}$ hours

Exercise 18

1 5.6   **2** 8.5   **3** 1.4   **4** 16.41   **5** 117.73

6 8.83   **7** 35.64   **8** 140.22   **9** 16.55   **10** 756.41

Exercise 19

1 0.48   **2** 7.38   **3** 17.5   **4** 340   **5** 12.1

6 1400   **7** 66.33   **8** 6.2   **9** 37.32   **10** 0.12

11 12.96   **12** 35.064

Exercise 20

1 5   **2** 15   **3** 11   **4** 12

5 16   **6** 24   **7** 11   **8** 23

9 8   **10** 24   **11** 2   **12** 5

Exercise 21

1 (a) 41 000   (b) 41 300   **2** (a) 6000   (b) 5800

3 (a) 84 000   (b) 84 200   **4** (a) 67 000   (b) 66 700

5 (a) 8000   (b) 7600   **6** (a) 3000   (b) 3100

7 (a) 43 000   (b) 43 200   **8** (a) 5000   (b) 5100

9 (a) 47 000   (b) 47 200   **10** (a) 1000   (b) 1000

11 (a) 1000   (b) 1200   **12** (a) 1000   (b) 1100

13 24 000   **14** 12 800   **15** £19 000

Exercise 22

1 12   **2** 13   **3** 15   **4** 10

5 44   **6** 6   **7** 14   **8** (a) 5   (b) 7

Exercise 23

1 (a) 3.86   (b) 3.860   **2** (a) 9.42   (b) 9.419

3 (a) 29.83   (b) 29.831   **4** (a) 0.01   (b) 0.014

5 (a) 0.98   (b) 0.975   **6** (a) 6.41   (b) 6.407

7 (a) 50.91   (b) 50.914   **8** (a) 4.89   (b) 4.886

9 (a) 36.06   (b) 36.058   **10** (a) 9.09   (b) 9.094

11 7.22   **12** 95.8   **13** 68.9

14 29.97   **15** 0.7857

Exercise 24

1 (a) 30   (b) 29.1   **2** (a) 6000   (b) 5650

3 (a) 70 000   (b) 73 400   **4** (a) 0.04   (b) 0.0375

5 (a) 20   (b) 23.5   **6** (a) 20   (b) 15.4

7 (a) 60   (b) 62.8   8 (a) 0.08   (b) 0.0810

9 (a) 500   (b) 468   10 (a) 4000   (b) 4090

11 0.126   12 10   13 0.66

14 290   15 4000

Exercise 25

1 90   2 200   3 500   4 4

5 160   6 1000   7 100   8 210

9 120   10 $\frac{1}{3}$ 11 15 000   12 800

Exercise 26

1 0.000 75   2 0.0098   3 0.000 037 5   4 1 600 000

5 0.001 01   6 736 000   7 6200   8 70 000

9 0.009 21   10 9 830 000

Exercise 27

1 7.0×10^{-2} 2 4.5×10^{3} 3 3.5×10^{-1}

4 8.0×10^{5} 5 8.0×10^{-3} 6 2.7×10^{-2}

7 2.4×10^{4} 8 6.9×10^{-3} 9 4.0×10^{3}

10 1.4×10^{4} 11 8.5×10^{-6} 12 9.0×10^{-4}

Exercise 28

1 (a) 7.8×10^{-4} (b) 0.000 78   2 (a) 1.2×10^{9} (b) 1 200 000 000

3 (a) 2.4×10^{6} (b) 2 400 000   4 (a) 3.2×10^{-6} (b) 0.000 003 2

5 (a) 3.84×10^{0} (b) 3.84   6 (a) 1.2×10^{8} (b) 120 000 000

7 (a) 1.2×10^{3} (b) 1200   8 (a) 6.48×10^{-3} (b) 0.006 48

Exercise 29

1 4.5   2 12.53   3 15.9   4 16.39   5 600

6 94.7   7 1300   8 20   9 52.2   10 600

11 20 m   12 1730 m^2 13 760 cm   14 7.4 m   15 534 m^2

Exercise 30

1 188 mm   2 £1069   3 6   4 51 g   5 1000

6 £8330   7 39   8 446 mm   9 412 mm   10 86 400

11 About 3200   12 About 35   13 About 40

14 About 10   15 About 200

Exercise 31

1 £535 500   2 3 408 005

3 (a) Five million, four hundred and seven thousand, eight hundred and ninety pounds

   (b) (i) £5 408 000   (ii) £5 407 900   (iii) £5 408 000

4 (a) 7776   (b) $\frac{1}{64}$ (c) 81   (d) 1   (e) 1600   (f) 243

5 (a) 21   (b) $\frac{7}{10}$ (c) $7\frac{5}{12}$ (d) $\frac{4}{21}$ (e) $1\frac{1}{6}$ (f) $1\frac{1}{4}$ (g) $12\frac{1}{4}$ (h) $\frac{4}{9}$

6 $8\frac{2}{5}$ inches   **7** 4   **8** $\frac{5}{6}$ **9** $\frac{4}{5}$ of 35 kg

10 (a) 30.80   (b) 5.54   (c) 5.92   (d) 4.80

11 (a) 7290   (b) 620   (c) 63.6   (d) 3.50

12 (a) (i) 0.0256   (ii) 2.56×10^{-2}

   (b) (i) 21 440 000   (ii) 2.144×10^{7}

   (c) (i) 15 000   (ii) 1.5×10^{4}

Exercise 32

1 $(600 \times \sqrt{36})/9 = 400$ **2** (a) £20 904   (b) 70, £300

3 (a) 31.284   (b) $\dfrac{90 \times 10}{20 + 10} = 30$

4 (a) 64p   (b) £34.27   (c) 35p   (d) 42p

5 6 days   **6** (a) £2.08   (b) 5 tins

7 (a) 49   (b) 27   (c) 16   (d) 5000   (e) 320

8 (a) $\frac{3}{4}$ (b) 6 tins   **9** (a) e.g. 0.34–0.49   (b) 3/4

10 (a) 0.6   (b) 66%, $\frac{2}{3}$, 0.67, 0.7   (c) (i) $1\frac{1}{6}$ (ii) 2   (iii) $7\frac{1}{2}$

11 (a) (i) 50, 30   (ii) 75   (iii) 79.36875   (b) 4.9×10^{11}

12 (a) 40 000   (b) 4000   (c) 3883.184998

13 (a) $£3.604 \times 10^{10}$ (b) £1071   **14** (a) 9.1×10^{-25} (b) 4.55×10^{-18}

15 (i) 12p   (ii) 22

16 (a) answer must be less than 17.8 because 0.97 is less than 1

   (b) 40, 60, 300

17 (a) (i) 4.5×10^{8} (ii) 6.5×10^{-9} (b) (i) 5.3×10^{-8} (ii) 4.6×10^{6}

18 (a) $\frac{1}{4}$ (b) $12\frac{1}{2}\%$

19 (a) 15 000   (b) 46.5

20 (a) 8.19×10^{13} (b) 2.7×10^{8}

21 (a) 24.86052632   (b) 25   **22** $£20 \times 150 = £3000$

Investigations

The important thing with coursework is not necessarily the correct answer, but the evidence you provide to show the process you have followed in getting near to, or reaching the answer.

1 The maximum and minimum lengths can be expressed to one decimal place only, but will have a difference of just less than 0.1 in this instance. The difference will become greater when you calculate the area, since the difference between each of the lengths and widths is then multiplied by itself. When the figures are expressed to two decimal places, the difference in length is then 0.01, and the difference in the area is greater again.

2 The general rules are that if you multiply two powers of the same number, you add the powers. If you divide powers of the same number, you take away the powers:

$$2^{n} \times 2^{m} = 2^{n+m} \qquad 2^{n} \div 2^{m} = 2^{n-m}$$

3 $\frac{1}{2}x + \frac{1}{4}x + \frac{3}{16}x + 2 = \frac{15x}{16} + 2$ so 2 is $\frac{1}{16}$ of the apples

The number of apples is therefore 32.

4 (a) One which works is G = 8, S = 27, B = 65 (b) G = 7, S = 49, B = 44

2 Percentages

Exercise 1

1 (a) 0.4 (b) $\frac{2}{5}$ **2** (a) 0.35 (b) $\frac{7}{20}$ **3** (a) 0.15 (b) $\frac{3}{20}$

4 (a) 0.44 (b) $\frac{11}{25}$ **5** (a) 0.27 (b) $\frac{27}{100}$ **6** (a) 0.825 (b) $\frac{33}{40}$

7 (a) 0.325 (b) $\frac{13}{40}$ **8** (a) 0.175 (b) $\frac{7}{40}$ **9** (a) 0.075 (b) $\frac{3}{40}$

10 (a) 0.1525 (b) $\frac{61}{400}$

Exercise 2

1 30%   **2** 50%   **3** 35%   **4** $37\frac{1}{2}$%   **5** 80%

6 132%   **7** $31\frac{1}{4}$%   **8** $31\frac{1}{4}$%   **9** $58\frac{1}{3}$%   **10** $93\frac{3}{4}$%

Exercise 3

1 75%   **2** 25%   **3** 25%   **4** $62\frac{1}{2}$%

5 $16\frac{2}{3}$%   **6** 50%   **7** 50%   **8** 50%

Exercise 4

1 0.4, 50%, $\frac{3}{5}$ **2** $\frac{1}{5}$, 32%, 0.35   **3** 0.3, 33%, $\frac{1}{3}$ **4** 70%, $\frac{3}{4}$, 0.80

5 0.25, 28%, $\frac{7}{20}$ **6** $\frac{3}{5}$, 63%, 0.65   **7** $\frac{9}{20}$, 0.55, 59%   **8** $\frac{5}{8}$, 0.7, 75%

Exercise 5

1 £8.00   **2** £1.08   **3** 16 g   **4** 60 mm   **5** 9 kg

6 3 cm   **7** 15 t   **8** £8.05   **9** £0.72   **10** 40 m

Exercise 6

1 £777   **2** 2312.5 g   **3** 708 g   **4** £736   **5** £325

6 112.8 m   **7** 420 ml   **8** £2.93   **9** £28.64   **10** £8.88

Exercise 7

1 £31.50   **2** 53 000   **3** £531.25   **4** £242.65   **5** 130 people

6 1770 t   **7** £3120   **8** £104

Exercise 8

1 £14.00   **2** £94.71   **3** £147.82   **4** £91.65   **5** £152.74

Exercise 9

1 (a) £817 (b) £467   **2** (a) £462 (b) £102

3 (a) £250 (b) £50   **4** (a) £296.88 (b) £71.88

5 (a) £5905.80 (b) £955.80   **6** (a) £626.25 (b) £51.25

Exercise 10

1 £468   **2** £63.00   **3** £11.93   **4** £222.75

5 5 yr 8 m   **6** 2 yr 2 m   **7** 7.03%   **8** £75

9 £166.67   **10** 2 yr 2 m

Exercise 11

1 £630.50	**2** £147.51	**3** £126.80	**4** £94.19
5 £88.36	**6** £10.31		

Exercise 12

1 £211.50	**2** £171.00	**3** £186.55	**4** £199.20
5 £3.96	**6** £4.08	**7** £26.80	**8** £21.60
9 £112.50	**10** £67.20	**11** £100.50	**12** £320.00
13 £104.00	**14** £28.25	**15** £69.68	**16** £118.20

Exercise 13

1 52.1% **2** $31\frac{1}{4}\%$ **3** $13\frac{1}{3}\%$ **4** $62\frac{1}{2}\%$
5 15% **6** 57.2% **7** 9.7% **8** 40%
9 (a) $46\frac{2}{3}\%$ (b) $53\frac{1}{3}\%$ **10** (a) 54.1% (b) 45.8%

Exercise 14

1 £87.20	**2** £160	**3** £620	**4** £64	**5** £250
6 £2400	**7** 250 kg	**8** £12 800	**9** £3800	**10** £18.00

Exercise 15

1

Decimal	Fraction	Percentage
0.9	$\frac{9}{10}$	90%
0.375	$\frac{3}{8}$	$37\frac{1}{2}\%$
0.45	$\frac{9}{20}$	45%
0.625	$\frac{5}{8}$	$62\frac{1}{2}\%$
0.6666	$\frac{2}{3}$	$66\frac{2}{3}\%$

2 $\frac{2}{3}$ of £139.53   **3** £8.05   **4** £1478.75
5 (a) £8694.25   (b) £394.25   **6** 1487.5 kg
7 £140   **8** £369.25   **9** £65.80
10 £172.42   **11** (a) £320   (b) £339.72
12 £68   **13** 20%   **14** 16%
15 £120   **16** £120.40   **17** £283.75
18 (a) £15.00   (b) £30.50

Exercise 16

1 (a) £130.22   (b) £136.74   **2** £817
3 15%   **4** (a) £34.37   (b) £558.40
5 $80\%, \frac{7}{8}, \frac{8}{9}, 0.9$ **6** £2280
7 (a) £4.80   (b) (i) 0.3   (ii) £3.60   (c) 7%   (d) $\frac{1}{50}$
8 (a) $\frac{13}{20}$ (b) £10 250   **9** (a) £1054   (b) 7%
10 (a) £17.10   (b) £31.00
11 (a) (i) £5.55   (ii) £44.86   (b) (i) £320   (ii) £4700
12 6p   **13** £36.00   **14** 60%   **15** (a) £61.80   (b) 1.23
16 (a) £247.50   (b) £256.00   (c) £264.75

1 Average weekly sales are 279 cases.

Piece rate: £120 ÷ 90 = £1.33 per document case produced

Time rate: £120 ÷ 36 = £3.33 per hour (0.4 hour per case)

Commission: £25 × 90 = £2250, £120 ÷ £2250 × 100 = 5% commission

An extra nine document cases are needed per week.

Piece rate: £1.33 × 9 = £12 extra

Time rate: 9 cases ÷ 0.4 hour = $22\frac{1}{2}$ hours extra at time and a quarter = £93.66

Commission: 5% on 9 × £25 = £11.25 extra

Clearly the time-rate figure may give the best profit for the workers, but the worst in terms of a deal for the manager. A compromise may be an arrangement which will pay by means of a combination of rates.

2 (a) 8 years   (b) $7\frac{1}{2}$ years   (c) $7\frac{1}{4}$ years

3 This investigation will give an opportunity for research into matters to do with the purchase of a house. Included in the calculations should be the cost of purchase, stamp duty, solicitor's fees, mortgage rates, insurance, etc. Monthly outgoings should include the mortgage repayments, building and contents insurance, local taxes and notional amounts for energy bills, repairs and maintenance.

3 Number relations

Exercise 1

1 1 : 4	2 1 : 2	3 3 : 2	4 1 : 3	5 1 : 4
6 2 : 3	7 2 : 5	8 6 : 7	9 2 : 1	10 1 : 2

Exercise 2

1 12 : 1	2 11 : 400	3 3 : 10	4 8 : 1	5 3 : 1
6 1 : 50	7 25 : 2	8 100 : 1	9 1 : 500	10 1 : 20
11 1 : 2	12 4 : 5			

Exercise 3

1 1 : 0.25	2 1 : 3	3 1 : 7.5	4 1 : 1.8	5 1 : 2.5
6 1 : 2.4	7 1 : 5	8 1 : 4	9 1 : 2.5	10 1 : 9

Exercise 4

1 $\frac{2}{7}$	2 0.2	3 25%	4 1.5	5 $\frac{1}{3}$
6 40%	7 0.5	8 40%	9 $\frac{7}{10}$	10 $2\frac{1}{2}$

Exercise 5

1 30	2 15	3 4	4 3	5 12
6 7	7 4	8 9	9 7	10 20

Exercise 6

1 20 cm	2 3.33 kg	3 6 kg	4 12.5 cm	5 120 kg
6 22.5 km/h	7 3240	8 280		

Exercise 7

1 £20 : £15   2 360 g : 240 g   3 £4.26 : £10.65
4 10.72 m : 37.52 m   5 12 cm : 20 cm   6 18 kg : 40 kg
7 45 cm, 30 cm   8 32 boys, 40 girl
9 400 g flour, 200 g fat   10 301

Exercise 8

1 20.4 tonnes   2 55 kg   3 198.1 m   4 175.5 kg
5 132 m   6 £9144

Exercise 9

1 £3.71   2 40p   3 $37\frac{1}{2}$ min   4 £13.00
5 70p   6 67.5 kg   7 £8.40   8 420

Exercise 10

1 $4\frac{1}{2}$ days   2 12 days   3 49 hours   4 4 days   5 3 hours
6 6 hours   7 75 boxes   8 18 days

Exercise 11

1 £187.20   2 £312.90   3 £84.15   4 £132.68
5 £240.80 + £548.25 = £789.05

Exercise 12

1 (a) 800 miles   (b) 1400 miles   2 (a) $1\frac{1}{4}$ hours   (b) $1\frac{1}{2}$ hours
3 40 m.p.h.   4 $1\frac{1}{2}$ hours   5 37 m/s   6 84 km
7 18 knots   8 3 km

Exercise 13

1 39 km/h   2 14 km/h   3 73 km/h   4 37 km/h
5 76 km/h   6 51 km/h   7 11 km/h   8 53 km/h

Exercise 14

1 782 schillings   2 136 500 lire   3 1339.20 marks   4 154.43 kroner
5 7592 francs   6 $1279.52   7 39072 peseta   8 140.92 punts
9 £153.41   10 £49.68   11 £2.97   12 £168.70
13 £1.31   14 £18.87   15 £7.78   16 £14.34
17 £39.58   18 £24.00   19 26 422.50 marks   20 £35.00

Exercise 15

1 −1 °C   2 −3 °C   3 −7 °C   4 −4 °C   5 2 °C
6 5 °C   7 −6 °C   8 −3 °C   9 −1 °C   10 3 °C
11 8 °C   12 11 °C   13 5 °C   14 3 °C   15 7 °C

Exercise 16

1 3   2 −4   3 −8   4 −4   5 0
6 −9   7 −3   8 −5   9 −12

Exercise 17

1 1   2 4   3 6   4 −9   5 1
6 −13   7 7   8 15   9 −7

Exercise 18

1 20	**2** 4	**3** −12	**4** −2	**5** −30
6 7	**7** −32	**8** 64	**9** 9	**10** 42
11 4	**12** −54			

Exercise 19

1 2	**2** 9	**3** 1	**4** −15	**5** −21
6 −12	**7** −4	**8** 5	**9** 8	**10** −36
11 −40	**12** −6			

Exercise 20

1 (a) 1, 2, 4, 8   (b) 1, 3, 5, 15   (c) 1, 2, 4, 7, 14, 28   (d) 1, 3, 13, 39
    (e) 1, 2, 4, 5, 8, 10, 20, 40   (f) 1, 2, 3, 4, 6, 8, 12, 24

2 (a) 6, 12, 18, …   (b) 5, 10, 15, …   (c) 9, 18, 27, …
    (d) 11, 22, 33, …   (e) 7, 14, 21, …

3 (a) 6   (b) 3   (c) 8   (d) 7   (e) 2   **4** 63, 70, 77, …

5 9, 8, 27, … (multiples of 9)

6 2, 3, 5, 7, 11, 13, 17, 19, 23, 29, 31, 37, 41, 43, 47, 53, 59, 61, 67, 71

Exercise 21

1 1, 4, 9, 16, 25, 36, 49, 64, 81, 100, 121, 144, 169, 196, 225, 256, 289,
    324, 361, 400

2 1, 8, 27, 64, 125, 216, 343, 512, 729, 1000, 1331, 1728, 2197, 2744,
    3375, 4096, 4913, 5832, 6859, 8000

3 (a) 7   (b) 9   (c) 2   (d) 5   (e) 13

4 2, 5, 10, 13, 17, 25

5 1, 121, 12321, 1234321, 123454321

6 9, 1089, 110889, 11108889, 1111088889

7 (a) 4.1231   (b) 3.1072   (c) 2.9833   (d) 1.9574   (e) 0.8944

Exercise 22

1 $2 \times 2 \times 3 \times 3$	**2** $2 \times 2 \times 2 \times 2 \times 2 \times 3$
3 $2 \times 2 \times 2 \times 3 \times 3 \times 3 \times 5$	**4** $3 \times 3 \times 3$
5 $2 \times 2 \times 2 \times 3 \times 3$	**6** $2 \times 2 \times 2 \times 3 \times 3 \times 5$
7 $2 \times 2 \times 2 \times 3 \times 5$	**8** $2 \times 2 \times 5 \times 7 \times 7$
9 $3 \times 4 \times 5 \times 7 \times 7$	**10** $2 \times 2 \times 2 \times 2 \times 2 \times 5 \times 5 \times 5$
11 $2 \times 2 \times 2 \times 5 \times 5 \times 13$	**12** $2 \times 3 \times 167$
13 $3 \times 3 \times 3 \times 3 \times 3 \times 3$	**14** $2 \times 2 \times 2 \times 2 \times 3 \times 13$
15 $5 \times 5 \times 29$	

Exercise 23

1 $5:2$	**2** $1:8$	**3** $2:7$	**4** $1:13$
5 $3:20$	**6** $3:5$	**7** $12:5$	**8** $10:3$
9 $5:1$	**10** $1:0.25$	**11** $1:0.2$	**12** $1:0.625$
13 $1:0.0888$	**14** 60%	**15** $\frac{3}{10}$	**16** $\frac{1}{4}$
17 75%	**18** 0.4	**19** $\frac{7}{15}$	**20** 0.9

21 8 kg   **22** 120 kg   **23** 30 cm   **24** 16 cm : 32 cm

25 £8.10 : £18.90   **26** 11.26 kg : 50.67 kg

27 24 cm, 32 cm, 40 cm   **28** £96, £76.80, £67.20

29 69p   **30** £59.60   **31** $5\frac{1}{4}$ h   **32** 980

33 £596.05   **34** £220.24   **35** 50 m.p.h.   **36** 7 miles

37 60 m.p.h.   **38** £64.29   **39** 1 134 000 pta

40 (a) 4, 9, 25   (b) 8, 27   (c) 7, 11, 13, 29

Exercise 24

1 (a) 200 miles   (b) $\frac{1}{2}$ hour   **2** (a) £25   (b) £84

3 Medium 5.2 g/p

4 (a) flour 345 g, butter 225 g, sugar 150 g, 3 eggs   (b) 177°   (c) 130

5 (a) 48   (b) $2^2 \times 3^2$ (c) 4, 9   **6** (a) £100, £80   (b) 60%

7 £396, £324, £252

8 (a) (i) 35 °C   (ii) 4 °C   (b) 4 °C   (c) −7 °C

9 London (95p > 80p)

10 (a) (i) 8 kg   (ii) £1.28   (b) 5p/kg

11 (i) 125   (ii) 6   (iii) 72

12 (a) $2 \times 3^2 \times 7$ (b) $2^4 \times 3 \times 7$ (c) $2^2 \times 3 \times 7$

13 (a) (i) e.g. -2×5 (ii) e.g. $-3 \div 3$ (b) −28

14 (a) 4950 Rand   (b) (i) 945 Rand   (ii) £90

15 (a) $10 460   (b) £11 or £12

16 (a) £9.40   (b) 75   (c) $37\frac{1}{2}$%

17 (a) (i) 38.2%   (ii) 63 g   (b) 105 g

Investigations

1 1.618 to three decimal places.

The numbers make up the Fibonacci series: 1, 1, 2, 3, 5, 8, 13, …, where each successive number is the sum of the two previous numbers.

2 $3^3 = 27 = 6^2 - 3^2$ $3^2 = 9 = 1 + 3 + 5$

$4^3 = 64 = 10^2 - 6^2$ $4^2 = 16 = 1 + 3 + 5 + 7$

$5^3 = 125 = 15^2 - 10^2$ $5^2 = 25 = 1 + 3 + 5 + 7 + 9$

the series is the differences   the series is successive
between the squares of   adding of odd numbers
consecutive triangular numbers

3 Use the pound as the common currency to which others relate. The important factor, though, on world currency markets, is that each currency relates to others: the pound itself is not stable.

Commission is also an important consideration in buying and selling currencies. For this reason, when going abroad, you should only change that amount of currency which you feel you will need; to change too much money will mean you incur additional charges for changing this currency back.

4 Patterns and relationships

Exercise 1
  1 21p   **2** 56p   **3** 98p
  4 £2.66   **5** £14   **6** £70

Exercise 2
  1 10   **2** 25   **3** 46
  4 37   **5** 61   **6** 157

Exercise 3
  1 (a) 40 cm^2 (b) 54 m^2 (c) 8.51 cm^2 (d) $30\,000 \text{ km}^2$
  2 (a) 26 cm   (b) 33 m   (c) 12 cm   (d) 700 km
  3 (a) 20 m/s   (b) 70 m/s   (c) 150 m/s   (d) 220 m/s
  4 (a) 60°   (b) 45°   (c) 24°   (d) 90°
  5 (a) £1.10   (b) £1.55   (c) £2.30   (d) £5.30
  6 (a) 50 min   (b) 56 min   (c) 97 min   (d) 31 min
  7 (a) 15 h   (b) 14 h   (c) 11 h   (d) $9\frac{1}{2}$ h

Exercise 4
  1 (a) 15   (b) 50   (c) 80   **2** (a) 60   (b) 180   (c) 15
  3 (a) 18   (b) 26   (c) 12   **4** (a) 5   (b) 2   (c) 15
  5 (a) 90   (b) 75   (c) 390   **6** (a) 39   (b) 100
  7 (a) 15   (b) 23   (c) 0   **8** $23\frac{1}{3}$ **9** $8\frac{1}{20}$ **10** 7

Exercise 5
  1 (a) 0.39 m^2 (b) 3900 cm^2 **2** $27\,000 \text{ m}^2$
  3 (a) 5.1 m^2 (b) yes; area of wall is 9.5 m^2 **4** £31.84
  5 2160 cm^3 **6** 3.74 cm^3 **7** $6 \, (.084) \text{ m}^3$ **8** $17.4(36) \text{ m}^2$

Exercise 6
  1 multiply by 2   **2** subtract 1   **3** multiply by 3
  4 add 5   **5** divide by 10   **6** subtract 3
  7 multiply by 10, then add 1   **8** multiply by 2, then add 1
  9 multiply by 4, then subtract 1   **10** multiply by itself (square)

Exercise 7
  1 $y = 2x$ **2** $y = x - 1$ **3** $y = 3x$ **4** $y = x + 5$
  5 $y = x/10$ **6** $y = x \div 3$ **7** $y = 10x + 1$ **8** $y = 2x + 1$
  9 $y = 4x - 1$ **10** $y = x^2$

Exercise 8
  1 (a) $£C = £12 + £1.70 \times h$ (b) $£C = £12 + £(1.7 \times 10) = £29$
  2 (a) $m - 30$ (b) $£C = £12 + £[(m - 30) \times 0.20]$
      (c) $£C = £12 + £(70 \times 0.20) = £12 + £14 = £26$
  3 (a) $£H = £8.50 + £(1.50 \times d)$ (b) $£H = £8.50 + £(1.50 \times 9) = £22$

4 (a) $£M = £(2.50 \times h) + £(3.50 \times s)$

(b) $£M = £(2.50 \times 6) + (3.50 \times 5) = £15 + £17.50 = £32.50$

5 (a) $£P = £240 + £(45 \times c)$ (b) $£P = £240 + £(45 \times 8) = £600$

Exercise 9

1 $G = 47.4$	2 $m = 57.276$	3 $r = 4.5$	4 $Y = 4.8$
5 $h = 2.48$	6 $J = 64$	7 $A = 277.92$	8 $t = 0.4$
9 $d = 322.7$	10 $x = 3.802$		

Exercise 10

1 (i) $T = 17.440\ 164$ (ii) 17.4 2 (i) $R = 288.808\ 66$ (ii) 289

3 (a) (i) $w = 269.22$ (ii) 269 (b) (i) $w = 265.066\ 32$ (ii) 265

(c) (i) $w = 669.204$ (ii) 669 4 (i) $b = 6.871\ 435\ 4$ (ii) 6.87

5 (a) (i) $d = 14.6$ (ii) 14.6 (b) (i) $d = 0.56$ (ii) 0.560

(c) (i) $d = -1.6$ (ii) -1.60

Exercise 11

1 2^6	2 x^8	3 y^6	4 a^5	5 4^5
6 2^{10}	7 t^6	8 10^9	9 m^5	10 10^5
11 b^{12}	12 x^{20}			

Exercise 12

1 $6a^2$	2 $30t^2$	3 $7y^4$	4 $12z^5$	5 $16b^6$
6 $8p^3q^2$	7 $28s^3t$	8 $160x^6y^5$	9 $8a^3b^3$	10 m^6n^6
11 $32c^{10}d^5$	12 10^6	13 6×10^7	14 $80a^3b^2$	15 $54x^6y^6$

Exercise 13

1 4	2 5^2	3 r^3	4 S^4	5 $12x^5$
6 a^4	7 $2b$	8 q^2	9 10^4	10 $8z^2$
11 $20x^2y^3$	12 10^8			

Exercise 14

1 $\dfrac{1}{y^3}$	2 $\dfrac{5}{a^2}$	3 $\dfrac{a}{b}$	4 $\dfrac{5x}{y^3}$	5 $\dfrac{1}{3pq}$
6 $2mn$	7 $\dfrac{3}{y}$	8 $\dfrac{d}{c}$	9 $\dfrac{5z^2}{2y}$	10 $\dfrac{2}{a^3}$
11 $\dfrac{2y}{3x}$	12 2			

Exercise 15

1 $8x$	2 $5 + y$	3 $6b - 2a$	4 $3w$	5 $4g - 4h$
6 $c + 1$	7 $6a - 2b$	8 $4p - q$	9 $x + 3$	10 0
11 $15h - 8k$	12 $14q$	13 $15a - 6b + 2$	14 $4x + 14y - z$	

Exercise 16

1 $7c$	2 $3m + 8$	3 $5x$
4 $2v - 6$	5 $18a - 3$	6 $8 - 3a^2$
7 k^3	8 $6q^2 + 4p$	9 $10x - 10y$
10 $4y - 4x$	11 $4d^4$	12 $5r^3 - 2r$

13 $3ab^2 + 2a^2b$　　　　**14** $11t^3$　　　　**15** $p^2 + 2pq - 15$

16 $4w^2$　　　　**17** $9a$　　　　**18** 0

Exercise 17			

1 $4c + 20$　　　　**2** $5a - 10$　　　　**3** $12x + 3$

4 $18k - 12h$　　　　**5** $50 + 60f$　　　　**6** $35x - 5y$

7 $2r^2 + 2r - 12$　　　　**8** $56 - 24h$　　　　**9** $3x^3 + 6x$

10 $15y^3 + 12y^2 + 9y$　　　　**11** $23 + 4j$　　　　**12** $p - 24q$

13 $30t + 100$　　　　**14** $7a + 4$　　　　**15** 12

Exercise 18			

1 $b^2 - 5b$　　　　**2** $t^2 + 3t$　　　　**3** $y^3 - 3y^2$

4 $5p^2 + 8p$　　　　**5** $z + 2z^2 - 3z^3 + 4z^4$　　　　**6** $m^3 + 4m^2$

7 $8h^2 - 9h$　　　　**8** $3d^2 + 21d$　　　　**9** $6x^2 - 60x$

10 $25x^4 + 5x^2$　　　　**11** $4v^4 - 12v^3 + 4v^2$　　　　**12** $2pr^2 + 2prh$

13 $15x^2y - 6xy^2$　　　　**14** $2a^3b + 8a^2b^2$　　　　**15** $10x^3 + 15x^3y - 25x^2y^2$

Exercise 19			

1 $7x + 6y$　　　　**2** $3c - 2d$　　　　**3** $23a - 24$

4 $5p - 23q$　　　　**5** $7a^3 + 3b$　　　　**6** $3ab - 2ac + 2bc$

7 $4 - 3x^2$　　　　**8** $3b - 2a$　　　　**9** $60 - 6x^3 + 5x$

10 $2p^2 + 7p - 9$

Exercise 20			

1 $x^2 + 3x + 2$　　　　**2** $x^2 + 11x + 30$　　　　**3** $2x^2 + 7x - 4$

4 $a^2 + 6a + 9$　　　　**5** $2y^2 - 17y - 30$　　　　**6** $x^2 - 1$

7 $6t^2 - 19t + 15$　　　　**8** $5m^2 + 26m + 5$　　　　**9** $25c^2 + 60c + 36$

10 $100x^2 - 1$

Exercise 21			

1 $2(a + 2b)$　　　　**2** $2(3p - q)$　　　　**3** $10(10x - y)$

4 $a(3 + 4b)$　　　　**5** $r(pq + st)$　　　　**6** $n(m - 4)$

7 $4t(2g + 3h)$　　　　**8** $a(3b - 4c + 5d)$　　　　**9** $x(2y - 3z)$

10 $t(u + 5t)$　　　　**11** $cd(c - d)$　　　　**12** $a(2b^2 - 6b + 1)$

13 $5(s^3 + 4)$　　　　**14** $xyz(x + y + z)$　　　　**15** $12d^2(3d - 1)$

16 $ap(2 + p^2)$　　　　**17** $ax(a + x)$　　　　**18** $y(3 - 2y^2)$

19 $a^3bc(a - b)$　　　　**20** $2\pi r(r + h)$

Exercise 22		

1 (a) $43, 48$　　　(b) each term is 5 greater than the previous term

2 (a) $52, 49$　　　(b) each term is 3 smaller than the previous term

3 (a) $162, 486$　　　(b) each term is 3 times the previous term

4 (a) $6, 3$　　　(b) each term is half of the previous term

5 (a) $25, 32$　　　(b) the differences increase by 1 each time

6 (a) $56, 72$　　　(b) the differences increase by 2 each time

7 (a) $55, 46$　　　(b) each term is 9 smaller than the previous term

8 (a) 34, 55 (b) each term is the previous two terms added

9 (a) 12, 12 (b) two sequences written alternately: one increases by 1 each time, the other decreases by 2 each time.

10 (a) 53, 68 (b) the differences increase by 2 each time

Exercise 23

1 22, 25 **2** 32, 40 **3** 38, 45 **4** 24, 30 **5** 30, 26
6 42, 68 **7** 62, 78 **8** 24, 25 **9** 145, 185 **10** 106, 128

Exercise 24

1 (a) $2n + 1$ (b) 15, 101 **2** (a) $5n - 1$ (b) 34, 249
3 (a) $3n + 9$ (b) 30, 159 **4** (a) $n + 4$ (b) 11, 54
5 (a) $10n - 3$ (b) 67, 497 **6** (a) $4n + 2$ (b) 30, 202
7 (a) $2n + 8$ (b) 22, 108 **8** (a) $(0.5)n$ (b) 3.5, 25
9 (a) $n - 3$ (b) 4, 47

Exercise 25

1 (a) 50, 65 (b) $n^2 + 1$ **2** (a) 72, 98 (b) $2n^2$
3 (a) 35, 48 (b) $n^2 - 1$ **4** (a) 144, 196 (b) $4n^2$
5 (a) 75, 101 (b) $2n^2 + 3$ **6** (a) 38, 51 (b) $n^2 + 2$
7 (a) 40, 53 (b) $n^2 + 4$ **8** (a) 43, 57 (b) $n^2 + n + 1$
9 (a) 48, 63 (b) $n^2 + 2n$ **10** (a) 42, 55 (b) $n^2 + 6$

Exercise 26

1 (a) $\frac{1}{7}, \frac{1}{8}$ (b) $\dfrac{1}{n + 1}$ **2** (a) $\frac{1}{12}, \frac{1}{14}$ (b) $\dfrac{1}{2n}$

3 (a) $\frac{7}{10}, \frac{8}{11}$ (b) $\dfrac{n + 1}{n + 4}$ **4** (a) $\frac{11}{13}, \frac{13}{15}$ (b) $\dfrac{2n - 1}{2n + 1}$

5 (a) $\frac{8}{18}, \frac{9}{20}$ (b) $\dfrac{n + 2}{2n + 6}$ **6** (a) $\frac{11}{12}, \frac{13}{14}$ (b) $\dfrac{2n - 1}{2n}$

7 (a) $\frac{6}{14}, \frac{7}{16}$ (b) $\dfrac{n}{2n + 2}$ **8** (a) $\frac{6}{17}, \frac{7}{20}$ (b) $\dfrac{n}{3n - 1}$

9 (a) $\frac{9}{12}, \frac{10}{13}$ (b) $\dfrac{n + 3}{n + 6}$ **10** (a) $\frac{17}{18}, \frac{20}{21}$ (b) $\dfrac{3n - 1}{3n}$

Exercise 27

1 63, 102, 165; each term is the sum of the two previous terms

2 47, 76, 123; each term is the sum of the two previous terms

3 81, 149, 274; each term is the sum of the three previous terms

4 105, 193, 355; each term is the sum of the three previous terms

5 896, 2448, 6688; each term is twice the sum of the two previous terms

6 109, 177, 287; each term is the sum of the two previous terms + 1

ANSWERS

Exercise 28

1 (a) £21 (b) £34.50 (c) £75
2 (a) 15 (b) 210 (c) 5050
3 (a) £36 (b) £78 (c) £252
4 (a) 4.2 (b) 65.4 (c) 0
5 (a) 33 (b) 9.416
6 (a) 66 (b) 66.05
7 $4x + 5y$ 8 $6p + 4$ 9 $3x + 2y$
10 $17 - 5x$ 11 $5x + 15$ 12 $7x - 20$
13 $8x - 12$ 14 $7x - 13$ 15 $2x + 19y$
16 $7x^2 + 11x - 31$ 17 $x^2 + 5x + 6$ 18 $2x^2 + 7x - 15$
19 $x^2 - 20x + 100$ 20 $x^2 - 100$ 21 51, 66
22 25, 12.5 23 $5x^6, 6x^7$ 24 67, 131
25 50, 43

Exercise 29

1 (a)(i) $\frac{1}{81}$ (ii) 1 (b) $2a^2b^2c$
2 $4 \rightarrow 24$ $10 \rightarrow 120$ $n \rightarrow n(n + 2)$
3 (a) ⊔⊔⊔⊔⊔ (b)

Pattern number	1	2	3	4	5	6	7
Number of sticks	3	5	7	9	11	13	15

(c) (i) 31 (ii) (Pattern no. × 2) + 1 (d) $S = 2n + 1$
4 (a) $80x$ (b) $80r + 60t$ (c) $80g + 120 = 1080$
5 (a) (i) 2, –1 (ii) Subtract 3 from previous term
  (b) $20 - 3n$ (c) –130
6 (a) (i) $3q^3$ (ii) $8x - 28$ (b) $7a^2 + 22ab$
7 (a) (i) 29 (ii) $4n - 3$ (b) $(4n - 3)^2$

Investigations

1 3rd differences: 0 0 0 …
Fourth, fifth, etc. differences will all be zeros.
(a) 6 7 9 12 16 21 27 …
  1st differences: 1 2 3 4 5 6 …
  2nd differences: 1 1 1 1 1 …
  3rd differences: 0 0 0 0 …
  4th differences: 0 0 0 …
Third, and subsequent, differences are all zero.
(b) 2 8 18 32 50 72 98 …
  1st differences: 6 10 14 18 22 26
  2nd differences: 4 4 4 4 4
Third, and subsequent, differences are all zero.

(c)

| | 1 | 8 | 27 | 64 | 125 | 216 | 343 | 512 | 729 | 1000 |

1st differences: 7 19 37 61   91 127 169 217 271

2nd differences: 12 18 24 30 36 42 48 54

3rd differences: 6   6   6   6   6   6   6

Fourth, and subsequent, differences are all zero.

(d)

| | 2 | 2 | 4 | 6 | 10 | 16 | 26 | 42 | 68 | 110 | 178 |

1st differences: 0   2   2   4   6   10 16 26 42 68

2nd differences: (2) 0   2   2   4   6   10 16 26

3rd differences: (–2 2) 0   2   2   4   6   10

4th differences: (4   –2   2) 0   2   2   4

5th differences: (–6   4   –2   2) 0   2

The differences are the same as the original sequence, moved along one term.

(e)

| | 2 | 3 | 5 | 9 | 17 | 33 | 65 | 129 | 257 | 513 |

1st differences: 1   2   4   8   16 32 64 128 256

2nd differences: 1   2   4   8   16 32 64 128

3rd differences: 1   2   4   8   16 32 64

All differences are the same, being increasing powers of 2.

The next two terms in each sequence are:

(a) 34, 42   (b) 128, 162   (c) 1331, 1728   (d) 288, 466
(e) 1025, 2049

2 A   For any three consecutive numbers, x, y, z, from the sequence, the difference between $x \times z$ and y^2 is always 1.

B   Dividing each term by the *previous* one gives a sequence which approaches the number 1.618 ...

Dividing each term by the *subsequent* one gives a sequence which approaches the number 0.618 ...

The ratio 1 : 1.618 is the same as the ratio 0.618 : 1; it is called the **golden ratio**, and appears much in classical art and sculpture.

5 Formulas, equations and inequalities

| **Exercise 1** | **1** 121 | **2** £414 | **3** 28p | **4** 17 |
| | **5** £1.74 | **6** 26p | **7** 532 | |

Exercise 2	**1** $x = 3$	**2** $k = 6$	**3** $t = 22$	**4** $y = 10$
	5 $x = 16$	**6** $r = 20$	**7** $y = 8$	**8** $p = 55$
	9 $z = 0$	**10** $v = 80$	**11** $t = 40$	**12** $t = 6$

ANSWERS

Exercise 3

1 $x = 16$	**2** $y = 30$	**3** $t = 18$	**4** $p = 16$
5 $m = 200$	**6** $s = 14$	**7** $x = 90$	**8** $t = 64$
9 $s = 25$	**10** $v = 5$	**11** $x = 800$	**12** $z = 100$
13 $d = 0$	**14** $x = 30$		

Exercise 4

1 $x = 2$	**2** $k = 5$	**3** $t = 4$	**4** $y = 12$
5 $y = 9$	**6** $p = 8$	**7** $x = 6$	**8** $y = 10$
9 $t = 14$	**10** $d = 6$	**11** $d = 60$	**12** $s = 0$

Exercise 5

1 $x = 2$	**2** $k = 3$	**3** $t = 1$	**4** $y = 5$
5 $x = 10$	**6** $r = 4$	**7** $y = 9$	**8** $p = 6$
9 $x = 20$	**10** $v = 1$	**11** $t = 5$	**12** $x = 6$
13 $y = 7$	**14** $a = 6$	**15** $b = 5$	

Exercise 6

1 $x = -3$	**2** $k = -4$	**3** $t = -\frac{1}{2}$	**4** $y = 7$
5 $x = -3$	**6** $r = 6\frac{2}{3}$	**7** $y = 4$	**8** $p = -4$
9 $x = -5$	**10** $z = -2\frac{1}{2}$	**11** $b = 1\frac{1}{2}$	**12** $c = -2$
13 $h = 10$	**14** $y = -1$	**15** $m = -6\frac{2}{3}$	**16** $r = -\frac{2}{5}$
17 $t = \frac{2}{3}$	**18** $g = 10$	**19** $c = 4\frac{1}{2}$	**20** $x = -11$

Exercise 7

1 $t = 7$	**2** $H = 1$	**3** $n = 8$	**4** $c = 5$
5 $x = 8$	**6** $x = -1$	**7** $s = -2$	**8** $x = 2$
9 $b = 3$	**10** $w = -2$	**11** $r = 3\frac{1}{2}$	**12** $z = 1$
13 $x = 1$	**14** $y = 8$	**15** $x = -1\frac{1}{2}$	**16** $k = 1$
17 $p = 2$	**18** $v = 3$	**19** $g = 3\frac{1}{2}$	**20** $t = 4$

Exercise 8

1 $x = 4$	**2** $t = 2$	**3** $n = 5$	**4** $p = 5$
5 $x = 2$	**6** $t = 5$	**7** $s = 2$	**8** $x = 2$

Exercise 9

1 (a) £$(X + 12)$ (b) £$(2X + 12)$
  (c) $2X + 12 = 50$: $X = 19$. Jack has £19, Jill has £31
2 $9x + 20 = 177.5$: $x = 17.5$, each payment is £17.50
3 $c + (c + 1) = 37$: $c = 18$, Charles is 18 years old
4 $t + (t + 3) + t + (t + 3) = 46$ or $4t + 6 = 46$: $t = 10$ cm
5 $a + b + o = 2b + b + (23 + b) = 143$ or $4b + 23 = 143$: $b = 30$, the apple weighs 60 g, the banana weighs 30 g and the orange weighs 53 g
6 $3j + 3j + j = 14$: $j = 2$ kg, parents each pick 6 kg, Judy picks 2 kg
7 $s + 2s + 2s = 30$ m: $s = 6$ m, lengths are 12 m, 12 m and 6 m
8 $60t + (40 \times 2t) = 980$ or $140t = 980$: $t = 7$, she bought 7 tulips and 14 daffodils

Exercise 10

1 $x = \pm 5.48$ **2** $x = \pm 7.07$ **3** $x = 2.35$

4 $x = 3.91$ **5** $x = 3.29, -3.79$ **6** $x = \pm 7.07$

7 $x = 2.33$ **8** $x = 18.34, -16.34$

Exercise 11

1 $x = 1, y = 2$ **2** $a = 6, b = 2$ **3** $p = 5, q = 1$ **4** $x = 2, y = 7$

5 $m = 6, n = 8$ **6** $s = 3, t = 3$ **7** $a = 4, b = 5$ **8** $x = 10, y = 1$

9 $m = 4, n = 3$ **10** $y = 1, z = 0$

Exercise 12

1 $x = 4, y = 6$ **2** $a = 1, b = 2$ **3** $p = 5, q = 3$ **4** $u = 10, v = 3$

5 $x = 7, y = 1$ **6** $c = 4, d = 3$ **7** $x = 2, y = 8$ **8** $p = 1, q = 3$

9 $s = 5, t = 5$

Exercise 13

1 $d = 2, e = 5$ **2** $x = 10, y = 4$ **3** $p = 7, q = 6$ **4** $x = 12, y = 8$

5 $a = 13, b = 7$ **6** $u = 4, v = 5$ **7** $a = 3, b = 4$ **8** $s = 2, t = 3$

9 $x = 49, y = 1$

Exercise 14

1 $x = 5, y = -1$ **2** $a = 3, b = 7$ **3** $p = 9, q = 7$ **4** $a = 3, b = 2$

5 $u = 4, v = 5$ **6** $y = 9, z = 1$ **7** $d = 8, e = 2$ **8** $x = 2, y = 2$

9 $x = 5, y = 0$

Exercise 15

1 $x = 4, y = 2$ **2** $x = 5, y = 2$ **3** $x = 3, y = -1$ **4** $x = 7, y = 2$

5 $x = 4, y = -2$ **6** $x = -2, y = 5$ **7** $x = 1, y = 6$ **8** $x = 2, y = -3$

9 $x = 10, y = 5$ **10** $x = 5, y = -4$ **11** $x = \frac{1}{2}, y = 4$ **12** $x = 20, y = 3$

13 $x = 3, y = \frac{3}{2}$ **14** $x = 2, y = -5$ **15** $x = \frac{5}{2}, y = -1$

Exercise 16

1 $3b + s = 27$, $b + 2s = 24$: $b = 6\text{p}$, $s = 9\text{p}$

2 $4n + s = 28$, $2n + 3s = 34$: $n = 5$ g, $s = 8$ g

3 $4A + 3B = 30$, $3A + 6B = 30$: $A = 6$ cm, $B = 2$ cm

4 $5X + 4Y = 46$, $2X - 3Y = 0$: $X = £6$, $Y = £4$

5 $3a + 2o = 88$, $a + 3o = 76$: $a = 16\text{p}$, $o = 20\text{p}$

Exercise 17

1 $d = c - 5$ **2** $n = 3m - 12$ **3** $x = y + 2$ **4** $s = 10 - 4r$

5 $p = \dfrac{t}{2}$ **6** $h = \dfrac{5g}{3}$ **7** $p = \dfrac{m + 5}{2}$ **8** $k = \dfrac{a - 4}{3}$

9 $V = \dfrac{k}{P}$ **10** $z = \dfrac{x}{m}$ **11** $v = \dfrac{330}{f}$ **12** $d = \dfrac{w}{6}$

Exercise 18

1 $R = \dfrac{V}{I}$ **2** $b = d - 3a$ **3** $q = \dfrac{2p}{3}$ **4** $r = \dfrac{C}{2\pi}$

5 $m = \dfrac{y - c}{x}$ **6** $x = \dfrac{z - 3}{2}$ **7** $v = at + u$ **8** $d = \dfrac{x}{3} + 4$

9 $C = \frac{5}{9}(F - 32)$ **10** $V = \dfrac{kT}{P}$

Exercise 19

1 $t = 40$ **2** $x = -0.6$ **3** $u = 20$ **4** $b = 6$
5 $p = 11$ **6** $m = 4$ **7** $p = 7$ **8** $C = 8\frac{1}{2}$
9 $y = 5\frac{1}{2}$ **10** $M = 4$ **11** $w = 5\frac{1}{2}$ **12** $C = 10$
13 $c = 2\frac{1}{2}$ **14** $u = 20$

Exercise 20

1 $x > 2$ **2** $k < 34$ **3** $t > 9$ **4** $y > 7$
5 $x < 7$ **6** $r > 10$ **7** $y < 6\frac{1}{2}$ **8** $p > -5$
9 $z < -3\frac{1}{4}$

Exercise 21

1 $x < 3$ **2** $k < 17$ **3** $t > 3$ **4** $y > -3$
5 $x < 8$ **6** $y < 1$ **7** $n < 3$ **8** $x < -\frac{20}{3}$
9 $z < 14$

Exercise 22

1 $t = 5, 6, 7, 8, 9$ **2** $x = 1, 2, 3, 4, 5, 6, 7, 8, 9$
3 $s = -4, -3, -2, -1, 0, 1,$ **4** $n = 2, 3, 4, 5, 6, 7, 8, 9, 10$
5 $x = 1, 2, 3, 4, 5$ **6** $t = -3, -2, -1, 0, 1, 2, 3$
7 $x = -9, -8, -7, -6, -5, -4, -3$
8 $m = 11, 12, 13, 14, 15, 16, 17, 18, 19, 20$
9 $n = 0, 1, 2, 3, 4, 5, 6, 7, 8, 9$

Exercise 23

1 $-3 < x < 3$ **2** $-5 < c < 5$ **3** $-6 \leqslant s \leqslant 6$ **4** $-8 < x < 8$
5 $-7 < x < 7$ **6** $-2 < k < 2$ **7** $-\frac{3}{2} \leqslant x \leqslant \frac{3}{2}$ **8** $-20 \leqslant n \leqslant 20$
9 $-\frac{1}{2} < d < \frac{1}{2}$ **10** $0.1 \leqslant x \leqslant 0.1$

Exercise 24

1 $x = 5$ **2** $x = 13$ **3** $x = 8$
4 $x = 6$ **5** $x = 7$ **6** $x = 11$
7 $x = 10$ **8** $x = 9$ **9** $x = 5$
10 $x = 8$ **11** $x = -4$ **12** $x = -8$
13 $x = 2\frac{1}{2}$ **14** $x = 1\frac{1}{4}$ **15** $x = 2$
16 $x = 2.35$ **17** $x = 4.14$ **18** $x = 4.79$
19 $x = 5.85$ **20** $x = 3.45$ **21** $x = 7.53$
22 $x = 2.86$ **23** $x = 4.64$ **24** $x = 7, y = 5$
25 $x = 10, y = 7$ **26** $x = 2, y = 3$ **27** $x = 8, y = 2$

28 $x = 6, y = 1$ **29** $x = 8, y = 2\frac{1}{2}$ **30** $x = 7, y = -2$

31 $x = \frac{2}{3}, y = \frac{1}{3}$ **32** $y = \dfrac{x}{4}$ **33** $k = 3h + 5$

34 $k = \dfrac{h+5}{3}$ **35** $k = \dfrac{h}{3} + 5$ **36** $n = 3(m - 2p)$

37 $F = \dfrac{9C}{5} + 32$ **38** $t = \sqrt{\dfrac{s}{10}}$ **39** $u = \sqrt{v^2 - 2as}$

40 $x > 7$ **41** $x < 5$ **42** $x < 19$

43 $x > 30$ **44** $x > 4$ **45** $x > 4$

46 $x > 2\frac{1}{2}$ **47** $x > 2$ **48** $-12 < x < 12$

49 $5 < x < 11$

Exercise 25

1 (a) $x = 5$ (b) $y = 4$ (c) $p = 3\frac{1}{5}$ (d) $x = -4\frac{1}{2}$ (e) $x \leqslant 2\frac{1}{2}$

2 2.8   **3** (a) $x = 2, y = \frac{1}{2}$ (b) $-3, -2, -1, 0, 1, 2, 3$

4 (a) $x = 6$ (b) $x = 3\frac{1}{2}, y = \frac{1}{2}$ (c) 2, 3   (d) $x = 2$ or $x = 3$

5 $x = 1.3$ **6** (a) (i) $2(5x + 2)$ (ii) $2x(3x + 2)$ (b) $A = 112$

7 $t = 2.44$ **8** (a) $a = 1\frac{1}{2}$ (b) $b = 4$ (c) $c = 5\frac{3}{5}$

9 (a) $n = -2, -1, 0, 1, 2$ and 3   (b) $x > -3$

10 (a) $3x(x - 2)$ (b) $3x^2 - 10x - 8$ (c) $t = \dfrac{4w - 3}{5}$

11 (a) $x = 5$ (b) $x = 12\frac{1}{2}$ (c) $x = 24$ (d) $x = 8$

12 $x = 2, y = -3$ **13** (a) $13x - 4$ (b) (i) $y \geqslant -2$ (ii) $x \geqslant 5$ or $x \leqslant -5$

14 (a) $4 + x$ (b) $2(4 + x + 1 + x) = 10 + 4x$ (c) $x = 6$

15 (a) $4x + 20$ (b) (i) $4x + 20 = 180$ (ii) $44°$

16 (a) (i) $x = 4$ (ii) $x = -3$ or $x = 4$

(b) $x = 5, y = -1$ (c) $n = -1, 0, 1$

Investigations

1 A (a) (i) no change   (ii) inequality sign has to be reversed

(b) (i) no change   (ii) inequality sign has to be reversed

B If $\dfrac{1}{x} < k$, then $x > \dfrac{1}{k}$

If $\dfrac{-1}{x} < k$, then $x > \dfrac{-1}{k}$

6 Graphical representation

Exercise 1

1 H = (−2, 4)
I = (7, −3)
J = (−5, −2)
K = (0, −4)
L = (−4, 1)

2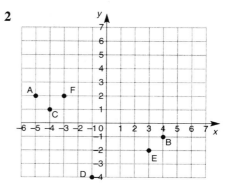

Exercise 2

1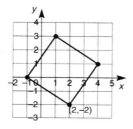

2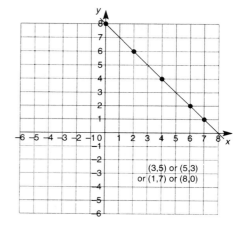

(3,5) or (5,3)
or (1,7) or (8,0)

3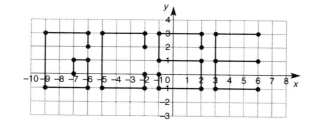

Exercise 3

1

x	−3	−2	−1	0	1	2	3	4
x + 2	−1	0	1	2	3	4	5	6

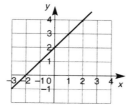

2

x	−3	−2	−1	0	1	2	3	4
x − 1	−4	−3	−2	−1	0	1	2	3

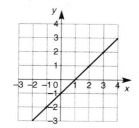

3

x	–3	–2	–1	0	1	2	3	4
$2x + 5$	–1	1	3	5	7	9	11	13

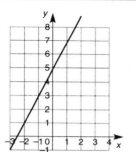

4

x	–3	–2	–1	0	1	2	3	4
$5 - x$	8	7	6	5	4	3	2	1

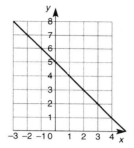

5

x	–3	–2	–1	0	1	2	3	4
$3x - 5$	–14	–11	–8	–5	–2	1	4	7

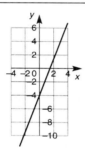

6

x	–3	–2	–1	0	1	2	3	4
$\frac{x}{2} + 7$	$5\frac{1}{2}$	6	$6\frac{1}{2}$	7	$7\frac{1}{2}$	8	$8\frac{1}{2}$	9

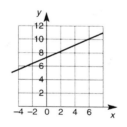

7

x	–3	–2	–1	0	1	2	3	4
$\frac{x}{2} - 1$	$-2\frac{1}{2}$	–2	$-1\frac{1}{2}$	–1	$-\frac{1}{2}$	0	$\frac{1}{2}$	1

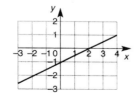

8

x	0	1	2	3	4	5	6	7	8
$15 - 2x$	15	13	11	9	7	5	3	1	–1

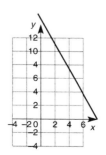

9

x	0	1	2	3	4	5	6	7	8	9	10	11	12
$10 - x$	10	9	8	7	6	5	4	3	2	1	0	−1	−2

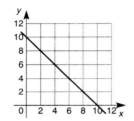

10

x	−3	−2	−1	0	1	2	3	4
$2x - 2$	−8	−6	−4	−2	0	2	4	6

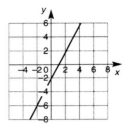

Exercise 4

1

x	−3	−2	−1	0	1	2	3	4
$y = 8 - x$	11	10	9	8	7	6	5	4

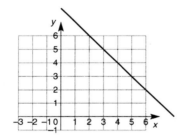

2

x	−3	−2	−1	0	1	2	3	4
$y = 2x - 3$	−9	−7	−5	−3	−2	1	3	5

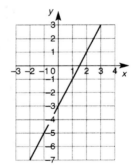

3

x	−3	−2	−1	0	1	2	3	4
$y = x + 2$	−1	0	1	2	3	4	5	6

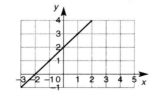

4

x	−3	−2	−1	0	1	2	3	4
$y = 12 - x$	15	14	13	12	11	10	9	8

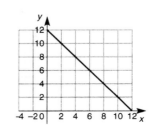

5

x			-3	-2	-1	0	1	2	3	4
$y = x + 4$			1	2	3	4	5	6	7	8

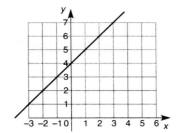

6

x			-3	-2	-1	0	1	2	3	4
$y = 2x + 4$			-2	0	-2	4	5	8	10	12

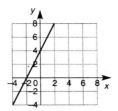

7

x			-3	-2	-1	0	1	2	3	4
$y = 2x + \frac{5}{2}$			$-3\frac{1}{2}$	$-1\frac{1}{2}$	$-\frac{1}{2}$	$2\frac{1}{2}$	$-4\frac{1}{2}$	$6\frac{1}{2}$	$9\frac{1}{2}$	$10\frac{1}{2}$

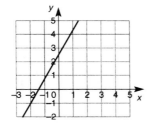

8

x			-3	-2	-1	0	1	2	3	4
$y = 2x + 3$			-3	-1	1	3	5	7	9	11

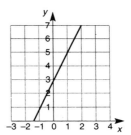

9

x			-3	-2	-1	0	1	2	3	4
$y = 2x - \frac{2}{3}$			$-6\frac{2}{3}$	$-4\frac{2}{3}$	$-2\frac{2}{3}$	$\frac{2}{3}$	$-1\frac{1}{3}$	$3\frac{1}{3}$	$5\frac{1}{3}$	$7\frac{1}{3}$

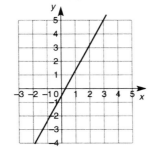

10

x			-3	-2	-1	0	1	2	3	4
$y = \frac{x}{2} + 4$			$2\frac{1}{2}$	3	$3\frac{1}{2}$	4	$4\frac{1}{2}$	5	$5\frac{1}{2}$	6

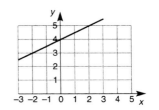

Exercise 5

1 (0, 3), (1, 4), (2, 5), (3, 6) etc.

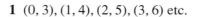
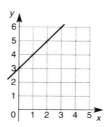

2 (0, −1), (1, 1), (2, 3), (3, 5) etc.

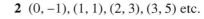
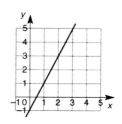

3 (0, 2), (1, 3), (2, 4), (3, 5) etc.

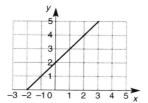

4 (1, 0), (4, 1), (7, 2), (10, 3) etc.

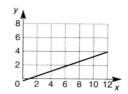

5 (0, 4), (2, 5), (4, 6), (6, 7) etc.

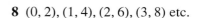
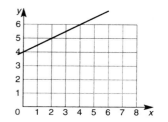

6 (0, −1), (1, 2), (2, 5), (3, 8) etc.

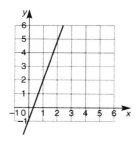

7 (3, 9), (4, 8), (5, 7), (6, 6) etc.

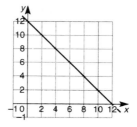

8 (0, 2), (1, 4), (2, 6), (3, 8) etc.

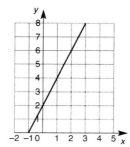

9 (4, 0), (5, 1), (6, 2), (7, 3) etc.

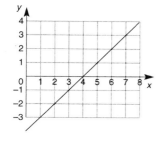

10 (1, 9), (2, 8), (3, 7), (4, 6) etc.

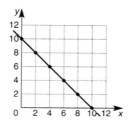

11 (4, 0), (6, 1), (8, 2), (10, 3) etc.

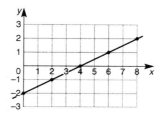

12 $(0, 16), (1, 14), (2, 12), (3, 10)$ etc.   **13** $(0, 3), (3, 2), (6, 1), (9, 0)$ etc.

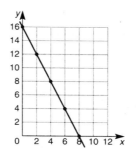

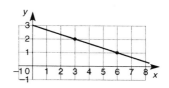

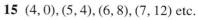

14 $(0, 8), (3, 6), (6, 4), (9, 2)$ etc.   **15** $(4, 0), (5, 4), (6, 8), (7, 12)$ etc.

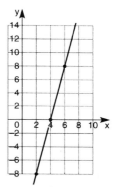

Exercise 6 **1** $(0, 1)$ **2** $(0, -4)$ **3** $(0, -3)$ **4** $(0, 5)$ **5** $(0, -2)$
6 $(0, 3)$ **7** $(0, -1)$ **8** $(0, \frac{3}{4})$ **9** $(0, \frac{1}{2})$

Exercise 7 **1** (a) 2 (b) −1 **2** (a) 3 (b) 4 **3** (a) 5 (b) 2
4 (a) 1 (b) −7 **5** (a) $\frac{1}{2}$ (b) 2 **6** (a) $\frac{2}{3}$ (b) −2
7 (a) −1 (b) 3 **8** (a) −2 (b) 0 **9** (a) −3 (b) 10

Exercise 8 **1** $1, 2; y = x + 2$ **2** $\frac{1}{2}, 1; y = \frac{x}{2} + 1 \ (2y = x + 2)$
3 $2, -2; y = 2x - 2$ **4** $-1, 4; y = -x + 4(x + y = 4)$
5 $-2, 6; y = -2x + 6(2x + y = 6)$ **6** $\frac{1}{2}, -2; y = \frac{x}{2} - 2(2y = x - 4)$

Exercise 9 **1** $x = 2, y = 3$ **2** $x = 4, y = 1$ **3** $x = 3, y = -2$
4 $x = -2, y = 4$ **5** $x = -1, y = -3$ **6** $x = 0, y = 4$

_____ **Exercise 10**

1

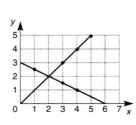

$x = 3, y = 1$

2

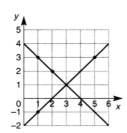

$x = 2, y = 2$

3

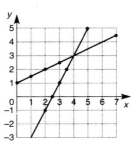

$x = 4, y = 3$

4

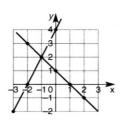

$x = -1, y = 2$

5

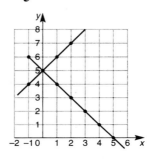

$x = 0, y = 5$

6

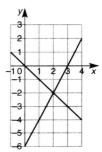

$x = 2, y = -2$

_____ **Exercise 11**

1

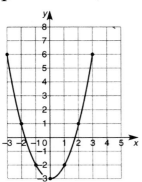

2

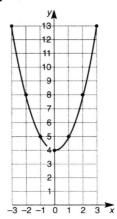

3

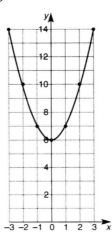

4

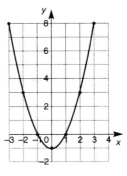

5

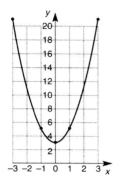

6

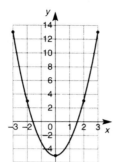

7

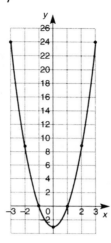

8

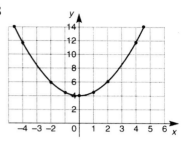

9

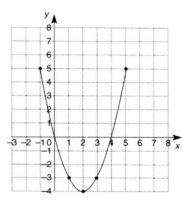

Exercise 12

1 (a) $x = 2.8$ and -2.8
  (b) $x = 2.35$ and -2.35

2 (a) $x = 2$ and -2
  (b) $x = 3.3$ and -3.3

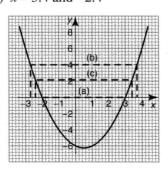

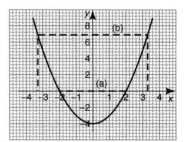

3 (a) $x = 3$ and -2
  (b) $x = 3.7$ and -2.7
  (c) $x = 3.4$ and -2.4

4 (a) $x = 4$ and -1
  (b) $x = 3.3$ and -0.3

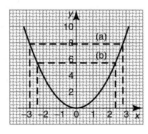

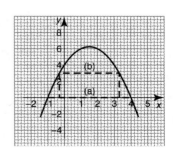

5 (a) $x = 2.5$ and -2
   (b) $x = 1.5$ and -1

6 (a) $x = 3.7$ and -0.7
   (b) $x = 3.7$ and -0.7

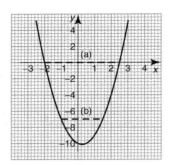
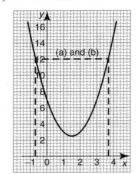

Exercise 13

1 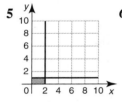   **2** 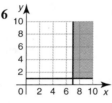   **3** 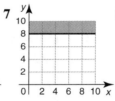   **4**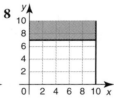

5 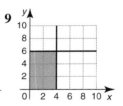   **6** 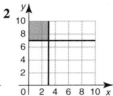   **7** 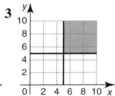   **8** 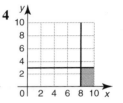   **9**

Exercise 14

1 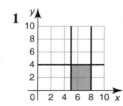   **2** 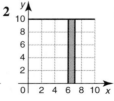   **3** 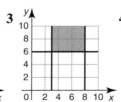   **4**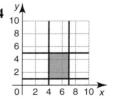

5 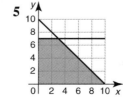   **6** 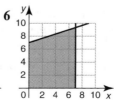   **7** 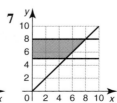   **8**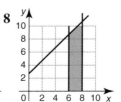

Exercise 15

1 (a) 1400 (b) 60 km/h (c) 1 h (d) 10 km
   (e) 1 h (f) 1.5 h (g) 46.7 km/h
2 (a) 1000 (b) $\frac{1}{2}$ h (c) 70 km (d) 1 h
   (e) third (f) 60 km/h
3 (a) 20 cm (b) 1.15 p.m. (c) 200 cm/h
   (d) 1.15 p.m. and 1.30 p.m. (e) 160 cm/h
   (f) 1.33 p.m. (g) 15 min (h) 100 cm/h
4 (a) 66.7 km/h (b) 100 km/h (c) 4.30 p.m. (d) 5.00 p.m.
5 (a) $\frac{1}{2}$ h (b) 10.00 p.m. (c) 50 km (d) 10.42 a.m.
   (e) Steve's (f) $\frac{1}{2}$ h

Exercise 16

1 (a) $(-2, 10), (5, 10)$ (b) $(-2, -6), (5, -6)$ (c) $(1, 6), (1, -2)$

2 (a)

x	0	1	2	3	4
y	12	9	6	3	0

(b)

x	-4	-3	-2	-1	0
y	0	3	6	9	12

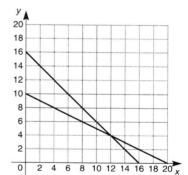

(c) Area of triangle = 48 sq. units.

3 (a) $(0, 16), (16, 0)$
   (b) $(0, 10), (20, 0)$
   (c) $(12, 4)$

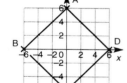

4 AB: $y = x + 6$
   BC: $x + y = -6$
   CD: $y = x - 6$
   DA: $x + y = 6$

5

x	-4	-3	-2	-1	0	1	2	3	4
y	20	13	8	5	4	5	8	13	20

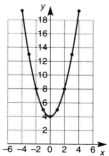

(a) $y = 4$
(b) $-3 < x < 3$

6

x	0	1	2	3	4	5	6	7	8
y	15	10	7.5	6	5	4.3	3.75	3.3	3

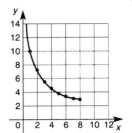

(a) $y = 4$

(b) $x = 3.5$

(c) $y = 0.1 \left(\frac{30}{300}\right)$

As x becomes larger and larger, y becomes smaller and smaller, getting nearer and nearer to zero, but never quite reaching zero.

7

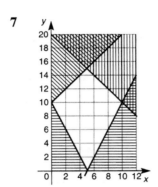

Shape is a kite

Exercise 17

1 $x = 1.2, y = 1.4$

2 (a)

x	−3	−2	−1	0	1	2
y	−3	−1	1	3	5	7

(b)

(c) (i) $y = 6$ (ii) $x = -1.75$

3 (a) (b) (i) min $y = -4.25$ (ii) $x = 2.56$ or -1.56

4 $y \leqslant 6, y \geqslant x$

5 (a) 3

(b) $y = 3x + 1$

6 (a)

x	−3	−2	−1	0	1	2	3
y	−17	0	5	4	3	8	25

(b)

(c) $x = 0, -1.4$ or 1.4

7 (a) $y = x + 2$ (b)

(b)

(c) $x = 3.3, y = 1.3$

8 (a)

x	-2	-1	0	1	2	3	4
y	25	13	5	1	1	5	13

(c) $x = -0.7$ and 3.7

(d) $2x^2 - 6x - 5 = 0$

9 (b) $x = 0.8$ $y = 1.4$

10 (b) Find the x-coordinate of the point where lines meet

11 $a = -\frac{3}{5}$ $b = 3$

12 (a)

x	-2	-1	0	1	2	3	4
y	6	1	-2	-3	-2	1	6

(c) $x = -0.7$ and 2.7

13 (a) $A = (0, -1)$ $B = (2, 0)$

(b) $\frac{1}{2}$ (c) Lines are parallel (same gradient)

(d) $x + y = 2$

14 (i) (d)   (ii) (a)   (iii) (f)

Investigations

1 (i)

x	-4	-3	-2	-1	0	1	2	3	4
y	16	9	4	1	0	1	4	9	16

(ii)

x	-4	-3	-2	-1	0	1	2	3	4
y	19	12	7	4	3	4	7	12	19

(iii)

x	-4	-3	-2	-1	0	1	2	3	4
y	9	2	-3	-6	-7	-6	-3	2	9

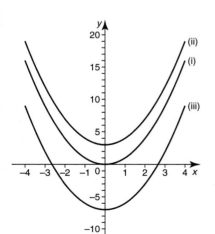

All three graphs are identical in shape, but moved vertically.

Extension

(i)

x	−4	−3	−2	−1	0	1	2	3	4
y	9	4	1	0	1	4	9	16	25

(ii)

x	−6	−5	−4	−3	−2	−1	0	1	2
y	9	4	1	0	1	4	9	16	25

(iii)

x	2	3	4	5	6	7	8	9	10
y	25	16	9	4	1	0	1	4	9

All three graphs are identical in shape, but moved horizontally.

2 All such lines are parallel with those shown in the diagram.

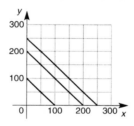

Extension

All such lines are parallel with those shown in the diagram.

As *K* increases, the lines move further away from the origin.

If *K* = 0, the line passes through origin.

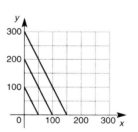

(i)

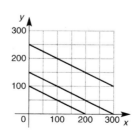

(ii)

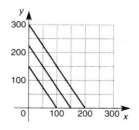

7 Measures

Exercise 1

1 70 mm	**2** 400 cm	**3** 0.043 km	**4** 6.25 cm	**5** 1.25 kg
6 310 ml	**7** 1370 g	**8** 130 cl	**9** 3000 m	**10** 3.51 m
11 30 ml	**12** 2000 kg	**13** 0.2 g	**14** 0.4 l	**15** 0.7 t
16 0.003 kg	**17** 49.8 cm	**18** 70 ml	**19** 113.2 mm	**20** 963 cm

Exercise 2

1 1.05 litres   **2** 2550 metres   **3** 1500 bags   **4** 48.6 kg

5 25   **6** 4 kg 725 g   **7** 10.5 kg

8 750 mm, 35 m, 0.072 km, 78 m, 0.3 km, 0.4 km, 550 m, 1.5 km

9 0.012 l, 0.02 l, 0.14 l, 1.3 l, 270 cl, 400 cl, 600 cl, 750 cl

10 112 kg, 0.2 t, 300 kg, 0.8 t, 0.85 t, 875 kg, 1.4 t, 1500 kg

Exercise 3

1 6 ft $11\frac{1}{2}$ in	**2** 14 pints	**3** 8 st 13 lb	**4** 12 oz	**5** 5 ft 5 in
6 110 yd	**7** 10 ft	**8** 35 oz	**9** 7 yd 1 ft	**10** 5 fl. oz
11 $6\frac{1}{2}$ cwt	**12** 2 ft $7\frac{1}{4}$ in			

Exercise 4

1 9 in	**2** 7 ft 2 in	**3** 6 gal 5 pt	**4** 660 yd	**5** $1\frac{3}{4}$ tons
6 $13\frac{1}{8}$ gal	**7** 11 st	**8** 16 st	**9** $4\frac{3}{4}$ oz	**10** 48

Exercise 5

1 22 lb	**2** 15 cm	**3** 24 km	**4** 7 kg	**5** 10.29 l
6 $33\frac{3}{4}$ miles	**7** 7 pt	**8** 20 kg	**9** 60 cm	**10** 40 km
11 237.5 cm	**12** 1.19 kg	**13** $4\frac{1}{2}$ m	**14** 40 ft	**15** 60 miles

Exercise 6

1 6.14 kg	**2** 85 cm	**3** $207\frac{1}{2}$ miles	**4** 6.6 lb	**5** 14 oz
6 12 m	**7** 6.56 gal	**8** 17.6 lb	**9** 8 m	**10** 6 ft

Exercise 7

1 kg	**2** cm	**3** km	**4** cm
5 litres	**6** cm	**7** cm	**8** ml
9 litres	**10** km	**11** ml	**12** mm

Exercise 8

1 (a) 17 cm	(b) 17.5 cm^2		**2** (a) 17 cm	(b) 18 cm^2
3 (a) 28 m	(b) 24 m^2		**4** (a) 25 m	(b) 19 m^2
5 (a) 28 cm	(b) 28.75 cm^2		**6** (a) 28 cm	(b) 24 cm^2
7 (a) 30 cm	(b) 38.5 cm^2			

Exercise 9

1 9 cm^2	**2** 20 cm^2	**3** 20 m^2	**4** 20 m^2	**5** 27 cm^2
6 42 cm^2	**7** 30 m^2	**8** 6.75 m^2		

Exercise 10

	Rectangles					Triangles		
	Length	Breadth	Area	Perimeter		Base	Height	Area
1	3 m	2 m	6 m^2	10 m	**9**	4 m	3 m	6 m^2
2	9 m	5 m	45 m^2	28 m	**10**	10 m	14 m	70 m^2
3	4 cm	3 cm	12 cm^2	14 cm	**11**	18 cm	12.5 cm	112.5 cm^2
4	6 cm	4 cm	24 cm^2	20 cm	**12**	24 cm	16 cm	192 cm^2
5	10 m	7.5 m	75 m^2	35 m				
6	18 cm	4.5 cm	81 cm^2	45 cm				
7	40 cm	12.5 cm	500 cm^2	105 cm				
8	30 cm	25 cm	750 cm^2	110 cm				

Exercise 11

1 24 cm^2 **2** 22 cm^2 **3** 24 cm^2 **4** 24 cm^2
5 53.4 cm^2 **6** 25.6 cm^2 **7** 26.25 cm^2 **8** 8.4 m^2
9 21.875 cm^2

Exercise 12

1 37.70 cm **2** 69.11 cm **3** 25.13 cm **4** 40.84 cm
5 9.42 cm **6** 34.56 cm **7** 163.36 cm **8** 31.42 cm
9 23.88 m **10** 87.96 cm **11** 6.37 cm **12** 13.53 m
13 38.20 m **14** 47.75 mm **15** 28.65 cm **16** 20.05 m

Exercise 13

1 188.5 cm **2** 34.5 mm **3** 204.2 cm **4** 40 023.89 km
5 942.48 cm **6** 21.36 m

Exercise 14

1 78.5 m^2 **2** 201.06 m^2 **3** 113.10 cm^2
4 38.48 m^2 **5** 19.63 cm^2 **6** 132.73 cm^2
7 18.86 cm^2 **8** 45.36 cm^2 **9** 50.27 m^2
10 78.54 cm^2 **11** 4.55 cm **12** 5.64 m
13 7.57 mm **14** 5.47 cm **15** 2.52 m

Exercise 15

1 201.06 m^2 **2** 113 m^2 **3** 9.62 m^2 **4** 4.52 m^2
5 1.60 m **6** 4.6 m **7** 706.19 cm^2 **8** 138.54 cm^2
9 38.48 cm^2 **10** 17.36 m^2

Exercise 16

1 54 cm^3 **2** 40 cm^3 **3** 330 cm^3
4 141.37 cm^3 **5** 603.19 cm^3 **6** 200 cm^3
7 96.21 cm^3 **8** 48 cm^3 **9** 15 cm^3
10 60 cm^3 **11** 112.5 cm^3 **12** 150 cm^3

Exercise 17

1 2.5 cm	**2** 1.78 cm	**3** 7.08 m	**4** 4.58 mm
5 1.99 m	**6** 3.5 m	**7** 3 cm	**8** 1.27 m

Exercise 16

1 132 m^2	**2** 132 cm^2	**3** 26 cm^2	**4** 30 cm^2
5 156 cm^2	**6** 84 cm^2	**7** 42 cm^2	**8** 30 cm^2
9 3600 cm^2	**10** 660 cm^2	**11** 620 cm^2	**12** 960 cm^2

Exercise 19

1 030°	**2** 300°	**3** 310°	**4** 110°	**5** 225°
6 025°	**7** 115°	**8** S20°E	**9** S5°W	**10** N30°W
11 S22°E	**12** N25°E	**13** N75°E	**14** N65°W	**15** S70°E

Exercise 20

Check the compass directions and 3-figures bearings you have drawn.

Exercise 21

1 (a) 100 km	(b) 132 km	(c) 276 km	(d) 288 km
2 (a) 7.5 km	(b) 14 km	(c) 41.5 km	(d) 42 km
3 (a) 87.5 km	(b) 30 km	(c) 242.5 km	(d) 169.25 km
4 (a) 3 km	(b) 8.4 km	(c) 60.6 km	(d) 72.6 km
5 (a) 175 km	(b) 42 km	(c) 532 km	(d) 616 km

Exercise 22

Bearings should be ±2° of those shown below, and distances ±0.5 km.

1 (a) 033°	(b) 32.4 km		**2** (a) 277°	(b) 9.6 km
3 (a) 052°	(b) 15 km		**4** (a) 187°	(b) 10.5 km
5 (a) 242°	(b) 23.1 km		**6** (a) 062°	(b) 23. km
7 (a) 213°	(b) 32.4 km		**8** (a) 350°	(b) 16.5 km
9 (a) 072°	(b) 26.7 km		**10** (a) 232°	(b) 37.8 km
11 (a) 016°	(b) 15.6 km		**12** (a) 170°	(b) 16.5 km

Exercise 23

1 30 m	**2** 5 km	**3** 200 m	**4** 400 m	**5** 1.25 km
6 8.75 km	**7** 1.25 km	**8** 600 m	**9** 4.8 km	**10** 2.175 km

Exercise 24

1 1.65 cm and 1.75 cm	**2** 8.25 m and 8.35 m
3 10.35 km and 10.45 km	**4** 9.5 cm and 9.15 cm
5 4.45 m and 4.55 m	**6** 7.95 m and 8.05 m
7 2.95 cm and 3.05 cm	**8** 4.845 cm and 4.855 cm
9 2.125 mm and 2.15 mm	**10** 7.245 cm and 7.255 cm
11 8.945 cm and 8.955 cm	**12** 2.05 mm and 2.15 mm
13 14.505 m and 14.515 m	**14** 8.385 m and 8.395 m
15 7.115 cm and 7.125 cm	

Exercise 25

1 50 mm	**2** 40 ml	**3** 3500 kg	**4** 2 kg	**5** 752 cm
6 0.7 m	**7** 17	**8** 45 kg	**9** 30 pt	**10** 4 yd
11 24 oz	**12** 4 ft 8 in	**13** 90 cm	**14** 5.71 l	**15** 64 km

16 (a) 15.4 cm (b) 14.4 cm^2 **17** (a) 27 cm (b) 35.5 cm^2

18 (a) 40 cm (b) 64 cm^2 **19** 40 cm^2 **20** 60 cm^2

21 136 cm^2 **22** 8.75 cm^2 **23** (a) 31.42 cm (b) 78.54 cm^2

24 (a) 37.70 cm (b) 113.10 cm^2 **25** (a) 9.42 cm (b) 7.07 cm^2

26 (a) 22.0 cm (b) 38.48 cm^2 **27** 48 cm^3 **28** 157.1 cm^3

29 432 cm^3 **30** 166 cm^2 **31** 39 cm^2 **32** 468 cm^2

33 (a) N44°E (b) 044° **34** (a) S44°W (b) 224°

35 (a) N45°W (b) 315° **36** (a) S65°E (b) 115°

Exercise 26

1 (a) 147 cm (b) (i) 121.5 cm (ii) 4 feet

2 (a) 18 000 cm^3 (b) 8%

3 (a) 7.8 cm (b) 500 m^3

4 (a) 3 cm (b) No – volume is 20 cm^3 < 24 cubes

5 (a) 2.6 m^2 (b) 3.9 m^3 (c) 17 420 kg

6 (a) 11 cm^2 (b) (i) 25.7 cm (ii) 39.3 cm^2

7 30.9 cm^2 **8** (a) 18.8 m (b) 28.3 m^2

9 (i) 9.5 cm (ii) 10.5 or 10.4999 …

10 3.989 cm **11** 31.5 – 31.6 mpg **12** 95.4 cm^2

13 216 cm^3 **14** 37 m^2 **15** 506.25 cm^2

Investigations

1

Year	Value	Error
1700 BC	3.160 493 8	0.6%
250 BC max	3.845 070 4	22.4%
250 BC min	3.142 857 1	0.04%
AD 100	3.162 277 7	0.65%
AD 300	3.155 555 5	0.4%
AD 500	3.141 592 9	0.000 008 4%

All values of π shown are *greater* than today's value of π, 3.1415927. The most accurate value used throughout Europe was the Greek minimum value (250 BC) of $\frac{22}{7}$. Indeed, this approximation continued to be in common use until calculators were introduced into schools and colleges in the 1980s: $\frac{22}{7}$ was easy to remember, and both numbers were small and, therefore, easy to handle in calculations done by hand. Although the Chinese value (AD 500) was more accurate, these two 3-digit numbers were not easy to handle.

2 The area is maximised when the sides are all at their maximum value, that is, all the same length.

$$16 \div 3 = 5.3333, \qquad 5.3333^2 = 28.44 \text{ ft}^2$$

For a length x of fencing, the maximum area of the pen will, therefore, be

$$\left(\frac{x}{3}\right)^2 = \frac{x^2}{9}$$

3 This investigation uses the idea that if the dimensions are increased to a percentage P, then the volume will be increased to a percentage P^3.

An increase of 10% takes the percentage to 110%, or 1.10. The volume will be increased by a factor of $(1.10)^3 = 1.331$, or 33.1%.

An increase of 100% (doubling) takes the percentage to 200%, or 2.0. The volume will increased by a factor of $(2.0)^3 = 8$, or an increase of 700%.

8 Geometry and trigonometry

Exercise 1

1 Not congruent **2** Congruent **3** Congruent **4** Not congruent
5 Congruent **6** Not congruent **7** Congruent **8** B, C
9 A, D **10** A, C **11** B, D **12** A, D
13 B, C **14** B, D **15** C, D

Exercise 2

1 (a) 102° (b) Obtuse **2** (a) 39° (b) Acute
3 (a) 82° (b) Acute **4** (a) 105° (b) Obtuse
5 (a) 68° (b) Acute **6** (a) 39° (b) Acute
7 (a) 142° (b) Obtuse **8** (a) 150° (b) Obtuse
9 (a) 120° (b) Obtuse **10** (a) 205° (b) Reflex
11 (a) 48° (b) Acute **12** (a) 278° (b) Reflex

Exercise 3

1 104° **2** 67° **3** 57° **4** 87° **5** 100°
6 70° **7** 70° **8** 113°

Exercise 4

1 (a) 36° (b) Isosceles **2** (a) 50° (b) Isosceles
3 (a) 60° (b) Equilateral **4** (a) 60° (b) Right-angled
5 (a) 65 (b) Isosceles **6** (a) 120° (b) Equilateral
7 (a) 45° (b) Right-angled and isosceles
8 (a) 90° (b) Isosceles and right-angled

Exercise 5

1 $a = 60°$, $b = 70°$ **2** $c = 65°$, $d = 70°$ **3** $e = 75°$, $f = 40°$

4 $g = 10°$, $h = 42°$ **5** $i = 100°$, $j = 55°$ **6** $k = 70°$, $l = 40°$

7 $m = 40°$, $n = 40°$ **8** $p = 80°$, $q = 60°$

Exercise 6

1 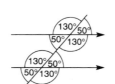 **2** 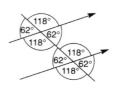 **3**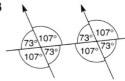

4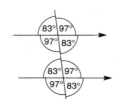

5 $a = 55°$, $b = 50°$ **6** $108°$

7 $e = 22\frac{1}{2}°$, $d = 22\frac{1}{2}°$ **8** $60°$

9 $g = 50°$, $h = 60°$ **10** $i = 65°$, $j = 115°$, $k = 50°$

11 $l = 90°$ **12** $m = 65°$, $n = 75°$, $p = 40°$

Exercise 7

1 $114°$ **2** $57°$ **3** $47°$ **4** $88°$

Exercise 8

1 Square, rhombus **2** Trapezium **3** Square

4 Square, rectangle **5** Parallelogram, rhombus

6 Trapezium **7** Square, rectangle, rhombus

8 Trapezium **9** Square **10** Square

Exercise 9

1

	Cube	Cuboid	Pyramid	Tetrahedron	Cylinder	Cone
Faces	6	6	5	4	2	1
Vertices	8	8	5	4	0	1
Edges	12	12	8	6	0	0

2 Faces + Vertices = Edges + 2

3 (a) Cuboid (b) Cuboid (c) Cylinder

Exercise 10

1 Tetrahedron **2** Pentagonal prism **3** Cylinder

4 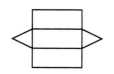 **5** 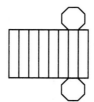 **6**   **7**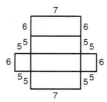

8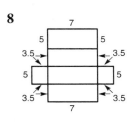

9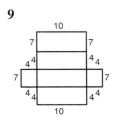

10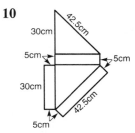

11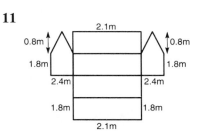

12 GE, BHD, IKA, MO, QS, ZX

Exercise 11

Check diagrams have been drawn correctly.

Exercise 12

1 Divide lengths by 5 **2** Divide lengths by 10
3 Divide lengths by 20 **4** Divide lengths by 12
5 Divide lengths by 100 **6** Divide lengths by 8

Exercise 13

1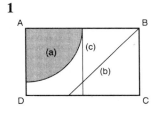

2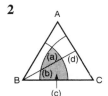

3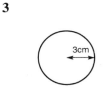

4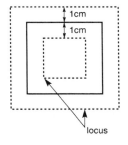

5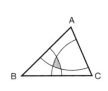

6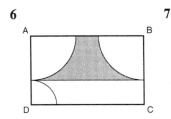

7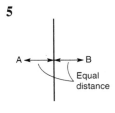

Exercise 14

| **1** 6.7 cm | **2** 13.1 cm | **3** 11.7 cm | **4** 12.3 cm | **5** 7.7 cm |
| **6** 9.0 m | **7** 8.35 m | **8** 4.8 m | **9** 6.9 cm | **10** 6.5 m |

Exercise 15

1 5.63 cm	**2** 3.94 m	**3** 66.2 mm	**4** 4.08 cm
5 10.4 m	**6** 6.16 cm	**7** 22.0 cm	**8** 154 mm
9 4.78 cm	**10** 3.86 m	**11** 5.56 m	**12** 6.01 cm
13 25.9 m	**14** 5.77 m	**15** 6.16 m × 7.88 m	

Exercise 16

1 45.6°   **2** 63.6°   **3** 67.6°   **4** 46.2°
5 41.8°   **6** 22.9°   **7** 44.4°   **8** 38.4°
9 50.0°   **10** 39.3°   **11** 48.6°   **12** 1.9°
13 20.5°   **14** 33.7°   **15** 67.4°, 112.6°

Exercise 17

1 10.7 cm   **2** 12.9 m   **3** 349 mm   **4** 212 mm
5 4.53 m   **6** 54.0 cm   **7** 40.6 cm   **8** 4.90 m

Exercise 18

1 50°   **2** 70°   **3** 120°
4 37°   **5** 84°   **6** 50°
7 $x = 75°, y = 75°$ **8** $x = 68°, y = 58°$ **9** $x = 65°, y = 55°$
10 $x = 70°, y = 55°$ **11** 99°   **12** 18
13 Trapezium   **14** Square, rhombus   **15** Cylinder
16 Cone
17   **18** 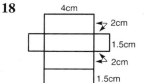   **19** Tetrahedron

or alternative

20–22: Check the accuracy of the drawings.

23 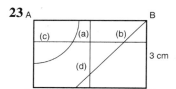   **24** 5.32 cm   **25** 7.68 cm
26 8.43 cm   **27** 10.8 cm
28 31.4°   **29** 5.33 cm
30 9.23 cm   **31** 13.4 cm
32 53.9°

Exercise 19

1 (a) $x = 50°, y = 40°$ (b)(i) kite
(ii) $p = 100°, q = 118°$
2 (a) 4.3 cm³   (b)

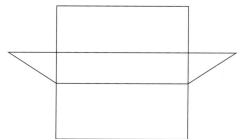

3

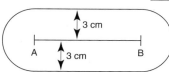

4 (a) 120°   (b) 300°

5

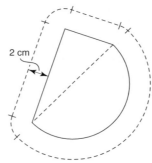

2 cm

6 (a) 125 cm   (b) 40 cm   (c) 140°   (d) 118.5 cm

7 (a) (i) 33°   (ii) 95°   (b)(i) 108°   (ii) 36°   (iii) 36°

8

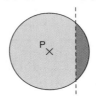

P Q

9 (a) 13.99 inches   (b) 37.5°

10 (a) 59°, vertically opposite   (b) 121°, e.g. supplementary

11 (a) 12.9 m   (b) 39.7°

12 (a) check drawing   (b) 50°   (c) acute

13 (a) (i) check drawing   (ii) 9.5 km ± 0.1 km   (iii) 42° ± 0.2°
   (b) (i) 10.6 km   (ii) 340.7° ± 0.1°

14

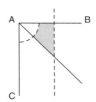

A   B

C

15 (a) 41.57 cm^2 (b) 8 cm   **16** (a) isosceles   (b) 80°

17 2.08 m   **18** (i) 54°   (ii) 46°

Investigations

1

Diagram	1	2	3	4	5	10
Number of interconnectors	4	10	19	31	46	166

The formula for the series is:

Number of interconnectors $= 1 + \dfrac{3n}{2}(n+1)$

2 There are many Pythagorean triplets. Four triplets with small numbers
   are: 3, 4, 5; 8, 15, 17; 5, 12, 13; 7, 24, 25

Other triplets can be formed by creating multiples of these, e.g:

$(3, 4, 5) \times 5 = 15, 20, 25$

3 There is no unique answer to this practical investigation. Your work should show evidence of a variety of strategies attempted, in order that a wide range of different envelopes can be produced. Some conclusions can be reached depending on the range of envelopes produced.

9 Symmetry

Exercise 1

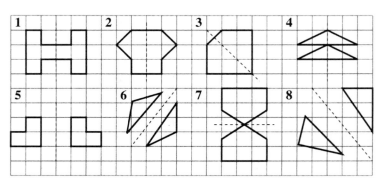

Exercise 2

1   2   3   4   5

6   7   8   9   10

Exercise 3

1

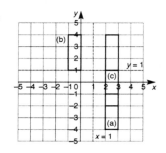

2

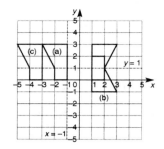

3

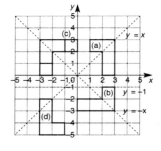

Exercise 4

1 9   **2** 3   **3** 4   **4** 6   **5** 4   **6** 3

7 2   **8** 3   **9** 4

Exercise 5

1 8   **2** 5   **3** 3   **4** 5

5 2   **6** 4   **7** 6   **8** 4

9   **10**   **11**   **12**

Exercise 6

1 Rotation, clockwise, 90°   **2** Rotation, clockwise, 135°

3 Rotation, 180°   **4** Rotation, clockwise, 90°

5 Rotation, clockwise, 90°   **6** Rotation, anticlockwise, 135°

7 Rotation, anticlockwise, 90°   **8** Rotation, clockwise, 90°

Exercise 7

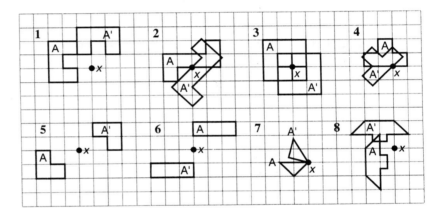

Exercise 8

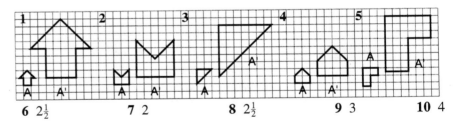

6 $2\frac{1}{2}$ **7** 2   **8** $2\frac{1}{2}$ **9** 3   **10** 4

Exercise 9

1 Enlargement s.f. 2, point of enlargement (0, 0)

2 Enlargement s.f. 2, point of enlargement (3, 0)

3 Enlargement s.f. 2, point of enlargement (0, 1)

4 Enlargement s.f. 3, point of enlargement (1, 1)

5 Enlargement s.f. 2, point of enlargement (0, 0)

6 Enlargement s.f. 2, point of enlargement (0, 4)

7 Enlargement s.f. 3, point of enlargement (0, 3)

8 Enlargement s.f. 2, point of enlargement (2, 6)

9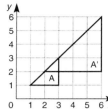

10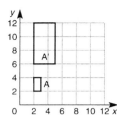

11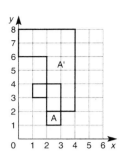

12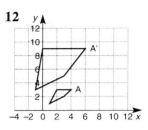

1 8	**2** 5	**3** 9	**4** 12
5 10	**6** 15	**7** 20	**8** 18
9 2520	**10** 4140°	**11** 5400°	**12** 6120°

13 (a) Yes 18 (b) No (c) Yes 24

14 (a) Yes 10 (b) Yes 9 (c) No

Regular polygon	No. of sides	Sum of interior angles	Size of interior angle	Size of exterior
Triangle	3	180°	60°	120°
Quadrilateral	4	360°	90°	90°
Pentagon	5	540°	108°	72°
Hexagon	6	720°	120°	60°
Heptagon	7	900°	128.57°	51.42°
Octagon	8	1080°	135°	45°
Nonagon	9	1260°	140°	40°
Decagon	10	1440°	144°	36°
Undecagon	11	1620°	147.27°	32.72°
Dodecagon	12	1800°	150°	30°

1

squares tessellate   triangles tessellate   hexagons tessellate

2 The following tessellate: (b) , (c) , (d) , (e) , (g) , (j) , (k)

1 $\begin{pmatrix} 6 \\ 0 \end{pmatrix}$ **2** $\begin{pmatrix} 3 \\ 2 \end{pmatrix}$ **3** $\begin{pmatrix} -3 \\ -2 \end{pmatrix}$ **4** $\begin{pmatrix} 3 \\ -2 \end{pmatrix}$ **5** $\begin{pmatrix} -6 \\ 0 \end{pmatrix}$

6 $\begin{pmatrix} -3 \\ 2 \end{pmatrix}$ **7** $\begin{pmatrix} 5 \\ 2 \end{pmatrix}$ **8** $\begin{pmatrix} -2 \\ -1 \end{pmatrix}$ **9** $\begin{pmatrix} -5 \\ 0 \end{pmatrix}$ **10** $\begin{pmatrix} -4 \\ -3 \end{pmatrix}$

11 $\begin{pmatrix} 4 \\ 3 \end{pmatrix}$ **12** $\begin{pmatrix} -4 \\ 2 \end{pmatrix}$ **13** $\begin{pmatrix} 1 \\ 4 \end{pmatrix}$ **14** $\begin{pmatrix} -8 \\ -1 \end{pmatrix}$

15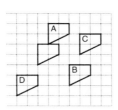

16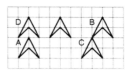

Exercise 14

1 A rotation of 90° anticlockwise

2 A reflection in the line $y = -x$

3 A rotation of 180° about the origin O

4 A translation of $\begin{pmatrix} 4 \\ -3 \end{pmatrix}$

5 A reflection in the line $y = x$

6 A rotation of 90° anticlockwise

7 A reflection in the y-axis

8 A reflection in the x-axis

Exercise 15

1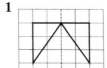

2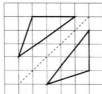

3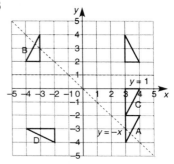

4 (a) 1 (b) 4

5 (a) 3 (b) 2 (c) 3 (d) 0

6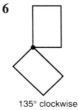

135° clockwise

7

180°

8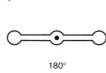

45° anticlockwise

9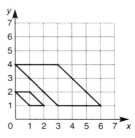

10 No

11 24

12 8

13 (a) $\begin{pmatrix} 5 \\ 1 \end{pmatrix}$ (b) $\begin{pmatrix} 0 \\ -4 \end{pmatrix}$ (c) $\begin{pmatrix} -4 \\ 1 \end{pmatrix}$ (d) $\begin{pmatrix} 4 \\ -1 \end{pmatrix}$

Exercise 16

1 (a)

(b)

2 (a) 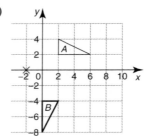 (b)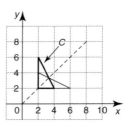

3 (a) 90° anticlockwise about the origin

(b) Reflection about the line $y = x$

(c)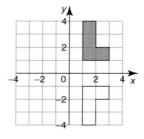

4 (a) (i) 45° (ii) 135°

(b) The two adjacent interior angles of an octagon add up to 270°, so 360° − 270° = 90°

5 (a) The line $x = -1$

(b) Rotation 90° clockwise about the origin

6 (a) 20 cm² (b) 12 cm, 15 cm (c) 9

7 (a) 120° (b)(i) 60° (ii) 150° (c) equilateral

8 (a) 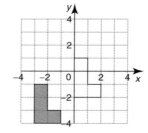 (b)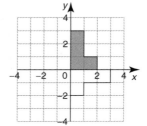

(c)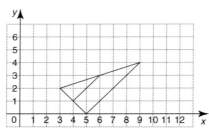

9 (a) Pentagon   (b) $108°$ (c) (i) angle D = angle E (ii) $36°$

10 (a), (b)

(c) Translation of $\binom{-4}{3}$

11 (a) reflection of A in y-axis, or reflection of D in x-axis

(b) (i) Translation of $\binom{4}{0}$ (ii) Reflection in the line $x = 2$

(c) Rotation of $180°$ about the origin.

Investigations

1 Scale factor area = (scale factor length)^2

Scale factor volume = (scale factor length)^3

2 It is easier if the scale diagram is drawn on squared paper. There are many extensions to this investigation, such as: What is the maximum possible number of rebounds? Try different sizes of snooker table.

3 The rule is: total of interior angles = $180° \times (n - 2)$ where n is the number of sides of the polygon.

---

10 Collecting and processing

Exercise 11

1 Heading could be 'number of occupants', and easier to summarise if there were columns with headings:

Number of occupants					
1	2	3	4	5	6

2 There are no questions about the quality of each meal, the available choice, or other meals which could be provided and which may prove popular. You could have two recording sheets:

(a)

Meal	Number eaten

(b)

Questionnaire
Meal eaten: _____
Was your meal:
 (i) satisfactory? ☐
 (ii) good value? ☐
Was there enough choice? <u>YES/NO</u>
If not, what other meals would you like to see on the menu?

3 There may need to be a column for 'Second choice', for when the first choice of newspaper is sold out.

4 It is easier to count the cars coming in, and going out, as, while you are counting empty spaces, there may be a large influx or exodus of cars.

Exercise 2

1 (a) There are no criteria for deciding an order of preference.

  (b) It is not clear whether (i) the numbers 1, 2, 3, 4, 5 are to be entered, one in each box (ii) any number from 1 to 5 can be entered in any of the boxes.

For each of the three criteria, put ONE tick against EACH name.
Which lecturer, in your opinion:

	Knows the subject?			Maintains interest?			Helps Learning?		
	a lot	some	not much	a lot	some	not much	a lot	some	not much
Mr James									
Mr Anderson									
Mrs Robson									
Mr Islam									
Mrs Oates									

You could ask about knowledge of the subject, maintaining interest, and helping you to learn, as three criteria. Also, it may help to allow, say, three levels of response, to questions.

2 The question does not ask how often any meal is eaten.

1 Do you eat at the College canteen regularly?

YES ☐   NO ☐   (please tick)

2 If YES, over an average two-week period, (i.e. 10 days), write in the number of times you have eaten one of the following meals.

	Number of times
Sausage	
Pizza	
Stir-fry	
Roast meat	
Vegetarian	
Baked potato	
Hamburger	
Other	

3 What other meals of about the same cost would you eat, if they were available?
(List up to three.)
  (i) _____
  (ii) _____
  (iii) _____

Please tick which of these countries you visited on your main holiday for the three years shown.

	1991	1992	1993
France			
Spain			
Belgium			
Germany			
Greece			
U.S.A.			
Other:			
please state			

3 The time of year is not asked for; it would be better to ask for the main holiday, possibly over the last three years.

4 Instead of 'What are you intending to do?', give alternatives, e.g. 'Do you intend to
(a) continue studying
(b) seek employment
(c) have a break?

Exercise 3

1 (a) 961 °C (b) 2570 °C (c) copper, gold, lead and silver (d) magnesium (e) gold (f) more (8.18 g/cm3)

2 (a) 2015 (b) 1600 (c) 3 h 15 min (d) 2 h 41 min (e) 0023

3 (a) £159.34 (b) £194.61 (c) £2000 (d) £143.13

4 (a) £59.99 (b) £4.00 (c) 78 × 78 (d) £9.50 (e) £5.50

Exercise 4 The column showing the tally marks has been omitted.

1

Mark	Frequency
0	3
1	2
2	3
3	2
4	4
5	3
6	7
7	5
8	5
9	4
10	2
	40

2

Fruit	Frequency
apple	8
banana	2
grape	2
kiwi	1
melon	3
orange	5
pear	3
	24

3

Minutes late	Frequency
0	12
1	6
2	5
3	3
4	4
5	2
6	0
7	1
8	1
9	1
	35

4

Level	Frequency
5	5
6	18
7	16
8	7
9	4
	50

Exercise 5

1

Number of tomatoes	Frequency
0–4	0
5–9	1
10–14	1
15–19	6
20–24	6
25–29	5
30–34	5
	24

2

Number of words	Frequency
0–2	2
3–5	4
6–8	8
9–11	15
12–14	9
15–17	2
	40

3

Number of books	Frequency
21–25	1
26–30	7
31–35	6
36–40	7
41–45	6
	27

Exercise 6   The column showing the tally marks has been omitted.

1

Amount (£)	Frequency
0–9.99	4
10–19.99	15
20–29.99	8
30–39.99	7
40–49.99	4
50–59.99	2
	40

2

Weight (kg)	Frequency
0.50–0.99	5
1.00–1.49	12
1.50–1.99	14
2.00–2.49	5
2.50–2.99	4
	40

3

Duration (min)	Frequency
80–89	7
90–99	13
100–109	9
110–119	7
120–129	4
	40

Exercise 7

1 mode = 4, median = 5

2 mode = 13, median = 15

3 mode = 7, median = 6

4 mode = 51, median = 52

5 mode = 8, median = 6

6 mode = 24, median = 28

7 mode = 11, median = 11

8 (a) 13 m (b) 14 m

9 (a) 16 (b) 15

10 3, 4, 4, 6, 7, 8, 9

Exercise 8

1 modal group = 200–299 mm, median height (estimate) = 258 mm

2 modal group = 2–3.99 m, median length (estimate) = 3.33 m

3 modal group = 60–79 points, median score (estimate) = 65 points

4 modal group = £60–£89.99, median amount (estimate) = £79.50

Exercise 9

1
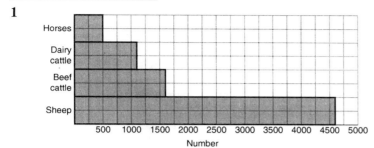

2
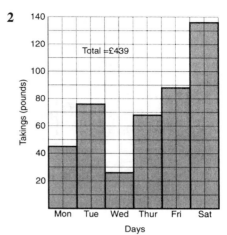

3
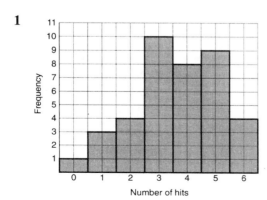

4
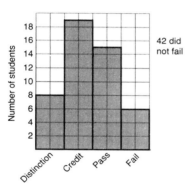

42 did
not fail

5
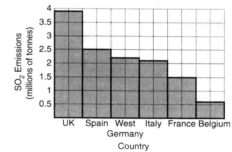

Exercise 10

1
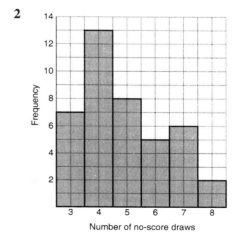

mode = 3 hits,
median (estimate) = 3.75 hits

2

mode = 4 draws (0–0),
median (estimate) = 4.63 draws (0–0)

ANSWERS

3

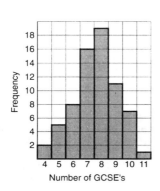

Number of GCSE's

mode = 8 GCSEs
median (estimate) = 7.71 GCSEs

4

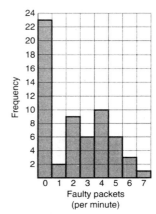

Faulty packets
(per minute)

mode = 0 packets,
median (estimate) = 2.1/2.2 packets

Exercise 11

1

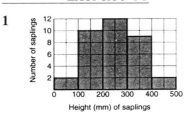

Height (mm) of saplings

2

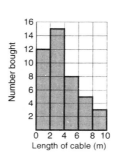

Length of cable (m)

3

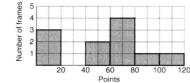

Points

Exercise 12

1

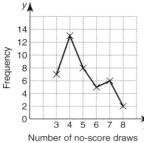

Number of hits

2

Number of no-score draws

3

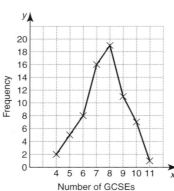

Number of GCSEs

4

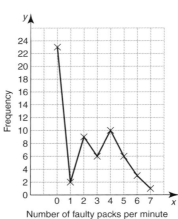

Number of faulty packs per minute

Exercise 13

1 £118.43   **2** 99.75 kg

3 Sandra (58.17; Tracey's mean score is 56.43)   **4** 14 °C

5 $\frac{30}{24} = 1.25$ winners   **6** (a) $\frac{54}{20} = 2.7$ min   (b) No

7 $\frac{350}{23} = 15.22$ pigeons   **8** $\frac{299}{20} = 14.95$ students

Exercise 14

1 $\frac{385}{30} = 12.83$ m   **2** $\frac{766}{33} = 23.21$ eggs   **3** $\frac{348.5}{11} = 31.77$ points

4 $\frac{52.5}{17} = 3.09$ faulty components

Exercise 15

1 £399.99 − £293.23 = £106.76

2 (a) Dean: range = 126 − 2 = 124; Ian: range = 133 − 1 = 132

    (b) Dean: mean = 54.1; Ian: mean = 60.7; Ian's is better.

3 (a) Betty: mean = 81; Moira: mean = 81

    (b) Betty: range = 7 (84 − 77); Moira: range = 20 (93 − 73)

    (c) Betty is more consistent.

    (d) Could choose either; there are arguments for both.

4 Total for 5 days = 743 × 5 = 3715. Total for 6 days = 750 × 6 = 4500. Attendance on day 6 = 4500 − 3715 = 785.

5 (a) £52.32 × 2 = £104.64

    (b) Edwin's takings = £45.62 × 3 = £136.86. Total takings = £241.50; hence mean takings = £48.30.

    (c) They need to take £330 − £241.50 = £88.50. (£330 = £55 × 6)

Exercise 16

1

Mark	0	1	2	3	4	5	6	7	8	9	10
Frequency	1	3	1	3	7	9	7	4	2	0	3

(a) 5   (b) 9   (c) 8

2

Mark	1–10	11–20	21–30	31–40	41–50
Frequency	6	8	12	11	8

(a)

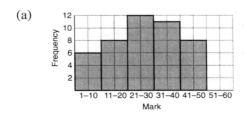

(b)   11 + 8 = 19

(c)   6 + 4 = 10

3

Letter	Frequency
T	1
X	1
Y	2
A	2
B	2
C	1
D	6
E	2
F	3
G	3
H	3
J	2
K	2
Total	30

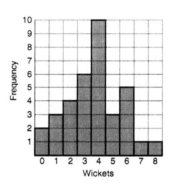

(a) D
(b) T
(c) 20

4

Wicket	Frequency
0	2
1	3
2	4
3	6
4	10
5	3
6	5
7	1
8	1
Total	35

(a) 2   (b) 4   (c) 10   (d) 3 + 8 + 18 + 40 + 15 + 30 + 7 + 8 = 129
(e) 129 ÷ 35 = 3.69

5 mode = 9, median = 8, mean = 7.5, range = 4
6 mode = 30, median = 31, mean = 33, range = 15
7 mode = 18, median = 18, mean = 19, range = 16
8 mean = (775 + 1320 + 3500 + 2960 = 2145) ÷ 60 = 178(0.3) cm.
9 (a)

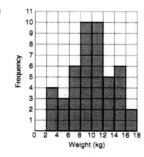

(b) 46 trees
(c) 13 trees
(d) mean = $\frac{458}{46}$ = 9.96 kg

10 (a)

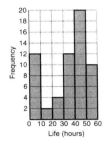

(b) 40–50 hours

(c) 40 hours

(d) 34.3 hours (2060 ÷ 60)

Exercise 17

1 (a)

Birth weight w kg	Tally	Frequency
$2.00 \leqslant w < 2.50$		0
$2.50 \leqslant w < 3.00$	III	3
$3.00 \leqslant w < 3.50$	IIII	4
$3.50 \leqslant w < 4.00$	II	2
$4.00 \leqslant w < 4.50$	I	1

(b) (i) 5   (ii) 5   (iii) 1

2 (a) $1575 \div 115 = 13.7$

(b) (ii) Mean of girls is higher, range is same.

3 (a) £17 500

(b) Median, as it is lower than the mean.

4 (a) 16.2   (b) $x = 20$

5 (a) (i) 60

(b) (ii) Machine A has a higher mean (more matches per box), and a more uniform spread than Machine B, although the range is about the same.

6 (a) 56.3 kg   (b) (i) 690.3 kg   (iii) 54.6 kg

7 (a) 29 (b) 9   (c) 6   (d) 8   (e) 6

8 (a) 6.07

(b) Manufacturer's claim is that mean is 6.24 hours. Although the estimated mean is a little below this, he is justified in his claim.

9 (a) 6   (b) 457.15 g

10 (a) 52   (b) 11   (c) Mean score increases (from 6.5 to 6.88 ...)

11 (a) 42   (c) 339.3 g

(d) Means are the same, first sample less tightly clustered (greater range).

12 (a) (i) 174   (ii) 180   (iii) 19

(b) Rovers team marginally taller, and with a much greater range that City team (1.9 to 7).

13 (a) (i) $20 \leqslant t < 24$ (ii) 23.05 min   (b) 14.41 min.

14 (a)

Mid-point	18	23	28	33	38	43	48

(b) 30.7 mph

(c)

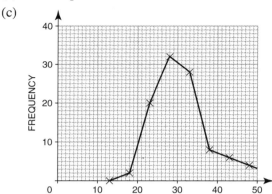

15 (a) (b) $\frac{3}{30} = \frac{1}{10}$

(c) First, as the mean is greater (about 30) than the second (about 13)

16 (a) $110 \text{ g} \times 1000 = 110 \text{ kg}$

(b) Orchard B, as there is less variation in weight (range is 12) than Orchard A (range is 24)

Investigations

1 There is likely to be only a relatively minor change in mean value, or in the general appearance of a bar graph.

2 The more uniform ('normal') the spread of results, the better the rule works.

11 Representing and interpreting

Exercise I

1 (a) 1788, on Monday (b) Tuesday (c) 12 (Wed–Thur) (d) 1795.6

2 (a) Wednesday is half-day, Thursday is late-night opening

(b) More people do not work on Saturdays.

(c) 18.7 customers

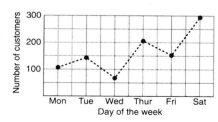

3 (a)
   (b)   1200–1300
   (c)   1100
   (d)   2 hours

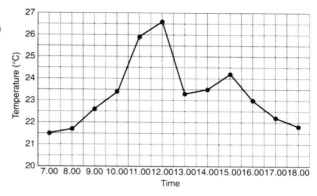

4

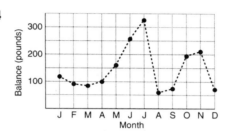

   (a)   August
   (b)   £69
   (c)   Feb, Mar, Aug, Dec

Exercise 2   Conversion graphs should be drawn for all questions 1–9.

1 (a) 7.7 lb   (b) 4.55 kg

2 (a) €13.125   (b) £16.33

3 (a) 28.35 kg   (b) 22.2 gallons

4 (a) 2.84 ℓ   (b) 4.84 pints

5 (a) 20.125 miles   (b) 2 hours 52 mins

6 (a) 8800 francs   (b) suitable graph   (c) £665.91   (d) 3080 francs

7 (a) £5.84   (b) 6.91 kg

8 (a) 158°F   (b) 37.8°C

9 $-40°C = -40°F$

Exercise 3

1

E	A	S	T
152°	92°	76°	40°

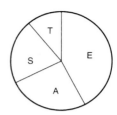

2

Fish	Sausage	Pie	Fishcake	Spring Roll
72°	78°	51°	96°	63°

3

A	B	C	Admin.
180°	108°	54°	18°

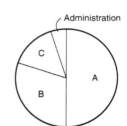

4 (a) plain
   (b) plain, salt and vinegar
   (c) 1st week 35, 2nd week 30

5 BBC1: 217, BBC2: 83, ITV: 250, C4: 50

6

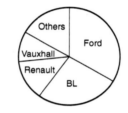

7

8 (a) 80°, 80°, 80°, 120°
   (b)

Exercise 4

4

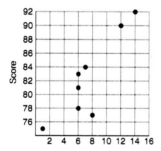

Higher handicap
means higher score.

5

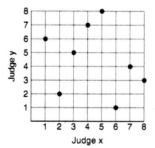

No evidence of
similar opinions.

6

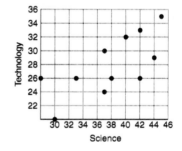

There is evidence of a link;
higher science score mean
higher technology scores.

4

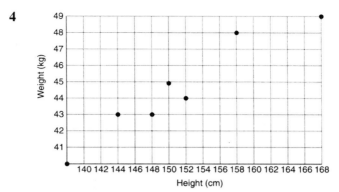

Yes, taller means heavier.

Exercise 5 (All answers are approximate, as they are read from graphs.)

1 (a), (b)

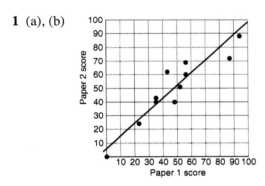

(c) 60 marks   (d) 56/57 marks

2 (a)

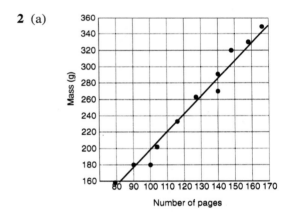

(b) 276 g   (c) 96 pages

3 (a)

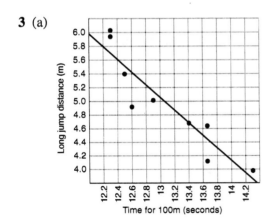

(b) 5 m

4 (a)

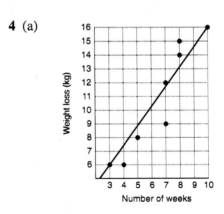

(b) Yes   (c) 8 weeks

Exercise 6

1 (a) Cumulative frequencies: 1 5 16 43 81 93 97 100

(b)
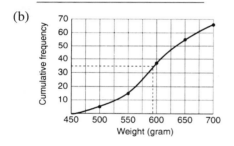
Speed of cars (km/h)

2 (a) Cumulative frequencies: 4 12 27 49 67 81

(b)
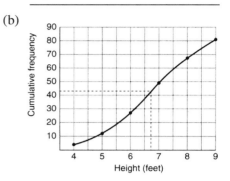
Height (feet)

3 (a) Cumulative frequencies: 5 15 37 55 66

(b)
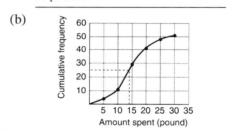
Weight (gram)

4 (a) Cumulative frequencies: 4 11 29 41 48 51

(b)
Amount spent (pound)

Exercise 7

1 41 km/h   **2** 6.7 ft   **3** 593 g   **4** £14.50

Exercise 8

1 10.3 cm, 12.7 cm, 2.4 cm   **2** £64 000, £108 000, £44 000

3 100p, 168p, 68p

4 2.07 kg, 2.4 kg, 0.33 kg

5 2.8 min, 6.2 min, 3.4 min

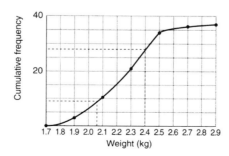
Weight (kg)

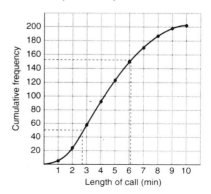
Length of call (min)

Exercise 9

1 (a) Saturday (b) £60 (c) Tue, Thu, Fri, Sat (d) £375

2 (a)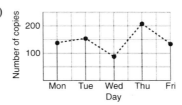

(b) 240 copies
(c) Wed
(d) 720 copies

3 A:4, B:7, C:12, D:8, E:5

4

Day	M	Tu	W	Th	F	Total
Copies	138	154	86	208	134	720
Angle	69°	77°	43°	104°	67°	360°

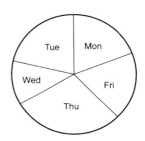

5

Age	19	20	21	22	23	24
Number	6	3	2	4	4	5
Angle	90°	45°	30°	60°	60°	75°

(a) 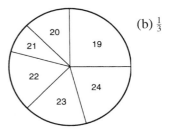 (b) $\frac{1}{3}$

6 (a) (b)
(c) 73 kg
(d) 183 cm

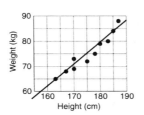

7 (a)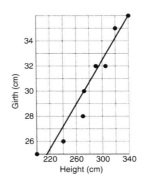

(b) $32\frac{1}{2}$ cm
(c) 245 cm

8 Cumulative frequency 1 4 8 14 24 32 38 43 47 50

(a)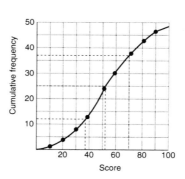

(b) 51/52

(c) lower quartile = 37/38
upper quartile = 68

9 Cumulative frequency 5 23 56 108 150 176 184

(a)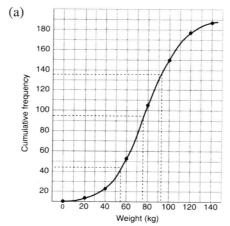

(b) 73–75 kg

(c) lower quartile = 53 kg
upper quartile = 92 kg
interquartile range = 39 kg

Exercise 10

1 (a)

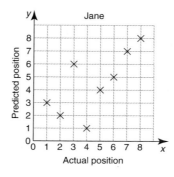

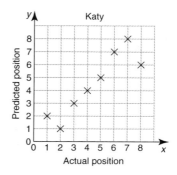

(b) Katy makes a better prediction, as her graph shows more positive
correlation (is less scattered) than Jane's.

2 (a) (i) 69%   (ii) 14%

(b)

	1995	2035
Median age	35	40
Upper quartile age	56	62
Lower quartile age	20	20
Interquartile range	36	42

(c) Little change for younger people (below 30) but more people in the range 30–90 in 2035. (Greater mean and U.Q. by 5 to 6 years)

3 (a)

(b) Positive

(c)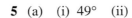

(d) 96

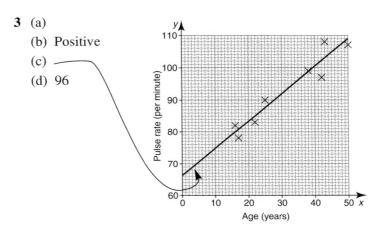

4 (a) 22(23)   (b) (i) 55 h   (ii) 5.5 h.

(c) Retired people – same average hours of sleep, but a wider range than students (8 compared to 5.5).

5 (a) (i) 49°   (ii)

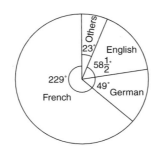

(b) (i) 56°   (ii) 1200

6 (a), (c)

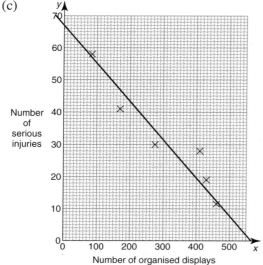

Number of serious injuries (y-axis) vs Number of organised displays (x-axis)

(b) The more organised displays, the fewer serious injuries occur.

(d) (i) 55 (ii) 360

(e) About 421

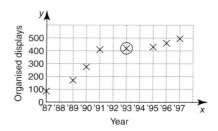

Organised displays vs Year

7 (a) (i)

Cumulative frequency
20
150
302
394
480
498
500

(a) (ii)

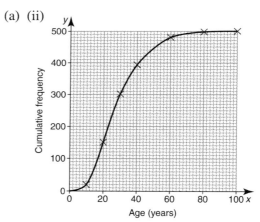

Cumulative frequency vs Age (years)

(b) (i) 26 (ii) 20 (c) 90

8 (a)

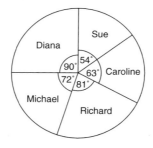

Pie chart: Sue 54°, Caroline 63°, Richard 81°, Michael 72°, Diana 90°

(b) £$\frac{4.20}{7} \times 9$

= £5.40

9 (a)

Age (less than)	30	40	50	60	70	90
Cumulative frequency	2	20	47	65	77	80

(b)

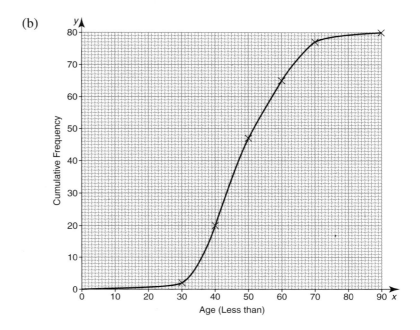

10 (a) (i)

Cumulative frequency
0
2
11
30
55
75
85
93
96

(a) (ii)

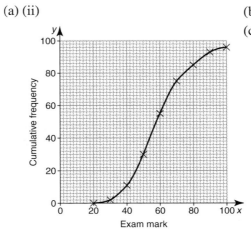

(b) (i) 57   (ii) 20

(c) Paper 2 – similar range but higher median (61 as against 57), although there is not a lot in it.

11 (a)

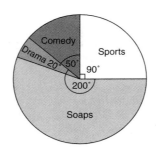

(b) $192 \times \frac{60}{360} = 32$ people for sport. Hence *second* survey had more people for sport.

12 (a) (i) 7   (ii) 17

(b) (i)

$t \leqslant 0$	$t \leqslant 5$	$t \leqslant 10$	$t \leqslant 15$	$t \leqslant 20$	$t \leqslant 25$	$t \leqslant 30$	$t \leqslant 35$
0	4	16	32	41	47	49	50

(ii)

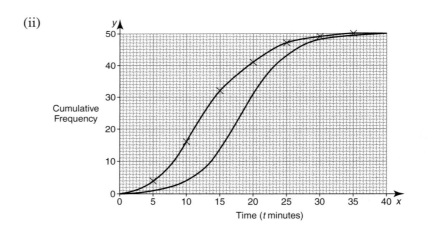

(c) (i)   Median = $12\frac{1}{2}$ minutes

(ii)   Yes – median is much shorter time (was 18 min) and more pupils had solved the problem more quickly than before (e.g. 16 had solved it in 10 mins or less, compared with 4 previously)

13 (a)

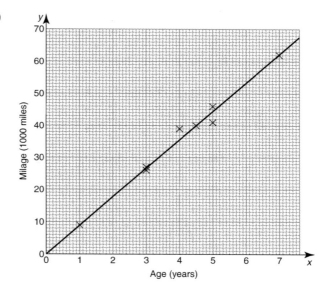

(b) Positive correlation   (c) 6 years old

14 (a)

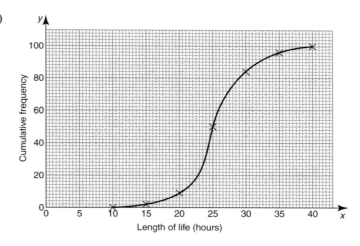

(b) 10   (c) (i) 25   (ii) 6

Investigations   **1** (There are other advantages/disadvantages than those stated here.)

Bar chart

Advantages: ● easy to compare heights of bars in a diagram
        ● easy to draw
        ● can display easily a wide range of values

Disadvantages: ● applying different ways of grouping can alter
          the bar chart

Pie chart

Advantages:
- can be rotated, hence gives equal weighting to all sectors
- easy to compare two or more pie charts

Disadvantages:
- angles need to be calculated
- awkward to distinguish small sectors
- less clear, if there are many sectors

2 (a) Estimate the distances of each point from the line, and check that the sum of the distances of points *above* the line is equal to the sum of the distances *below* the line.

  (b) Alter the position of the line slightly, and repeat.

  (c) Check that the total of the distances of *all* points from the line is small.

12 Probability

Exercise 1

1 (a) P = 0.5 or 50%, Q = 0.25 or 25%, R is almost 1 or 100%, S is about 0.03 or 3%, T = 0.01 or 1%

  (b)

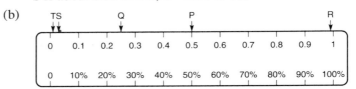

Exercise 2

1 (a) $\frac{2}{3}$ (b) $\frac{1}{3}$

2 (a) $\frac{1}{7}$ (b) $\frac{2}{7}$ (c) $\frac{5}{7}$

3 (a) $\frac{1}{6}$ (b) $\frac{2}{6} = \frac{1}{3}$ (c) $\frac{3}{6} = \frac{1}{2}$ (d) $\frac{5}{6}$

4 (a) $\frac{5}{12}$ (b) $\frac{7}{12}$ (c) $0\left(\frac{0}{12}\right)$ – impossible   (d) $\frac{12}{12} = 1$ – certain

5 (a) $\frac{5}{12}$ (b) $\frac{4}{12} = \frac{1}{3}$ (c) $\frac{8}{12} = \frac{2}{3}$ (d) $\frac{9}{12} = \frac{3}{4}$ (e) $0\left(\frac{0}{12}\right)$ – impossible

6 (a) $\frac{10}{200} = \frac{1}{20}$ (b) 51 tickets

Exercise 3

7 (a) $\frac{1}{37}$ (b) $\frac{2}{37}$ (c) $\frac{4}{37}$ (d) $\frac{7}{37}$ (e) $\frac{12}{37}$ (f) $\frac{18}{37}$

1 $\frac{3}{23}$ 2 $\frac{22}{30}$

3 (a) $\frac{6}{12} = \frac{1}{2}$

  (b) four hearts, two clubs, a diamond and a spade

4 (a) (i) $\frac{3}{20}$ (ii) $\frac{5}{20} = \frac{1}{4}$ (iii) $\frac{12}{20} = \frac{3}{5}$ (iv) $0\left(\frac{0}{20}\right)$

  (b) (i) 9   (ii) 15   (iii) 36   (iv) none

Exercise 4

1 (i) $\frac{8}{20} = 0.4$ (ii) $\frac{6}{14} = 0.428$;   (ii) is more likely

2 (i) $\frac{3}{8} = 0.375$ (ii) $\frac{2}{5} = 0.4$;   (ii) is more likely

3 (i) $\frac{13}{52} = 0.25$ (ii) $\frac{1}{5} = 0.2$;   (i) is more likely

4 (i) $\frac{5}{7} = 0.71$ (ii) $\frac{3}{4} = 0.75$;   (ii) is more likely

5 (i) $\frac{4}{100} = 0.04$ (ii) $\frac{15}{350} = 0.0428$;   (ii) is more likely

Exercise 5

1 $\frac{5}{36}$ 2 $\frac{6}{36} = \frac{1}{6}$ 3 $\frac{18}{36} = \frac{1}{2}$ 4 $\frac{5}{36}$ 5 0

Exercise 6

1 $\frac{1}{4}$ 2 $\frac{1}{8}$ 3 (a) $\frac{8}{10} \times \frac{8}{10} = \frac{64}{100} = \frac{16}{25}$ (b) $\frac{2}{10} \times \frac{2}{10} = \frac{4}{100} = \frac{1}{25}$

4 (a) $\frac{4}{5}$ (b) $\frac{4}{5} \times \frac{4}{5} = \frac{16}{25}$ 5 $\frac{3}{4} \times \frac{2}{3} = \frac{6}{12} = \frac{1}{2}$

Exercise 7

1 (a) 0.5   (b) 0.7   (c) 0.5

2 (a) 0.28   (b) 0.12   (c) 0.28

3 (a) 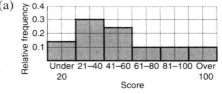   (b) (i) 0.45   (ii) 0.2   (iii) 0.3

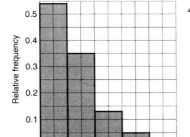

4 (a)

Age	0–19	20–29	30–39	40–49	50+
Number	27	13	6	3	1
Relative frequency	0.54	0.26	0.12	0.06	0.02

(b)   (i) 0.54   (ii) 0.2   (iii) 0.98

Exercise 8

1 (a) $\frac{9}{12} = \frac{3}{4}$ (b) $\frac{8}{12} = \frac{2}{3}$ 2 (a) $\frac{5}{6}$ (b) $\frac{4}{6} = \frac{2}{3}$

3 (a) $\frac{7}{12}$ (b) $\frac{5}{12}$ 4 (a) $\frac{6}{16} = \frac{3}{8}$ (b) $\frac{4}{16} = \frac{1}{4}$ (c) $\frac{11}{16}$

5 (a) $\frac{8}{12}$ (b) $\frac{5}{13}$ (c) $\frac{9}{13}$

Exercise 9

1 0.7   2 0.665   3 (a) $\frac{1}{16}$ (b) $\frac{14}{16} = \frac{7}{8}$

4 (a) $\frac{5}{18}$ (b) $\frac{15}{18} = \frac{5}{6}$ (c) $\frac{8}{18} = \frac{4}{9}$ 5 (a) $\frac{1}{22}$ (b) $\frac{15}{22}$ (d) $\frac{7}{33}$

Exercise 10

1 (a) $\frac{6}{8} \times \frac{6}{8} = \frac{9}{16}$ (b) $\frac{2}{8} \times \frac{2}{8} = \frac{1}{16}$ **2** $\frac{2}{4} \times \frac{2}{4} = \frac{1}{4}$ **3** $\frac{3}{5} \times \frac{3}{5} = \frac{9}{25}$

4 $\frac{2}{5} \times \frac{2}{5} = \frac{4}{25}$ **5** $\frac{5}{6} \times \frac{5}{6} = \frac{25}{36}$ **6** $\frac{21}{28} \times \frac{21}{28} = \frac{9}{16}$

7 $\frac{6}{10} \times \frac{6}{10} \times \frac{6}{10} = \frac{216}{1000} = \frac{27}{125}$, so Betty is not correct

8 $\frac{4}{5} \times \frac{4}{5} = \frac{16}{25}$

Exercise 11

1

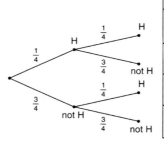

Outcome	Probability
HH	$\frac{1}{4} \times \frac{1}{4} = \frac{1}{16}$
H (not H)	$\frac{1}{4} \times \frac{3}{4} = \frac{3}{16}$
(not H) H	$\frac{3}{4} \times \frac{1}{4} = \frac{3}{16}$
(not H) (not H)	$\frac{3}{4} \times \frac{3}{4} = \frac{9}{16}$

(a) $\frac{1}{16}$

(b) $\frac{9}{16}$

(c) $\frac{6}{16} = \frac{3}{8}$

2

Outcome	Probability
RR	$0.2 \times 0.2 = 0.04$
RD	$0.2 \times 0.8 = 0.16$
DR	$0.8 \times 0.2 = 0.16$
DD	$0.8 \times 0.8 = 0.64$

(a) 0.64

(b) 0.32

(c) 0.04

3

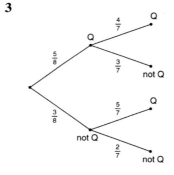

Outcome	Probability
Q, Q	$\frac{5}{8} \times \frac{4}{7} = \frac{5}{14}$
Q, not Q	$\frac{5}{8} \times \frac{3}{7} = \frac{15}{56}$
not Q, Q	$\frac{3}{8} \times \frac{5}{7} = \frac{15}{56}$
not Q, not Q	$\frac{3}{8} \times \frac{2}{7} = \frac{3}{28}$

(a) $\frac{5}{14}$

(b) $\frac{15}{28}$

(c) $\frac{3}{28}$

4

Outcome	Probability
SS	$0.4 \times 0.6 = 0.24$
SG	$0.4 \times 0.4 = 0.16$
GS	$0.6 \times 0.6 = 0.36$
GG	$0.6 \times 0.4 = 0.24$

(a) 0.24

(b) 0.24

(c) 0.52

5 (a)

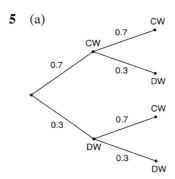

Outcome	Probability
CW, CW	$0.7 \times 0.7 = 0.49$
CW, DW	$0.7 \times 0.3 = 0.21$
DW, CW	$0.3 \times 0.7 = 0.21$
DW, DW	$0.3 \times 0.3 = 0.09$

(b) (i) 0.49

(ii) 0.51

6 (a)

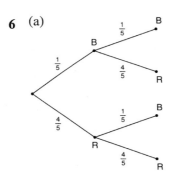

Outcome	Probability
BB	$\frac{1}{5} \times \frac{1}{5} = \frac{1}{25}$
BR	$\frac{1}{5} \times \frac{4}{5} = \frac{4}{25}$
RB	$\frac{4}{5} \times \frac{1}{5} = \frac{4}{25}$
RR	$\frac{4}{5} \times \frac{4}{5} = \frac{16}{25}$

(b) (i) $\frac{8}{25}$

(ii) $\frac{17}{25}$

Exercise 12

1 (a) 0.512 (b) 0.104

2 (a) $\frac{5}{28}$ (b) $\frac{55}{56}$ (c) $\frac{1}{56}$

3 (a)

Outcome	Probability
CCC	$0.7 \times 0.7 \times 0.7 = 0.343$
CCD	$0.7 \times 0.7 \times 0.3 = 0.147$
CDC	$0.7 \times 0.3 \times 0.7 = 0.147$
CDD	$0.7 \times 0.3 \times 0.3 = 0.063$
DCC	$0.3 \times 0.7 \times 0.7 = 0.147$
DCD	$0.3 \times 0.7 \times 0.3 = 0.063$
DDC	$0.3 \times 0.3 \times 0.7 = 0.063$
DDD	$0.3 \times 0.3 \times 0.3 = 0.027$

(b) (i) 0.027

(ii) 0.784

4

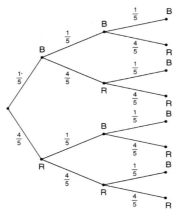

Outcome	Probability
BBB	$\frac{1}{5} \times \frac{1}{5} \times \frac{1}{5} = \frac{1}{125}$
BBR	$\frac{1}{5} \times \frac{1}{5} \times \frac{4}{5} = \frac{4}{125}$
BRB	$\frac{1}{5} \times \frac{4}{5} \times \frac{1}{5} = \frac{4}{125}$
BRR	$\frac{1}{5} \times \frac{4}{5} \times \frac{4}{5} = \frac{16}{125}$
RBB	$\frac{4}{5} \times \frac{1}{5} \times \frac{1}{5} = \frac{4}{125}$
RBR	$\frac{4}{5} \times \frac{1}{5} \times \frac{4}{5} = \frac{16}{125}$
RRB	$\frac{4}{5} \times \frac{4}{5} \times \frac{1}{5} = \frac{16}{125}$
RRR	$\frac{4}{5} \times \frac{4}{5} \times \frac{4}{5} = \frac{64}{125}$

(a) $\frac{64}{125}$ (0.512)

(b) $\frac{48}{125}$ (0.348)

(c) $\frac{12}{125}$ (0.096)

(d) $\frac{1}{125}$

5

Outcome	Probability
Ch Ch Ch	$\frac{6}{8} \times \frac{5}{7} \times \frac{4}{6} = \frac{5}{14}$
Ch Ch Cu	$\frac{6}{8} \times \frac{5}{7} \times \frac{2}{6} = \frac{5}{28}$
Ch Cu Ch	$\frac{6}{8} \times \frac{2}{7} \times \frac{5}{6} = \frac{5}{28}$
Ch Cu Cu	$\frac{6}{8} \times \frac{2}{7} \times \frac{1}{6} = \frac{1}{28}$
Cu Ch Ch	$\frac{2}{8} \times \frac{6}{7} \times \frac{5}{6} = \frac{5}{28}$
Cu Ch Cu	$\frac{2}{8} \times \frac{6}{7} \times \frac{1}{6} = \frac{1}{28}$
Cu Cu Ch	$\frac{2}{8} \times \frac{1}{7} \times \frac{6}{6} = \frac{1}{28}$
Cu Cu Cu	$\frac{2}{8} \times \frac{1}{7} \times \frac{0}{6} = 0$

(a) $\frac{5}{14}$

(b) $\frac{9}{14}$

Exercise 13

1 (a) $\frac{4}{6}\ (=\frac{2}{3})$ (b) $\frac{2}{6}\ (=\frac{1}{3})$ **2** (a) $\frac{5}{8}$ (b) $\frac{3}{8}$

3 (a) $\frac{9}{16}$ (b) $\frac{7}{16}$

4 (a) $\frac{3}{7}$ (b) $\frac{5}{7}$ (c) $\frac{5}{7}$ (d) 0

5 (a) $\frac{7}{16}$ (b) $\frac{1}{16}$ (c) $\frac{9}{16}$

6 $\frac{7}{20}$ **7** $\frac{3}{15}\ (=-\frac{1}{5})$ **8** (a) $\frac{6}{8}\ (=\frac{3}{4})$ (b) $\frac{3}{8}$

9 (a) $\frac{5}{20}\ (=\frac{1}{4})$ (b) $\frac{5}{20}\ (=-\frac{1}{4})$ (c) $\frac{11}{20}$

10 (a) $\frac{6}{10}\ (=\frac{3}{5})$ (b) 0 (c) $\frac{7}{10}$

11

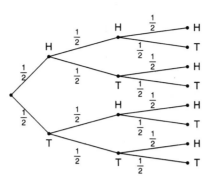

Outcome	Probability
HHH	$\frac{1}{2}\times\frac{1}{2}\times\frac{1}{2}=\frac{1}{8}$
HHT	$\frac{1}{2}\times\frac{1}{2}\times\frac{1}{2}=\frac{1}{8}$
HTH	$\frac{1}{2}\times\frac{1}{2}\times\frac{1}{2}=\frac{1}{8}$
HTT	$\frac{1}{2}\times\frac{1}{2}\times\frac{1}{2}=\frac{1}{8}$
THH	$\frac{1}{2}\times\frac{1}{2}\times\frac{1}{2}=\frac{1}{8}$
THT	$\frac{1}{2}\times\frac{1}{2}\times\frac{1}{2}=\frac{1}{8}$
TTH	$\frac{1}{2}\times\frac{1}{2}\times\frac{1}{2}=\frac{1}{8}$
TTT	$\frac{1}{2}\times\frac{1}{2}\times\frac{1}{2}=\frac{1}{8}$

(a) $\frac{1}{8}$

(b) $\frac{3}{8}$

(c) $\frac{4}{8}(=\frac{1}{2})$

12 $p(BB)=\frac{30}{90}$

$p(WW)=\frac{12}{90}$

$p(BB\text{ or }WW)=\frac{42}{90}$

$(=\frac{7}{15})$

Outcome	Probability
BB	$\frac{6}{10}\times\frac{5}{9}=\frac{30}{90}$
BW	$\frac{6}{10}\times\frac{4}{9}=\frac{24}{90}$
WB	$\frac{4}{10}\times\frac{6}{9}=\frac{24}{90}$
WW	$\frac{4}{10}\times\frac{3}{9}=\frac{12}{90}$

Exercise 14

1 (a)

		Diamond card				
		1	2	3	4	5
Heart card	1	0	1	2	3	4
	2	1	0	1	2	3
	3	2	1	0	1	2

(b) $p(3)=\frac{2}{15}$

2 (a) She has not thrown the dice enough times to prove any statement.

(b) Keith's – green has occurred more often than blue, even though there are two blue and only one green face.

3 (a)

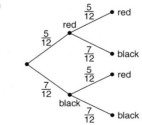

(b) (i) $p(\text{red, red})=\frac{25}{144}$ (ii) $p(\text{different})=\frac{35}{72}$

385

4 (a) $0.85 \times 0.6 = 0.51$ (b) $0.85 \times 0.4 = 0.34$

5 (a) Red (b)(i) 0.1 (ii) 0

6 (a)

	5	6	7	8
1	4	5	6	7
2	3	4	5	6
3	2	3	4	5
4	1	2	3	4

(b) $\frac{8}{16} = \frac{1}{2}$

7 (a) (i) 0.2 (ii) 0.4
   (b) (i) 0.0625 (ii) 0.12

8 (a) (i) $\frac{4}{29}$ (ii) $\frac{17}{29}$

   (b) (i)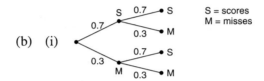

   S = scores
   M = misses

   (ii) 0.42

9 (i)

5	6	7	8	9	10
4	5	6	7	8	9
3	4	5	6	7	8
2	3	4	5	6	7
1	2	3	4	5	6
	1	2	3	4	5

   (ii) $p(2) = \frac{1}{25}$ (iii) $p(8, 9, 10) = \frac{6}{25}$

10 (a)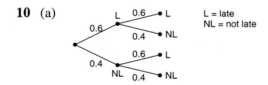

   L = late
   NL = not late

   (b) (i) 0.16 (ii) 0.84 (1–0.16)

11 (a) (i) 0.2 (ii) 0.9 (iii) 0.7 (iv) 48
   (b) (i) She has not taken out enough sweets to determine the probability of each type.
   (ii) *Either*: take *one* sweet out 100 times (replacing it each time, and shaking the container) and note which type it is.

   Or: take a larger sample (say 30), and count how many of each type. Then repeat this experiment 20 times or more.

12 (a) $0.2 \times 30 = 6$ days

(b)   (i)

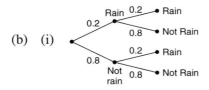

(ii) $0.8 \times 0.2 = 0.16$

Investigations

1 The theoretical probabilities are:

p(heart first) = 0.25

p(heart third) = 0.145 (2941 ...)

The most likely position is *first*.

(p(H first) = 0.25, p(H second) = 0.19,

p(H third) = 0.145, p(H fourth) = 0.11)

2

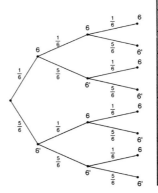

Outcome	Probability
666	$\frac{1}{6} \times \frac{1}{6} \times \frac{1}{6} = \frac{1}{216}$
666'	$\frac{1}{6} \times \frac{1}{6} \times \frac{5}{6} = \frac{5}{216}$
66'6	$\frac{1}{6} \times \frac{5}{6} \times \frac{1}{6} = \frac{5}{216}$
66'6'	$\frac{1}{6} \times \frac{5}{6} \times \frac{5}{6} = \frac{25}{216}$
6'66	$\frac{5}{6} \times \frac{1}{6} \times \frac{1}{6} = \frac{5}{216}$
6'66'	$\frac{5}{6} \times \frac{1}{6} \times \frac{5}{6} = \frac{25}{216}$
6'6'6	$\frac{5}{6} \times \frac{5}{6} \times \frac{1}{6} = \frac{25}{216}$
6'6'6'	$\frac{5}{6} \times \frac{5}{6} \times \frac{5}{6} = \frac{125}{216}$

From the diagram:

p(no 6s) = $\frac{125}{216}$

= 0.579

p(one 6) = $\frac{75}{216}$

= 0.347

p(two 6s) = $\frac{15}{216}$

= 0.069

p(three 6s) = $\frac{1}{216}$

= 0.0046

On average, every set of 216 throws will pay out:

$(75 \times £1) + (15 \times £2) + (1 \times £10) = £75 + £30 + £10 = £115$

The total money taken in will be £216. The game is *not* fair, and is weighted in favour of the stallholder, who makes on average £101 on every 216 throws (or 47p each throw).

(This may well be satisfactory in so far as a village fête is concerned.)

Here are two ways of making a profit of about £2 every ten throws (there are many others):

(a)   If 50p is paid out for no 6s, then the total pay-out for 216 throws, on average, will be: $(125 \times 50p) + £115 = £177.50$.

Profit will be $£216 - £177.50 = £38.50$

This is $\frac{£38.50}{216} = 17.8p$ per throw = £1.78 for 10 throws.

(b) If, instead, the payments are: £1 for one 6, £5 for two 6s and £24 for three 6s, then the pay-out for 216 throws, on average, will be:

$(75 \times £1) + (15 \times £5) + (1 \times £24) = £174$.

Profit on 216 throws is $£216 - £174 = £42$

This is $\frac{£42}{216} = 19.4$p per throw $= £1.94$ for 10 throws

(If the pay-out for throwing three 6s was lowered to £22.80, the average takings would be exactly £2 for every ten throws.)

Index